INVENTING
PLACES

INVENTING PLACES

STUDIES IN CULTURAL GEOGRAPHY

Edited by
Kay Anderson and Fay Gale

1992

Longman Cheshire

WILEY HALSTED PRESS

Published in Australia by
Longman Cheshire Pty Limited
Longman House
Kings Gardens
95 Coventry Street
Melbourne 3205 Australia

Offices in Sydney, Brisbane, Adelaide and Perth. Associated companies, branches and representatives throughout the world.

Published in North and South America by
Halsted Press: an imprint of John Wiley & Sons, Inc. ISBN 0-470-21871-1

Copy-edited by Adrienne Linley
Set in 10/12 pt Times
Produced by Longman Cheshire Pty Ltd
Printed in Malaysia — VP

National Library of Australia Cataloguing-in-Publication data

Inventing places : studies in cultural geography.

   Includes bibliographies and index.
   ISBN 0 582 86875 0.

   1. Human geography. 2. Human geography - Case studies. I.
Anderson, Kay. II. Gale, Fay, 1932- .

304.2

Library of Congress Cataloging-in-Publication date

Inventing places : studies in cultural geography / edited by Kay
   Anderson and Fay Gale.
         p.   cm.
         Includes bibliographical references and index.
      ISBN 0-470-21871-1
1. Human geography.   2. Landscape assessment.   3. Geographical
perception.   I. Anderson, Kay.   II. Gale, Fay.
GF90.I58 1992
304.2--dc20

The mural used on the cover was prepared by James Covill on a wall provided for the purpose by courtesy of Holden's Engine Company, Port Melbourne. The cover photograph is by Malcolm Cross.

Contents

Constructing geographies: identities of exclusion

Constructing geographies: culture and capital

Constructing geographies: culture and nature

The land in cultural context

Notes on contributors

John Agnew is Professor of Geography at Syracuse University. He researches and writes on the political and urban geography of Italy and the United States. His recent publications include an Italian translation of *Place and Politics* (1991) and 'From political methodology to geographical social theory?' in R.J. Johnston et al. (eds), *Developments in Electoral Geography* (London, 1990).

Kay Anderson is Lecturer in Geography at the Australian Defence Force Academy (University of NSW). She was the joint recipient of the 1987 Dissertation Award from the Urban Geography Speciality Group of the Association of American Geographers. In addition to contributing chapters to books, she has published articles in the *Annals, Association of American Geographers, Environment and Planning D: Society and Space, Australian Geographical Studies* and *The Canadian Geographer*. She is also author of *Vancouver's Chinatown: Racial Discourse in Canada, 1875-1980* (McGill-Queen's University Press, 1991). Her current project is the cultural history of the Aboriginal housing project in the Sydney suburb of Redfern.

Jacquelin Burgess lectures in cultural geography at University College, London. For many years, she has been researching and teaching courses which explore the connections between environmental meanings and the mass media. She is joint editor, with John Gold, of *Valued Environments* and *Geography, The Media and Popular Culture*. She is currently working on a project concerned with popular understandings of climatic change.

Mona Domosh is an Assistant Professor of Geography in the College of Liberal Arts at Florida Atlantic University. She has published in the fields of urban cultural geography and feminist theory.

James Duncan is Professor of Geography at Syracuse University. He has published in cultural geography and geographic thought. He is the author of *The City as Text: The Politics of Landscape Interpretation in the Kandyan Kingdom* (Cambridge University Press, 1990), co-editor of *The Power of Place* (Unwin Hyman, 1989) and *Writing Worlds* (Routledge, 1992).

Kevin Frawley is an environmental planner with the National Capital Planning Authority in Canberra. Previously a Lecturer in Geography at the Australian Defence Force Academy (University of NSW), he has a long-standing interest in Australian forest and land management, forest history, natural area planning and conservation ideas.

Fay Gale is Vice-Chancellor of the University of Western Australia, an Officer of the Order of Australia and a Fellow of the Academy of the Social Sciences in Australia.

She is a cultural geographer who has worked extensively at the interface of Aboriginal and European relations in Australia. Her research has concentrated on the differences between the ways Aboriginal people viewed and used the land and the ways adopted by people of European origin in Australia. She has published numerous books in various areas of cultural geography, in addition to numerous book chapters and journal articles.

Jon Goss is Assistant Professor of Geography at the University of Hawaii. He has researched and published on the urban built environment and third world urbanisation.

Peter Jackson teaches Geography at University College in London. He is author of *Maps of Meaning: An Introduction to Cultural Geography* (Unwin Hyman, 1989) and co-author of *Exploring Social Geography* (George Allen & Unwin, 1984). His current research focuses on the social geography of British and Canadian racism.

Jane M. Jacobs is a cultural geographer. She has worked on Australian Aboriginal land rights and the management of Australian cultural heritage sites. She received her PhD from University College, London, having examined the cultural politics of urban conservation.

David Ley is Professor of Geography at the University of British Columbia. He researches and teaches in the field of urban and social geography, emphasising processes of change in Canadian downtowns and inner-city neighbourhoods, including the office sector and gentrification. He is the author of over fifty articles and a number of books, including *A Social Geography of the City* and *Re-Presenting Cultural Geography* (co-edited with James Duncan).

Janice Monk is Executive Director of the Southwest Institute for Research on Women and Adjunct Professor of Geography, University of Arizona. Her recent publications have mainly been in feminist geography, including landscape studies and curriculum concerns.

Kris Olds is a researcher at the Centre for Human Settlements, University of British Columbia. He has examined housing evictions resulting from Expo 86, and is beginning a comparative international project on the housing impacts of hallmark events.

Eric Pawson is Senior Lecturer in Geography at the University of Canterbury, NZ, after training as a historical geographer at the University of Oxford. In New Zealand he has examined processes of British imperialism and their impact on indigenous cultures and landscapes, and is currently heavily involved in the production of a historical atlas of New Zealand.

David Sibley is a Senior Lecturer in the School of Geography, Hull University, England. He has worked for a number of years on responses to Gypsy communities in Europe. His other research interests include the production of knowledge in social science and the home environments of teenage problem drinkers.

Hilary Winchester is Senior Lecturer in Geography at the University of Newcastle, NSW, and has held academic appointments at Plymouth Polytechnic, UK, and the University of Wollongong, NSW. She undertook both undergraduate and postgraduate training at Oxford University, UK. She has written one book and about thirty articles, including publications in *Environment and Planning D: Society and Space* and *Transactions of the Institute of British Geographers*. Her main academic interests are in urban social geography.

Elspeth Young is an Associate Professor in Geography at the Australian Defence Force Academy (University of NSW). Since the mid 1970s she has studied land issues and the socioeconomic transformation of remote aboriginal communities, primarily in Australia's central desert but more recently in Canada and Alaska. These issues are presented in her book *The 'Third' World in the 'First': Development and Enterprise in Remote Indigenous Communities in Canada and Australia* (Routledge).

Acknowledgements

This book is the outcome of a combination of enthusiasm and frustration on our part as teachers, students and researchers of cultural geography. In the past the task of assembling reading lists for undergraduate cultural geography courses has left us weary and unsatisfied. We harboured a nagging concern that the intellectual rewards of the field were being denied to students as long as practising cultural geographers wrote to, and for, each other. If cultural geography were to join the mainstream of undergraduate course offerings in university departments, as we believed it should, a gap in the market seemed in need of a plug.

Our first debt of gratitude, therefore, goes to the many authors who attempted to write for their undergraduate audience. We have learnt this is no simple task. Our primary acknowledgement, however, must go to our cultural roots, the Department of Geography at the University of Adelaide, which in Aboriginal terms was 'the land that grew us up'. Of different generations, nevertheless we are both graduates of the cultural geography that emanated from that department. It was an early offshoot of the Sauer Berkeley School, adapted and metamorphosed to interpret the Australian landscape. The theme developed from the cultural imprint on the land through cultural imperialism to an appreciation of the dynamics of cultural construction and the 'invention' — both symbolic and material — of places and landscapes.

Our special thanks also go to Julie Kesby of the Department of Geography and Oceanography at the Australian Defence Force Academy, who formatted the chapters, assisted with the index, and generally helped oversee the project. We are also grateful to Paul Ballard for his cartographic services and to the department in general for providing facilities that supported the project.

Kay Anderson
Fay Gale
Canberra and Perth

1 Introduction

Kay Anderson and Fay Gale

The variety of social groups described in the language of culture in recent commentaries about contemporary western societies suggests that the term 'culture' has grown significantly in scope and application in the last decade. Social scientists, journalists and policy-makers alike have seen fit to ascribe a coherence of vision and practice to domains once glossed over as mere ripples in our relatively homogeneous metropolitan societies. Corporate culture, popular culture, pub culture, retail culture, service culture, cultures of racism, regional cultures, enterprise cultures and patriarchal cultures are just a few of the centres of meaning and action that are attracting fresh anthropological notice.

Not long ago, 'culture' was portrayed by most commentators on society as the preserve of just two groups: first, of those non-western people and nations whose artefacts, customs, rituals and landscapes had apparently escaped the trajectory of 'progress' in whose image the cosmopolitan west had been made. Second, the term was applied to that category of westerners, removed by privilege from ordinary folk, who were known to have a peculiar penchant for opera, literature and art. 'High' culture was their artistic and intellectual creation and its possession rendered them 'cultured'. In both usages of the term, culture was the 'thing' or sphere occupied by the exotic. Now, however, there is a range of local worlds in both western and non-western contexts whose modes of understanding, speaking and behaving are the subject-matter of the topical field called 'cultural geography'.

This volume grows out of the freshly recovered interest by geographers in the commonsense subjectivities of people at home and abroad. It seeks to devote to advanced capitalist societies like Australia, New Zealand, the United States, Britain and Canada the kind of quizzical attention usually reserved for the distant — both the non-western 'other' and local classes of elites. The 'ways of seeing' (Berger 1972) of those two groups can be enjoined to a range of groups that cohere around shared visions, languages and codes of practice. Such 'textual communities', in the words of Stock (1983), are the focus of the recently invigorated field of cultural geography to which this collection contributes.

To what tendencies does the recently expanded use of the word 'culture' refer? What processes does the term's currency reveal? A range of answers to this question is possible. First, it might signal the proliferation of reference groups that have emerged during the recent phase of economic and cultural restructuring in the west when old lines of class division are being fractured around new sources of identity and political mobilisation. Environmental lobbies, for example, are forging new ways of seeing and relating to nature that are rallying people of all political persuasions and class affiliations. Other oppositional cultures of disabled groups, racialised minorities and peace activists, to name just a few, are combining — often on a local basis — around visions of alternative futures.

A second explanation for the growing currency of the term 'culture' is possible. It has been argued by some geographers that ever more flexible regimes of capital accumulation are structuring western societies, and that increasingly specialised economic complexes are taking (and requiring for their maintenance) a corresponding diversity of ideological forms (see, for example, Harvey 1989; Huxley & Kerkin 1988; ch. 10 below). Cases in point are our increasingly differentiated consumer culture, including the niche occupied by the heritage industry, and the appearance of downtown 'spectacles' (like Darling Harbour in Sydney and Covent Garden in London) that attract thousand of pleasure-seekers and transform declining sites into profit. These visible testimonies to the 'post-modernity' of the contemporary urban condition are for some interpreters the 'cultural clothing' of late capitalism.

Finally, it might be suggested that the new expansiveness of the term 'culture' reflects shifts in academic fashion. The twin critiques of post-modernism and feminism have prompted social scientists to renounce totalising explanatory models and confront the relativity of all forms of knowledge, both popular and scientific. In particular, the loss of the sense of an absoluteness of western accounts of history (see Said 1978; Young 1990) has precipitated a self-consciousness about European culture's own historical relativity. In an intellectual setting where claims to universal (ungendered, ethnocentric) truths are being rapidly abandoned and all knowledges contextualised, an important project has emerged. It is one that seeks to show how people's frames of mind and action are situated within the cultural worlds they inhabit — an anthropology that remains to be done for the west, with its multiplicity of cultures, and that forms the focus of this collection of introductory essays.

People within cultural worlds

Whatever the complex origins of the textual communities that characterise all societies, it is important that their myriad forms and effects be made the subject of closer investigation. This undergraduate collection of readings is devoted to precisely such an exposition, describing select ways of seeing the world that resonate in the everyday experience of all of us. We all as humans rely on visions and vocabularies to help us interpret our experience, our relationship to others and the world at large, and social change. Often without being aware of it, each of us imposes a 'plot' on our daily existence, picking and choosing and arranging detail to make sense of it and prepare each day for the next one. This is the creative act of living, and while elements of our narrative plot belong to us as individuals, we share many visions and actions with the people who occupy our cultural worlds.

To be sure, much of people's 'sense-making' is so ordinary as to be unworthy of geographers' notice. The taken-for-granted minutiae of dress conventions, traffic rules, table manners, types of humour, concepts of time, funeral rituals, subtleties of fashion shifts and definitions of personal beauty are probably beyond the purview of geographers. Other acts of imaginative construction, however, command the critical attention of social scientists. Think, for example, of the markers of human skin colour and the anatomical features distinctive to each sex. The beliefs among Europeans (and other cultural groups) that 'races' exist naturally and that gender roles likewise owe their origin to differences we can simply take for granted have made the cues of skin colour and sexual difference far more culturally significant than their mere physical reality. Many westerners also believe that nature and animals exist at a lower point on the 'chain of being' than humans; that commodities hold some inherent 'magic' that will give them status and identity; that the artefacts of the past possess 'character'; that the (green and pleasant) English countryside is the model of landscape beauty; that rural life is 'simple' and so on. These 'inventions' (Hobsbawm & Ranger 1983) require analysis because, far from being irresistible truths, they are the cultural stuff out of which broad moral and material systems are made. They are 'maps of meaning' (Clarke et al. 1976; see also Jackson 1989), that whether 'right' or 'wrong' are picked up by people, groups and institutions. They are acted upon, reproduced and hardened into seeming 'fact' in a continuous process that is constitutive of both social structure and real world topographies. If culture can be defined at all, then, it refers to these shared codes of understanding, communication and practice that set one of many contexts for human thought and action.

In this book, we follow in the path established by critics of the American Berkeley School of Geography (see Duncan 1980; Agnew et al. 1984; Jackson 1989; Ley 1983). Carl Sauer, a dominant figure in the Berkeley School, worked with a view of culture as a 'way of life' and inspired some forty years of study into the differences from region to region in the activities of human communities. The focus was mainly on rural landscapes which were 'read' by Sauer and his students for cues of (sequent) human occupance. Wagner and Mikesell's (1962) collection called *Readings in Cultural Geography* was one important text to be influenced by the Berkeley School. The editors conceived of cultures as assemblages of 'verifiable common characteristics' that provide 'a means of classifying areas according to the character of the human groups that occupy them' (Wagner & Mikesell 1962, 2). In a similar vein, world regional geography of the 1950s and 1960s classified the globe's populations into 'culture worlds', as if cultures and regions were homogeneous entities. These 'worlds', including the Oriental and Arab regions, were conceived by world regional geographers of the time such as Russell and Kniffen (1951) as 'unified subdivisions' whose 'traits' and 'similar ways of changing landscapes' made their occupants 'alien to the inhabitants of other culture worlds'.

Since the mid 1970s, a number of geographers have distanced themselves from the tradition of Berkeley cultural geography, dismissed by some critics as the 'geography of artifacts' (Goss 1988). We do not wish to rehearse the difficulties with this tradition of cultural geography, nor to overstate the magnitude of recent shifts away from it. For the purposes of the perspective illustrated in this book, however, we recall two major points of the Berkeley School critique, one relating to culture, the other to landscapes.

First, the authors in this book share the view that culture is a *process* in which people are actively engaged. The contributors see culture as a dynamic mix of symbols, beliefs, languages and practices that people create, not a fixed thing or entity governing humans. Back in the 1920s, Sauer had suggested that culture was such an independent force moulding people and landscapes in its image. Others since Sauer's time have rightly argued, however, that the decisive agents in constructing group life and landscapes are not customs but people. People interpret and grasp their worlds — and indeed reality itself — with the use of symbols and vocabularies that equip them to participate actively in the construction of cultures and geographies. 'We are all intellectuals', Horne (1986, ch. 1) writes, and people often, without knowing it, impose bias on the ordering of experience. While the forms of such bias might support the label of 'customs', to do so risks eclipsing some important points about social life. First, it carries the danger of depicting people as passive recipients of thoughts and behaviours handed down to subsequent generations. While it is true that people live with and through 'realities' they inherit, it is also the case that people re-present those realities according to their own motivations and always possess the capacity to question and criticise, and so create fresh hypotheses about existence. Second, the term 'customs' conjures up images of 'things' that are uniformly imbibed across whole societies, whereas societies are complexly differentiated by class, ethnicity, gender, age and so on. It is more appropriate to speak therefore in terms of multiple cultures, rather than unitary national ones. Third, the terminology of 'customs' carries images of traditional and rural settings, when, certainly in a country like Australia, the dominant culture is overwhelmingly metropolitan. Finally, the language of customs has a conservative current, directing attention to the continuity of cultural systems and obscuring their vulnerability to revision, adaptation and manipulation.

The cultural process by which people construct their understandings of the world is an inherently geographic concern. In the course of generating new meanings and decoding existing ones, people construct spaces, places, landscapes, regions and environments. In short, they construct geographies. By the term 'geographies' we refer to a range of empirically specifiable phenomena that have cultural (and other) factors as their underpinning. Some of these geographies — such as the erection of religious buildings or, in the case of Australia's Aboriginal population, the distribution of sacred sites — reflect and reactivate visions and practices that are unambiguously cultural. Other geographies, such as the building of suburban estates or the mining of uranium, emerge out of actions that are less conspicuously cultural. They are not deliberate acts of cultural construction but nonetheless, when excavated for their meaning, bear the stamp of culturally distinctive beliefs and responses. In the case of outlying suburban estates, we can find within their constitution sets of assumptions about the cultural separation of 'home' and 'work' and the respective gender roles that attach to each activity. Likewise, the mining of the earth for elements such as uranium relies on beliefs about the separation of humans from nature and on culturally-bound resource appraisals.

In constructing cultures, therefore, people construct geographies. They arrange spaces in distinctive ways; they fashion certain types of landscape, townscape and streetscape; they erect monuments and destroy others; they evaluate spaces and places and adapt them accordingly; they organise the relations between territories at a range of scales from the local to the international. In direct and indirect ways, both wilful and unintentional, people construct environments, regions and places. However, geographies do not just exist 'out there' as inert reflections of cultures, a point which brings us to the second element of the Berkeley School critique we wish to recall.

In 1925 Sauer wrote 'Culture is the agent, the natural area is the medium, the cultural landscape is the result' (p. 46), a view which led cultural geographers of Sauer's time to envisage landscapes (and spatial arrangements) as mere artefacts of culture. However, just as cultures are constitutive of geographies, so are our geographies inherent to the culture-building process. Human geographies are under continuous invention and transformation by actions whose underlying fields of knowledge are themselves recreated through geographic arrangements. People's cultures and their geographies intersect and reciprocally inform each other, we argue, in process, in time.

The chapters in this book illuminate both sides of this dynamic relationship between culture and geography. The second chapter underlines the fundamental point (above) that there is human selectivity in all representations of reality. One source of this variability is the broadly shared cultural outlook people bring to everyday life. In New Zealand the divergence in 'ways of seeing' between Maori and pakeha people has had far-reaching implications for the nature of past and present society — its land use, economy and politics. Other sources of variability in human geographies are internal to the western cultural tradition. Three chapters therefore examine the making of identities and geographies surrounding such foci as status, place and business affiliations. Chapter 3 examines elite group status and landscape construction in a Canadian city over a hundred-year period; chapter 4 assesses the role of identification to place in the electoral geography of post-war Italy; and chapter 5 addresses the links between business connections and architectural forms in nineteenth-century New York City. Each of the authors demonstrates that places, landscapes and buildings are 'fields' in which in-group identifications (inclusive identities) are constructed and communicated, with important bearings on broader regimes (of status and politics).

Of course, group identities have multiple sources, and can be ascribed by non-group members as well as negotiated among like-minded people. Four chapters pursue the theme of identity ascription, examining the ideologies out of which exclusionary identities have been conferred and territories assigned to categories of people who are deemed 'different'. People's beliefs relating to race are the focus of chapters 6 and 7; chapter 6 examines the distorted representations of North American Indians and their landscapes rendered by image-makers such as photographers, and chapter 7 addresses the perceptions of Gypsy people and places in England. Chapters 8 and 9 then examine the ideologies which have organised sexual difference in cross-cultural and Australian settings. In combination, the four chapters demonstrate that in the service of patriarchal and European world views distinctive geographies have been drawn to mark cultural boundaries between an ingroup of 'us' and an outgroup of 'them'.

Other contributors to the book develop their analyses from the side of the dialectic of culture and geography occupied by the environment. Increasingly ascendant in western culture and economy are images surrounding people's pursuit of commodities (ch. 10) and entertainment experiences (ch. 11). Many inner-city environments bear the stamp of consumer culture, and the two chapters are important in bringing different emphases to its explanation. An equally popular current in contemporary western culture and economy is the idealisation and packaging of the past. The break with modernist aesthetics has been made in many cities, including London, where groups (with different purposes) attach 'heritage value' to settings and buildings once deemed to be defunct (ch. 12).

If our urban environments have been adapted in the image of people's belief systems, so also do our physical landscapes provide a window on cultural constructs. The evolution of Australian environmental attitudes over the last century is discussed in chapter 13, while chapter 14 examines the influence of the media in shaping public knowledge about, and outcomes for, a section of London's marshland designated for redevelopment. Chapter 15 then concludes, and with chapter 2 frames, the book by highlighting once again the fundamental relativity of environmental moralities. It underlines that point by contrasting the perceptions of land and resources on the part of European and indigenous populations in remote parts of North America and Central Australia. The terrain covered by the contributors ranges widely indeed, but the chapters are united conceptually by a respect for ordinary folk knowledge and the geographies it informs and re-forms.

Institutions as cultural domains

Most of the chapters in this book have more ambitious conceptual aims than describing people's distinctive understandings of the world. Uncovering such understandings constitutes an essential, but preliminary, step in cultural analysis. Many authors are also concerned with the sources and shapers of cultural knowledge, the penetration of such knowledge into macro moral and material fields, and the functions that cultural understandings perform. Central to these concerns is the role institutions play in the processes of cultural construction.

Just as people frame their actions in terms of shared definitions of situations, so do organisations and institutions operate as cultural domains. They too rely on cognitive constructions about their roles and functions. Universities, banks, the military complex, the levels of state, the church, corporations, schools, the media and even families impose some narrative form onto their activities, binding members to the unit and justifying their existence to themselves and society at large. For example, of all the things that families might say about themselves they often specify the priority of 'blood ties' as their defining characteristic; the military invokes the 'defence of nation' as its rationale; the state claims to have the 'public interest' as its raison d'être; immigration departments often proclaim their mission is to 'protect the fabric of the nation', as do environmentalist groups for the whole earth. Finally, sectors of the media purport to be 'objective informers of the public', as if the facts of news somehow speak for themselves.

We might legitimately counter that such pronouncements are themselves 'factual', moreover that they are morally defensible. We wish to suggest that the important point, however, is not the 'truth' or otherwise of such positions — as if such definitive things as absolute truths and iron-clad moralities exist in social life — but rather their selectivity, their cultural and historical specificity and their partiality. To be sure, discourses about the 'public interest', 'family', the 'nation' and even high-sounding rhetoric about global commitment can serve partisan interests, promote elitist goals and perform ignoble functions. The cultural ideal of 'family' — understood in the west as a nuclear unit of man, woman and children — is often surrounded in popular and official discourse by rhetoric that eclipses the political struggles required for the unit's maintenance. It also tends to marginalise the practice and concept of alternative domestic arrangements. Newspaper publishers and editors, for another example, make strategic judgements about what their readers (buyers) wish to hear, when selecting from an infinity of events the things that seem newsworthy. So, for example, the complexity of Ethiopia becomes reduced in readers' minds to the cycles of war, flood and famine that plague helpless, black folk. In both examples of the rhetoric surrounding the family and the so-called facts of news, patriarchal and ethnocentric cultural assumptions are being reproduced through institutions that give them legitimacy.

The discourses that organisations articulate to interpret themselves to each other and the world at large can clearly uphold unequal relations between people and places. Powerful institutions (including nations) can even work to ensure that what are partial, culturally-bound interpretations of reality are accepted as 'natural' and 'correct' by the public at large. Think, for example, of the widely held view that freeways facilitate the flow of traffic and goods. Few people would dispute the truth of such a view. However, implicit within such a 'truth' has been an ethos, a world view governed by the language of efficiency (rather than, for example, environmental impact) which has tended to marginalise alternative visions of, and proposals for, urban transportation. Such has been the cultural strength of economists and oil magnates in urban planning circles that many democratically-elected politicians have been persuaded to accept efficiency arguments that, when implemented, empower certain groups and neighbourhoods over others (and possibly endanger us all). Social life is replete with struggles for imaginative dominance of precisely this kind, and one of the goals of cultural geography is to uncover them from the multiple contexts in which they are embedded.

Culture and power

If frames of mind are sources of cultural understanding and identity for people and institutions, they are also sources of control, conflict and contest. While all of us participate in symbolising the world, people do not enjoy equal access to the conditions for creating those shared symbols. Struggles for imaginative supremacy are perhaps as endemic as those that course, both overtly and latently, between economic classes in advanced capitalist societies.

It will be clear from the above comments that some of the visions that groups and institutions use to interpret the world emerge from structures of domination and oppression. The meaning surrounding the label 'Australian' is a case in point. It often conjures up in the popular and official imagination associations of 'white', male and rural origins, a myth that, for all its popular appeal, masks significant and enduring lines of social division in Australian society. Women have no conceptual space in this version of an 'Australian', neither do settlers of non-white European background, or, remarkably, city-dwellers. Yet the myth is immensely powerful and still forms the raw material from which media representations of the country are drawn. More seriously, it has long informed public and private sector policies in relation to the life chances of excluded groups. Australian women continue to experience wage and other forms of discrimination, and racialised minorities, including Aboriginal people, do not by any means enjoy equality with 'white' Australians in the rewards of citizenship.

The example highlights the general point that cultural inventions (in this case the imagined community called 'Australians') penetrate far beyond the gestalt field of people's minds and hearts into tangible institutional spheres such as the workplace and public policy where people's material circumstances are determined. Meanings surrounding spaces and places (see Shields 1991) can even extend to the nation-state where they can influence the configuration of geopolitical alliances and rivalries (Anderson 1983). Culture does not occupy an autonomous sphere, therefore, and cultural geographers need continually to confront the connections between culture, human geographies and the workings of power. This is especially so if we are to avoid a style of self-congratulatory discourse analysis where the researcher is consumed by the task of deconstructing knowledges to the neglect of the conditions, impacts and political functions of people's cultural conceptions.

Culture and resistance

The process by which cultural understandings become constructed and reproduced through time and space is complexly negotiated. It involves not just the efforts of powerful groups to secure conceptual and instrumental control, but also the struggles of weaker groups to resist definitions that exclude and marginalise them. For an example, it is helpful to consider the challenges made by poor, inner-city dwellers in advanced capitalist societies during the 1960s to the dominant definition of their neighbourhoods as 'slums' (or, in the words of civic bureaucracies of the time, 'revenue sinks' in need of 'rationalisation'). The struggle of such residents continues into the present when upwardly mobile professionals have reclassified the same old homes and districts as 'places of character', fit for gentrification. There are also myriad examples of resistance strategies on the part of Aboriginal Australians and their indigenous counterparts in New Zealand, the United States and Canada to the racialised ascriptions and practices that accompanied their dispossession. Likewise, a range of women's groups in western societies contest essentialist assumptions about gender difference that justify male privilege and female subordination. The gaps in dominant cultures are being exposed, therefore, by new and insistent voices.

We noted above that dominant groups and institutions have the power to 'make over' the world in the image of select interests by defining for all groups what is considered 'natural'. A number of chapters make this clear, while at the same time being alert to people's capacity to subvert the messages they receive. People can decode messages in ways not intended by their producers. This is not always or necessarily a self-consciously oppositional process on the part of disgruntled groups, any more than the exertion of control by powerful groups is always a deliberate act of engineering of the public imagination. The processes of cultural reproduction are infinitely more complex and subtle than that, showing evidence of both compliance and resistance, accommodation and conflict. Moreover, the processes are mediated through, and re-formed by, specific geographic settings. The contingencies introduced by geographic variation deny researchers anything as easy or satisfying, or for that matter possible, as generalisable models of human behaviour. Precisely because of the time-space relativity of our subjects' knowledge and our own more 'scientific' observations, the aim of cultural geography is to produce contextualised interpretation, not universalistic explanation.

This book demonstrates that our landscapes are valuable documents on the power plays from which social life is constructed, both materially and rhetorically. The visionary struggles on the part of differentially empowered groups are the focus of chapters on the cultural politics of land tenure and resource use, heritage sites, redevelopment locations, gendered landscapes, racialised settings, elite and corporate streetscapes, and electoral outcomes. The authors bring evidence to show how the hegemonic 'projects' of colonialism, modernism, patriarchy, racism, status supremacy, certain political regimes and redevelopment agendas are realised in and through distinctive geographies. Some authors also examine the linkages between cultural and economic determinants of human geographies. These geographies include retail

complexes, corporate landscapes, heritage settings and European land-use transformations. It is certainly the case that ways of seeing combine with ways of being and
doing, to an extent that renders false any separation of the material and symbolic
domains. Nor is the dominance of powerful groups a unidirectional event. As chapters
11 and 14 demonstrate, potentially profitable projects (such as urban redevelopments
and World Fairs) are open to various interpretations by people who lack the power of
definition.

Developments within human geography in the 1980s

A number of geographers have already pointed to the weakness of the research field
called behavioural geography that gave us 'mental maps' in the 1970s (for example,
Jackson & Smith 1984). Like the tradition of subcultural studies in sociology in the
1950s and 1960s (for example, Whyte 1943; Suttles 1968), perception studies failed to
situate the workings of the human mind in the broader contexts that informed it. While
helpfully showing that the 'facts' of situations (say, of the physical distance between
places) are less decisive in influencing behaviour than people's construction of the facts
(the cognitive distance between places), behavioural geography failed to investigate the
preconditions for, and functions of, human perceptions. It reminded us that people see
and evaluate the same things differently, but ignored the issue of why certain
interpretations come to prevail over others in the struggle between groups for
imaginative dominance. For that matter, it ignored groups and institutions, focusing
almost exclusively on individuals. All these limitations left it open to the charge of
idealism, and silent to the power plays and conflicts that reside within ideological fields.

For some years, during the late 1970s and 1980s, Marxist geographers seized the
explanatory ground by situating people's versions of reality in the sphere of 'ideology'.
According to those geographers, capitalism moulded the consciousness of people to
meet the need of the economic system for continual capital accumulation. There was no
call to examine the forms of people's sense-making because they were deemed to be
(false) reflections of more decisive economic pressures. The radical critique precipitated
many developments within human geography and certainly expanded the scope and
ambition of the subject's substantive concerns and explanatory frameworks. Behavioural
geographers and humanistic geographers of the late 1970s who studied people's 'sense
of place' were forced to confront the limits of their questions and answers about human
subjectivity.

Since the late 1980s a range of human geographers has become attentive to the
linkages between the ideological and material dimensions of social life (for example,
Kobayashi & Mackenzie 1989; Jackson 1989). The rise of the post-modern attitude or
outlook has been especially decisive in opening up possibilities of dialogue between
explanatory paradigms by challenging all claims to universal truths. Thus, while cultural
geographers choose to emphasise the forms and effects of people's understandings of
the world, they would not claim that cultures belong to a free-floating realm any more
than those with a materialist bent would now argue that culture is mere icing on the
economic base of capitalism. The way is perhaps cleared for further engagement of
organising frameworks, both constructivist and materialist.

What cultural geographers do insist upon, however, is the need to take seriously
people's ideas and values, especially those which are constitutive of broader moral and

material systems (see also Philo 1991). The everyday knowledge of ordinary and elevated folk — however distorted, contradictory, partial and biased — makes its own contribution to macro social and spatial structures, economic and political arrangements, environmental quality and other conditions. Precisely because people's cultural knowledge forms a building block from which broader regimes are formed and transformed, we dedicate a book to the exposition of some of its more influential forms. By listening to the micro-order of people's sense-making, we can, as Knorr-Cetina and Cicourel (1981, 42) argue, 'hear the macro-order tick'.

Methodological considerations

Retrieving data about people's cultural conceptions from the contexts that shape them is a difficult task, and one persistently undervalued by geographers trained in seemingly more rigorous paradigms. Struggles for imaginative dominance as to what constitutes 'good' geography and indeed 'geography' itself, exist no less between schools of geographers. One of the credibility problems that cultural geographers face is in the types of data sets they use and generate. It is often alleged by critics that sample populations are too small, that conclusions cannot be 'disproven', and that the findings do not propel us toward models of geographical reality. These and other charges have recurred in different guises in the authenticity debates which have raged for decades between positivist and non-positivist researchers.

Yet it is precisely because cultural geographers are so conscious of the inconclusive nature of such methodological debates and the philosophical issues on which the debates turn, that they take care in the way they use and combine a range of techniques. Cultural geographers see no need to argue the merits of qualitative methods over the quantitative since both have a contribution to make to the task of uncovering people's constructions of the world and their sociospatial articulation. It should not be presumed that the interest in cultural mythology breeds whimsical accounts without rigour or concern for what happens on the ground. The necessity for empirical work has been emphasised since Carl Sauer first led the revival in cultural geography in the 1920s. The Berkeley School was deeply committed to observation (though not usually its extension into experimentation) and, equally, contemporary cultural geographers are careful to measure the empirically specifiable impacts of ways of seeing the world on social patterns, practice and policy.

During the late 1950s and 1960s methodological debates carved the discipline of geography into two quite distinct fields and even, in some universities, into separate departments of human and physical geography. During this time, quantification dominated human geography, people were abstracted from their environment, space was seen as a geometric plane, and geography was assumed to be 'culture-free'. For a time geography even appeared not to be located in space, so committed were its proponents to abstraction. But the discipline of geography survived this watershed and a period of re-evaluation followed. How wise had it been to separate people from their environment? Had regional geography — where space had been viewed in unity with the people who moulded it — been prematurely rejected? The 1970s saw a revival of people-centred geographies, claiming allegiance to no one specific methodology but insisting that the methodology used would be determined by the subject matter at hand, not by any one school of thought or the whims of academic fashion.

Thus, as will be evident in this book, the research procedures of cultural geographers range across a wide spectrum of techniques including observation, the use of interview schedules and questionnaires often favoured by sociologists, participant observation approaches common to anthropologists, the integration of quantitative records, and the analysis of texts such as photographs, speeches, council minutes and newspaper accounts. 'Deconstruction' has been the name given to the technique for analysing (historicising) such texts, and in geography it has been adapted to the task of 'reading the landscape' (Meinig 1979). While few of the contributors to this book undertake 'deconstructionism' in the strict sense of its post-structuralist founder Derrida (1967), many adopt a version of it. This can be found in chapters 3, 6, 9 and 12 which, in different ways, unpack folk knowledges and their geographies, and nest them within the contexts that historically surround them. Other chapters are intellectual histories of a more conventional, but no less incisive kind.

For the cultural geographer, then, a range of techniques is appropriate, and often several may be used in concert to uncover the connections between visions, practices and geographies. The task requires an equally diverse range of skills: a sensitivity to people's subjectivity, a keen eye to the topographies that people fashion, a conscientious contextualising of the connections between people and place, a commitment to rigorous documentation and plausible argumentation, and an honest confrontation with our values and the relativity of our own interpretations. As the challenges of cultural geography are considerable so too are its rewards, which this book hopes to communicate.

References

Anderson, B. 1983, *Imagined Communities*, Verso, London.

Agnew, J., Mercer, J. & Sopher, D. 1984, *The City in Cultural Context*, Allen & Unwin, Boston.

Berger, J. 1972, *Ways of Seeing the World,* Penguin, Harmondsworth.

Clarke, J., Hall, S., Jefferson, T. & Roberts, B. 1976, 'Subcultures, cultures and class: a theoretical overview', in S. Hall & J. Henderson (eds), *Resistance Through Rituals,* Hutchinson/Centre for Contemporary Cultural Studies, London, pp. 9–74.

Derrida, J. 1967, *De la Grammatologie, Les Editions de Minuit, Paris* (translated as J. Derrida 1974, *Of Grammatology*, John Hopkins University Press, Baltimore).

Duncan, J. 1980, 'The superorganic in American cultural geography', *Annals, Association of American Geographers,* 70, pp. 181–98.

Goss, J. 1988, 'The built environment and social theory: towards an architectural geography', *Professional Geographer*, 40, 4, pp. 392–403.

Harvey, D. 1989, *The Condition of Postmodernity: An Enquiry into the Origins of Cultural Change,* Blackwell, Oxford.

Hobsbawm, E. & Ranger, T. 1983, *The Invention of Tradition*, Cambridge University Press, Cambridge.

Huxley, M. & Kerkin, K. 1988, 'What price the Bicentennial? A political economy of Darling Harbour', *Transition*, Spring, pp. 57–64.

Horne, D. 1986, *The Public Culture: The Triumph of Industrialism*, Pluto Press, Sydney.

Jackson, P. 1989, *Maps of Meaning*, Unwin Hyman, London.

Jackson, P. & Smith, S. 1984, *Exploring Social Geography*, George Allen & Unwin, London.

Knorr-Cetina, K. & Cicourel, A. (eds) 1981, *Advances in Social Theory and Methodology: Toward an Integration of Micro- and Macro- Sociologies,* Routledge & Kegan Paul, Boston.

Kobayashi, A. & Mackenzie, S. (eds) 1989, *Remaking Human Geography*, Unwin Hyman, London.

Ley, D. 1983, *A Social Geography of the City*, Harper & Row, New York.

Meinig, D. (ed.) 1979, *The Interpretation of Ordinary Landscapes,* Oxford University Press, New York.

Philo, C. 1991, 'Delimiting human geography: new social and cultural perspectives', in C. Philo (compiler), *New Words, New Worlds: Reconceptualising Social and Cultural Geography*, proceedings of a conference, Aberystwyth, pp. 14–27.

Russell, B. & Kniffen, D. 1951, *Culture Worlds*, Harper & Row, New York.

Sauer, C. 1925, *The Morphology of Landscape,* University of California Publications in Geography, 2, pp. 19–53.

Said, E. 1978, *Orientalism,* Pantheon Books, New York.

Shields, R. 1991, *Places on the Margin: Alternative Geographies of Modernity*, Routledge, London.

Stock, B. 1983, *The Implications of Literacy,* Princeton University Press, Princeton.

Suttles, G. 1968, *The Social Order of the Slum*, University of Chicago Press, Chicago.

Wagner, P. & Mikesell, M. 1962, *Readings in Cultural Geography*, University of Chicago Press, Chicago.

Whyte, W. 1943, *Street Corner Society* (2nd edn 1955), University of Chicago Press, Chicago.

Young, R. 1990, *White Mythologies: Writing History and the West,* Routledge, London and New York.

The land in cultural context

2 Two New Zealands: Maori and European

Eric Pawson

Introduction

At the beginning of 1990, the fourteenth Commonwealth Games were held in Auckland. The location and timing were no accident. The Games had been brought to New Zealand's largest city to initiate celebrations marking 150 years of the birth of the country as a modern state. The opening ceremony trumpeted this theme. Eschewing the high-tech extravaganzas of recent Olympics, it was a lavish spectacle of New Zealand's bicultural history, a massive choreographed display by thousands of people carpeting the arena. Brightly outfitted, but with minimal props, they enacted the Maori story of creation and occupation of the land, and the subsequent arrival of the Europeans, culminating with the signing of the Treaty of Waitangi in 1840. The show was witnessed by national teams of athletes from the Commonwealth, each previously escorted into the stadium by Maori warriors in traditional dress.

The underlying message of the occasion was clear. Here, hosting representatives of a fraternity of nations, was a country that wanted to be seen as a model of cultural fraternity, in which the descendants of European colonists coexist easily with an indigenous people, the Maori. The message was to serve an obvious purpose. Not only was it to confirm to a global television audience New Zealand's widely assumed place as a harmonious society, but also to reinforce to New Zealanders themselves that this was indeed the case. As a spectacle it worked. Even the most sceptical local onlooker could not help but be moved by a sense of national pride.

The sceptic, however, must ask questions. Was the spectacle honest? Do Maori and European[1] in fact share a joint home in harmony? Is this the real story of the last 150 years? Is New Zealand an unusual example of a co-operative, bicultural venture in a modern, intensively competitive world? To explore such questions, as this chapter will, is an exercise in cultural geography. It must dissect the meanings of culture to two very different peoples in order to assess the ways in which they have lived with each other and the land that they occupy. It is necessarily also an exercise in historical reconstruction as, without an appreciation of the past, the circumstances of the present cannot be understood. So 'thinking historically is no luxury; on the contrary it is an essential part of doing human geography' (Driver 1988, 504).

Cultural contexts

The signing of the Treaty of Waitangi in 1840 marked the formal annexation by the British Empire of the territories that Europeans called New Zealand. For perhaps half a century before this, coastal peripheries of the North and South Islands had been part of the 'informal' empire, visited and temporarily settled by European sealers, whalers and traders. Such activities had been tolerated, even welcomed, by coastal Maori peoples as opportunities for trade and the acquisition of European goods. However, because of distance, expense and limited resources, the question of annexation had not been favoured earlier. Indeed, a series of British parliamentary acts from 1817 onwards had recognised the New Zealanders, i.e. the Maori, as sovereign peoples (Orange 1987).

This situation could not long prevail. Nineteenth-century Britain was the leading impulse in a rapidly developing European crucible of capitalism, a country seeking ever widening horizons for trade, capital export and emigration. The European world was in ferment and Britain in particular was becoming industrialised, urbanised and conspicuously class divided. Between 1815 and 1914, as many as ten million Britons (Baines 1985, 45) accompanied British capital overseas in search of improved opportunities for labour. Most went to North America, with much smaller streams to South America, South Africa, the tropical colonies and Australasia. As a field of European settler colonisation, New Zealand was one of the last significant links in a worldwide chain of British emigration. However, it caught the eye of a prominent theorist of colonisation, Edward Gibbon Wakefield, whose New Zealand Company was ready to plant settlements there by the late 1830s. It was a desire to control these settlements, to minimise the threat of antagonising the Maori, and, to a limited extent, to protect Maori interests, that the Treaty of Waitangi was offered by the British Crown to the Maori in 1840 (Adams 1977; Orange 1987). In this regard, the British were maintaining a long tradition.They almost always acted to secure the consent of indigenous peoples through treaties as a condition of the constitutionality of their imperium (McHugh 1989; Williams 1989).[2]

The Treaty of Waitangi is thus the founding document of New Zealand as a modern state. However, ever since it was signed it has been the subject of ongoing confusion. In order to understand why this is — and to provide a window into the nature of relations between European colonisers and indigenous peoples the world over — it is necessary to explore the very different cultural contexts of the two treaty partners. In so doing, it is useful to focus on the twin themes of competition and co-operation, these being essential arbiters in the analysis of how cultures are constructed. To a greater or lesser extent for every culture, these themes characterise the manner of relationships between people, and between people and nature. They not only describe such relationships as practised, but are also employed in cultural mythologies to represent and proscribe experience. At the risk of caricature, because neither theme is by any means absent in the other, it can be said that the guiding motif of nineteenth-century British life was that of competition, whereas pre-European Maori culture was organised on more co-operative principles. The British colonisation of New Zealand thus brought together two peoples whose underlying cultural assumptions and practices were very different.

By the early decades of the nineteenth century, populations in northern Europe were growing rapidly. From this fact, inescapable in the evidence of early censuses and expanding cities, Wakefield drew his conclusions about the necessity of emigration to accommodate 'surplus' people. Malthus, however, used it to derive a very different result, his infamous 'natural law' of the inevitability of strife, famine and war as populations outstripped their means of subsistence. That the latter was, for Britons, being continually augmented by the expansion of empire did nothing to diminish the powerful appeal of Malthus' argument. It was this portrayal of competitive struggle that Darwin appropriated in his own theory of evolution as the mechanism to explain processes of adaptation to environment by those species fittest to survive (Young 1985). Although Darwin himself was often reluctant to draw moral conclusions from nature, his followers had no such hesitation. The theory of evolution was in turn used to explain and celebrate the apparent material progress of Europe, as well as to justify the intense dog-eat-dog laissez-faire capitalism on which it was based (Peet 1985). Hence a prominent Darwinist such as Huxley could write that '... so long as ... man increases and multiplies without restraint, so long will peace and industry not only permit, but they will necessitate, a struggle for existence as sharp as any that ever went on under the regime of war' (Huxley 1894, 209).

Thus competition between individuals, families, classes and companies in an increasingly atomistic capitalist society was legitimated by recourse to a powerful natural analogy. Wealth among people who had long lived by the rules of the marketplace (Macfarlane 1978) was measured in ownership of commodities and control of the means of production. The drive to imperialism was little more than the desire to commodify the rest of the world and extend British access to an ever widening stock of resources in order to stay ahead in the struggle between states (Pawson 1990). In this, access to land was critical, as its possession yielded not only food and raw materials but conferred on its new owners a status denied them in the more crowded conditions of home.

Inevitably this drive brought Europeans into conflict with indigenous peoples who measured wealth in very different ways, did not regard land as a tradeable commodity and did not use it in ways Europeans considered productive. From the evolutionary standpoint of the latter, such peoples belonged to 'lesser races' (fig. 2.1), towards whom European attitudes became increasingly racist in the nineteenth century (Horsman 1981). However, the Maori were assigned a higher place in the perceived 'order of races' than those such as Australian Aborigines, because the British respected their military prowess, cultural artifacts and willingness to embrace the habits of trade and literacy. Nonetheless, they were condemned for the 'beastly communism' of a social order based on networks of kinship centred on affiliation to hapu (family groups) and iwi (tribes),[3] and for lacking an ethic of capital accumulation. Although rivalry and competitive combat between hapu and iwi were commonplace, within and often between them social self-esteem depended on what was given and the interests of the individual were subordinate to those of the group. This contrasted sharply with European ways, in which social self-esteem was a product of what was acquired, and group interests were subordinate to those of the individual (Kawharu 1989).

Even so, it would be a mistake to assume that an understanding of co-operative values was entirely absent from European traditions. This re-emerged strongly in nineteenth-century socialism. Marx, while praising Darwin's model as 'the basis in natural science of our own views', i.e. his own progressive theory of historical materialism, nonetheless

EUROPEAN CULTURAL VIEWS

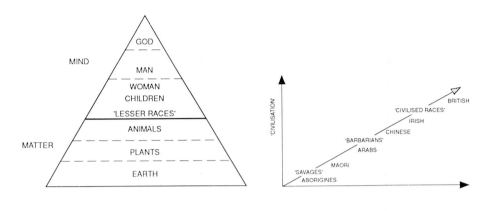

a of Nature

b of Progress and Race, from a British perspective

MAORI CULTURAL VIEWS

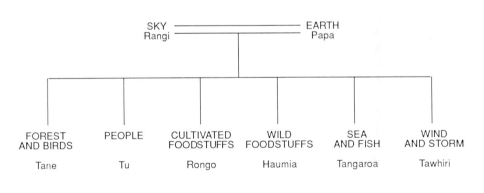

c of the Environmental Family

Figure 2.1: Cultural contexts.
Sources: constructed by author from various sources, e.g. Thomas (1984) and Yoon (1986).

based his model of human nature on a concept of 'other beingness'. This has been described as 'a capacity unique to members of the human species for empathising and cooperating with fellow members of the species' (Conway 1987, 33). Kropotkin, reacting strongly against the views of Huxley and other Darwinians, developed a natural analogy of 'mutual aid', derived from myriad examples of co-operation between members of the same species. While accepting a struggle for existence between species, he asked who were the fittest to survive. The answer was that 'we at once see that those animals that acquire habits of mutual aid are undoubtedly the fittest' (Kropotkin 1914, 6). As a renowned geographer-anarchist, he urged respect for the other peoples of the world (Kropotkin 1885), a message that was too inconvenient for most Europeans at the time to hear.

It was too inconvenient because of conflict over the one resource Europeans particularly desired on the global periphery: the land of indigenous peoples. Maori attitudes to land shared much with those of other indigenes. The land was regarded as 'the sacred trust and asset of the people as a whole' (Sinclair 1981, 86). Under customary tenure land was held tribally, with families and their kin being allocated rights of use and occupation according to the needs of individuals and the group. However, the 'mana' of the land, that is its integrity and creative power, was vested in the chief, and only the chief with the consent of the group could alienate land. Iwi territory was maintained by the ability of the group to defend it against others, and the precedence of the group over the individual in this context was summarised by the aphorism 'a house that stands alone will be consumed by fire' (Walker 1982, 70). So the Maori had a strong sense of place and attachment to land which they verbalised in the form of 'motto-maxims' identifying their mountain, river and iwi on formal oral occasions (Yoon 1986, 47–59).

Maori culture was thus centred upon nature, which provided both material and spiritual sustenance. The features of land and water bodies were woven through with spiritual meaning, and the Maori creation myth, which explained the descent of all living things from the children of Rangi (the skyfather) and Papa (the earth mother), portrayed all of nature, including people, as linked in one holistic environmental family (fig. 2.1). Although the mythology established the primacy of people in nature and validated their right to use its resources, people were not regarded as above nature and had to observe well-developed rules of propitiation and conservation. People did not own the land, they belonged to it. To the Maori, nature was sacred (Yoon 1986; Durie 1987).

It was certainly not sacred to Europeans. Although there has been much debate about White's (1967) characterisation of 'the orthodox Christian arrogance towards nature' (see Attfield 1984; Passmore 1974), it is clear that Christian Europe assigned spiritual significance only to the relationship between people and God. Europeans saw themselves as above nature, a belief mythologised in Genesis when Adam was given dominion over the animals. Theirs was a combative relationship with the natural world, for having erred in the Garden of Eden, people were made to sweat for their livelihoods thereafter. Europeans undoubtedly saw in creation a natural order, a 'chain of being' stretching from God to man, woman, the 'lesser races', down to the beasts and plants (fig. 2.1), a model which reflected the class divisions of their own societies (Thomas 1984). Lacking spiritual significance, nature was to be used for material benefit and land commodified for individual use and gain.

These were the two very different cultural contexts that the parties to the Treaty of Waitangi brought to the signing of the document in 1840. A brief statement of three articles, it was prefaced by a preamble in which the Crown offered a partnership to the Maori,[4] establishing a co-operative context that would have been readily appreciated by representatives of a culture structured on group relationships. The extent to which a written document would have been accurately understood by chiefs versed only in oral negotiation is, however, debatable, particularly given crucial differences between the

English and Maori language versions of the treaty, and problems of translating concepts central to one culture into the language of another (Biggs 1989). What is clear is that the Maori version that was signed by the chiefs guaranteed them 'te tino rangatiratanga,' the chiefly power over land, and ceded to the Crown only 'kawanatanga,' or governorship, while the English version secured the Crown's sovereignty over all New Zealand.[5] That which mattered most to the Maori, that which they thought, and many still think, the treaty protected, was the very thing that experience proved was to be taken away. As an influential chief said in 1840 'the shadow of the land goes to the Queen, but the substance remains with us'. Just a year later he revealed his fear that 'the substance of the land would pass to the European and only the shadow would remain with the Maori people' (in Asher & Naulls 1987, 13).

The clash of cultures

This fear was to prove accurate. By the turn of the century, the territories of New Zealand were all but entirely in European hands (fig. 2.2). The European population had grown at a rate unforeseen by the Maori in 1840: from 11 500 three years later, to 79 000 in 1860 and 770 000 by 1900. As the strength of the European position relative to that of the Maori increased, the force of the obligations of co-operation spelt out in the treaty's preamble, as well as that of the guarantees specified in its articles, diminished. That this was not yet so in the late 1840s, when state authority was threatened in the far north, was recognised by a former British Prime Minister, Sir Robert Peel. In a private letter in 1848 he wrote: 'If the obligations of good faith vary with the military skill and prowess of the parties to a Treaty, the New Zealanders [i.e. the Maori] have put in a claim to be respected which it has become prudent on our part to recognise' (in Adams 1977, 245).

With the passage of authority from direct British rule to local settler government in 1853, respect and prudence ceased to be on the agenda. In fact, throughout the British Empire, as the substantive power of the coloniser over the colonised grew, politicians and judges moved to dismiss indigenous rights claimed in reliance upon treaties (Williams 1989).

The question that arises, however, is how the Maori were stripped of so much land, and hence material and cultural well-being, when the treaty specifically guaranteed their rights to all that they wished to keep. A first explanation is that initially the nature of land transactions were not understood by the Maori in European terms. The concept of individualised use rights was well established among them, but that of individual land ownership was not. It is likely that European offers of guns, goods and money were interpreted as purchasing only rights of occupancy. The granting of such rights had been commonplace as gestures of mutual aid to allies and kinsfolk made destitute in war (Ward 1974, 29). There would have been every reason to extend the same privilege to Europeans, to enable them to associate with iwi to share the benefits of trade (Durie 1987, 78).

The Maori were not slow to appreciate the value of trade. Far from being culturally static, as traditional European historiography has assumed of indigenous peoples the world over, their entire millenium in New Zealand had seen continual adaptations to changing circumstances. They had discovered upon arrival from migrations from 700 AD onwards that their treasured Pacific Island fruits and vegetables, such as breadfruit and bananas, would not grow in New Zealand's cooler climate. Consequently they changed their diet to one of birdmeat and shellfish. As these resources became increasingly scarce, they not only introduced explicitly conservational themes into their environmental mythologies, but also developed horticultural economies based on vegetables like taro, yams and kumara (Davidson 1984). European vegetables and

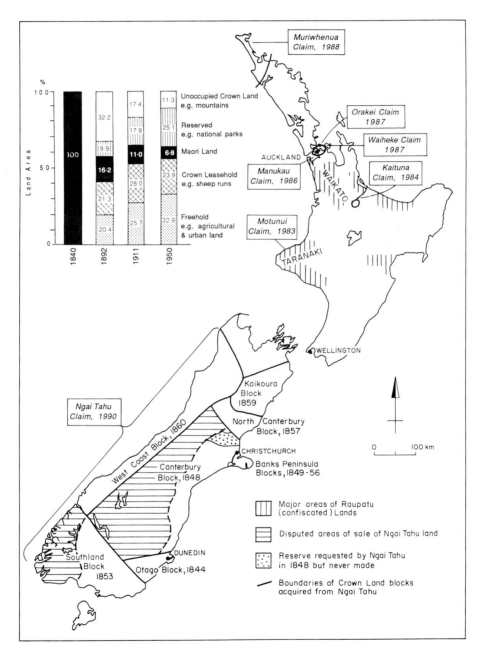

Figure 2.2: Land purchases, confiscations and claims.
Sources: constructed by author from various sources, including O'Regan (1989, 243–5).

cereals, and animals such as pigs, were readily incorporated from stocks left by Captain Cook and later navigators. It was thus a short step to the exchange of surplus food with new European residents for trade goods. So successful were their co-operative economies in this regard that it is considered that in the 1840s and early 1850s, the Maori supplied the bulk of the food consumed in the new European settlements of Auckland and Wellington (Asher & Naulls 1987, 12–14).

However, land given in exchange for money, cattle and other items of trade did not come back. There is no doubt that this was appreciated relatively quickly. Some chiefs took advantage of the situation by selling land that did not belong to them, such as conquered territories they had not occupied and, according to customary rights, therefore did not own. This was the case with the Kaikoura and North Canterbury blocks in the South Island (fig. 2.2). Consequently, as Crown agents, using such divide and rule tactics, moved to purchase increasingly large areas in the 1850s for a rapidly growing European population, the Maori began to lose control of the situation. The vast Canterbury and Southland blocks passed to the Crown in 1848 and 1853 respectively, and the boundaries of what was agreed in the sale have been disputed ever since (fig. 2.2). As elsewhere, iwi wishes to retain their sacred sites, settlements and cultivated and food gathering districts were ignored. Due to the Crown's assumption of sovereignty, English land law was presumed to apply to the whole of these blocks, with the proviso that valued iwi territories should be 'handed back' to be held under Crown title. According to the guarantees in the treaty, they should never have been taken; most were never handed back either (O'Regan 1989, 242–50).

Similar processes of land acquisition in the North Island, where the Maori population was much more numerous, generated fierce resistance. It is only recently that the lengths taken by indigenous peoples everywhere to contest the loss of their lands have been recognised in historical writing (Pawson 1990). Imbued with the same Eurocentric traditions as the actors about whom they have written, historians have long assumed that peoples of the global periphery were too weak and 'uncivilised' to compete militarily and, from this standpoint, suppressed evidence to the contrary. The extent of resistance in New Zealand's North Island has, however, been extensively documented by James Belich. Although some Maori, taking advantage of circumstances to settle old scores, sided with the Crown, there was widespread iwi co-operation designed to curb land alienation. In response to this, the state precipitated a series of armed conflicts in the 1860s that 'were more akin to classic wars of conquest than we would like to believe' (Belich 1986, 80). Governor Grey, himself an astute politician, elicited an imperial commitment of 12 000 professional soldiers for the wars, more than were available for the defence of England at the time. Although maximum Maori strength was closer to 2000 men, they exacted victory after victory. The numerical norms of imperial warfare were completely reversed and awareness of the conflicts was suppressed in European memory, unlike the heroics of British campaigns in Africa or Asia.

The success of Maori military resistance was due to better strategy and tactics, based in part on more intimate knowledge of the landscape. It also owed much to effective means of intertribal mutual aid. British troops were frequently drawn away from homeland areas into dense bush and left to attack fortifications that were often deliberately left empty. These fortifications were essentially trench systems designed to protect the Maori from superior enemy fire power: the victory at Gate Pa in 1864 was won when assaulting British troops were massacred from such protective hidden positions, having advanced after an artillery bombardment roughly twenty times as intense as that later used in the initial Allied assault on the Somme in the First World War. The Maori had perfected trench warfare a century before Europeans did so (Belich 1986, 295). In order to resist incursions in two arenas simultaneously, namely Taranaki and the Waikato, chiefs circulated their warriors between the two districts, periodically substituting man for man in order to enable hapu to maintain food production. In these ways, iwi organisation resisted a standing army.

European justification for such blatant violation of the treaty was simple. As the Minister of Justice said in 1870, '... [we require] the detribalization of the Natives — to destroy [their] principle of communism which stood as a barrier in the way of all attempts to amalgamate the Native Race into our own social and political system.' The Prime Minister considered that 'the want of force has been the one great cause of failure of all attempts ... to raise and civilise the Natives' (in Pawson 1987, 310). Both echoed Wakefield's earlier forecast that the only choice for the Maori lay between 'amalgamation and extermination' (in Miller 1974, 97). They were expected, in other words, to conform to a model of British society, to make do with a minimal amount of land, or to die.

Substantive sovereignty was eventually enforced over much of the North Island by the simple expedient of land confiscation and individualisation of title. More than 1.6 million acres of prime tribal lands, over which the British had won some authority, were confiscated (fig. 2.2) and Maori land courts established to break the principle of communal holding over much of the remainder. These courts required a limited number of Maori claimants to their own land to register title in person, failure so to do resulting in its loss. The cohesion of iwi and hapu was undermined, just as intended, by conflict between those who wished to retain their titles and those who did not, the latter often forced to sell to recoup the costs of the court proceedings (Sorrenson 1981). In such ways the precepts of a capitalist culture were used to break the authority of a co-operative one.

These conflicts were to guarantee the success of European settler capitalism. The landscape, once secured, was remade according to British models of productivity. It was asserted that 'it is colonisation that gives the real value to land' (in Burns 1983, 212), echoing theorists such as Adam Smith and Wakefield. 'Victory over environment' — a splendidly Darwinian metaphor — was exacted in the rapid draining of swamps, clearance of the North Island forests and burning of the South Island tussock grasslands. Such was the transformation of the 'wastelands', a common European term for territories that had sustained the material and social life of the Maori for a millenium. According to one geographer, this landscape transformation had taken twenty centuries in Europe and four in North America, but was engineered in only one in New Zealand (Cumberland 1941, 529).

Over substantial parts of New Zealand, the intricate pre-colonial geographies of the Maori were erased. A new iconography of landscape (Cosgrove & Daniels 1988) was created. As a first step, it was renamed in a replay of the process of asserting dominion spelt out in the mythology of Genesis. Military associations were often appropriately recalled, as in the towns of Wellington, Napier and Hastings, and the regions of Marlborough and Nelson. As Yoon (1980) pointed out, only smaller urban centres in regions of remnant Maori populations retained predominantly Maori names, and only in such areas is a preponderance of Maori names for landscape features to be found.

Two of New Zealand's most prominent mountains, Cook and Egmont, are named after English sailors.

Landscapes were redesigned according to the simplified requirements of the surveyor and farmer, leading one geographer to compare the appearance of the Canterbury plains to the geometrical artwork of the Dutch painter Piet Mondrian (Holland 1983, 26). The new capitalist economy depended on imported northern hemisphere species of flora and fauna, their introduction being referred to by Crosby (1986) as part of a process of 'ecological imperialism'. Once again the agents of this imperialism were the European settlers, although imported plants and animals were often credited with superior competitive qualities in a 'battle' against native species. A local botanist considered the 'defeat' of the latter to be 'almost certain' (Travers 1869, 299–300), echoing the view of a renowned authority, Joseph Hooker, that 'many of the small local genera of Australia, New Zealand and South Africa, will ultimately disappear' (in Crosby 1986, 165).

The key element of ecological imperialism for the Maori, however, was introduced infections against which they had limited immunity. As had happened throughout the Americas and in Australia, epidemics, bronchitis, tuberculosis and sexually transmitted diseases took a heavy toll during the 'fatal contact' with Europeans. A population that may have been as numerous as 120 000 in the early 1800s had fallen to about 56 000 by 1858. The nadir of 42 000 was reached at the turn of the century (Pool 1977, 234–5). As early as 1837 a colonist remarked that '... the natives are perfectly sensible of this decrease ... they conclude that the God of the English is removing the aboriginal inhabitants to make room for [European families]' (Crosby 1986, 250).

Later interpretations were overtly Darwinian. Darwin himself, using examples from New Zealand, Tasmania and Hawaii in 1870, concluded that 'when civilised nations come into contact with barbarians, the struggle is short' (Darwin 1901, 283). One of the most striking icons in the remade landscape was erected on a hill above Auckland, close to the site of the Commonwealth Games stadium. It is a memorial obelisk to the Maori people, with a lone imported pine, where once stood a sacred totara tree.

Loss and recovery of memory

If thinking historically in this way reveals such a stark picture of a clash of cultures, why has European New Zealand long fostered a reputation for benevolent cultural relations (see Sinclair 1971)? This reputation is partly a product of historical amnesia, as Belich (1986) has shown, but it also stems from the long relative isolation of the two cultures from each other. After the wars of the 1860s, the only iwi to flourish were those in the centre and on the northern and eastern fringes of the North Island. They had held onto land remote from the main towns, much of it of marginal quality in European eyes. Hence, as late as the 1940s three-quarters of the Maori population lived in rural districts still largely characterised by their own cultural values. 'This segregation — geographical, social, cultural — was the artificial basis for New Zealand's reputation for sound race relations' (King 1985, 189).

Many nineteenth-century European colonists had retained a lingering respect for the Maori and regarded them as wayward children who could still be 'civilised' according to the norms of the now dominant culture. The contemporary term for this was the 'amalgamation of the races' (Ward 1974). Pearson (1990) characterises such attitudes as ethnocentric and assimilationist. They stand in contrast to the racist and exclusionary stance Europeans often adopted towards the few Chinese and Indians in the country. In common with other British settler colonies, the New Zealand parliament passed a stream of legislation between 1870 and 1920 designed to exclude or limit the numbers of Asians. Maori men, however, were given the franchise as early as 1867. This apparently enlightened move was integral to the process of amalgamation. It was designed to encourage their participation in a democratic method that Joseph Schumpeter once defined as a means of 'arriving at political decisions in which individuals acquire the power to decide by means of a competitive struggle for the people's vote' (Schumpeter 1952, 269). The intention was clear: to weaken Maori allegiance to the consensual forums of the hapu and iwi. Democracy ensured that as a minority, the Maori vote could always be overridden by that of the majority, a factor reinforced by Maori representation long being restricted to only four specially created parliamentary seats.[6]

This was one means by which the agencies of the state were used to normalise the values of the European and marginalise those of the Maori. The courts moved in the same direction, from having confirmed treaty rights in the 1840s when the Maori were still in the majority, to denying their validity by the 1870s. In fact in 1877, the Chief Justice declared the Treaty of Waitangi 'a simple nullity', a position subsequently endorsed by the Privy Council in London and widely accepted in New Zealand until the 1970s (Sorrenson 1989, 151). Schools, too, were used as a means of cultural reproduction, inculcating the individualised ethics and the language of the coloniser (Walker 1990). Maori people, as the original hosts, found themselves being hosted in their own land.

The Maori did gain materially, however, from the extensive health and welfare measures first established around the turn of the century when New Zealand's new welfare state was widely regarded as 'the social laboratory of the world'. In response, far from dying out, the Maori population began to expand, reaching 64 000 in 1926 and over 295 000 by 1986.[7] Throughout these years they never forgot the treaty guarantees made to them in 1840, as the evidence of continual petitions to parliament and directly to the British Crown signify (Orange 1987; Walker 1990). From the 1950s, increasing numbers migrated to the cities until, by the 1970s, three-quarters of all Maori people lived in close proximity to Europeans. In these circumstances, their relative levels of deprivation became very visible (table 2.1). Some young, urbanised Maori began to urge their people to adopt methods of action taking on the European state in European terms. Protest became more vigorous, culminating in a well-supported land rights march the length of the North Island to parliament in 1975. In the same year, the third Labour government, whose party had been allied with Maori political forces since the 1930s, moved to give statutory recognition to the Treaty of Waitangi for the first time.

The *Treaty of Waitangi Act 1975* established the Waitangi Tribunal as a permanent, roving commission. It was charged with interpreting the principles of the treaty and applying them in hearing claims from the Maori for redress from perceived breaches of the treaty. Its mandate, however, was not retrospective; it covered only grievances arising from Crown policies or practices currently or thereafter in force. Neither could it enforce its findings; it could only make recommendations to the government of the day. Little happened until Chief Judge Durie, himself a Maori, was appointed chairman in the early 1980s. He transformed the tribunal, taking it to the marae (Maori meeting place) and turning it into a vigorous but non-adversarial arena of debate. Maori as well as English was used as its language; Maori protocol was observed in its operation

Table 2.1:   Measures of the relative material positions of European and Maori[1] in New Zealand, 1986

	European	Maori
Proportion of population	81.2	9.0
Employment status, %[2]		
Employers	7.6	1.5
Self-employed	10.1	3.1
Wage or salary earners	75.1	78.7
Unemployed	5.6	15.7
Occupational status, %[3]		
Professional, technical	16.1	5.8
Administrative, managerial	6.2	0.9
Production, labourers	30.2	56.0
Educational status, %[4]		
No school qualifications	46.4	70.2
Tertiary qualifications	31.6	12.7
Criminal status,[5] rates per 10 000		
Trialled and sentenced in court	2.7	18.7

1 Ethnic categories, based on self determination, used in NZ census 1986. Only those declaring themselves to be of one ethnic origin are included. Pacific Islanders, Asians and those declaring to be of more than one ethnic origin are omitted.
2 Of those aged fifteen years or over, in or seeking full or part time paid work: NZ census 1986.
3 Of those aged fifteen years or over, in full time paid work: NZ census 1986.
4 Of those aged fifteen years or over: NZ census, 1986
5 District and High Courts: Justice Statistics 1986.

(Temm 1990). This conscious attempt to provide a forum for the Maori, free of monocultural bias, won increasing respect and hope from the Maori themselves. Some important claims were heard in the mid 1980s (fig. 2.2). When the then National Party government rejected the tribunal's findings on the first of these (at Motunui in 1983), there was sufficient outcry from many Maori and Europeans to cause not only a political about-face but to increase considerably the cross-cultural profile of the tribunal itself.

The claims of the mid 1980s (at Motunui, Kaituna and Manukau) came from the peoples of Taranaki and the Waikato who had been rendered largely landless after the confiscations of the 1860s. They could speak with unified voices as the confiscations had, ironically, spared them the tribally divisive processes of land individualisation. Being landless, their claims concerned the pollution of water resources on which they partly relied for food. In its findings, the tribunal bared fundamental differences in the prevailing environmental attitudes of the two cultures. Water bodies have often been used by Europeans as convenient sewers; for the Maori, water is endowed with spiritual properties that must be fostered in order to sustain stocks of fish and shellfish. Hence, using water to dispose of industrial wastes or sewage is offensive in Maori eyes, even if treatment to scientifically determined standards has taken place.

The Motunui claim was prompted by a proposal to build an ocean outfall pipe from a new industrial plant on the Taranaki coast. It was feared that this would pollute the extensive shellfish beds of the Ati-Awa, which were already suffering contamination from another outfall pipe used to discharge sewage and factory wastes. The tribunal recommended that the new outfall not be built (it was not) and that land disposal methods be initiated to replace the other outfall pipe. The Kaituna claim resulted from a proposal by the Ministry of Works to discharge treated sewage from the resort city of Rotorua into the Kaituna River. The river is the outlet of Lake Rotorua and valued as a fishery by the Ngati Pikiao people. For many years, Rotorua's waste had been emptied into the lake, and despite being treated to a higher degree than that of almost any other New Zealand town or city, had caused dangerous eutrophication (high levels of nutrients, encouraging the growth of algae) in a water body that is a major recreational resource. However, the tribunal criticised the proposal as 'a mechanical answer ... coming from the mind of an engineer', betraying a lack of ecological awareness that would result simply in the problem being transferred further along the same ecosystem. Again, it recommended land-based disposal, a method used for sewage in Melbourne, Australia, for more than a century. Such a scheme has since been put into effect. The Manukau case, brought by the Tainui, was more complex, but revealed how this extensive harbour had long received Auckland's waste, destroying tribal fisheries, to many of which access had already been denied by local planning authorities. A comprehensive clean up campaign was recommended, and work begun.

In these cases, the tribunal won growing respect from many Europeans for the care with which it heard and interpreted evidence, and the attainable resolutions that it promoted (Sorrenson 1989). It also raised the expectations of the Maori. Its reports are a unique record of Maori environmental values and of previously hidden histories. In exploring the meaning of the principles of the treaty, it drew on the evidence of a new generation of constitutional lawyers (in Kawharu 1989). As a result, the view of the treaty as a 'simple nullity' has been declared 'clearly untenable ... as a matter of international law' (Kingsbury 1959, 121). Instead, the tribunal defined the treaty as a partnership between the Crown and the Maori, 'the foundation of a developing social contract, not merely a historical document' (Sorrenson 1989, 162). This position was broadly endorsed by the Labour Party, seeking to retain the Maori vote after a decade out of office. Upon the election of the fourth Labour government in 1984, the deputy Prime Minister, himself a constitutional lawyer, assumed responsibility for the formulation of a treaty policy. A year later Labour amended the Treaty of Waitangi Act to enable the tribunal to hear Maori claims resulting from treaty violations extending back to 1840.

This measure opened the floodgates to a series of land claims from Maori people all over New Zealand. By the late 1980s, few had been settled and a backlog of 150 cases had built up. Appointments to the tribunal were substantially increased to enable it to work on different claims simultaneously. One of the first to be heard under the new Act was from the Ngai Tahu, whose grievances arise from loss of ancestral lands in an area covering seven-eighths of the South Island (fig. 2.2). Their argument was not for the return of all these lands, but for compensation for the Crown's failure to make requested reserves at the time of the original purchases and its very liberal interpretations of the boundaries of territories the tribe had agreed to sell. Of the rectitude of the Ngai Tahu claim there is no doubt: this was admitted by a Royal Commission in 1879 (which prompted the government of the day to disband it), and another in 1944, which resulted in the ongoing payment of a small annuity to the tribe. The relevant question was the realistic extent of compensation, and whether it should be in cash, shares in state-owned enterprises (such as the Land and Forestry Corporations), return of title to the extensive Crown leasehold lands occupied by sheep farmers, or a combination of all three with greater iwi representation on decision making bodies such as National Parks boards

(O'Regan 1989). The outcome of this complex claim is bound to have far-reaching implications for how other land claims, such as those to raupatu, the confiscated territories in the North Island, may be settled.[8] In 1988, the tribunal issued a major report on the fisheries component of the Muriwhenua claim, spurred by a government move to privatise access to all of New Zealand's offshore fisheries (Cant 1990). It not only established the impressive extent to which the peoples of Northland harvested the fisheries in the mid-nineteenth century, but observed that the Crown never purchased any fisheries rights from the Maori, despite these rights having been specifically guaranteed in the treaty. It recommended that the two treaty partners immediately negotiate a resolution.

A key question to arise since 1985 is whether, after 150 years of European domination, Maoridom still possesses adequate iwi structures to manage the extent of resources that are being claimed and might reasonably be granted to settle demonstrable historical injustices (Kawharu 1989). Managerial and professional skills are not widely available among the Maori (table 2.1), and the urbanisation of their population since 1950 has removed many from their original territories and left them ignorant of iwi affiliations. In greater Auckland, which today houses one-third of New Zealand's Maori, there are three traditional iwi groupings. Once these people are accounted for, over 100 000 Auckland Maori remain. How, asks Sir Hugh Kawharu, one of the country's most respected Maori elders, is the rangatiratanga of these people to be defined? How can they benefit from the return of tribal assets? (Kawharu 1990).

Notwithstanding such problems, the Treaty of Waitangi is now, for the first time since the 1850s, at the forefront of national consciousness. In a celebrated case in 1987, the Court of Appeal, the highest court in the land, found in favour of the national Maori Council in its attempt to restrain the potential privatisation of state assets involved in claims before the Waitangi Tribunal. In its findings, the court reaffirmed the treaty as a living partnership between the Crown and the Maori, and one which the judges considered the Crown had an active responsibility to promote (Temm 1990). It is this decision that Ranganui Walker, a prominent Maori activist and writer, has hailed as 'pitch[ing] New Zealand firmly into the post-colonial era' (Walker 1990, 265) (fig. 2.3).

Conclusion: two metaphors

The second half of the 1980s, the years of the fourth Labor government, was certainly a period of momentous change in New Zealand. Labor's record was to prove extremely ambivalent. On the one hand, it pursued radical social programmes designed to settle Maori grievances. It established for the first time a Ministry of Women's Affairs and enacted pay equity legislation. It gave considerable attention to environmental matters and introduced a widely recognised non-nuclear policy. On the other hand, its economic programme was libertarian in the extreme, a product of capture by New Right forces (Jesson 1987). A protected economy was opened up to free market forces, and many state assets were either corporatised or sold (Kelsey 1990). Labor was clearly guided by two overriding metaphors: one of co-operation, aimed at more constructive dialogue between the Maori and Europeans, women and men, and people and the environment; and one of vigorous competition, overtly promoted to make companies and individuals 'leaner and fitter' in striving for success within the dictates of international capitalism.

Figure 2.3: Cultural relations. The motif used by the Waitangi Tribunal on the cover of its reports. The Tribunal's own description is that this motif invokes 'the signing of the Treaty of Waitangi and the consequent development of Maori-European history interwoven in New Zealand, in a pattern not yet completely known, still unfolding'. Reproduced courtesy of the Waitangi Tribunal.

It is arguable how much of substance was actually achieved within the framework of the first metaphor. Certainly, many of the initiatives taken had the potential to change long-standing patterns of social relations in New Zealand. However, it was the impact of the policies of the second metaphor that seemed more material to most people, be they Maori or European. New Zealand became an increasingly class-divided society. Unprecedented displays of conspicuous consumption at one end of the scale were matched by growing levels of distress at the other. As BMWs became more popular, the queues of jobless people lengthened. Unemployment levels reached 200 000 in a country that thirty years before had regarded one thousand people out of work as unacceptable (Gould 1982). Maori people, traditionally marginalised, were disproportionately affected (table 2.1). At the very time when 'the grimmer realities of New Zealand race relations' in the past (Belich 1986, 299) were becoming more public, grim realities were being reproduced in the present. It was clearly in the interests of the state to obscure this, particularly in 1990. It was feared that the 150th anniversary of the signing of the treaty would be used by some Maori for vigorous protest over material conditions and to highlight the slow speed at which treaty claims were being resolved (Pawson 1991). Hence the resort to spectacle, such as the carnival production of the Commonwealth Games, to entertain, but also to divert, simplify and conceal more pressing issues.

However, in respect of relations between Maori and the European state in New Zealand, which metaphor will have a greater long-term effect? The experience of the 1980s clearly showed that, following Giddens (1981), the state can be both a force for emancipation and the defender of the interests of the powerful. However, when not only principles, but power and resources, are at stake, a capitalist state is likely to give primacy to the competitive pressures of its own cultural context. By 1990, this was becoming very clear (Kelsey 1990). For instance, the Labour government sought to use the opportunity provided by the tribunal's report on the Muriwhenua fishing claims to find a resolution to all iwi fishing claims. The Maori partners to the treaty sought a half share of a fisheries resource which they had never sold to the Crown, yet over which they had nearly completely lost control. After lengthy negotiations, the government overrode the tribunal's recommendation that an agreed settlement be reached, and enacted legislation that guaranteed iwi only 10 per cent. Then, after Labour lost office in 1990, due to widespread discontent with its economic programme, a National government was elected. It quickly moved to repeal the pay equity legislation and to reverse Labour's moves to delegate limited authority and control of state funds to iwi authorities.

Despite the context of historical understanding of cultural relations that this chapter has sought to portray, there is now much wider recognition of the validity of Maori cultural values. The vitality of Maoridom has been spurred by the renewed recognition given to the Treaty of Waitangi. As the founding document of modern New Zealand, it is no longer a European lost memory, but whether it can or will be used, in the words of the chairman of the tribunal, as part of a process 'to put an end to this driving need that permeates our western society, to own, possess and dominate the landscape, and to re-establish a corner of the world where one can simply belong' (Durie 1987, 80–1) is another matter.

Notes

1   The term 'European' is used in this chapter not only to describe the peoples of Europe who migrated throughout the world in the nineteenth century (most of the immigrants to New Zealand being Britons), but also to describe the majority population in New Zealand today. The Maori term for such people is 'pakeha'. This word was unknown before European contact, as was the term 'Maori' itself. The indigenous people of New Zealand identified themselves primarily on the basis of family and tribal affiliation, e.g. Ngati Toa, Ngai Tahu.

2   An exception to this occurred in Australia, as the Aborigines were then considered to possess an insufficient degree of political organisation to enter into a treaty. To quote the British Select Committee on Aborigines (1837): 'destitute are they even of the rudest forms of civil polity' (in McHugh 1989, 57).

3   The Maori equivalent of the English word 'tribe' is 'iwi'. Many Maori and European writers tend to use the two words interchangeably. Iwi were not the basic building blocks of Maori society; this privilege belonged to whanau (the extended family) and hapu (groupings of families), themselves allied by kin relations into iwi. For a lucid discussion of Maori concepts, see Walker (1990).

4   The treaty partners were the British Crown, represented at the signing by a newly appointed Governor, and Maori tribes, represented by their chiefs. Today the Crown partner is in effect the government of New Zealand. Constitutionally, its authority is still derived from the Crown, via an appointed Governor General. Sir Paul Reeves, Governor General from 1985-90, is himself a Maori.

5   Full discussions of the two treaty texts are to be found in Orange (1987), Kawharu (1989) and Walker (1990). On the problems inherent in conveying the concepts of one culture in the language of another, Biggs gives an example from English to Japanese, exposed by retranslation into English. 'Liberty and the pursuit of happiness' becomes 'licence to commit lustful pleasures'! (1989, 303).

6   In fact, the Maori who met the individualised property qualification, which of course few could, were permitted to vote in European electorates from 1852. The 1867 Act allowed all Maori men to vote but only in four special Maori electorates. In the 1890s, the property qualification was abolished, the franchise was extended to women and 'half-castes' were permitted to vote in either European or Maori seats. This choice was not open to all Maori until 1975 (Sorrenson 1986).

7   Until this date, the census defined all persons of half or more Maori origin as Maori for statistical purposes. In the 1986 census, self identification as the basis of ethnic origin was used for the first time. The figure of 295 000 was those declaring themselves to be Maori. It rose to 390 000 with the inclusion of those declared as owning two ethnic origins, 'European–Maori'.

8   The tribunal's report was published in 1991. It said 'that the theme that constantly arises in (our) findings and indeed almost as constantly conceded by the Crown, is the failure of the Crown to ensure Ngai Tahu were left with ample land for their present and future needs'. Almost all aspects of the claim were upheld, except for those concerning the boundary disputes shown on figure 2.2. However, it made few specific proposals for recompense, this being a matter of negotiation between Ngai Tahu and the Crown. It did urge that a sum of not less than NZ $ 1 million be paid to the Ngai Tahu to enable them to engage professional assistance in the negotiations (Waitangi Tribunal, Ngai Tahu Report 1991, Wellington).

References

Adams, P. 1977, *Fatal Necessity: British Intervention in New Zealand, 1830-1847*, Auckland University Press, Auckland.

Asher, G. & Naulls, D. 1987, *Maori Land*, New Zealand Planning Council, Planning Paper No. 29, Wellington.

Attfield, R. 1984, *The Ethics of Environmental Concern*, Basil Blackwell, Oxford.

Baines, D. 1985, *Migration in a Mature Economy, Emigration and Internal Migration in England and Wales, 1861-1900*, Cambridge University Press, Cambridge.

Belich, J. 1986, *The New Zealand Wars and the Victorian Interpretation of Racial Conflict*, Auckland University Press, Auckland.

Biggs, B. 1989, 'Humpty Dumpty and the Treaty of Waitangi', in I.H. Kawharu (ed.), *Waitangi, Maori and Pakeha Perspectives of the Treaty of Waitangi*, Oxford University Press, Auckland, pp. 300–12.

Burns, P. 1983, *Te Rauparaha, A New Perspective*, Penguin, Auckland.

Cant, R.G. 1990, 'Waitangi: treaty and tribunal', *New Zealand Journal of Geography*, 89, pp. 7–12.

Conway, D. 1987, *A Farewell to Marx: An Outline and Appraisal of his Theories*, Penguin, Harmondsworth.

Cosgrove, D. & Daniels, S. (eds) 1988, *The Iconography of Landscape, Essays on the Symbolic Representation, Design and Use of Past Environments*, Cambridge University Press, Cambridge.

Crosby, A.W. 1986, *Ecological Imperialism: The Biological Expansion of Europe 900-1900*, Cambridge University Press, Cambridge.

Cumberland, K. 1941, 'A century's change: natural to cultural vegetation in New Zealand', *Geographical Review*, 31, pp. 529–54.

Darwin, C. 1901, *The Descent of Man and Selection in Relation to Sex*, John Murray, London.

Davidson, J.M. 1984, *The Prehistory of New Zealand*, Longman Paul, Auckland.

Driver, F. 1988, 'The historicity of human geography', *Progress in Human Geography*, 12, 4, pp. 497–506.

Durie, E. 1987, 'The law and the land', in J. Phillips (ed.), *Te Whenua, Te Iwi, The Land and the People*, Allen & Unwin, Wellington, pp. 78–81.

Giddens, A. 1981, *A Contemporary Critique of Historical Materialism*, Macmillan, London.

Gould, J. 1982, *The Rake's Progress? The New Zealand Economy Since 1945*, Hodder & Stoughton, Auckland.

Holland, P.G. 1983, 'Plants and lowland Canterbury landscapes', *Proceedings of the Twelfth New Zealand Geography Conference*, New Zealand Geographical Society, Christchurch, pp. 25–31.

Horsman, R. 1981, *Race and Manifest Destiny: The Origins of American Racial Anglo-Saxonism*, Harvard University Press, Cambridge, Mass.

Huxley, T.H. 1894, *Evolution and Ethics and Other Essays*, Macmillan, London.

James, C. 1987, *The Quiet Revolution: Turbulence and Transition in Contemporary New Zealand*, Allen & Unwin, Wellington.

Jesson, B. 1987, *Behind the Mirror Glass: The Growth of Wealth and Power in New Zealand in the Eighties*, Penguin, Auckland.

Kawharu, I.H. 1989, 'Introduction', in I.H. Kawharu (ed.), *Waitangi, Maori and Pakeha Perspectives of the Treaty of Waitangi*, Oxford University Press, Auckland, pp. x–xxiii.

Kawharu, I.H. 1990, 'The quid pro quo in the treaty', Radio New Zealand broadcast.

Kelsey, J. 1990, *A Question of Honour? Labour and the Treaty 1984-1989*, Allen & Unwin, Wellington.

King, M. 1985, *Being Pakeha*, Hodder & Stoughton, Auckland.

Kingsley, B. 1989, 'The Treaty of Waitangi: some international law aspects', in I.H. Kawharu (ed.), *Waitangi, Maori and Pakeha Perspectives of the Treaty of Waitangi*, Oxford University Press, Auckland, pp. 121–57.

Kropotkin, P. 1885, 'What geography ought to be', *The Nineteenth Century*, 18, pp. 940–56.

Kropotkin, P. 1914, *Mutual Aid: A Factor of Evolution*, Extending Horizons Books, Boston.

Macfarlane, A. 1978, *The Origins of English Individualism: The Family, Property, and Social Transition*, Basil Blackwell, Oxford.

McHugh, P. 1989, 'Constitutional theory and Maori claims', in I.H. Kawharu (ed.),*Waitangi, Maori and Pakeha Perspectives of the Treaty of Waitangi*, Oxford University Press, Auckland, pp. 25–63.

Miller, J. 1974, *Early Victorian New Zealand: A Study of Racial Tension and Social Attitudes 1839-1852*, Oxford University Press, Wellington.

Orange, C. 1987, *The Treaty of Waitangi*, Allen & Unwin, Wellington.

O'Regan, T. 1989, 'The Ngai Tahu Claim', in I.H. Kawharu (ed.), *Waitangi, Maori and Pakeha Perspectives of the Treaty of Waitangi*, Oxford University Press, Auckland, pp. 234–62.

Passmore, J. 1974, *Man's Responsibility for Nature: Ecological Problems and Western Traditions*, Duckworth, London.

Pawson, E. 1987, 'Order and freedom: a cultural geography of New Zealand', in P.G. Holland & W.B. Johnston, *Southern Approaches, Geography in New Zealand*, New Zealand Geographical Society, Christchurch, pp. 305–29.

Pawson, E. 1990, 'British expansion overseas, 1730-1914' in R. Butlin & R. Dodgshon (eds), *An Historical Geography of England and Wales*, 2nd edn, Academic Press, London, pp. 521–44.

Pawson, E. 1991, '1990 and the Treaty', *New Zealand Geographer*, 47, 1, pp. 32–5.

Pearson, D. 1990, *A Dream Deferred : the Origins of Ethnic Conflict in New Zealand*, Allen & Unwin/Port Nicholson Press, Wellington.

Peet, R. 1985, 'The social origins of environmental determinism', *Annals of the Association of American Geographers*, 75, 3, pp. 309–33.

Pool, D.I. 1977, *The Maori Population of New Zealand 1769-1971*, Auckland University Press, Auckland.

Schumpeter, J. 1952, *Capitalism, Socialism and Democracy*, 4th edn, Allen & Unwin, London.

Sinclair, K. 1971, 'Why are race relations in New Zealand better than in South Africa, South Australia or South Dakota?', *New Zealand Journal of History*, 5, 2, pp. 121–7.

Sinclair, D. 1981, 'Land: Maori view and European response', in M. King (ed.), *Te Ao Hurihuri The World Moves On: Aspects of Maoritanga*, Longman Paul, Auckland, pp. 115–39.

Sorrenson, M.P.K. 1981, 'Maori and pakeha', in W. H. Oliver (ed.), *The Oxford History of New Zealand,* Oxford University Press, Wellington, pp. 168–93.

Sorrenson, M.P.K. 1986, *A History of Maori Representation in Parliament,* Report of the Royal Commission on Electoral Reform, Wellington, B1–64.

Sorrenson, M.P.K. 1989, 'Towards a radical reinterpretation of New Zealand history: the role of the Waitangi Tribunal', in I.H. Kawharu (ed.), *Waitangi, Maori and Pakeha Perspectives of the Treaty of Waitangi,* Oxford University Press, Auckland, pp. 158–78.

Tauroa, H. 1982, *Race Against Time,* Human Rights Commission, Wellington.

Temm, P. 1990, *The Waitangi Tribunal: The Conscience of the Nation,* Random Century, Auckland.

Thomas, K. 1984, *Man and the Natural World: Changing Attitudes in England 1500-1800,* Penguin, Harmondsworth.

Travers, W.T.L. 1869, 'On the changes effected in the natural features of a new country by the introduction of civilised races', *Transactions New Zealand Institute*, 2, pp. 299–330.

Walker, R. 1982, 'Development from below: institutional transformation in a plural society', in I. Shirley (ed.), *Development Tracks*, Dunmore Press, Palmerston North, pp. 69–89.

Walker, R. 1990, *Ka Whawhai Tonu Matou: Struggle Without End,* Penguin, Auckland.

Ward, A. 1974, *A Show of Justice: Racial Amalgamation in Nineteenth Century New Zealand,* Australian National University Press, Canberra.

White, L. 1967, 'The historical roots of our ecologic crisis', *Science*, 155, pp. 1203–7.

Williams, D. 1989, 'Te tiriti o Waitangi — unique relationship between Crown and tangata whenua?', in I.H. Kawharu (ed.), *Waitangi, Maori and Pakeha Perspectives of the Treaty of Waitangi,* Oxford University Press, Auckland, pp. 64–93.

Yoon, H.-K. 1980, 'An analysis of place names for cultural features in New Zealand', *New Zealand Geographer,* 36, 1, pp. 30–4.

Yoon, H.-K. 1986, *Maori Mind, Maori Land, Essays on the Cultural Geography of the Maori People from an Outsider's Perspective*, Peter Lang, Berne.

Young, R.M. 1985, *Darwin's Metaphor: Nature's Place in Victorian Culture,* Cambridge University Press, Cambridge.

Constructing geographies:
identities of inclusion

3 Elite landscapes as cultural (re)productions: the case of Shaughnessy Heights

James Duncan

Introduction

This chapter examines the way in which a particular elite landscape, Shaughnessy Heights in Vancouver, Canada, has been produced. Shaughnessy Heights is not simply a cultural production in the sense that it is the product of a particular group of people at a particular time and place. It is also, as I will argue below, a cultural (re)production in the double sense that it not only reproduces a cultural landscape model from another place and time (nineteenth-century England), but also reproduces a particular class distinctiveness and model of elite consumption within contemporary Canadian society. By tracing the history of Shaughnessy Heights from its founding by the railroad as a speculator suburb in the early twentieth century until the early 1980s when it was defined as a historic resource, I will show how cultural production is enmeshed within a whole sociopolitical complex of development companies, zoning boards, city planning departments, city council, and heritage committees. Particular attention will be paid to the period of the late 1970s and early 1980s when the Shaughnessy Heights Property Owners' Association successfully steered a new and highly restrictive zoning code and neighbourhood design guidelines, which institutionalised an elite landscape model, through the City Planning Department and City Council. The final section of this chapter explores some working-class responses to the institutionalisation of this elite landscape model.

Cultural (re)production

The term 'culture' is used in a variety of ways in the English language. One is to refer to 'high' culture, or what is at times termed civilisation, a body of elite knowledge or canon encompassing what is thought to be most valuable in art, literature and social mores. Such knowledge is transmitted by an intellectual elite both within universities (in Western Civilisation courses, for example) and outside such formal institutions in the form of books, films, and lectures on literary and art criticism for an educated public. A second notion of culture, the one that concerns us in this chapter, is a more democratic notion. In this second usage, which is drawn from twentieth-century anthropology, culture is not the exclusive preserve of elites within a society, but something in which all members of a society participate equally. It is the way of life of a people. In this usage, for example, a night out at the pub is every bit as much a part of English culture as the plays of Shakespeare or the paintings of Constable. Although I subscribe to this more democratic view of culture, I wish to qualify in a small but important way the manner in which we think about it. Most people consider culture something that we simply 'have' because we are all born into a particular culture (and social class, for that matter) that existed before we came into the world and will continue long after we die. It is precisely this collective quality of culture that makes it appear to be something external to us as individuals. I would argue, however, that it is analytically more useful to think of culture as something that we actively (re)produce rather than something external to us.

What are the implications of people (re)producing rather than simply having culture? The major one is that it allows us to deal with the question of agency; that is, people are not portrayed by social science as passive carriers of culture, rather their culture is something that they not only learn, but also sustain, defend, resist, and even create or reject. When viewed in this way, we can see that culture as a system of ideas is inextricable from the social structuration of a society and from political process. For example, we can see the interlinkage between cultural ideas of race and gender on the one hand, and political practice on the other, in current debates in the United States over the role of women or African Americans within the society. Similarly, we can see cultural definitions of home and neighbourhood being worked out politically and economically in city councils, zoning board meetings and lawsuits between property owners.

This chapter explores the (re)production of culture by examining the behaviour of an elite group in Vancouver, Canada. While all groups engage in such (re)production, the production process is more clearly discernible at some times than at others. For example, during times of conflict, when a group feels threatened, cultural production processes which are normally submerged from view and operate at a deep level, rise closer to the surface. At such times people highlight cultural assumptions in order to frame arguments against their adversaries. During such periods of 'foregrounding' or, to use Giddens' (1979, 5) terms, the shift from practical to discursive knowledge, cultural assumptions are open to review and contest both within the group that holds the views and from others. While cultural assumptions rise closer to the surface during such times of conflict, they nevertheless remain partially submerged, for people develop an awareness of the strategic effect of their arguments on others and thus selectively highlight or mask their beliefs in order to forward their cause. This can be illustrated by considering the attempt by the board members of the Shaughnessy Heights Property Owners' Association to convince a largely sympathetic City Planning Department and a rather less sympathetic City Council to support their plan to rezone the neighbourhood and institute design guidelines on all future development. Until the members of the board of the Property Owners' Association met with planning officials they operated with a largely unarticulated understanding of their own cultural assumptions about what their neighbourhood should look like and how best to institute changes. The meetings with city officials forced them to articulate their assumptions then refine them in light of how they thought city officials would react to them. In the two years that I was an observer at meetings between board members and city officials, I witnessed not only a foregrounding of cultural assumptions by board members, but also a subsequent repackaging of these ideas in order to make them acceptable to both planners and city councillors who did not necessarily share all of these assumptions. The result of this process was a cultural production, a neighbourhood that conformed to a particular elite style which is termed Anglophile. This style will be examined in more detail later.

If the notion of 'having' culture seems too passive to capture the contested nature of cultural process, how might we conceptualise it more effectively? For our purposes perhaps the most satisfactory conception of culture has been put forward by Raymond Williams (1982). He (p. 13) defines culture as 'the signifying system through which necessarily (though among other means) a social order is communicated, reproduced, experienced and explored'. He argues that cultural practice and cultural production are not 'simply derived from an otherwise constituted social order but are themselves major elements in its constitution' (1982, 12–13). Williams distinguishes cultural production from other kinds of social organisation such as the political or economic systems and from more specific systems of signs while emphasising that, as a signifying system, culture is embedded in other systems as a constitutive component. Williams cites dwellings as an example of this interpenetration. While dwellings primarily satisfy the need for shelter, they also signify a particular kinship or family system and further signify internal social differentiations (1982, 211). In certain cases, especially among elites, the signifying factor overrides the normally primary factor of shelter. There are several advantages to Williams' definition of culture. One is that cultural systems, although analytically distinct from social and political systems, are conceptualised as dialectically related to the latter. Another is that such a definition emphasises both the systematic quality of culture (as a structured system of signs) and its processual quality as something which is temporal, dynamic, contested and reaffirmed.

Anglophilia as a cultural system

We will now elaborate the rather abstract notion of culture as a signifying system. In the case of the Shaughnessy elite, the system of signs is adopted from a nineteenth-century English upper-class cultural model. This system of signs is expressed in different media: in language, in dress, in demeanour, in institutions such as social clubs and private schools, and in the residential landscape.

This chapter will focus upon the landscape, not only because it is an essential part of geography, but because it is one of the central (and for an individual and the city government the costliest) elements in a cultural system. Landscapes are ordered assemblages of objects which act as a signifying system through which a social system is communicated, reproduced, experienced and explored. By acting as a signifying system a landscape does more than simply fulfil obvious, mundane functional requirements. For example, residential dwellings do more than provide shelter from the elements. Rather, by encoding within a landscape various conventional signs of such things as group membership and social status, individuals are able to tell morally charged 'stories' about themselves and the social structure of the society in which they live. A number of authors, including Firey (1945), Lowenthal and Prince (1965), Duncan (1973), Duncan and Duncan (1980, 1984), Pratt (1981), Hugill (1986), and Wyckoff (1990), have argued that landscapes are a major repository of symbols of social status.

The importance of the residential landscape as a symbol of individual or group identity varies cross-culturally (Duncan 1981, 1985; Rapoport 1981). In highly individualistic capitalist societies such as Australia, Canada and the United States, where status is largely achieved rather than being ascribed by membership in a caste or kin group, such as in South Asia, a major means of communicating social identity is through the private 'conspicuous' consumption of objects. The dwelling, together with the status level of the neighbourhood, is one of the principal symbols of social status. The creation and preservation of residential landscapes serve as part of the vehicle through which the integrity of a social group is maintained. Landscapes and the other elements of a culture are used to define membership in a social group through reaffirmation of members' values, and exclusion of non-members. The process not only involves conscious sociopolitical action, but also the unintended consequences of collective action based on unarticulated, 'taken-for-granted' values. A residential landscape helps in the reproduction of a class or status group because it is an important repository of symbols of social class and ethnic heritage. Increasingly subtle variations allow it to continue to serve this function for a particular social group.

Having reviewed the role played by the landscape in a cultural system, let us now outline a particular cultural model (the Anglophile), then examine the manner in which the Shaughnessy elite of Vancouver have made use of this signifying system, and the way the economic and political systems of the city have interpenetrated it. At the heart of this landscape system stands the English country house and garden. Of course the real English country house and garden as a cultural system are not simply mortar, stone, wooden beams and overgrown perennial beds, but a complex web of social and place relations which could not be exactly reproduced outside England. What can be created, however, is a simulation, a sign system which stands for an emulated system of relations. However, it is actually more complicated than this. There is no simple relation between the simulated and the authentic, as the nineteenth- and early twentieth-century English version which serves as an original for the twentieth-century Vancouver version is itself a simulation of an earlier version with its own somewhat different symbolic code.

In the late eighteenth century, the urban English upper and upper middle classes adopted an increasingly romantic view of the countryside and country pursuits. These attitudes became formalised in the nineteenth century in the form of idealised country residences situated on the peripheries of English cities (Lowenthal & Prince 1965, 189–90). The effect sought was the picturesque, a landscape that evoked a mood of nostalgia for the rural past. Within an urban context, the picturesque had the qualities of closeness, variety and intimacy, and the ever-recurring contrasts of tall and low, large and small, wide and narrow, straight and crooked, closes and retreats and odd leafy corners (Pevsner 1957, 105).

Architects and landscape architects sought to make the new look like the old and blend unobtrusively into a 'naturalised' setting (Girouard 1981, 228). During the latter half of the nineteenth century, nostalgia for the life of the gentry was signified within English cities by 'Old English' style houses. By the early twentieth century this nostalgia was manifested in the rage for 'Tudor' style houses and diffused from urban elites to the more modest structures of the middle classes (Wiener 1981, 66). Coupled with this Tudor revival was a dramatic increase of interest in the preservation of old buildings. The result of these two trends was 'a generalised historicity and rusticity — the purpose of which was to convey a feeling of old rural England, rather than to adhere to any particular and consistent style' (Wiener 1981, 650). According to Raymond Williams (1973, 248), this yearning for an idealised past on the part of generations of upper and middle-class English people was deeply ironic because in the late nineteenth and twentieth centuries in England 'there was almost an inverse proportion ... between the relative importance of the working rural economy and the cultural importance of rural ideas'.

When the country house style was transferred to England's colonies and former colonies it became doubly coded, signifying not only the status of gentry which it did in England, but also an abstract concept of Englishness which was seen by Anglophile elites as the most prestigious ethnic identity. Such a landscape model is to be found in such geographically diverse locations as hill stations in India (Kenny forthcoming) and Sri Lanka (Duncan 1989), the suburb of Toorak in Melbourne, Australia (Ley forthcoming), many major cities around the United States (Hugill 1986; Wyckoff 1990), and most of the large cities of Canada (Ley forthcoming).

Shaughnessy Heights as a cultural (re)production 1907-83

Shaughnessy Heights serves as a fine example of how Anglophilia as a cultural system is fundamentally interconnected with the economic and political systems of a society.[1] For example, the English cultural model was initially used in Vancouver to achieve a particular end, the sale of land by the Canadian Pacific Railroad (CPR) to an elite. Increasingly, however, this link between a particular Anglophile cultural model and the economic goals (profits for CPR from the sale of land) which that cultural model was designed to support could only be sustained by enmeshing it within a political framework both at the provincial and municipal levels, as CPR sought to protect the value of its undeveloped land in the area by restricting the free market in land through zoning regulations. By the 1970s, however, the relationship between this cultural model, economic goals and the local political framework had been redefined. The Anglophile houses in Shaughnessy were no longer a way for the railway to make money. Rather, they were seen as part of the heritage of the city of Vancouver, and therefore something to be protected through legislative action from an economic rationality that argued that a greater profit was often to be made by subdividing large lots and tearing down early twentieth-century mansions.

In 1884 CPR was granted 2428 ha (6000 acres) of land in Vancouver in exchange for extending the transcontinental railroad to that fledgling port city. In 1907 CPR began clearing 140 ha (345 acres) immediately to the south of the central business district which it hoped to convert into the most prestigious residential suburb in the city. The suburb was to be named Shaughnessy Heights after the current president of CPR, Lord Thomas Shaughnessy. The railroad then retained the services of Frederick Todd, a landscape architect from Montreal who was greatly influenced by the work of Frederick Law Olmsted, the American landscape architect whose romantic English-inspired 'country in the city' designs were the rage during the latter part of the nineteenth century. Taking advantage of the hilly topography of the subdivision, streets were laid out in a sinuous fashion to follow contours, and sewer and water lines were built. The lots ranged in size from 810 m^2 (one-fifth of an acre) to 6000 m^2 (1.5 acres) and the area was transected by several handsome boulevards and a 2 ha (5 acre) park (fig. 3.1). It is estimated that before a single house was built $1 million were spent on developing the

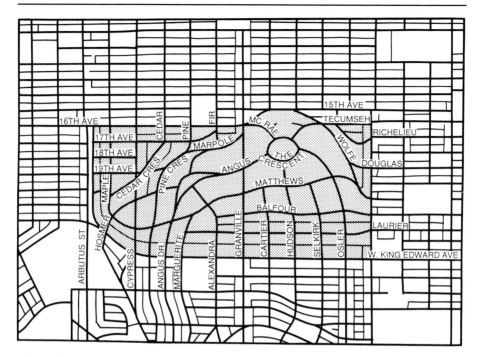

Figure 3.1: Map of Shaughnessy Heights (the shaded area represents Shaughnessy Heights).

land. CPR planned, however, to recover this sum many times over through the sale of lots to the wealthy citizens of this rapidly growing city. The railway threw the full weight of its prestige behind the development of Shaughnessy Heights in order to make it the kind of high status Anglophile environment that would appeal to businesspeople and professionals. Streets were named after four of its directors, prominent local figures, and a Canadian and British Prime Minister. In 1909, to show his confidence in the project, Richard Marpole, the local head of CPR, built the first house in the area.

Land was sold in the subdivision for $25 000 per hectare ($10 000 per acre), a large sum of money for undeveloped land in those days. Only single family dwellings were permitted, with a minimum price of $6000. In order to entice investors to build in Shaughnessy Heights CPR loaned buyers 90 per cent of the price of the land (at 6 per cent for eight years) and 66 per cent of the price of the building (up to a maximum of $5000). Altogether the company set aside the huge sum of $5 million for loans on homes. Such loans were, however, only available if the plans for the building met the standards set by CPR. Building plans were carefully checked, not only to ensure that they adhered to the price guidelines, but also for their overall appearance including positioning on the lot, house style, and quality of building materials. Thus from the beginning there were design controls on housing which would ensure that the house and lot would conform to the English country house style. The only zoning restrictions at this time, however, were that the area remain single family residential. The result was a residential area of very large lots with Victorian and Tudor style mansions, many of which had gate houses and stables (fig. 3.2). The average lot size was nearly 1500 m² (16 000 ft²), compared to 370 m² (4000 ft²) for single-family detached housing in middle-class sections of the city. Approximately half of the Shaughnessy Heights houses are still over 370 m² (4000 ft²) in area. In other words, these houses exceed the average lot size of nearby middle-class areas.

By 1914, 243 houses had been completed, approximately 40 per cent of the present stock. The company sought to protect its investment by safeguarding the exclusive nature of the development and its control over the area's appearance. To achieve this, in 1914 it paid for a group of Shaughnessy residents to travel to Victoria in order to convince the provincial government to allow Shaughnessy Heights to break away from the municipality of Point Grey (then an independent suburb of Vancouver) and become a separate municipality. Point Grey also sent a delegation to oppose the secession. Although the provincial legislature rejected the proposal for secession, it created the Shaughnessy Heights Settlement Act which allowed the area to become a separate ward of Point Grey with the important proviso that taxes collected in the area were to be used solely for its benefit. These funds were not only spent on schools but also on maintaining highly manicured parks and streetscapes (fig. 3.3).

Although in 1922 Point Grey became the first municipality in Canada to pass zoning regulations, these controls were not seen as restrictive enough by CPR. The railway, therefore, once again turned to the provincial government which in December 1922 passed the Shaughnessy Heights Building Restriction Act, removing zoning control from Point Grey and creating a special provincial zoning prohibiting subdivision. The Act further stipulated that any resident was entitled to take out an injunction against a zoning violator. It was correctly assumed that the threat of legal action by CPR or affluent residents would dissuade any would-be violators. To further safeguard the Anglophile single-family character of the area, which was seen as crucial to maintaining

Figure 3.2: A Shaughnessy mansion.

Figure 3.3: A Shaughnessy streetscape.

high property values, CPR placed restrictive covenants on Shaughnessy deeds forbidding multiple family occupancy of homes. All these controls were apparently secured with the approval of residents, who saw a convergence of their interests with those of CPR. By the end of the 1920s CPR had created a housing development which not only was a financial success but which was increasingly seen by its residents as an important part of their status as the elite of this growing western Canadian city. As such, the Anglophile landscape created to make money for CPR simultaneously became a part of the cultural reproduction of the Vancouver elite.

The Depression, however, brought to an end both the period of growth and the era of harmony between the interests of CPR and property owners. As a result of the financial crisis, many prominent residents were forced to file for bankruptcy and sell their mansions. Although property values declined to a fraction of their earlier market value, taxes remained at their previous levels, contributing to the financial crisis. Residents began to take in boarders illegally and many single-family homes were converted to rooming houses. In 1938 the Shaughnessy Heights Property Owners' Association (SHPOA) was formed, with the primary goal of combatting the conversion of mansions to multiple-occupancy units. The leaders of SHPOA were successful businessmen and professionals who, unlike some of their neighbours who had fallen on hard times, were financially secure and committed to the area as a place to live. One of SHPOA's first acts was to file a petition in 1939 with the provincial government to extend the Building Restriction Act to 1970. The provincial government not only accepted this proposal, but granted SHPOA the right to register complaints against and prosecute violators of the act.

The advent of the Second World War, however, further undermined SHPOA's goal of maintaining a financially stable single-family area of large houses. Because of the housing shortage in Canada during the war years, in 1942 the federal government permitted the establishment of multi-family dwellings in all areas previously zoned as single-family. This law accelerated what the Depression had started — the wholesale conversion of single-family houses into rooming houses. Furthermore, there were subdivisions of large properties. After the war SHPOA appealed to the provincial government to ban all existing rooming houses, but the government compromised and banned all conversions after 1955. Any single-family houses converted before that date could remain as legal non-conforming uses. A survey conducted in 1957 showed that 30 per cent of the houses in the area were multiple-occupancy. As these represented a disproportionate number of the largest mansions, SHPOA was concerned that this severely compromised the elite nature of the area and thus the claims of the residents to high status.

During the post-war economic recovery, Shaughnessy regained a good deal of its prestige and popularity with executives. They found the area convenient to the city business area, and house prices, which had still not recovered from the effects of the Depression, were also affordable. Existing houses and undeveloped building lots sold quickly. Most of the houses that were built during these decades, though large by city standards, were smaller than the mansions built forty years earlier. Many of these large bungalows were built on smaller, one-fifth of an acre lots, creating a discernible shift in landscape aesthetics away from the English country house look towards a new Californian model which was more middle-class. With the return of prosperity, rooming houses were slowly reconverted to single-family housing. Although members of SHPOA were delighted by these recovered mansions, they were dismayed by the increase in smaller houses which in their opinion undermined the 'exclusive' character of the area. Once again, SHPOA discovered its limits. As long as minimum lot size was adhered to there was little the Association could do to prevent the appearance of bungalows or Spanish colonials. For the Anglophile elite, different models of housing undermined the image that they wished to foster in the area. What SHPOA members could do, however, was to be vigilant in detecting violations of the zoning code. Members actually patrolled the neighbourhood looking for any signs of building activity or code violations. Any suspected violators were reported to SHPOA's legal committee or directly to the provincial government.

In 1970 the Building Restriction Act expired and the City of Vancouver assumed responsibility for Shaughnessy's zoning. The City established a new zoning category for Shaughnessy, setting the minimum lot size at 882 m² (9500 ft²) and the minimum frontage at 26 m (85 ft). It was hoped both by SHPOA and the City Planning Department that this would provide greater protection against subdivision than had previously existed. However, as the average lot size in the heart of Shaughnessy was 3950 m² (42 500 ft²) and the average frontage 47.5 m (156 ft), there still remained the possibility of subdivision. As an added safeguard, therefore, the City's Director of Planning was given some discretion over subdivision. Since SHPOA felt that the City in the past had been insufficiently vigorous in prosecuting zoning violators, it convinced the City to change its charter to allow SHPOA itself to prosecute violators. As it turned out, even these extraordinary provisions were not sufficient to preserve all of the houses and large lots.

Although the pace of demolition and subdivision were slowed, the activities could not be halted, and after six years of working within the context of the 1970 zoning category, SHPOA decided that a new zoning law would better conserve what remained of the Anglophile landscape. To this end, in 1976 a private firm was commissioned by SHPOA to propose a new plan for Shaughnessy that would reflect the members' Anglophile landscape taste and desire to retain the district's elite Anglophile character. A modified version of this plan was sent to the City Planning Department in 1978. The Planning Department, which favoured neighbourhood self-determination and heritage preservation, was broadly supportive of the proposal and recommended that a Working Committee be formed to assist the Planning Department in drawing up a new Shaughnessy Plan. This Working Committee was composed of ten members of SHPOA, three owners of rooming houses, two tenants, a member of the Vancouver Heritage Advisory Committee, and a representative of the City Planning Department. The composition of the committee, which had the approval of the City Planning Department, was a clear acknowledgement of the pre-eminence of SPHOA in Shaughnessy. Its members numerically dominated the committee, thereby ensuring that the final results would reflect their views. Of the three owners of boarding houses, only one, a rather timid person who was treated with benign condescension by the members of SHPOA, attended regularly. The tenants on the committee had been recruited by SHPOA and did not appear to represent the true interest of tenants in the area, which normally would be the retention of affordable rental accommodation.

Before discussing the workings of the committee it is important to establish the sociopolitical context of these deliberations. The immediate political context during the early to mid 1970s was a City Council dominated by The Electors' Action Movement (TEAM), a liberal political party whose platform was the 'liveable city'. It included a concern both on the part of City Council and the TEAM-appointed Director of Planning for the issues of quality of life, landscape aesthetics and neighbourhood protection. The 'Goals for Vancouver' survey of 5000 people in 1979 sampled attitudes in order to help set the goals for city planning in the 1980s. The responses to this survey placed great emphasis upon aesthetics, preserving green spaces, supporting the individual character and identity of neighbourhoods, and preserving 'heritage and character' areas. The Planning Department and the City Council adopted these goals, which well suited the arguments about Shaughnessy that SHPOA had put forward during the previous forty years. The Association could argue that its desire for heritage preservation and green space was not merely in its own interest, but was endorsed by the city as a whole. Seventy years earlier, when the first house was built by CPR in what was clearly a development suburb, the cultural model of Anglophilia had been a marketing strategy designed to sell land. By 1979 the relationship between cultural and economic forces in Shaughnessy Heights had shifted, so that the development of imitation English houses had become an important part of Vancouver's heritage to be preserved for the citizenry at large. An aesthetic value that had been pressed into service for economic motives had entered the realm of high culture and was to be protected from the economic sphere (developers who wished to make a profit from subdivision and the demolition of large mansions). It was only by tightly enmeshing this culture model of Anglophilia into a political framework of zoning laws, heritage committees and design guidelines that it could be saved from what were portrayed as unrestrained economic forces. Of course, economic forces were still very much implicated in this cultural model. Large mansions in Shaughnessy cost millions of dollars, and zoning controls provided a kind of hidden subsidy to the residents of the area, many of whom could not have afforded to be surrounded by such a landscape had there existed an unrestricted market in land.

If liveability was on Vancouver's political agenda in the late 1970s there was also the countervailing reality of a housing shortage of near crisis proportions. A rental vacancy rate consistently below 1 per cent and a shortage of land for building were raising housing costs to unprecedented levels. Shaughnessy was characterised by low housing densities on land near the heart of the city. It was uncertain whether arguments over green space, heritage and neighbourhood protection would prevail over arguments for more plentiful and affordable housing.

The very general goals of the Shaughnessy Planning Committee were to try to preserve the 'English country house in the city' appearance of the area and maintain its single-family residential status. This overall goal implied several subgoals: first, to halt subdivision of large lots; second, to provide financial incentives to owners of the largest mansions so that they would not demolish them; third, to encourage owners of rooming houses to convert them either to single-family structures or to 'strata title' tenure so that houses would remain owner-occupied and the outside appearance of the house would remain unchanged; fourth, to create a set of guidelines so that all new building in the area would conform to SHPOA's English country house ideal.

Since the appearance of the landscape was of crucial importance to the SHPOA committee members, their attention focused on the content of the proposed design guidelines and its implementation. The guidelines controlled everything from house style and siting on the lot to types of windows and planting. The issue of responsibility for ensuring the guidelines were followed was the subject of intense debate. In the end it was decided that SHPOA members were to compose a majority of a design committee, thereby guaranteeing that the English country house ideal would be reflected in all new development in the area.

Much of the discussion in the planning meetings revealed the 'old money' values of SHPOA members, set against newcomers whom they considered to be *nouveaux riches* bringing new housing tastes to Shaughnessy and thereby threatening the status of the old elite. One of the committee members described the type of landscape she wanted to maintain in Shaughnessy: 'We are striving for tasteful seclusion, privacy, trees, [and] setbacks. We hate tacky bungalows with their open lots. They look functional, like they are for living and nothing else. We love old Tudors, Victorians, things which are authentic.' However, for political reasons in the official minutes of their meetings and in the final draft of the plan to be presented to the City Council, the committee members tried their best to downplay the image of the area as a haven of the upper class and portray it as a park-like, 'heritage' landscape for all Vancouver citizens to enjoy. As one member put it: 'We should decrease in emphasis the "well to do exclusiveness" of the area [which appeared in an early draft of the plan]. Is this good public relations? Does it add to our claim of historic preservation? We must present Shaughnessy as an area of historical significance to people in Burnaby [an outer suburb], etc. Perhaps the mention of rich people will turn them off.' A second member of SHPOA agreed: 'Yes, remove the reference to helping people maintain large properties. The press will pick this up as a preoccupation of ours. Do you want to see this printed in the press?' A planner for the city who attended some of the committee meetings made a welcome suggestion that showed his empathy for the SHPOA point of view: 'If you have an 8000 square foot house, you don't want one 5000 square feet of the same height behind it. Probably you want a smaller house beside it that would look like a coach house. This then wouldn't spoil the character of the 8000 foot house.' The committee was impressed and members began to espouse the idea. At a later meeting one said: 'We want coach houses next to large houses to make it appear like an estate'.

This argument, when combined with the Planning Department and City Council's strong belief in neighbourhood self-determination, made it difficult for even a left of centre Council to reject the Shaughnessy plan. The result was that in 1982 the City Council met and approved the Shaughnessy plan which, in the face of a citywide housing crisis, increased the minimum lot size in the area and displaced several hundred lower income renters.

The upper-class members of SHPOA did not invent the ideologies of the liveable city, green space, architectural heritage, neighbourhood protection and local control. These had been espoused primarily by middle-class liberal academics, bureaucrats and politicians with an eye to improving the quality of life in middle and working-class districts. SHPOA skilfully employed this ideology and its sometimes contradictory social consequences because it genuinely believed in the importance of green space, heritage and the right to self-determination. SHPOA members found the ideology of the liveable city congenial not simply because it was expedient for them, but because they recognised in it old English upper-class ideas about the importance of aesthetics, locality and history. In other words, the ideology of the liveable city had made traditional upper-class landscape tastes and ideals acceptable to the political left, centre and right alike. The exclusionary class interest of SHPOA had been intentionally masked by a rhetoric of the general interest, incidentally ensuring that the liveable city would continue to be more liveable for some than for others.

Shaughnessy Heights: the view from the working class

It is highly tempting, based upon the Shaughnessy story, to conclude that a group of upper-class residents manipulated liberal planners and politicians and that the big losers, despite the rhetoric of the general good, were the working-class people who were spoken for by these groups but from whom we have not heard directly. The voices of the working class reveal another side of the (re)production of elite landscape, that in some respects is infinitely more disturbing than the, at times, rather cynical manipulation of middle-class ideologies of green space, heritage and participation by an elite.

When fifty working-class residents of the predominantly low-income east side of the city were asked whether they felt that it was in the interest of the city as a whole to preserve and enhance the character of Shaughnessy, an astonishing 79 per cent said it was. Why, in the face of a housing crisis, would so many working-class people want to preserve something that did not appear to be in their material interests? The answer is complex. The residents who favoured the preservation of the character of Shaughnessy were able to articulate very little specifically about the history or even the components of Anglophile landscape taste but they nevertheless recognised it as a *general* elite model, thought it was beautiful and worth preserving. In a similar fashion, although they knew little of the details of the lifestyle of the Shaughnessy elite, I would argue that they supported the idea of reproducing that elite culture. Landscape symbolism, I believe, helps us to understand these working-class attitudes towards the elite. For these members of the working class Shaughnessy was not simply a material thing, a neighbourhood of mansions on one and a half acre lots. The landscape symbolically performed several functions. First, it provided a focus for working-class pride in the beauty of Vancouver. Although they infrequently passed through the neighbourhood, as residents of the city they could vicariously share in the Shaughnessy image, thus underpinning the official Planning Department view that Shaughnessy is part of every resident's heritage irrespective of social class. Second, it mediated between the reality of their working-class lives and the optimistic ideology of individualism so dominant in North America today. Shaughnessy did not raise issues of class conflict or a sense of social injustice as it might in some societies, but evoked individualistic feelings about aspirations, opportunities and personal worthiness. An important part of the ideology of western society is that anyone, no matter how humble his or her origins, can become wealthy. Informants expressed these sentiments when asked about preserving Shaughnessy. Some felt that it should be retained for its symbolic value. As one person said, 'Shaughnessy serves as an example to others'. The landscape conveys the promise of social mobility. A number discussed this theme in terms of a dream. One said, 'Shaughnessy is the last of the dream areas', suggesting that although it is not available to them in reality, it is in fantasy. Yet the notion of a 'dream world' has a double meaning, part fantasy, and part guide to what the future might hold. Some seemed to argue that it was a right of working-class people such as themselves that such places exist. 'People are entitled to their dream', one person said, while another said 'It would be awful to take away the dream of thousands of people'.

A second theme is the belief that the class structure of society is natural and just. Some even see it as based upon the differential worthiness of individuals. 'Of course there are class differences', one woman said, 'that's the way it has to be'. Another said, '... people must accept that some will have a higher standard of living'. There is a belief that the class system is just and people get what they deserve. 'Rich people worked hard for what they got and shouldn't have it taken away from them', another person said. The explanations were highly individualistic rather than social. Nothing was seen other than personal failings. As one person said, 'If people really wanted to get into Shaughnessy, they could'. Another impugned the motives of those whom she believed to be opposed to preserving the area by saying, 'People who don't want to preserve the area are simply envious of the rich'. Another argued against change by saying 'Increasing the density, especially with town houses, would mean lower income people would come in and that would take away from its niceness'.

The above statements bear a strong similarity to what Sennett and Cobb (1973) found when they interviewed poor people in the United States about success. The authors argued that the psychological impact on the poor of an ideology of individual responsibility for position in the class system was very great. In a society where it is believed that anyone can succeed if he or she has the personal qualities, those who remained at the lower end of the class system perceived themselves as personally responsible for their failure. They believed that failure stemmed not from a system of institutionalised inequality and differential access to opportunity but from individually generated inequality. Sennett and Cobb discuss the feelings of unworthiness associated with a lack of success in America. They call this the 'hidden injuries of class'. The other side of this coin is what might be termed the 'hidden benefits of class' as derived by a Shaughnessy elite who can gain the support of liberal planners and city politicians for their Anglophile landscape tastes because such tastes have been incorporated into the discourse of liberal planning under the guise of heritage preservation and green space. As such, public officials intervene on behalf of the residents to preserve a landscape and thereby reproduce an elite. The working class are also implicated in this process of reproducing an elite, as by supporting the idea that Shaughnessy is part of the heritage of all of the residents of the city and by preserving it as a fantasy of upward mobility they help ensure its preservation as a reality.

Conclusion

We have traced the history of a particular cultural production, an elite neighbourhood in Vancouver, Canada. In doing so we have seen that people do not simply possess culture, but must struggle over it, and that this is true even for the dominant classes. Shaughnessy Heights is not simply a cultural production (a material landscape) interpenetrated by political and economic structures; it is also a cultural (re)production in that it reproduces the meaning of belonging to an Anglophile elite in a western Canadian city. Finally, as I have tried to show by bringing in the voices of the working class, Shaughnessy as a class production also serves to reproduce class distinctions within Canadian society and, I would argue, to mystify the nature of class relations in a capitalist society.[2]

Notes

1   This case study is primarily based on two years of participant observation (1979-81) at meetings between the First Shaughnessy Citizens' Working Committee and the Vancouver City Planning Department.

2   I am indebted to the editors of this volume and to Nancy Duncan and Joanne Sharp for comments on earlier drafts of this chapter.

References

Duncan, J.S. 1973, 'Landscape taste as a symbol of group identity: a Westchester County Village', *Geographical Review*, 63, pp. 334–55.

Duncan, J.S. 1981, 'From container of women to status symbol: the impact of social structure on the meaning of the house', in J.S. Duncan (ed.), *Housing and Identity: Cross-Cultural Perspectives*, Croom Helm, London, pp. 36–59.

Duncan, J.S. 1985,'The house as symbol of social structure: notes on the language of objects among collectivistic groups', in I. Altman & C.M. Werner (eds), *Home Environments. Human Behaviour and Environment: Advances in Theory and Research*, vol. 8, Plenum, New York, pp. 133–52.

Duncan, J.S. 1989, 'The power of place in Kandy, Sri Lanka: 1780-1980', in J. Agnew & J.S. Duncan (eds), *The Power of Place: Bringing Together Geographical and Sociological Imaginations*, Unwin-Hyman, Boston, pp. 185–201.

Duncan, J.S. & Duncan, N.G. 1980, 'Residential landscapes and social worlds: a case study in Hyderabad, Andhra Pradesh', in D.E. Sopher (ed.), *An Exploration of India: Geographical Perspectives in Society and Culture*, Cornell University Press, Ithaca, pp. 271–86.

Duncan, J.S. & Duncan, N.G. 1984, 'A cultural analysis of urban residential landscapes in North America: the case of the anglophile elite', in J. Agnew, J. Mercer & D. Sopher (eds), *The City in Cultural Context*, Allen & Unwin, Boston, pp. 255–76.

Firey, W. 1945, 'Sentiment and symbolism as ecological variables', *American Sociological Review*, 10, pp. 140–8.

Giddens, A. 1979, *Central Problems in Social Theory,* University of California Press, Berkeley.

Girouard, M. 1981, *Life in the English Country House,* Penguin, Harmondsworth.

Hugill, P. 1986, 'English landscape tastes in the United States', *Geographical Review,* 76, pp. 408–23.

Kenny, J. (forthcoming), *Constructing an Imperial Hill Station: The Representation of British Authority in Ootacamund,* Cambridge University Press, Cambridge.

Ley, D. (forthcoming), 'Past elites and present gentry: neighbourhoods of privilege in Canadian Cities', in L. Bourne & D. Ley (eds), *The Changing Social Geography of Canadian Cities,* McGill-Queens University Press, Montreal.

Lowenthal, D. & Prince, H. 1965, 'English landscape tastes', *Geographical Review,* 55, pp. 186–222.

Pevsner, N. 1957, *London, Volume 1: The Cities of London and Westminster,* Penguin, Harmondsworth.

Pratt, G. 1981, 'The house as an expression of social worlds', in J.S. Duncan (ed.), *Housing and Identity: Cross-Cultural Perspectives,* Croom-Helm, London.

Rapoport, A. 1981, 'Identity and environment: a cross-cultural perspective', in J.S. Duncan (ed.), *Housing and Identity: Cross-Cultural Perspectives*, Croom-Helm, London.

Sennett, R. & Cobb, J. 1973, *The Hidden Injuries of Class,* Vintage, New York.

Wiener, M.J. 1981, *English Culture and the Decline of the Industrial Spirit,* Cambridge University Press, Cambridge.

Williams, R. 1973, *The Country and the City,* Chatto & Windus, London.

Williams, R. 1982, *The Sociology of Culture*, Schocken Books, New York.

Wyckoff, W.K. 1990, 'Landscapes of private power and wealth', in M.P. Conzen (ed.), *The Making of the American Landscape*, Unwin-Hyman, London, pp. 335–54.

4

Place and politics in post-war Italy: a cultural geography of local identity in the provinces of Lucca and Pistoia

John Agnew

Introduction

Intense loyalty to local football (soccer) clubs has become an important feature of everyday life for people, especially young men, all over Europe. Nowhere is this more the case than in Italy where fanatical adherence to 'the team' recalls older forms of identification with locality generally referred to in Italian as *campanilismo*. Italy is a relatively 'new' state, only unified under one national government in the 1860s, and local identities are still very strong. In the region of Tuscany (Toscana) in central Italy, the Florence team, Fiorentina, has the largest mass following relative to other major Italian football teams, reflecting the prominent position that the city of Florence has occupied historically within the region. However, in the province of Lucca, to the west of Florence between the Apennine mountains and the Tyrrhenian Sea, Juventus of Turin, the arch-enemy of Fiorentina in contemporary Italian football, has thirteen supporters' clubs to the five of Fiorentina, a figure roughly three times greater than any other Tuscan province. This is because the population of Lucca, a separate republic independent of Tuscany until 1847, has an identity distinct from the other Tuscan provinces. Even when there is no local team capable of challenging that of Florence, many *lucchesi* throw in their lot with a successful team in distant Turin rather than convert to support for Fiorentina.

The phenomenon of local identity is not unique to Italy. Regionally and locally-based political cultures characterise the United States, Canada and many European countries. Political geography, especially the geography of elections, has been relatively silent about this, probably because of that field's lack of attention to the concept of culture. In the Italian case this silence is difficult to fathom. It can be plausibly argued that if today 'localism' is in the ascendency again in Italy, as shown by the electoral success of essentially local and regional political movements (such as the *Lega Lombarda*, or Lombard League, in the region of Lombardia), Italy had never been strongly homogenised by an Italian national culture in the first place (Forgacs 1990). Why, then, should social science in general and political geography in particular have had difficulty seeing local identity and the cultural contexts from which it springs as essential for understanding political action?

In modern social science local identity has been viewed as either residual, something fading under the onslaught of modernisation and its political twin national identity, or primordial, related to a cultural drive in which culture is viewed as a fixed bundle of traits and beliefs formed in the distant past and reproduced unwittingly by local populations. In studies of Italian politics these have been the dominant perspectives. The 'residualists', the majority group among students of Italian politics, have stressed the slow emergence of the modern 'individual' engaged in opinion voting, with a decline in political action based on group identity or clientelism (for example, Parisi & Pasquino 1980). The 'primordialists' have emphasised the impact on political activities and voting behaviour of relatively fixed 'regional cultures' or subcultures, especially the Catholic subculture of north-east Italy, the Socialist subculture of central Italy and the clientelistic subculture of the south and Sicily (for example, Putnam et al. 1985).

In this chapter, after a review of these positions, I shall propose an alternative perspective. This sees local identity (or sense of place) as one dimension of a concept of place in which 'culture' is a dynamic phenomenon, a set of practices, interests and ideas subject to collective revision, changing or persisting as places and their populations change or persist in response to locally and externally generated challenges. Attention then turns to interpreting Italian electoral politics since the Second World War, first, at the level of the country as a whole and, second, with respect to two Tuscan provinces, Lucca and its neighbour towards Florence, Pistoia. These two provinces have been selected to illustrate the central theme of this chapter: What is possible politically is defined by the evolving cultures of specific places.

Local identity as residual or primordial

A widely-accepted premise of modern political science is that political outlooks and alignments are increasingly organised around national social cleavages to produce national patterns of political mobilisation. Increasingly, political differences are 'nationalised' as membership in national census categories displaces geographical location as the primary predictor of political behaviour. In Italy this point of view became popular among political scientists in the late 1960s. A major study of Italian political behaviour conducted between 1963 and 1965 argued that a 'nationalisation' of Italian politics had occurred between 1946 and 1963 (Galli & Prandi 1970). The pattern of an electorate divided into two parts, left and right, and spread throughout the country — as in other 'representative democracies' — had come to Italy (table 4.1). From this point of view, individual opinion voting had replaced identification with social group or locality as the main source of political identity (Parisi & Pasquino 1980). 'Modern' voting behaviour is seen as the expression of personal choice constrained by access to information and particular sociodemographic characteristics, such as class, age, education, etc.

Certainly, national and province-level election results in the period 1963–76 can be used to support this perspective. There was a tendency towards homogenisation in support for the major Italian political parties: the Christian Democrats (DC), the Communists (PCI) and the Socialists (PSI) (Agnew 1991). This could be explained partly in terms of 'saturation' of support for parties in some areas and partly in terms of common national processes of political mobilisation (Bartolini 1976; Parisi & Pasquino 1980). There was also a sense of greater electoral instability as voters became more

Table 4.1a: Political elections 1946–87, Constituent Assembly (1946) and Chamber of Deputies, per cent by party (seats in parentheses)

Party[a]	1946	1948	1953	1958	1963	1968	1972	1976	1979	1983	1987
DC	35.1 (207)	48.5 (305)	40.1 (263)	42.4 (273)	38.3 (260)	39.1 (266)	38.8 (267)	38.7 (292)	38.3 (262)	32.9 (225)	34.3 (234)
PCI	18.9 (104)	31 (183)[b]	22.6 (143)	22.7 (140)	25.3 (166)	26.9 (177)	27.2 (179)	34.4 (228)	30.4 (201)	29.9 (198)	26.6 (198)
PSI	20.7 (115)		12.8 (75)	14.2 (84)	13.8 (87)	14.5 (91)[b]	9.6 (61)	9.6 (57)	9.8 (62)	11.4 (73)	14.3 (94)
PSDI	-	7.1 (33)	4.5 (19)	4.5 (22)	6.1 (33)		5.1 (29)	3.4 (15)	3.8 (20)	4.1 (23)	3.4 (17)
PRI	4.4 (23)	2.5 (9)	1.6 (5)	1.4 (6)	1.4 (6)	2 (9)	2.9 (14)	3.1 (14)	3 (16)	5.1 (29)	3.7 (21)
PLI	6.8 (41)	3.8 (19)	3 (13)	3.5 (17)	7 (39)	5.8 (31)	3.9 (21)	1.3 (5)	1.9 (9)	2.9 (16)	2.1 (11)
PR	-	-	-	-	-	-	-	1.1 (4)	3.5 (18)	2.2 (11)	2.6 (13)
DP	-	-	-	-	-	-	-	1.5 (6)	0.8 (-)	1.5 (7)	1.7 (8)
PdUP	-	-	-	-	-	-	-	-	1.4 (6)	-[c]	-
MSI	-	2 (6)	5.8 (29)	4.8 (24)	5.1 (27)	4.4 (24)	8.7 (56)	6.1 (35)	5.3 (30)	6.8 (42)	5.9 (35)
Monarchists	2.8 (16)	2.8 (14)	6.9 (40)	4.8 (25)	1.7 (8)	1.3 (6)	-	-	-	-	-
Others[d]	9.5 (50)	2.5 (5)	2.7 (3)	1.7 (5)	1.3 (4)	6.0 (26)	4.0 (4)	0.8 (4)	2.7 (6)	3.2 (6)	5.8 (10)

Source: Istituto Centrale di Statistica (ISTAT).

[a] DC (Democrazia cristiana), PCI (Partito comunista Italiano), PSI (Partito socialista italiano), PSDI (Partito socialista democratico italiano), PRI (Partito repubblicano italiano), PLI (Partito liberale italiano), PR (Partito radicale), DP (Democrazia proletaria), PdUP (Partito di unita proletaria per il comunismo), MSI (Movimento sociale italiano).

[b] Parties presented joint election lists.

[c] Ran on PCI lists.

[d] Includes South Tyrol People's party (SVP), Sardinian Action party (PSA), Valdotaine Union (UV), and Socialist Party of Proletarian Unity (PSIUP). SVP generally accounts for three seats; PSIUP won twenty-three seats in 1968. The Greens won thirteen seats with 2.5 per cent in 1987.

volatile in their political affiliations (Barbagli et al. 1979). However, neither homogenisation nor electoral volatility in themselves can be taken as signals of a permanent shift from a geographically-fragmented to a nationally-homogeneous process of political mobilisation (Agnew 1988). As the huge literature on neighbourhood effects in voting suggests, opinion voting is not an isolated individual act but is subject to local social influences (Agnew 1987, ch. 4; Johnston 1986). Moreover, homogenisation and volatility have been insufficient in recent Italian electoral history to justify total abandonment of older models of political behaviour involving recourse to concepts of local identity and subculture. Even proponents of the trend towards nationalisation based on opinion voting stress, therefore, the important 'residual' role of identity and clientelistic (vote-favour exchange) voting as expressive of local histories and interests (for example, Parisi & Pasquino 1980).

Considerable empirical evidence now suggests that nationalisation of voting patterns was a feature of the period 1963–76 rather than a permanent trend (Pavsiv 1985; Agnew 1988). This has led to a revival of 'geographical' models of political behaviour which emphasise regional subculture and the persistence of regional 'types' of voting. Such models identify historical-cultural rather than socioeconomic factors as the primary determinants of political cleavages. The 'rootedness' of parties in particular areas through their organisation and institutional strength is given special weight as a factor producing socialisation into different political traditions. Key periods in the past — the years after unification, the period of labour organising early in the twentieth century, and the period after the collapse of fascism, 1943–46 — are viewed as critical in the establishment of regional political traditions. The Catholic subculture of north-east Italy, the Socialist subculture of the centre, and the clientelistic subculture of the south and Sicily, are regarded as the major traditions that have resulted.

There are perhaps three specific models that rely on fixed subculture-regional conceptions of political action: first, regional taxonomies of cultural traditions; second, historical studies of local political cultures; and, third, sociological studies of party-government and political subculture links. For reasons outlined later, none of these models is considered satisfactory.

The first involves identifying the most 'fundamental' geographical divisions in voting behaviour in terms of subcultural homogeneity. A number of taxonomies have been proposed, the earliest in 1967 (Dogan 1967), the most influential that of Capecchi et al. (1968), and the most recent those of Cartocci (1987) and Anderlini (1987). Over time, the taxonomies have shifted from a tripartite regional division, north-east, centre and south, with the north-west as a 'residual' region not easily characterised in subcultural terms, to an emphasis on the importance of the north-south division (Cartocci 1987) and local 'functional' regions defined partly in cultural terms (Anderlini 1987).

A second primordial model involves focusing upon local areas with a long history of political homogeneity, such as 'red areas' with strong support for the PCI in central Italy (for example, Bagnasco & Trigilia 1985; Baccetti 1987; Caciagli 1988) or 'white areas' with strong support for the Christian Democrats in the north-east (for example, Bagnasco & Trigilia 1984). Emphasis is placed upon the persistence of political alignments in the face of economic and social change, suggesting that political cultures defined in the past continue to exercise control over later political behaviour (for example, Tullio-Altan 1986; Putnam et al. 1985). Unlike the American literature (for example, Almond & Verba 1963), there is a positive tendency to see political culture as a phenomenon rooted in and emanating from local social institutions (especially clubs and associations) rather than directly 'internalised' psychologically by individuals (Caciagli 1988).

The third model focuses on the question of local institutions, particularly the dominance in them of particular political parties and particular organisational cultures. For some commentators (for example, Tarrow 1977; Galli 1984) local political systems, elsewhere as well as in Italy, when dominated by a single political party and political entrepreneurs of a particular complexion, use jobs, favours and a dominant local ideology to produce local populations with commitments to that party. The tautological nature of this position (dominance produces dominance) has led others to introduce 'subcultures' as a kind of social 'glue' or mediating variable for particular parties and their appeal. In examining the recent economic success of north-east and central Italy, for example, Trigilia (1986) and Bagnasco (1988) argue for the importance of local party dominance and social traditions in jointly creating the conditions of consensus and mediation of diverse interests necessary for the development of the dynamic small firms that have prospered in these Italian regions. Subcultures, party dominance and economic growth thus form a virtuous circle in these regions, whereas by implication they do not elsewhere, especially in the south (for detailed critiques see Bellini 1989; Blim 1990; Amin & Robins 1990).

All these models share a 'primordial' definition of culture and an orientation towards continuity rather than change in political behaviour. There are four specific drawbacks to them. First, there is little if any attention to the reconstruction of historical-geographical sequences in the development of Italian politics. Geography is seen in static rather than dynamic terms. Second, there is little emphasis on the local area as a 'theatre' of activities from which social and political commitments and political change emerge. Rather, the local is seen in terms of cultural persistence, resistance to change and the overwhelming weight of tradition.

Third, only *some* regions or localities are viewed as 'integrated' communities with territorial subcultures. Elsewhere, again especially in the south, communities are viewed as without the consensus or bonds of faith and trust that are taken as indicative of 'true' subcultures (for example, Trigilia 1986). The problem here is that those who cannot have a subculture pinned on them are left without culture at all! Kertzer (1980, 252-5) has suggested that the term 'hegemony' be reserved for those settings where political parties have acquired a certain role in consensus and institution-building — and the term subculture be dropped altogether so that all Italians can be thought of in cultural terms rather than just those in the north-east and centre (also Feltrin 1988, 298).

Fourth, culture, especially 'political culture', is seen in static and deterministic terms. Opinions, captured in surveys at particular points in time, are regarded as constitutive of political culture which, in turn, becomes a 'black box' of values and beliefs used to explain the self-same opinions. To avoid this tautological dead-end, culture is better thought of as a structure or system of 'signification' (set of symbols and commitments) that defines the range of possible actions (political and other) that a group or individual can undertake in a given society (Williams 1981; Allum 1988). More particularly, a political culture can be thought of as defining the limits of the 'possible' in political life, the intersubjective framework to which individual actors bring their own attitudes, values, interests and personalities (Taylor 1985). Allum (1988, 265) summarises this perspective as follows:

It can be affirmed, by reformulating a noted saying, that, 'culture proposes, man disposes'. Further, however, I would underline that political culture is not static, even if it is persistent: it changes over time even if slowly, as taught in the *18 Brumaire* of Marx, and changes above all in the course of political struggles that totally restructure practices and 'systems of signification', so that the 'sense' of yesterday is not always the 'sense' of today, and alternative politics that were unthinkable yesterday become suddenly possible today.

Place and politics

The critical issue for a geography of Italian politics, unaddressed by either residualists or primordialists, can be raised in terms of a simple empirical puzzle. It is that national (or other aggregate) averages are more or less representative of specific observations depending upon the degree of dispersion of all observations. The point is substantive more than statistical. National averages disguise a variety of local differences. By way of example, figure 4.1 shows the relationship between social class and vote in an imaginary country of four regions. In each region the correlation between class and vote is perfect, but for the country as a whole there is no relationship whatsoever. This extreme case illustrates a simple point: rather than seeing local variations as deviations from a national norm, the national norm is meaningless unless seen as constituted out of locally-specific situations (Agnew 1991).

The argument for this perspective is sociological. People are social beings rather than isolated individuals or members of census categories. It is in social contexts that

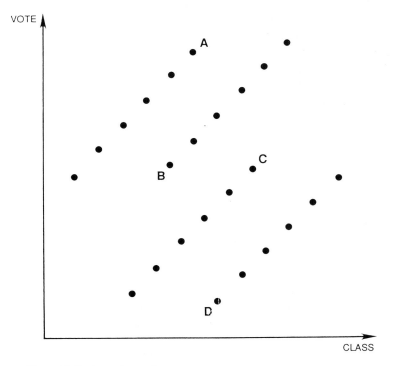

Figure 4.1: Regions, class and vote.
Source: Derivry & Dogan (1986, 158).

people acquire the practical reasons that lead them to act in some ways rather than others. These social contexts are formed geographically. Social relations are constituted in physical settings or locales that people cross into and out of constantly in the course of their everyday lives. Such locales are embedded in a wider territorial society according to locational constraints imposed by the activities of states and the demands of geographically extensive divisions of labour. Common experiences and interests create an emotional attachment and self-definition peculiar to the specific place in which the locales of enduring social relationships are concentrated. This is a local identity or sense of place (Agnew 1987).

What is possible politically is defined by the evolving cultures of specific places. Over time these can be more or less distinctive but, however similar or different, they are *formed* from the bottom up, out of everyday life. This does not mean to say that political dispositions are created in geographical isolation. That has been the fallacy of so many 'community' studies (Cooke 1990). Different places have different relationships to the national state, international economy, and secondary social organisations such as churches, labour unions and political parties. These differences affect the nature of local political cultures as local life adjusts to external challenges. The outcome of this process of social structuration is the geographically differential appeal of different political parties and movements that changes over time as changing 'local cultures propose and local people dispose'.

The geographical dynamics of Italian electoral politics, 1947–87

Italian electoral politics since the Second World War can be viewed in terms of either nationalisation and the rise of the individual opinion voter or regional cultures with static political profiles. Alternatively, it can be interpreted in terms of three political-geographical 'regimes' in which the places out of which Italy is made have had different degrees of similarity and difference at different times. After describing the case for the three regimes at the national level an attempt is made at explaining them by reference to two provinces in central Italy: Lucca and Pistoia.

The three regimes

The geography of Italian politics since 1947 can be characterised in terms of three distinctive geographical regimes that have dominated in different periods (see Agnew 1991). The first regime, dominant from 1947 until 1963, involved a regional pattern of support for the major political parties based upon place similarities that clustered regionally. The second, in effect from 1963 until 1976, witnessed the expansion of the Communist Party (PCI) out of its regional stronghold into a nationally competitive position with the Christian Democratic Party (DC). This had different causes in different places but the net effect was to suggest a nationalisation of the two major parties. The third, characteristic of the period since 1976, has seen increased support for minor parties, including regional parties such as the *Lega Lombarda*, the geographical 'retreat' of the PCI and a more localised pattern of political expression in general, reflecting the increased 'patchiness' of Italian economic growth and social change.

Figure 4.2: Italian provinces and voting regions used by Galli and Prandi (1970, 114). © 1970, The Twentieth Century Fund.

The regionalising regime

The period 1947-63 is that of the classical electoral geography of Italy established most definitively by Galli and his colleagues (Galli & Prandi 1970). They divided the country into six zones on the basis of levels of support for the three major parties, the PCI, DC and the Socialists (PSI), and the strength of the major political subcultures, the Socialist and the Catholic (fig. 4.2).

Zone 1, the industrial triangle, covered north-west Italy and included Piemonte, Liguria and Lombardia. This was the region in which industrial production was concentrated before the Second World War and in which most new industrial investment was concentrated in the 1950s. Socialists, Christian Democrats, and Communists were all competitive in this region.

Zone 2, *la zona bianca*, covered north-east Italy and included the provinces of Bergamo and Brescia in Lombardia, the province of Trento, the province of Udine, and all of Veneto except the province of Rovigo. The Christian Democrats were most strongly entrenched in this region and opposition was divided among a number of parties.

Zone 3, *la zona rossa*, covered central Italy and included the provinces of Mantova, Rovigo and Viterbo; the whole of Emilia-Romagna except for the province of Piacenza; Toscana except for Lucca (an 'isola bianca'); Umbria; and the Marche, except for the province of Ascoli Piceno. In this region the PCI was most strongly established, especially in the countryside but increasingly in the cities.

Zone 4, the south, included the province of Ascoli Piceno, Lazio (except Viterbo), Campania, Abruzzo e Molise, Puglia, Basilicata, and Calabria. This zone was historically the poorest and most marked by clientelistic politics. In the 1950s, the Christian Democrats and the right-wing parties dominated the zone but were faced with increasingly strong challenges from the PCI and PSI.

The final two zones, 5, Sicily, and 6, Sardinia, had more complex political alignments than the peninsular south. For example, the PCI was well-established in the southern provinces of Sicily (especially the sulphur mining areas) while Sardinia had a strong regionalist party.

There were strongly rooted cultural 'hegemonies' (party-based consensus building) in only two of these zones, la zona bianca and la zona rossa (Stern 1975; Muscarà 1987). However, in electoral terms, support for specific political parties was remarkably clustered regionally in 1953 (Rizzi 1986): the PCI in the centre, the PNM (monarchists) and MSI (neo-Fascists) in the south and Sicily, DC in the north-east and the south. In the 1950s, Italian politics followed a regional regime reflecting a similarity at the regional scale of place-based social, economic and political relationships.

The nationalising regime
The second period, 1963-76, marks a break with the regional pattern characteristic of the 1950s. Two electoral shifts were especially clear: the expansion of support for the PCI outside la zona rossa (along with its consolidation inside), particularly in the industrial north-west and parts of the south, and the breakdown of la zona bianca as a number of small parties made inroads in the previously hegemonic support for DC in parts of the north-east. The net effect of these changes was a seeming nationalisation of the major parties, even though they still maintained traditional areas of strength.

These political changes were the fruit of the major economic and social changes Italy underwent in the late 1950s and early 1960s. A major expansion occurred in manufacturing and industrial employment, especially in the north-west, as a phenomenal boom or 'economic miracle' drew the Italian economy away from its predominantly agrarian base.

At the same time that the industrial centres of the north-west were experiencing such dramatic economic and social change as a result of the economic boom and massive immigration, the rest of the country was experiencing shockwaves emanating from the north-west. The extreme south (Puglia, Basilicata and Calabria) was a major zone of emigration to the north-west and, with the exception of Taranto, without much industry. Where industry was established it created pockets of new social and economic relationships in the midst of a rapidly depopulating rural society. In all these places and among immigrants in the north, the PCI expanded its support in the late 1960s and early 1970s.

The other major feature of the period 1963-76 was the so-called breakdown of the Catholic subculture or dominant position in la zona bianca or north-east and the subsequent loss of DC voters. The argument is that DC, being largely an electoral rather than a mass party with a large membership, had relied heavily on affiliated organisations, many of a religious nature, to mobilise its support. However, in the 1960s, as a result of heavy outmigration from rural areas in the Veneto, Trento and Friuli, the constituent subregions of la zona bianca, and the growing industrialisation of some areas, such as Venice, Treviso, Trento and Pordenone, the traditional social networks and communal institutions upon which DC hegemony was based began to collapse (Parisi 1971; Sani 1977; Caciagli 1985; Chubb 1986).

The nationalising political-geographical regime peaked in 1976 when DC and PCI together accounted for 73 per cent of the national vote. Although this trend had distinctive causes relating to the geographically differentiated social and economic impacts of the economic miracle and their interplay with political and organisational traditions, it was widely interpreted as a permanent nationalisation of political life (Agnew 1988). DC and the PCI were now national political parties.

The localising regime

The 1979 election indicated a much more complex geography of political strength and variation than had been characteristic previously. Since then all parties have been less regionalised than in the past (Rizzi 1986). The 1983 and 1987 elections suggest a trend towards a localisation or increased differentiation of political expression. In 1983, DC lost 5.4 per cent nationally, but the PCI was not the beneficiary. Rather, it was smaller parties such as the PSI and the Republicans (PRI) in the north and the MSI in the south that gained most. In 1987, DC recovered somewhat from 1983 but without a major geographical expansion. The major loser this time was the PCI, which lost ground in the north-east, the north-west and some provinces of la zona rossa to the PSI and a variety of smaller parties including the Radicals (PR), the Greens, and Democrazia Proletaria (DP) (Leonardi 1987).

One cause of localisation was the increasingly differentiated pattern of economic change after a previous era of concentration. While the economic boom of the early 1960s concentrated economic growth increasingly in the north-west, by the late 1960s there was considerable decentralisation of industrial activity out of the north-west and into the north-east and the centre. This new pattern of differentiated economic growth led some commentators to write of the 'three Italies' — a north-west with a concentration of older heavy industries and large factory-scale production facilities, a north-east–Centre of small, family-based, export-oriented and component-producing firms, and a still largely underdeveloped south, reliant on government employment but with some of the small-scale development (for example, in the vicinity of Bari and Caserta) characteristic of the third Italy (north-east–centre) (see Bagnasco 1977). This terminology, though useful as a general characterisation of a new economic geography, masks both a much more uneven and differentiated pattern at a local scale and the linkages between localised development and the big firms of the north-west. High concentrations of employment in major growth industries have, in fact, been widely scattered (Cooke & Pires 1985).

Other causes have also contributed to the contemporary localising political-geographical trend. One of these has been the failure of parties to successfully adapt to recent social and economic change. In Trento and Udine (in the north-east), for example, DC has had problems adapting to the new economy. In large parts of the south and the north-west, the PCI has been unable to capitalise on earlier successes mainly because, in the south, it has neither had control over the state resources that lubricate the politics of many parts of that region, nor been able to build a permanent following. In the north-west, its major vanguard of unionised workers has been much reduced in economic importance at the same time that other parties have become better organised and the particular problems of southern immigrants have largely receded from the political agenda (Sassoon 1981; Caciagli 1985; Pasquino 1985).

The emergence of effective regional-level governments since 1970 has also reinforced the localisation of interests and sense of place. Where parties have achieved some strength and legitimacy through control over regional governments, they have been able to build local coalitions for national politics based upon the pursuit of local interests. The PCI, for example, has benefited from its control of or participation in the regional governments of Emilia-Romagna, Toscana and Umbria, but it has suffered elsewhere, and other parties such as DC or the PSI have benefited, because of its lack of control over patronage jobs and inability to write regional political agendas (Putnam et al. 1985).

Finally, the former successes of DC and the PCI in, respectively, la zona bianca and la zona rossa rested to a degree on the social institutions with which they were affiliated (unions, co-operatives, clubs, etc.), as well as social isolation. However, the shifting orientations of these institutions and the rise of the consumer society have opened up possibilities for the smaller parties. There is some evidence that, since the late 1960s, the ties between DC and the PCI and their supportive organisations, especially the unions, have weakened (Weitz 1975; Hellman 1987; Mershon 1987). The parties themselves are responsible for some of this. In order to expand nationally, they have often had to abandon or at least limit the ideological appeal that served so well in areas of traditional strength. They have also had to respond in some areas to 'new' movements, such as the Greens, which opened them up for both factionalism and essentially localised forms of organisation and ideology (Amyot 1981; Caciagli 1985). More generally, parties do not always travel well. Thus, in comparing north-east with central Italy, the question of compatibility between party style and local style arises. Stern (1975, 223) notes:

> the evolution of two very different forms of political hegemony, each with distinct characteristics that necessitate sharply contrasting forms of maintenance. The Christian Democratic variety that flourishes in northeastern Italy is fueled efficiently by a stable social organisation that deemphasises the place of politics in community life. In comparison the Communist variant thriving in central Italy accents the urgent attention that political matters should command among the local citizenry and thereby constantly reaffirms the relatively recent sense of legitimacy that underlies PCI control.

Of course, these hegemonies always have local roots and in some localities their power has been quite visible and persistent, as studies of Bologna and Vicenza suggest (Kertzer 1980; Allum & Andrighetto 1982). Although, as Tesini (1986) suggests for Bologna, things *could* have turned out quite differently. There is persistence in place as well as change. At present, and throughout Italy, however, support for all parties is more obviously localised than previously.

Lucca and Pistoia

Lucca and Pistoia are interesting provinces from the perspective of this chapter because in conventional 'primordialist' terms each represents a particular territorial subculture: Lucca, the Catholic subculture (la zona bianca) and Pistoia, the socialist subculture (la zona rossa). Although each, especially Lucca, can be reasonably portrayed as historically culturally distinctive, it is important to stress two points:

1 that their political complexion has not remained static over time; and
2 different *comuni* within the provinces have changed over time politically in different as well as similar ways to other *comuni*. [The major purpose of this section is to] explore these two points and suggest from the 'place perspective' how the cultural contexts of Lucca and Pistoia have changed so as to 'produce' the sequence of regimes at a national level.

The provinces of Lucca and Pistoia are located in northern Toscana, north of the river Arno to the west-north west of Florence (fig. 4.3). One of the oldest *autostrade* (four-lane highways) in Italy, dating from the 1930s, the 'Firenze–Mare', runs through the two provinces and connects them to Florence. In 1980 Lucca had a population of 388 904 and Pistoia of 267 151. The six *comuni* chosen for study, all of which grew in population and experienced considerable economic, especially small-scale industrial, development between 1960 and 1990 (Becattini 1975; Reyne 1983) had the following populations in 1981: Lucca, 91 246; Capannori, 44 041; Porcari, 6699; Pistoia, 92 274; Quarrata, 20 350; and Monsummano Terme, 16 511.

Politically the two provinces and the six *comuni* are diverse. In terms of electoral support for the two largest Italian political parties, Lucca and its *comuni* have been more dominated by support for the Christian Democrats than have been Pistoia and its *comuni* by support for the Communist Party (table 4.2). However, each province tended to go through three phases. In Lucca, the period 1946-58 was one of consolidation of support for DC. From 1963-76 the PCI emerged as a major competitor as the DC vote initially fell but, thereafter, generally was maintained. Since 1976 support for the DC fell, much more in *comuni* other than the three selected here, but parties other than the PCI, especially the PSI and the Verdi (Greens), gained in support. In Pistoia, the period 1946–58 was one of balance between the two major parties, except in Monsummano Terme where there was an early dominance by the PCI. From 1963–76 the PCI moved ahead of the DC, even though DC remained the major opposition party. Since 1976 the PCI vote stagnated and, most recently, declined, and the DC vote decreased substantially, with other parties such as the PSI acquiring the 'lost' votes. However, in Quarrata DC maintained its position much more than in the other *comuni*.

Overall, these trends conform to those for Italy as a whole described in the previous section. In the 1950s DC and PCI 'hegemonies' (ascendancy in social and political life based on social consensus) were in formation, although the DC hegemony in Lucca was

Figure 4.3: The provinces of Lucca and Pistoia, showing the six *comuni* referred to in the text and the *comuni* of Pisa and Florence.

much the strongest. In the 1960s DC and PCI became competitive on what was previously each other's turf, even though one party dominance was maintained or enhanced. After 1976, a greater heterogeneity in patterns of support for all political parties was apparent. Today, neither DC nor the PCI is the only alternative to the other in either Lucca or Pistoia. Recent local election and referendum results offer further evidence for this fragmentation (*La Stampa*, 9 maggio 1990; 5 giugno 1990).

A focus on the *comuni* can, perhaps, help explain what happened. Porcari and Quarrata changed the most politically. In 1953 DC was the majority party in each. Since then it has steadily weakened, largely to the benefit of the PCI, most clearly in Quarrata. In each case economic transformation and immigration played major roles. Prior to

Table 4.2:   Results of elections to the Constituent Assembly (1946), Chamber of Deputies (1948–87), Provinces of Lucca and Pistoia and three comuni from each: turnout (% eligibles voting) and % DC, PCI.

| | 1946 | | | 1948 | | | 1953 | | | 1958 | | |
	T	DC	PCI	T	DC	PCI	T	DC	PCI	T	DC	PCI
	(FDP)*											
Lucca	87.6	48.0	13.6	91.3	61.2	21.6	93.1	51.9	17.8	92.4	54.1	15.7
Lucca	85.4	49.5	12.2	92.5	63.8	16.2	94.8	54.9	15.8	94.8	56.5	12.5
Capannori	89.3	48.8	9.9	92.9	63.1	16.6	93.1	55.8	16.7	91.7	61.0	14.6
Porcari	92.6	46.5	11.8	93.7	60.9	21.4	95.3	55.8	22.8	94.0	56.6	21.4
Pistoia	94.5	29.8	34.5	95.2	40.1	47.2	96.4	35.0	37.1	96.1	34.5	37.8
Pistoia	93.4	28.7	34.4	97.1	39.7	47.2	96.9	34.4	37.3	97.0	34.4	37.5
Quarrata	94.0	24.3	42.3	95.7	50.3	39.3	97.4	46.6	28.3	97.5	46.8	29.2
Monsummano T.	94.2	20.8	46.9	96.1	32.5	55.2	96.9	26.4	49.4	96.7	24.0	50.4

| | 1963 | | | 1968 | | | 1972 | | | 1976 | | |
	T	DC	PCI	T	DC	PCI	T	DC	PCI	T	DC	PCI
Lucca	93.5	47.2	17.7	94.1	45.8	21.0	94.6	47.3	23.0	95.1	47.6	29.9
Lucca	95.2	49.7	13.3	95.5	49.2	15.6	95.9	51.6	16.8	96.5	54.2	22.8
Capannori	94.6	55.7	15.7	94.2	53.6	20.6	94.6	57.5	21.4	94.2	56.5	27.0
Porcari	94.1	49.7	23.4	94.6	48.4	28.8	96.0	49.6	30.2	96.6	47.9	38.3
Pistoia	96.6	30.2	42.7	96.3	30.3	44.6	96.5	30.2	45.3	96.5	30.7	50.5
Pistoia	98.5	30.1	41.5	96.9	30.1	43.4	96.9	30.2	44.1	97.2	30.4	49.8
Quarrata	97.1	43.6	36.5	97.5	42.0	40.9	97.2	41.8	42.0	96.3	40.1	47.3
Monsummano T.	96.0	20.3	56.0	96.2	21.6	56.4	96.3	20.1	56.4	96.5	22.6	62.2

| | 1979 | | | 1983 | | | 1987 | | | | | |
	T	DC	PCI	T	DC	PCI	T	DC	PCI			
Lucca	92.5	45.1	27.9	90.7	39.0	28.1	90.6	38.7	26.1			
Lucca	94.8	50.3	21.4	91.5	42.9	21.6	90.9	42.1	19.8			
Capannori	92.2	54.4	25.3	90.4	49.9	25.4	90.6	48.3	23.6			
Porcari	95.4	45.2	35.1	93.4	42.6	34.3	94.0	41.5	30.8			
Pistoia	94.5	29.8	48.7	92.5	25.4	48.9	93.3	25.7	45.4			
Pistoia	94.7	29.3	47.2	91.7	25.2	47.6	94.0	25.5	44.2			
Quarrata	95.2	39.3	45.6	93.2	34.6	45.8	93.5	34.9	41.7			
Monsummano T.	95.1	23.6	58.6	93.8	17.8	57.7	93.1	20.1	54.0			

*FDP = Fronte Democratico Popolare (inc. PCI)
Sources: 1946, 1948: M. Gabelli, 'Toscana elettorale 1946 e 1948', *Quaderni dell' Osservatorio Elettorale*, 20 (1988), 199-308; 1953-68 *Dalla Costituente alla Regione: Il Comportamento Elettorale in Toscana dal 1946 al 1970* (Florence: Giunta Regionale, 1972); 1972: Regione Toscana, *Il Comportamento Elettorale in Toscana: Una Prima Interpretazione* (Florence: Giunta Regionale, 1975); 1976-83: Regione Toscana, *Elezioni Senato e Camera 1976, 1979, 1983, 1987* (Florence: Giunta Regionale, 1976, 1979, 1983, 1987).

fascism Quarrata was a stronghold of the PPI (Partito popolare italiano), whose activists were founders of the local DC after the Second World War (Ballini 1981). However, the economy of the area changed from agricultural to industrial. Moreover, the area experienced considerable immigration, especially from other parts of Toscana and the Italian south. The PCI worked to extend its support in the area, partly through ancillary organisations such as social clubs. This strategy was successful for a time, but today

Figure 4.4: An aerial panorama of the city of Lucca looking west to east, the famous walls clearly demarcating the 'old' city.

these clubs attract mainly older men and are not major instruments of political mobilisation.

Porcari is likewise an area whose economy was transformed and which has also had a large immigration. In this case, however, the PCI was not particularly well-organised to exploit the grievances and aspirations of new voters, perhaps because PCI organisation in the province of Lucca is much inferior to that in the province of Pistoia. However, none of the parties is well-organised in Porcari and there is in general a much lower level of politicisation of local and national issues than is apparent in Quarrata.

This degree of political change is less true of the *comuni* that are seats of provincial government. They have relatively more diversified economies, although Lucca has a greater preponderance of larger firms and a weaker small firm sector than Pistoia. This reflects Lucca's greater dependence on outside capital and its long history of ties with northern Italy and overseas. Pistoia's economic development has been much more endogenous in origin, based on local artisans transforming themselves into small entrepreneurs. Also, in the *comuni* of Lucca and Pistoia, affiliation to the dominant local party is an important prerequisite for appointment to a wide range of jobs in the public sector. Local industries and local organisations, such as Chambers of Commerce, are still strongly tied to the two major parties. For example, banks and the Chambers of Commerce in both Lucca and Pistoia are strongly DC in orientation. There is also, perhaps, the most continuity in local social-spatial identity or sense of place. In both Lucca and Pistoia, but especially in Lucca, the historical centre of the city provides an emotive reference point for identity that is missing from the amorphous *comuni* of the 'urbanised countryside' such as the other four. In Lucca, the walls of the city stand as

Figure 4.5: A new communist manifesto? 'The firm as labour', a meeting with small and medium entrepreneurs, Palazzo dei Congressi, Florence, 4 February 1989.

an everyday reminder of the glorious past of Lucca and its political independence (Tazartes 1987). A merging of the civil and religious in a copenetration of physical symbols such as the walls and churches of the city, helps cement the self-image of *lucchesi* as citizens of a 'separate world' with its own distinctive politics (Camaiani 1979) (fig. 4.4). Given the Tuscan context of PCI dominance, DC has been the major beneficiary of this Luccan 'separatism'.

In Pistoia the physical damage to the city in the last years of Second World War, still apparent in places, is a constant reminder of the importance of those who resisted fascism. This has undoubtedly benefited the PCI which played the leading role in local resistance efforts (Risaliti 1976). The PCI has also been successful in Pistoia in politicising the working class population to its advantage. This was partly due to its success among the workers of the major local employer, *Breda costruzioni ferroviarie* (a major producer of railway vehicles and buses), but it also reflects the ability of the local party organisation to adapt to changing economic conditions, for instance through its strong support for the expansion of the small firm sector among local artisans and former share-cropping families (see figure 4.5 showing the announcement of a PCI conference in Florence on small and medium-sized firms).

Interestingly, DC in Lucca is all but invisible between elections, suggesting that the population there has a lower aptitude than that of Pistoia for political mobilisation on an everyday basis (on this issue in general see Stern 1975). Ironically, there appears to be a lower level of activity in voluntary organisations such as social clubs and the volunteer ambulance in Lucca than in Pistoia, including DC and PCI activists, even though Lucca has a long history of involvement with Catholic aid societies and is dominated by a political language emphasising mutual aid and an active social life based around parish and neighbourhood.

In Capannori and Monsummano Terme the hegemony of one of two major parties has been maintained against the trends in their respective provinces. Even though these *comuni* have changed the least electorally they have undergone tremendous economic and social change. In Monsummano Terme an established agrarian radicalism, based around the class conflict inherent in the system of share cropping dominant locally, was effectively harnessed by the local PCI which also successfully recruited southern immigrants into the party (Rossi & Santomassino 1981). The party has also been active in promoting and supporting the local shoe industry and in improving local physical infrastructure and housing.

In Capannori the industrialisation of the local economy has reinforced the dispersed settlement pattern of a *comune* which still looks to Lucca as its centre. Until 1978 the seat of the comune government was Lucca. Many workers also still farm small family-owned plots even when they work full-time at factory or workshop jobs. These 'peasant workers' identify closely with the city of Lucca, which is the centre for most social services. The important social role of the local priest in everyday life reinforces the persistence of a social catholicism which lends itself to support for DC. Rather than breaking down DC dominance, therefore, social and economic changes in Capannori have supported it. This is somewhat different, however, from the myth of a transcendental subculture persisting autonomously to constantly recreate the politics of the past.

A range of different processes, then, have operated to produce the shifts in support for the two major political parties that characterise both the provinces of Lucca and Pistoia and Italy as a whole. Rather than individualised opinion voting or primordial subcultures, therefore, explanation has been sought in the fluid, constantly reworked local political cultures of particular places.

Conclusion

The main purpose of this chapter has been to dispute dominant views of the link between local identity and politics by proposing an alternative perspective which views local identity as socially constructed and changing but ever-present rather than residual or primordial. In other words, local identity is part of the structuration of politics in place. In so doing the chapter offers a contribution in the specific context of Italian politics to the redefinition of the culture concept going on in contemporary human geography and social science.

The major advantages of the perspective laid out here are:

1 its ability to deal with changes in the geography (including dominant scale of expression) of electoral politics over time;
2 political culture is not equated with tradition but is seen as the intersubjective framework of practices, ideas and symbols in which political choices and activities are embedded;
3 *all* people live in cultural worlds that are made and remade through their everyday activities, not just those who live in areas where specific political parties have created systems of consensus or hegemony; and

4 cultural worlds are grounded geographically in the experience of place. Culture, therefore, is *inherently* geographical, defined in places and through local identity, and thus *internally related* to the geographical dynamics of politics.

Note

This section is based on fieldwork in Lucca and Pistoia in the spring of 1989. A number of local people were especially helpful to me: in Pistoia, Pierluigi Bartolini, Ivo Lucchesi, Sabino Catania and the Hon. Gerardo Bianchi; in Lucca, the Hon. Sergio Dardini, Armando Carnini and Walter Lencioni. Professor Agostino Palazzo, President of the Faculty of Political Sciences, the University of Pisa, and the author of an important study of politics and local economic planning in the province of Pistoia (Palazzo 1966), gave me valuable information on political and economic continuity and change in Pistoia and Lucca since 1970.

References

Agnew, J.A. 1987, *Place and Politics: The Geographical Mediation of State and Society*, Allen & Unwin, London.

Agnew, J.A. 1988, 'Better thieves than Reds? The nationalization thesis and the possibility of a geography of Italian politics', *Political Geography Quarterly*, 7, pp. 307–21.

Agnew, J.A. 1991, 'The geographical dynamics of Italian politics, 1947-1987', in L. Hochberg & C. Earle (eds), *The Geography of Social Change,* Stanford University Press, Stanford, CA, forthcoming.

Allum, P. 1988, 'Cultura o opinioni? Su alcuni dubbi epistemologici', *Il Politico,* 53, pp. 261–8.

Allum, P.A. & Andrighetto, T. 1982, 'Elezioni e elettorato a Vicenza nel dopoguerra', *Quaderni di Sociologia*, 30, pp. 355–97.

Almond, G. & Verba, S. 1963, *The Civic Culture*, Little, Brown, Boston.

Amin, A. & Robins, K. 1990, 'The re-emergence of regional economies: The mythical geography of flexible accumulation', *Society and Space*, 8, pp. 7–34.

Amyot, G. 1981, *The Italian Communist Party: The Crisis of the Popular Front Strategy*, St Martin's Press, New York.

Anderlini, F. 1987, 'Una modellizzazione per zone sociopolitiche dell' Italia repubblicana', *Polis*, 1, pp. 443–79.

Baccetti, C. 1987, 'Memoria storica e continuità' elettorale. Una zona rossa nella Toscana rossa', *Italia Contemporanea*, 167, pp. 7–30.

Bagnasco, A. 1977, *Tre Italie: La problematica territoriale dello sviluppo italiano*, Il Mulino, Bologna.

Bagnasco, A. 1988, *La costruzione sociale del mercato*, Il Mulino, Bologna.

Bagnasco, A. & Trigilia, C. 1984, *Società e politica nelle aree di piccola impresa. Il caso di Bassano*, Arsenale, Venice.

Bagnasco, A. & Trigilia, C. 1985, *Società e politica nelle aree di piccola impresa. Il caso di Valdelsa*, Franco Angeli, Milan.

Ballini, P.-L. 1981, 'La Democrazia Cristiana', in E. Rotelli (ed.), *La ricostruzione in Toscana, dal CLN ai partiti. Tomo II: I partiti politici*, Il Mulino, Bologna, pp. 21–248.

Barbagli, M., Corbetta, P., Parisi, A. & Schadee, H.M.A. 1979, *Fluidità elettorale e classi sociali in Italia*, Il Mulino, Bologna.

Bartolini, B. 1976, 'Insediamento subculturale e distribuzione dei suffragi in Italia', *Rivista Italiana di Scienza Politica,* 6, pp. 481–514.

Becattini, G. (ed.) 1975, *Lo sviluppo economico di Toscana*, IRPET, Florence.

Bellini, N. 1989, 'Il socialismo in una regione sola: Il PCI e il governo dell' industria in Emilia-Romagna', *Il Mulino*, 325, pp. 707–32.

Blim, M.L. 1990, 'Economic development and decline in the emerging global factory: Some Italian lessons', *Politics and Society,* 18, pp. 143–63.

Caciagli, M. 1985, 'Il resistibile declino della Democrazia Cristiana', in G. Pasquino (ed.), *Il sistema politico italiano,* Bari, Laterza, pp. 101–27.

Caciagli, M. 1988, 'Approssimazione alle culture politiche locali. Problemi di analisi ed esperienze di ricerca', *Il Politico*, 53, pp. 269–92.

Camaiani, P.G. 1979, *Dallo stato cittadino alla città bianca: La 'società cristiana' lucchese e la rivoluzione toscana,* La Nuova Italia, Florence.

Capecchi, V. , Cioni Polacchini, V., Galli, G. & Sivini, G. 1968, *Il comportamento elettorale in Italia,* Il Mulino, Bologna.

Cartocci, R. 1987, 'Otto risposte a un problema: La divisione dell' Italia in zona politicamente omogenee', *Polis,* l, pp. 481–514.

Chubb, J. 1986, 'The Christian Democratic party: Reviving or surviving?', in R. Leonardi & R.Y. Nanetti (eds), *Italian Politics: A Review,* vol. l, Frances Pinter, London, pp. 69–86.

Cooke, P. 1990, 'Locality, structure, and agency: A theoretical analysis', *Cultural Anthropology,* 5, pp. 3–15.

Cooke, P. & Pires, A. da Rosa 1985, 'Productive decentralization in three European regions', *Environment and Planning A,* 17, pp. 527–54.

Derivry, D. & Dogan, M. 1986, 'Religion, classe et politique en France: Six types de relations causales', *Revue Francaise de Science Politique,* 2, 36, pp. 157–81.

Dogan, M. 1967, 'Political cleavages and social stratification in France and Italy', in S.M. Lipset & S. Rokkan (eds), *Party Systems and Voter Alignments,* The Free Press, New York, pp. 129–95.

Feltrin, P. 1988, 'Le culture politiche locali: Alcune osservazioni critiche sugli studi condotti in Italia', *Il Politico,* 53, pp. 293–306.

Forgacs, D. 1990, *Italian Culture in the Industrial Era, 1880-1980,* Manchester University Press, Manchester.

Galli, G. 1984, *Il bipartitismo imperfetto: Comunisti e democristiani in Italia,* Mondadori, Milan.

Galli, G. & Prandi, A. 1970, *Patterns of Political Participation in Italy,* Yale University Press, New Haven.

Hellman, J.A. 1987, *Journeys Among Women: Feminism in Five Italian Cities,* Oxford University Press, New York.

Johnston, R.J. 1986, 'The neighbourhood effect revisited', *Society and Space,* 4, pp. 41–55.

Kertzer, D.C. 1980, *Comrades and Christians: Religion and Political Struggle in Communist Italy,* Cambridge University Press, New York.

King, R. 1985, *The Industrial Geography of Italy,* St Martin's Press, New York.

La Stampa 9 maggio 1990, 'Lo stato, il nuovo Barbarossa', p. 3; 'I risultati delle provinciali: Si conferma la sconfitta PCI nelle zone rossa', p. 8.

La Stampa 5 giugno 1990, 'A vuoto la consultazione su caccia e pesticidi: per la prima volta ha votato solo il 43.4%', p. l.

Leonardi, R. 1987, 'The changing balance: The rise of small parties in the 1983 election', in H.R. Penniman (ed.), *Italy at the Polls, 1983: A Study of the National Elections,* Duke University Press, Durham, NC, pp. 100–19.

Mershon, C.A. 1987, 'Unions and politics in Italy', in H.R. Penniman (ed.), *Italy at the Polls, 1983: A Study of the National Elections,* Duke University Press, Durham, NC, pp. 120–45.

Muscarà, C. 1987, 'Dalla geografia elettorale alla geografia politica: Il caso italiano delle aree bianca e rossa', *Bollettino della Società Geografica Italiana,* 4, pp. 269–302.

Palazzo, A. 1966, *Programmazione e unità locali di decisione,* Giuffre, Milan.

Parisi, A. 1971, 'La matrice socio-religiosa del dissenso cattolico in Italia', *Il Mulino,* 21, pp. 637–57.

Parisi, A. & Pasquino, G. 1980, 'Changes in Italian electoral behavior: The relationships between parties and voters', in P. Lange & S. Tarrow (eds), *Italy in Transition: Conflict and Consensus,* Frank Cass, London, pp. 6–30.

Pasquino, G. 1985, 'Il partito comunista nel sistema politico italiano', in G. Pasquino (ed.), *Il sistema politico italiano,* Laterza, Bari, pp. 126–68.

Pavsiv, R. 1985, 'Esiste una tendenza all' omogeneizzazione territoriale nei partiti italiani?', *Rivista Italiana di Scienza Politica,* 15, pp. 69–97.

Putnam, R., Leonardi, R., Nanetti, R.Y. & Pavoncello, F. 1985, 'Il rendimento dei governi regionali', in G. Pasquino (ed.), *Il sistema politico italiano,* Laterza, Bari, pp. 345–83.

Reyne, G. 1983, *L'industrie en Toscane: Etude d'Une Region Italienne Confronteé a La Crise,* thesis presented at L'Université de Nice, France.

Risaliti, R. 1976, *Antifascismo e resistenza nel Pistoiese,* Tellini, Pistoia.

Rizzi, E. 1986, *Atlante geo-storico, 1946-1983: Le elezioni politiche e il parlamento nell' Italia repubblicana*, GSI, Milan.

Rossi, M.G. & Santomassimo, G. 1981, 'Il partito comunista italiano: Introduzione', in E. Rotelli (ed.), *La ricostruzione in Toscana, dal CLN ai partiti. Tomo II: I partiti politici*, Il Mulino, Bologna, pp. 757–68.

Sani, G. 1977, 'Le elezioni degli anni settanta: Terremoto o evoluzione?', in A. Parisi & G. Pasquino (eds), *Continuità e mutamento elettorale in Italia*, Il Mulino, Bologna, pp. 67–102.

Sassoon, D. 1981, *The Strategy of the Italian Communist Party*, St Martin's Press, New York.

Stern, A. 1975, 'Political legitimacy in local politics: The Communist Party in northeastern Italy', in D.L.M. Blackmer & S. Tarrow (eds), *Communism in Italy and France,* Princeton University Press, Princeton, pp. 221–58.

Tarrow, S. 1977, *Between Center and Periphery: Grassroots Politicians in Italy and France,* Yale University Press, New Haven.

Taylor, C. 1985, 'Interpretation and the sciences of man', *Philosophy and the Human Sciences: Philosophical Papers 2,* Cambridge University Press, Cambridge, pp. 15–57.

Tazartes, M. 1987, *Una città allo specchio: Lucca fra cronaca e storia*, Mari Pacini Fazzi, Lucca.

Tesini, M. 1986, *Oltre la città rossa: L'alternativa mancata di Dossetti a Bologna (1956-1958)*, Il Mulino, Bologna.

Trigilia, C. 1986, *Grandi partiti e piccole imprese,* Il Mulino, Bologna.

Tullio-Altan, C. 1986, *La nostra Italia: Arretratezza socioculturale, clientelismo, trasformismo e ribellismo dall' Unità ad oggi,* Feltrinelli, Milan.

Weitz, P. 1975, 'The CGIL and the PCI: From subordination to independent political force', in D.L.M. Blackmer & S. Tarrow (eds), *Communism in Italy and France*, Princeton University Press, Princeton, pp. 541–71.

Williams, R. 1981, *Culture*, Fontana, London.

5 Corporate cultures and the modern landscape of New York City

Mona Domosh

> Like almost all the arts, even music, architecture has a representational function. Not only does it express the values (and land values) of a society, but also its ideologies, hopes, fears, religion, social structure, metaphysics. It may represent these facts or betray them; it may give the illusion of an unearthly realm ... or create in reality an earthly 'paradise'. This strange, double aspect of architecture — both to be and to represent a state of affairs — distinguishes it from other, purely expressive arts such as painting. (Jencks 1982, 178)

> However irrelevant to the conduct of business, a company's investment in bricks and mortar — its building — inevitably says something about its culture. After all, building investments are made or at least overseen by senior management. As much as they'd like to avoid the thought, most senior managers recognise that the buildings will likely outlive them; thus they try to create a setting that makes a statement to the world about their company, both deliberate and otherwise. (Deal & Kennedy 1982, 129–30)

Introduction

When corporate executives make decisions about the location and design of their buildings, they are indeed creating images of their companies; they are involved in the complex activity of communicating by symbol the culture of which they are a part. As Charles Jencks (1982) points out, those buildings both represent that culture and house it; they are functional and symbolic at the same time. In this sense, corporate buildings are no different from any other type of architecture; they both are and 'represent a state of affairs'. Yet, the corporate landscape is in many respects unique — given the highly-structured world of the corporation, and its complicated relationship to its employees and customers, the decisions concerning architectural form are rarely simple, and often involve the appeasement of seemingly contradictory needs. In addition, the corporate landscape is riddled with messages and codes that allude to the commercial nature of its enterprises, messages that are often not obvious from first appearances. What is it that corporations want to communicate to the world? Does a corporation wish to display its commercial motivations in its building, or an image untainted with the everyday workings of money-making? What other interests do corporations have in shaping the urban landscape? The answers to these questions are complex, varying through time and across the corporate world, dependent on the relationships between the business world, the architectural professions and changing societal values and ideals. This chapter will explore the answers to these questions by focusing on the creation of the business landscape of nineteenth-century New York, and, using that analysis, will suggest how that process has continued and changed throughout the early and late twentieth century. First, it is important to discuss in more detail the notion of corporate culture and its relationship to architecture and landscape.

There are, indeed, 'cultures' of corporations, but it would be difficult to argue that there is one corporate culture. Many companies have found it beneficial to develop policies that establish a type of ethos among its employees; this ethos or 'culture' is considered successful if it helps the company compete in its particular business environment. As Terrence Deal and Allan Kennedy discuss in their book *Corporate Cultures*:

> This business environment is the single greatest influence in shaping a corporate culture. Thus, companies that depend for success on their ability to sell an undifferentiated product tend to develop one type of culture ... that keeps its sales force selling. Companies that spend a great deal of research and development money before they even know if the final product will be successful or not tend to develop a different culture ... designed to make sure decisions are thought through before actions are taken. (Deal & Kennedy 1982, 13–14)

Thus, companies tend to develop a set of practices that serve to codify a particular value system and promote a type of self-representation. The construction of a building gives material expression to those practices, and in this sense participates in the definition of a corporate culture. A true 'reading' of the corporate landscape requires an understanding of these internal distinctions between types of business cultures. A company that bases its success on constant innovation will assuredly construct for itself a building different in type from a business that relies on an impression of stability for its success. Yet the image that a company wishes to promote, whether it is of innovation or stability, is dependent upon the larger business environment — that is, on how the world of business fits into the prevailing social, economic and cultural relations of the time. To 'read' the corporate landscape, then, requires an understanding both of the types of companies involved — the corporate 'cultures', in the words of Deal and Kennedy — and the historical and material conditions under which that landscape was created. This chapter will discuss changes in the types of business 'cultures', and their relationship to broader social and economic contexts, by focusing on the first self-conscious displays of commerce in the modern world, the early skyscrapers of lower Manhattan.

The context of skyscraper development

> The modern high building, whether it is beautiful or ugly, whether it expresses pleasant or disagreeable traits and truths, is distinctively of this day and this country, and containing all the other modes of enterprise it is comprehensively typical. (Steffens 1897, 38)

If, indeed, the skyscraper was typical 'of this day and this country', then it must have embodied at least some of the defining characteristics of its time. It did come to serve as the undisputed symbol of New York City, and as such, was laden with those extremes of emotion that the city has tended to generate (Strauss 1961; Trachtenberg 1979; Domosh 1985). Skyscrapers were invested with meaning by those who viewed them, but they of course were also created by people with certain intentions, intentions that developed out of circumstances particular to late nineteenth-century New York, and it is to an understanding of this context that we must first turn our attention.

As the self-proclaimed poet of Manhattan, Walt Whitman was the first literary figure to capture the essence and spirit of New York City. His poetry, in both form and content, expresses the energy, dynamism and diversity of the city that was to become the capital of the modern world. Nineteenth-century New York was a city of extremes and excess that, like Whitman's poetry, looked outward, toward the vistas of the American West for inspiration. Historian Edward Spann makes the point clear:

> Although it included a wide range of human existence, New York was best known in its extremes, as a city capable of shedding the most brilliant light and casting the deepest shadows. Perhaps no place in the world evoked such extremes of love and hate, often in the same person. In its slums, dirt, materialism, violence, congestion, rush, politics and municipal mismanagement, it could depress, degrade and offend, the human spirit. In its wealth, intelligence, power, opportunities, freedom, and in the seemingly endless wonders of its streets, it could exalt, exhilarate and, occasionally, even charm strangers and citizens alike. The new metropolis was radically imperfect, but its imperfections were those of a masterwork of collective human spirit and masterful presence in the world. (Spann 1981, 426)

By mid-century, New York had come to dominate the economic sphere of the nation, and by the 1890s, of the western world (Hammack 1982). That dominance resulted from both the city's strategic physical location — midway between the major population centres of America, with access to exceptionally good and well-protected harbours — and the ability of its population to take advantage of that location and establish innovative economic initiatives. One of the earliest of such innovations was the construction of the Erie Canal, which provided the only water route from inland America to a port and thereby enabled New York to capture much of the interior fur and agricultural trade. Because of the strong ties with the British market that such trade established, New York merchants were able to take over most of the cotton trade from Charleston and New Orleans merchants. As cotton was the prime export of America at the time, such a takeover provided New York with incredible mercantile supremacy. In 1830, 36.8 per cent of all importing and exporting in America passed through the port of New York, and by 1850, the percentage jumped to 71.2 per cent (Hammack 1982).

Such success in mercantile endeavours created strong ties to the capital supply controlled by Great Britain, and helped New York merchants to invest in what was to become one of the most lucrative enterprises of the century — railroads. Both Philadelphia and Boston merchants had tried their hands in such investments but, for various reasons, each had failed to supply the large amounts of capital necessary for success in railroad financing. Wall Street's rise to supremacy in the railroad finance world by 1860 had significant effects on the city's economy, bringing economic dominance to New York in the mercantile, financial and eventually industrial spheres (Chandler 1977).

Such economic dominance was intimately related to New York's social fabric. New York's innovative business class was in many senses both the cause and result of the city's economic position. The tone of the city was set by the competitiveness, heterogeneity and fluidity of its social classes. From its original inception as a trading post by the Dutch trading companies in the late seventeenth century, the raison d'être of the city was its economic functionings, without any illusions of religious or social control. Even in the early eighteenth century, New York was known for its tolerance of diversity, and throughout the century experienced waves of migrations from Europe that acted as prelude to the massive immigration of the nineteenth century. The original Dutch and then English elite classes controlled the city for short time periods, but were not able to maintain economic or cultural control over such a rapidly-expanding population (Jaher 1982). This heterogeneity and instability of New York's population continued to characterise the city throughout the nineteenth century, and helped create its competitive and innovative business culture by encouraging commercial risk-taking and discouraging conservative business policies.

It is from within this particular context that the impulse for businesses to build skyscrapers developed. Because of this instability and diversity, New York's business class in the late nineteenth century was continually striving for supremacy, looking to every possible invention or gimmick to gain the competitive edge. Skyscrapers, then, provided both a lucrative investment and a very legible advertisement for new and competitive industries. As a group whose wealth was of relatively recent vintage, New York's business class was socially unstable, and was seeking signs of status and cultural legitimacy. The ornate, historical-revival style skyscrapers acted as status symbols and cultural adornments for a class eager to display itself through any channel, including the landscape. Skyscrapers, then, fulfilled a combination of needs — for real estate investment, material symbolism, social status, and cultural legitimacy. Close analyses of the creation of two such buildings will serve to illuminate these points.

Cultural monuments to business supremacy: two New York examples

> Many large companies have long since recognised the commercial advantages of a splendid building which shall give outward and visible evidence of the magnitude of their resources ... the greatest companies imagining, and with some show of reason, it must be admitted, that those who occupied the largest and highest buildings will be endowed, in the popular mind, with the most wealth. (Ferree 1894, 304–5)

Pulitzer (World) building

When Joseph Pulitzer was considering the construction of a new building to house the expanding business of his newspaper, the *New York World*, he was faced with decisions concerning its location, size, design and designer. His purchase of the relatively small newspaper in 1883 had been prompted by more than strictly mercenary aims, although the newspaper industry at the time promised to be a lucrative one. Pulitzer, a relatively recent migrant to New York and not far removed from his Eastern European ancestry, was looking for a way of communicating both his newly-found economic and cultural status. The purchase and supervision of a newspaper provided Pulitzer with a platform from which he could contribute to the political and cultural dynamic of the city, while at the same time allowing him to display his concern for the 'common people', by treating his paper as a type of 'public' service.

Pulitzer's pioneering techniques in sensational journalism, combined with his use of large headlines and illustrations, turned the *World* into an immediate success, with the paper boasting a record-breaking circulation of 250 000 by 1886 (Bleyer 1927). The rapid growth of the paper necessitated the enlargement of its quarters on Park Row, and Pulitzer decided that a new and grand building be constructed as the home of the now famous *New York World*.

The newspaper industry in New York was a highly competitive one, with all of the daily newspapers vying for supremacy. Most of the papers were located near Park Row since it was close to both City Hall and Wall Street, and throughout the latter part of the 1870s these newspaper companies had participated in a building competition — that is, some of the newspapers began to express their status by constructing ornate and often tall structures. In 1875, the *New York Tribune* had taken that competition seriously when it constructed for itself what many consider the first skyscraper, thereby outdoing all its competitors by virtue of its height alone. It would have been difficult for anyone in Manhattan, let alone in the newspaper industry, to miss the overt symbolism of such a building. The *New York Times* had constructed for itself a new building on Park Row that was completed in 1888, and although it was no taller than the *Tribune* building, it was designed in the very latest architectural style. With his somewhat shaky ego and newly-found social status, Joseph Pulitzer was not about to let his paper be surpassed by the *Tribune* and the *Times*, and in his instructions to his architect for his new building, he made explicit his concern that the building be at least as fine as the *Times* building:

> The finish of the building is something I know very little about. I want to be sure that no false economy or niggardliness will mar the building inside. I want the finish to be creditable at least, if no more, and first-class in every respect, as the contract with Post [the architect] requires ... How is the *Times* building finished? Have you ever been through it? Can anything be suggested by which our finish can be improved? You remember Post's contract requires it to be at least as good as that of the *Times*. (quoted in Seitz 1924, 175)

The *World* building was meant to fulfil at least these two needs — that is, for more space for the expanded newspaper, and as a response to the building competition among the newspapers in New York. Yet Pulitzer seemed to have much more in mind when he insisted that his building be an 'architectural ornament to the metropolis' ('The Pulitzer Building' 1890). Pulitzer wanted his building to be praised for its aesthetic qualities, as much as he wanted it to be noticeable on the skyline. He hired the most popular commercial architect in the city, George Post, and instructed him to design a building that would be an aesthetic tribute to the city. In addition, Pulitzer spoke of his newspaper as a public service, as a voice for the common people, and his new building was also meant to express this public nature of the paper.

Pulitzer's demands for his new building were difficult to negotiate. The building was to advertise the new status of the newspaper, and therefore was meant to be a commercial statement. It was also to fulfil Pulitzer's aspirations of achieving elevated status for himself, and therefore was meant as an aesthetic adornment that would be praised by the city's arbiters of taste. The building was also to represent the public nature of a newspaper, its concerns for the virtues of everyday people. To further complicate matters, George Post, the architect, also had various personal and professional agendas in designing the building.

Post's choice of the Renaissance revival style for the new building was appropriate to these demands. The allusion to the Renaissance period served to associate the paper with the cultural creations of that era, as well as the public (as opposed to commercial) nature of the newspaper. Many of the civic structures built in the latter half of the nineteenth century in American cities were designed in similar styles, completing the association with public service that Pulitzer had demanded.

Completed in 1890, the new *World* building stood six storeys above any other building in the city (fig. 5.1). The uppermost of its sixteen storeys was topped by a gold dome in which were located Pultizer's and the editorial staff's offices. The classically inspired archways, columns and pedestals that adorned the exterior of the building gave the building a distinctive appearance, as did the four large torchbearers representing art, literature, science and invention. The choice of these four realms of human invention is instructive, in that, Pulitzer noticeably deleted any mention of commercial endeavours from the exterior form of the building. The building was to be a cultural monument to public service.

Given the complexity of the design process and the often conflicting demands, it is not surprising that the building had its critics. It failed most resoundingly as an aesthetic creation. The arbiters of taste in New York, mostly the architectural critics, judged the building a failure, arguing that 'for thoughtful and refined design, one looks everywhere in vain' ('The New World Building' *Record and Guide*, 1890). Yet as an advertisement of the paper to the public, it was an overwhelming success. Thousands of people came to the elaborate opening-day ceremonies, and the building continued to attract visitors for years, many choosing to ride the elevator to the top in order to view the city from the highest vantage point available. The new *World* building was apparently the talk of the town, with *Harper's Weekly* writing: 'The success of the *World* newspaper under the management of Mr. Pulitzer is one of the most important achievements of recent years. It is fitly crowned and attested by the erection of the great building ...' ('The New York "World", *Harper's Weekly*, 1890, 47).

What was not mentioned by *Harper's Weekly* is almost as significant as what was: the building was not admired for its architectural design, or floor-plan, or the feat of engineering that it represented; it was 'great' because it was tall. The connection between the owner and the building was explicit — the *World* had literally crowned itself for its success. The building, then, was a success as advertisement for the newspaper and a monument to Pulitzer, but less of a success as an aesthetic artifact.

By the mid 1890s, most of the newspapers in New York had completed the structures that were to house them for the next fifty years or so; the expansion of the industry had reached its peak. It is at this time that another type of business, the life insurance industry, became particularly involved in skyscraper development. Like the newspaper business, the life insurance industry was an incredibly competitive one, with many companies vying to capture the millions of dollars that the new urban dwellers were willing to spend to insure their newly-found wealth. Lacking other forms of material expression, and in need of larger and more offices, life insurance companies were very interested in constructing ornate and tall buildings. Between 1892 and 1896, life insurance companies were responsible for over 20 per cent of all significantly tall buildings constructed in Manhattan (Domosh 1985).

Metropolitan Life building

A relative newcomer to the industry, the Metropolitan Life Insurance Company expanded rapidly in the last decade of the nineteenth century. The company had outgrown its headquarters in lower Manhattan, and in 1893 took the risky step of moving

Figure 5.1: Pulitzer (World) Building, exterior view.
Source: Photo by George P. Hall & Son, n.d. Courtesy of the New York Historical Society, NYC.

uptown to Madison Square to build its new structure. The eleven-storey marble edifice was designed by architect Napoleon LeBrun in the Renaissance revival style, complete with a marble court that had a vaulted ceiling three storeys from the floor, and a stairway to the executive offices that was apparently modelled after the Paris Opera House (James 1947, 27). The rapid growth of the company necessitated expansion of the building only a few years after it opened, and company president James Hegeman decided to hire the sons of the deceased architect to design a building appropriate to the company's rising economic status.

Yet, similar to Pulitzer's decisions concerning his new building, the decisions about the type and design of the Metropolitan's new building were based on multiple needs. Certainly the need for more office space was a major concern, but the actual design of that space was given much thought by Hegeman himself. As a product of and participant in a particular type of corporate culture, Hegeman shared with other life insurance executives an ideological belief in the benign service role of their companies. As Equitable Life president James Alexander argued, 'assuredly, an institution which exists for the benefit of widows and orphans ... is one which ought not to be conducted on a low plane of competition' (Keller 1963, 26). Such an ideological stance permeated the public statements of the life insurance industry, legitimising their excess profits and lack of any apparent material product. More than many other types of businesses, life insurance could be construed as providing a public service for the good of society, and such associations were exploited artfully by the executives of the emerging industry.

When it came to the construction of a new addition to the main office building of the Metropolitan, Hegeman and his vice-president, Haley Fiske, were interested in creating a statement not only about the newly-found economic position of their company, but also of the public-mindedness of its 'mission'. Given the general Renaissance style of the main building, Hegeman decided that the addition would take the form of a tall tower that would use the campanile in St Mark's Square in Venice as its prototype. The choice was an apt one — the tower would enable the Metropolitan to continue the skyward commercial competition in which life insurance companies were actively involved, and the association with Venice and the Renaissance period would provide both cultural legitimacy and a message of civic-mindedness.

When completed in 1909, the fifty-storey tower was the tallest structure in New York (fig. 5.2) and the company wasted no time in exploiting that fact as advertisement for itself. On the exterior, from the twenty-fifth to the twenty-seventh floor was a large clock that apparently was visible over a mile away, and at the very top was an electric lantern that flashed out the time. Haley Fiske called this 'the light that never fails', making explicit the association with the company's public stature. The image of this beacon on top of the building, with those words encircling it, became the logo for the company, and was placed on all of its advertisements and correspondences (Domosh 1988). At the fiftieth storey was a public lookout from which, the company claimed, were visible the homes of over one-sixteenth of the entire American population (*The Metropolitan Life Insurance Company* 1908, 26).

As an advertisement for the company and a symbol of its new economic power, the Metropolitan tower was a success (Dublin 1943). New Yorkers seemed enamoured with the building, and millions rode the elevator to the top to see the panoramic view from the fiftieth floor. Whether its association to the precapitalist, civic-oriented Venetian Renaissance registered in many of the visitors' and viewers' minds is doubtful, although

Figure 5.2: Metropolitan Life Building
Source: From a postcard, n.d.

such association did enhance its recognition value and allowed it to be considered seriously as an aesthetic object. The notion of the incompatibility of art and commerce was being challenged by life insurance companies like the Metropolitan, who were using art (in this case an 'aesthetically-correct' architecture) to create a public identity for a corporate entity. That identity would serve the corporation well, particularly as its internal policies came under legislative attack in the last years of the nineteenth century (North 1952), and its role as a 'philanthropic' enterprise became increasingly suspect. Metropolitan's home office building and its branch offices were meant as clear expressions of a business that had public-minded goals at the forefront of its activities. Among the many urban guide-books that proliferated in the nineteenth century, Moses King's *Handbooks* were perhaps the most influential, and his 1894 description of the notable buildings of Manhattan alludes to the complete identification of the private insurance industry with public, philanthropic endeavours:

> All kinds of benevolent, semi-benevolent and philanthropic organisations are productive of wholesome results. But chief of all these are the numerous life insurance companies — the most practical kind of philanthropy ... Beside their benevolent work, these life corporations have been the prime causes of the city's architectural growth, for the life insurance buildings of New York surpass the office structures of any city in the world. (King 1894, quoted in Gibbs 1984)

The Metropolitan, along with the other life insurance companies in New York, apparently had succeeded in presenting to the public a civic-minded corporate identity, and its headquarters building was the material manifestation of that identity.

As a contender in the aesthetic game, however, the Metropolitan building was less than successful. By the time of its completion, the architectural critics were searching for a skyscraper style that would be representative of America and of the newly-emerging modern period. As a direct imitation of a structure from a different country and different time period, the Metropolitan tower was deemed inappropriate for its context. One critic compared it unfavourably to the Flatiron building (a twenty-storey structure completed several years earlier), saying that the tower 'belongs to an earlier people and a vanished race', while the Flatiron was a 'twentieth century giant' that 'stands on the threshold of vigorous new life and of vast architectural possibilities' (Corbin 1903, 262).

The Metropolitan tower certainly fulfilled the needs of the company for office space, and for a distinctive form of material expression and advertisement, yet it did not provide a form of aesthetic legitimacy for the company. The aesthetic constructs established by the arbiters of taste in New York excluded such buildings, since its style was deemed to be simply out of date. Like Pulitzer, Hegeman's status aspirations were never fulfilled.

Such a failure must not have bothered Hegeman very much — the building was far more a corporate entity than a personal one, whereas the *World* building had been very much a personal expression for Pulitzer. In fact, personal and corporate identities were intertwined for Pulitzer. The *World* was Pulitzer's own creation, and his new building was as much a statement of his personal prestige as it was an advertisement for the paper. Hegeman, on the other hand, was only one of many presidents of what was (and is) an incredibly large and complex corporation. The Metropolitan tower was more a corporate symbol than a statement of personal status.

During the relatively short time between the construction of the two buildings, a change had occurred in the type of economic structure that characterised New York.

Economic historians argue that the country was moving from a mercantile to a modern, industrial form of capitalism (Chandler 1977). Corporations began to replace individually-run businesses, distancing ownership from control. Business organisations grew larger and more complex, resulting in the creation of a new class of white-collar workers. Life insurance companies are one of the best examples of this type of new organisation, and the Metropolitan tower represents a transition stage between the personally-identified businesses of the mid nineteenth century and the corporate world of the early twentieth century. In this sense, the Metropolitan Insurance Co. belonged to a type of corporate culture different from that of the *New York World*; it is representative of a type of bureaucratic and hierarchical culture that began to take control of the urban landscape at the turn of the century.

The emergence of a modernist corporate landscape

Many of the new corporations that began to dominate the economic structure of the country in the early twentieth century had their headquarters in New York, which became the major centre for bankers, insurance workers, lawyers, engineers and managers (Hammack 1982). Skyscrapers were built to house these white-collar workers, but these buildings were neither personal statements nor corporate symbols. Instead, they were large, speculative structures built to earn the most rents from a particular piece of real estate. These massive office buildings began to provoke reaction both from architectural critics, who referred to the buildings as 'architectural aberrations', and from a newly-vitalised group of urban reformers who found their appearance and height unacceptable. Drawing their inspiration from a national reformist crusade often referred to as the city beautiful movement, this group of professionally educated middle and upper-class people translated the new aesthetic and vision of urban order into a language that American city-dwellers could understand. According to William Wilson, embedded in the city beautiful movement was an ideology that conflated the notions of beauty and utility (Wilson 1989). 'No structure or scene could be truly beautiful without being functional as well' (Wilson 1989, 83). With this conflation of interests, the large businesses that were beginning to control the urban landscape became quite vocal supporters of the attempts to 'beautify'; the functional city was to their financial benefit. New circulation routes in the city were beautiful because functional, and vice versa. In addition, the new city beautiful ideology spoke not only of the association of beauty and utility but also of efficiency, particularly the efficiency of the new factories and corporations. As Wilson writes, these urban reformers believed that 'the presumed efficiency of some private-enterprise factories and offices could be transferred to nonpecuniary concerns including the aesthetic' (Wilson 1989, 83). This confluence of the concepts of beauty, utility and efficiency produced an alliance of big business, design professionals and many politicians that was to shape the future of the American urban landscape (Boyer 1983; Wilson 1989).

   The irregularly-shaped, speculative skyscrapers of the late nineteenth and early twentieth centuries certainly did not fit into this prevailing aesthetic. The new corporate world was not particularly concerned with symbols of personal or individual corporate status. Instead, it was interested in the built environment as a means of promoting a certain corporate image, and as a way of facilitating the transportation and communication systems that were essential to its functioning and profit-making. The new design and planning professions found symbols of unbridled competition, as in the mammoth skyscrapers of the turn of the century, inappropriate and unacceptable (Domosh 1989). Commercial buildings were permissible if they took a secondary position to civic monuments, and if they participated visually in a compatible grouping of buildings. The landscape of the city beautiful was one 'where mere individualism was subordinated to the harmony of the greater good' (Wilson 1989, 283).

Proponents of the aesthetics and ideology of the city beautiful movement were from the beginning self-conscious about their efforts to create a rational landscape. These notions provided the underpinnings of what we call today modernism, and the modernist aesthetic became the dominant architectural style for the new corporate world. Modernism, as it was imported into American architecture from Europe throughout the first decades of the twentieth century, spoke of a fit between design and function. The now-famous dictum that form should follow function was more than a rallying cry — it indeed represented a celebration of function, of the workings of modern life. In this, modern design fitted the needs of modern industrial corporations. Instead of disguising the technological underpinnings of the modern world, modernism not only allowed for but encouraged a display of that technology. The simple, interchangeable parts of modern design reflected the structure of the new corporate world, and satisfied demands of corporations for flexible and expandable spatial arrangements. An architecture that suggested the eschewal of the past in favour of future progress suited corporations that identified themselves as the harbingers of a brave new world.

Yet modernism provided corporations with more than an architectural style; it provided an aesthetic justification for the efficiency and functionalism of the corporate world. David Ley summarised this merging of the interests of big business with urban design issues in his discussion of such modernist advocates as Le Corbusier:

> For Le Corbusier ... 'big business is today a healthy and moral organism' and other contemporaries agreed that the business corporation could 'introduce into city government the standardisation and scientific management already found in industry...'. (Ley 1989, 50)

Modernism indeed served modern corporations yet, as is noted above, the converse is also true — modern corporations served modern architecture. Not only did corporate executives provide many of the commissions for the first major structures of modernism (Jencks 1973; Doordan 1989), but they and the companies they ran served as the model for numerous modern architects. The standardisation of products essential to modern industrial production could be seen as a democratic innovation in that it allowed for the mass production of items for middle America. By so doing, mass production did indeed provide goods to people who previously could not afford them, and allowed for a rhetoric of social responsibility and democratic vision by the business world. Similarly, the standardisation of architecture made possible by new technology and celebrated by modernism could adequately provide for the many in an egalitarian society. Technology could be seen as liberating, and the machine-like functionings of the corporation provided a structure to make that possible. The business corporation was a model of efficiency, of technology used productively, of the egalitarianism of the machine, of management through an established hierarchy, and of rational order. These were the precepts of the new architects and urban planners of the 1920s and 1930s and, arguably, of the following three decades (Jencks 1973; Berman 1982). Guided by a similar ethos and armed with new machines and money, modern architecture and modern corporations created the modern city — a place of mass-produced, anonymous and interchangeable structures.

Unlike Pulitzer's *New York World*, modern corporations were not interested in using the built environment for personal statements or as advertisements. With other, more sophisticated means of advertising available, and with the degree of competitiveness somewhat dulled, the interests of corporations in shaping the built environment were perhaps more subtle. Buildings were used less as advertisements than as signs of group identity, a demand important both for both employees and customers, of a large, depersonalised corporation. Business corporations relied on a rational ordering of space in the city — on efficient transportation and infrastructure. Modernism fulfilled both these needs. We can think of modern architecture and the modern corporation as the products of the same cultural moment — each fulfilling the needs of the other.

Conclusion: toward a post-modern corporate landscape

The urban skylines of most western cities and, increasingly, the suburban fringe surrounding such cities, are dominated by structures built for corporations. All of these structures were meant to fulfil some basic needs for these corporations yet, as we have seen, those needs are neither simple nor unchanging, nor are they the same for all corporate 'cultures'. Many of the early skyscrapers in New York were built as much as statements of personal identity, business acumen and aesthetic legitimacy as they were to provide the space necessary to the incredible economic expansion of the city in the late nineteenth century. Although most were failures as bids for the legitimacy afforded by participation in 'high' culture, they were resounding successes as advertisements for their businesses, and as creators of the symbolic association of height with the new economic order.

As the nature of New York's economy and society changed, the landscape expression of the corporate world also changed. Corporate needs for a rational ordering of space coincided with the aesthetic of modernism, and the repetitious lines of the new glass boxes were perfect representations of the modern industrial organisations. The relationship between business elites and the design professionals was altered in the early years of the twentieth century — the ideology of the city beautiful movement and the aesthetics of modernism provided an agenda for urban reformers that was in the best interests of both groups. In addition, corporations were becoming increasingly prominent participants in both the political and economic life of cities, and therefore were extremely influential members of the coalitions that shaped our modern cities. The conflict between commerce and art that seemed to afflict nineteenth-century business leaders was no longer an issue. The needs of one were the expression of the other.

It is difficult to ascertain exactly how corporations will shape the post-modern world. Post-modernism speaks a rhetoric antithetical to the functional needs of the late twentieth-century corporation. New construction projects are meant to be place and culturally specific, to be small-scale, and to contain allusions to historical precedent, local vernacular styles or personal identity. Yet most large corporations have become, if anything, more powerful and internationalised since 1970, and an architecture with place-specific symbolism may not seem the most appropriate. However, if the emergence of the office park is any indication, the image that some types of corporations wish to convey is different from their modern counterparts. The imagery of office parks is decidedly anti-urban and anti-machine, representing a rural or suburban ideal, yet underlying it is a very modernist conception — the ordered and controlled world of the corporation, effectively removed from outside contact and shielded from the day-to-day encounters that an urban setting would provide. It would seem, then, that the corporate world is re-situating itself, but its cultural and economic investment in the landscape suggests a situation fundamentally the same as that of the modernist era. Indeed if such relatively new buildings as the Trump Tower represent a continuing trend in office building construction, some of the same impulses that shaped the nineteenth century city are still alive in our post-modern world.

References

Berman, M. 1982, *All That is Solid Melts into Air: The Experience of Modernity,* Simon & Schuster, New York.

Bleyer, W.G. 1927, *Main Currents in American Journalism*, Houghton Mifflin Co., New York.

Boyer, M.C. 1983, *Dreaming the Rational City: The Myth of American City Planning,* MIT Press, Cambridge, MA.

Chandler, A.D. 1977, *The Visible Hand: The Managerial Revolution in American Business,* The Belknap Press, Cambridge, MA.

Corbin, J. 1903, 'The twentieth century city', *Scribners*, 33, 259–272.

Deal, T. & Kennedy, A.A. 1982, *Corporate Cultures: The Rites and Rituals of Corporate Life*, Addison-Wesley Publishing Co., Reading, MA.

Domosh, M. 1985, 'Scrapers of the Sky: The Symbolic and Functional Structures of Lower Manhattan', unpublished PhD thesis, Clark University.

Domosh, M. 1988, 'The symbolism of the Skyscraper: case studies of New York's first tall buildings', *Journal of Urban History*, 14, 321–45.

Domosh, M. 1989, 'New York's first Skyscrapers: conflict in design of the American commercial landscape', *Landscape,* 30, 34–8.

Doordan, D. 1989, 'Corporate culture as symbol and icon', paper presented at the Hagley Museum and Library corporate culture seminar series.

Dublin, L.I. 1943, *A Family of Thirty Million*, The Metropolitan Life Insurance Co., New York.

Ferree, B. 1894, 'The high building and its art', *Scribners*, 15, 297–318.

Gibbs, K.T. 1984, *Business Architectural Imagery in America, 1870-1930,* UMI Research Design, Ann Arbor, MI.

Hammack, D.C. 1982, *Power and Society: Greater New York at the Turn of the Century,* Russell Sage Foundation, New York.

Jaher, F.C. 1982, *The Urban Establishment: Upper Strata in Boston, New York, Charleston, Chicago, and Los Angeles,* University of Illinois Press, Urbana, Illinois.

James, M. 1947, *The Metropolitan Life*, Viking Press, New York.

Jencks, C. 1982, *Architecture Today*, Harry N. Abrams Inc., New York.

Jencks, C. 1973, *Modern Movements in Architecture*, Garden City, Anchor Press/Doubleday, New York.

Keller, M. 1963, *The Life Insurance Enterprise, 1885-1910,* Harvard University Press, Cambridge, MA.

Ley, D. 1989, 'Modernism, post-modernism, and the struggle for place', in J. Agnew & J. Duncan (eds), *The Power of Place*, Unwin Hyman, Boston, pp. 44-65.

The Metropolitan Life Insurance Company, 1908, The Metropolitan Life Insurance Company, New York.

'The new World Building', 1890, *Record and Guide*, 14 June.

'The New York "World"', 1890, *Harper's Weekly*, 34, 47.

North, D. 1952, 'Capital accumulation in life insurance between the Civil War and the investigation of 1905', in William Miller (ed.) *Men in Business*, Harvard University Press, Cambridge, MA, pp. 238–53.

'The Pulitzer Building', 1890, *New York World*, 10 December.

Seitz, D.C. 1924, *Joseph Pulitzer: His Life and Letters*, Simon & Schuster, New York.

Spann, E. 1981, *The New Metropolis*, Columbia University Press, New York.

Steffens, J.L. 1897, 'The modern business building', *Scribners*, 22, 37–61.

Strauss, A. 1961, *Images of the American City*, The Free Press, New York.

Trachtenberg, A. 1979, *Brooklyn Bridge: Fact and Symbol*, The University of Chicago Press, Chicago.

Wilson, W.H. 1989, *The City Beautiful Movement*, Johns Hopkins University Press, Baltimore.

Constructing geographies:
identities of exclusion

6 Constructions of culture, representations of race: Edward Curtis's 'way of seeing'

Peter Jackson

Introduction: representing 'the other'

John Berger's *Ways of Seeing* (1972) provides some radical insights into the problem of visual representation. Berger demonstrates that pictorial images carry multiple meanings and that their interpretation involves political as well as aesthetic judgements. Reference to his title is particularly apt in the context of the present chapter which deals with 'representation' in both the political and aesthetic senses of that term. For any claim by one group to 'represent' another is itself a form of power, exercised over subordinate groups by those more powerful than themselves. Recent years have witnessed some significant challenges to this virtual hegemony in the power of representation, with the development of history-from-below (Samuel 1981), the feminist critique of masculinist forms of knowledge (Harding 1986), and the growing realisation of a 'crisis of representation' throughout the human sciences (Marcus & Fischer 1986).

In his brilliant study of *Orientalism* (1978), Edward Said demonstrates the extent to which representations of other cultures reflect the 'domestic' concerns of their author's own society rather than providing a faithful portrait of those they claim to represent. Yet, with few exceptions (e.g. Anderson 1987), geographers have shown little interest in turning their analytical gaze onto their own society's constructions of cultural difference or applying a comparative perspective to their own culture as well as to those of more 'exotic' societies overseas. Again with few exceptions (e.g. Cosgrove & Daniels 1988), the problem of visual interpretation has been seriously neglected in comparison with the burgeoning attention paid to such literary concerns as landscape biography (Samuels 1979), problems of narrative (Sayer 1989), or the metaphor of landscape-as-text (Duncan 1990; Barnes & Duncan 1992). Yet the interpretation of visual images poses as many challenges as the critical exegesis of literary texts.

The present chapter focuses on representations of 'race' and constructions of cultural difference. Examining a series of photographic images of North American Indians from the early years of this century, it demonstrates how particular images of 'race' are related to historically and culturally specific forms of domination. It shows how racism changes shape according to the particular context, as ideologies shift with changing material conditions (Jackson 1987). Finally, it shows that many different 'readings' of any given set of images are possible, reflecting the different interests of the observer. Rather than attempting to identify any single photographic message, this chapter demonstrates a number of ways of reading Curtis's photographs, aiming to contextualise his work in terms of contemporary 'ways of seeing'. In keeping with this emphasis on complexity — on the multiple 'maps of meaning' (Jackson 1989) with which we make sense of the world — the chapter concludes with a discussion of some of the diverse ways in which the photographer has himself been represented.

The photographs in question result from the virtual obsession of Edward Sheriff Curtis (1868-1952), who set out to make a permanent record of the culture and society of North American Indians. Curtis was born in rural Wisconsin, moving to Seattle with his family in 1887. He began to photograph Indians in the 1890s, having earlier specialised in portraiture and landscape photography. In 1899 he joined the E.H. Harriman expedition to Alaska as official photographer. The following year he devoted himself full-time to photographing Indians, taking more than 40 000 photographs over the next thirty years. In 1905, he met President Theodore Roosevelt who became one of Curtis's most ardent supporters, providing him with an introduction to the American banker, J. Pierpont Morgan, who loaned him the capital to begin publication of his massive undertaking. Published privately over more than twenty years and sold by subscription, the work was entitled *The North American Indian, being a series of volumes picturing and describing the Indians of the United States and Alaska* (Curtis 1907-30). Each set comprised twenty volumes of illustrated text with a further twenty portfolios containing more than 700 photogravures. Never having made much money from the project, Curtis died in relative obscurity in 1952 (Graybill & Boesen 1976).

Contextualising Curtis

While this chapter takes the form of a case study, it would be wrong to exaggerate the uniqueness of Curtis's photographic vision. Instead, he will be approached as representative of a 'way of seeing' which was widely shared among his contemporaries. For, as Berkhofer's (1978) work has unequivocally shown, the image of the 'white man's Indian' has been an extremely persistent one, exercising a powerful effect on a whole range of issues concerning the rights of native peoples from land claims to political sovereignty, commercial exploitation to human welfare. Before evaluating Curtis's work, therefore, it is necessary to outline something of the political and economic, cultural and intellectual contexts in which it was produced.

Born in 1868, Curtis grew up in the period of westward expansion when the United States saw its national destiny in terms of the occupation of the entire continent. These territorial ambitions dictated United States policy towards native Americans, which went through several phases during the nineteenth century. From an initial emphasis on removal and resettlement west of the Mississippi, policy was modified during the 1840s and 1850s, under the so-called peace policy through which the government took over responsibility for natives' education, concentrating Indians on reservations, denying them self-government and religious freedom. In 1871, after the conquest of native Americans was virtually complete, the policy of treaty-making with particular tribes was superseded by a new emphasis on detribalisation and assimilation. Under the provisions of the *General Allotment Act 1887*, each family was 'allotted' a quarter-section of 160 acres, held in trust for twenty-five years by the Secretary of the Interior. Ostensibly designed to reduce the effects of 'tribal communalism', the Act led to a drastic reduction in Indian land over the next fifty years. When Curtis's study was being published (1907-30), many native Americans had still not been granted citizenship, a right that was finally bestowed in 1924. While several reports by the Bureau of Indian Affairs had urged the settlement of long-standing claims against the federal government arising from broken treaties and similar abuses, an Indian Claims Commission was not established until 1946.

Clearly, there were economic and political imperatives for westward extension of the frontier, but there were also cultural and ideological forces that made the American public eager to hear about the 'backwardness' and 'inferiority' of the Indian 'race'. Popular attitudes were given greater legitimacy through various forms of 'scientific' racism (Jones 1980). Victorian anthropology lent scientific credibility to the categorisation of human beings according to physical criteria such as skin colour, facial characteristics and 'cranial capacity'. By such criteria, 'races' were ordered hierarchically and inferences about social attributes (from sensuality to leadership potential) were inferred directly from physical traits. The Victorian penchant for scientific measurement and classification was soon brought to bear on the question of 'racial' origins and human evolution, providing scientific legitimation for imperial expansion overseas. It was this mind-set that Curtis inherited and applied in the context of America's expanding western frontier. Observations of physical 'type' led directly to inferences about human culture and, with equal inexorability, to judgements about moral worth. As Berkhofer has shown, scientific observers were as prone as explorers and settlers to mix ideology with ethnography.

Ethnographic description according to modern standards could not truly be separated from ideology and moral judgement until both cultural pluralism and moral relativism were accepted as ideals. Not until well into the twentieth century did such acceptance become general among intellectuals, and even then only a few whites truly practised the two ideals in their outlook on native Americans (Berkhofer 1978, 27).

Belief in the inherent superiority of the white 'race' provided ample justification for the subjugation of other 'races', including the extermination of many thousands of Indians. Only much later in the twentieth century has it come to be generally acknowledged that the concept of 'race' has no sound biological basis (Banton 1987; Rex & Mason 1986). To speak as though separate 'races' exist other than as social constructions is to perpetuate the kind of racist ideology from which discriminatory practices inevitably follow.

One final context for the interpretation of Curtis's work is the growing importance of photography for 'political' as well as for recreational and 'artistic' purposes which took place during Curtis's lifetime. While photography was still considered marginal as an art form in the 1890s, the invention of small hand-held cameras, such as Eastman's Kodak, increased its popularity until it rivalled that of the bicycle. The craze for popular photography was soon supplemented by more serious practitioners who (like Curtis) used the camera for ethnographic purposes or (like Jacob Riis and Walker Evans) for political commentary and social reform. Jacob Riis's *How the Other Half Lives* (1890) is often regarded as a pioneering work of photojournalism. His studies of street life among New York's tenement poor were, no less than Curtis's Indian photographs, carefully posed for maximum impact. His work reached massive audiences through serialisation in *Scribner's Magazine* and reproduction of some of the more dramatic pictures in the *New York Sun*. Walker Evans' photographic preface to *Let Us Now Praise Famous Men* (Agee & Evans 1939), a study of the lives of impoverished Alabama sharecroppers, also achieved considerable renown with selected highlights published in popular journals like *Atlantic Monthly*. The work has since achieved classic status within the history of photography as well as fulfilling its contemporary role within the progressive politics of the Farm Security Administration who commissioned the work. Besides their political and artistic significance, each of these studies constitutes a kind of cultural record of particular 'ways of seeing'. This is part of the context in which to approach an interpretation of Curtis's oeuvre.

Pictures at an exhibition

The current re-evaluation of Curtis's work began at an exhibition, organised by the Smithsonian Museum, that toured various American museums in the early 1980s. Entitled *The Vanishing Race and Other Illusions: A New Look at the Work of Edward Curtis*, the exhibition presented a critical interpretation of Curtis's photographs. The exhibition's title refers to one of Curtis's most famous images *The Vanishing Race — Navaho* (1904) (fig. 6.1), about which he wrote: 'The thought which this picture is meant to convey is that the Indians as a race, already shorn of their tribal strength and stripped of their primitive dress, are passing into the darkness of an unknown future' (Curtis 1907). The photograph shows a group of Navaho Indians on horseback, receding from the camera and about to enter a dark canyon. One of the Indians looks wistfully over his shoulder towards the viewer, suggesting both the Indians' uncertain future and the viewer's complicity in their fate.

Viewing the exhibition in Chicago in 1983, I was both attracted by Curtis's sepia-tinted photographs and appalled at the lengths to which he had evidently gone to construct an 'authentic' picture of Indian life, amounting in some cases to complete fabrication. The exhibition was designed to draw attention to these 'illusions' which were also the subject of an accompanying book (Lyman 1982). Among the deceptions which Curtis employed, Lyman notes the use of props which the photographer himself gave his subjects (feather headdresses, beads and wigs); posing and framing his subjects in particular ways (often inside the studio tent which he took with him on all his expeditions); cropping and retouching his photographs (with the help of his darkroom assistant Adolph F. Muhr) to obliterate every sign of 'European' influence such as parasols and automobiles.

Similarly, for his musical celebration of *The North American Indian*, Curtis borrowed tepees and other props from the American Museum of Natural History in New York to serve as stage sets. The musical selections were not 'authentic' Indian songs but 'arrangements' specially written for the occasion by the Boston composer H.F.B. Gilbert. As opposed to 'mere adaptations of Indian melodies', one contemporary observer notes, they were 'original compositions ... filled with the particularly rich quality of Mr Gilbert's imagination' (Arthur Farwell, quoted in Gidley 1987, 70). Far from being an 'authentic' record of Indian life, Curtis's representations are what anthropologists today call 'partial truths' (Clifford 1986a): incomplete and necessarily biased accounts that tell us as much about the expectations of Curtis's viewers as about their ostensible subject matter.

Figure 6.1: The Vanishing Race — Navaho (E.S. Curtis, 1904).
Source: Smithsonian Institution photo no. 90-14320

The very choice of subjects, picture captions, titles and accompanying texts were all designed to portray an 'authentic' and abiding 'Indianness'. Curtis's photographs represent a highly selective and idealised version of pre-contact Indian culture and of the landscapes with which that culture was thought to be associated. One could argue that Curtis's deceptions merely involved the exercise of artistic licence — the kind of creative manipulation of the medium that gives photography its claim to the status of art. Yet Curtis himself, and his promoters, claimed that his work measured up to the strictest standards of 'scientific accuracy'. However we approach these issues, Curtis's photographs clearly merit closer scrutiny and should be judged by the standards appropriate to ethnographic evidence as well as in terms of their artistic merit. We should also guard against the tendency to exaggerate Curtis's uniqueness. Rather, it is the extent to which he mirrors the 'way of seeing' characteristic of his day that gives his work its general significance for cultural geography.

Art and illusion

In the general introduction to volume 1 of *The North American Indian*, Curtis describes his objective as having been to make 'a comprehensive and permanent record of all the important tribes of the United States and Alaska that still retain to a considerable degree their primitive customs and traditions' (Curtis 1907, vol. 1, xiii). Like many of his anthropological contemporaries, Curtis's work was infused with a sense of impending crisis which drove him to try to make a documentary 'record' of his subject matter before it 'vanished' for all time. As Curtis himself explained:

> The great changes in practically every phase of the Indian's life that have taken place, especially within recent years, have been such that had the time for collecting much of the material, both descriptive and illustrative, herein recorded, been delayed, it would have been lost forever. (Curtis 1907, vol.1, xvi)

However, the goal of capturing an 'authentic' version of Indian culture led Curtis to deny certain aspects of change, leading him to 'reconstruct' what had recently 'vanished'. As a result, Curtis documents little of the impact of cultural change, creating the illusion of a relatively untouched aboriginality.

The tension between scientific accuracy and artistic licence was a feature of Curtis's work. He refers to it himself in an early letter to J.P. Morgan, soliciting funds for *The North American Indian*. Writing in 1906, Curtis describes his work as aiming for both 'scientific accuracy' and 'artistic merit' (quoted in Lyman 1982, 60). President Roosevelt was to express the same tension when he wrote the foreword to the first volume, describing Curtis as 'both an artist and a trained observer whose work has far more than mere accuracy, because it is truthful' (Curtis 1907, vol. 1, foreword). One of Curtis's earliest critics, writing in the journal *Camera Craft* in 1901, similarly noted the 'immense ethnological value' of Curtis's photographs but also claimed that 'most of them are really picturesque, showing good composition and interesting light effects' (Arnold Genthe, quoted in Lyman 1982, 53). Curtis discusses this issue in his own introduction to the series where he argues that:

> ... the fact that the Indian and his surroundings lend themselves to artistic treatment has not been lost sight of, for in his country one may treat limitless subjects of an aesthetic character without in any way doing injustice to scientific accuracy or neglecting the homelier phases of aboriginal life. (Curtis 1907, vol. 1, xiii)

There is not simply a tension here between 'scientific accuracy' and 'artistic treatment'. The very notion of 'scientific accuracy' is itself a cultural construction and a highly significant one in the context of Curtis's work, for Curtis claimed to have photographed Indian life 'directly from Nature', showing 'what actually exists or has recently existed ... not what the artist in his studio may presume the Indian and his surroundings to be' (Curtis 1907, xiii–xiv). Yet, while Curtis travelled extensively throughout North America to photograph his subjects in the field, there were clear limitations to his dedication to the principle of observation from nature. His photographs of Indians 'on the warpath' and his pictures of the Hopi snake dance and similar rituals were obvious re-enactments where subjects were paid to adopt militaristic poses or to perform 'secret' ceremonies in front of the camera. Thus, in an article on 'Posing the American Indian' that compares Curtis with other contemporary photographers, Margaret Blackman describes Curtis's 'romanticised view' as having been 'tempered with the ethnographer's concern for accuracy' (Blackman 1980, 71). She praises the 'ethnographic accuracy' with which Curtis costumed his subjects, but goes on to admit that he carried with him 'a wardrobe of museum props' in order to effect the appropriate pre-contact image of his subjects.

Curtis employed a variety of visual and textual strategies to engage his audience and to persuade them of his claims to verisimilitude. In the text he wrote to accompany his 'musicale', for example, Curtis speaks directly to the audience, emphasising the authority that comes from long first-hand experience: 'I want you to see this beautiful, poetic, mysterious, yet simple life, as I have grown to see it through the long years with the many tribes' (quoted in Gidley 1987, 75). It is, however, in the visual representation of Indian culture and landscape that Curtis's deceptions are most pronounced.

Documenting the deceptions

Lyman (1982) provides a catalogue of the photographic deceptions that Curtis employed in the construction of an anthropological illusion. Here, there is only space to illustrate a handful of Curtis's attempts to fabricate an 'authentic' view of Indian landscape and society. Curtis employed a variety of techniques to sustain the illusion of an undiluted aboriginality. In his representations of people, he frequently used airbrushing to remove signs of 'European' influence: trouser braces, parasols, manufacturers' names on 'traditional' materials, automobiles and so on. In some cases, Curtis went to extreme lengths to remove 'unauthentic' details, such as the medal or clock that appears in the negative but not in the finished version of *In a Piegan Lodge* (1910) (figs 6.2 and 6.3). Most remarkable, however, is the transformation that Curtis worked on his translator and informant, A.B. Upshaw, depicted by Curtis in the full regalia of a 'traditional' Crow Indian (*Upshaw — Apsaroke* 1905), but shown some seven years earlier in much less exotic attire by the Omaha photographer F.A. Rinehart (*A.B. Upshaw — Interpreter* 1898) (figs 6.4 and 6.5). Elsewhere, too, the deceptions are so crude that it is easy to catch Curtis out: in two separate photographs, a Shunkala man and a Hitdatsa appear in identical costumes, such as those that Curtis carried with him.

Landscape representations were subject to similar photographic manipulation. In this case, the illusion that Curtis sought to sustain was of an idealised pre-contact society, living in complete harmony with nature. In *Pima Water Girl* (1907), for example, Curtis uses extensive airbrushing to give an irrigation ditch the appearance of a natural pool. Other landscape elements were more contradictory. The sheep in *Navaho Flocks* (1904), for example, were clearly a European introduction but apparently presented less of a challenge to Curtis's idealised 'way of seeing'. They were simply assimilated as a 'natural' part of the aboriginal landscape.

Curtis's landscapes are entirely consistent with his 'way of seeing' Indian culture, in harmonious relation with externalised nature. The way that Curtis posed his subjects in the landscape stresses their inseparability from the natural world. Curtis's caption to *A Son of the Desert — Navaho*, for example, reads:'In the early morning this boy, *as if springing from the earth itself*, came to the author's desert camp. Indeed, he seemed a *part of the very desert* ...' (quoted in Graybill & Boesen 1976, emphasis added).

The *Scout — Apache* similarly shows 'the primitive Apache in his mountain home'. 'Nature' and 'culture' are even more closely fused in subjects like *Chipewyan Tipi Among the Aspens* where the family group and their tepee blend in harmoniously with their sylvan setting. Curtis's Indians are depicted gaining their livelihood directly from nature. Their handicrafts are displayed as skilful transformations of natural materials. Even their portraits are captioned with Indian names that bear witness to the close association between human beings and the natural world (Slow Bull, Black Eagle, Two Moon).

The representation of Indian life as peculiarly close to nature enabled Curtis's contemporaries to portray the Indian as an evolutionary predecessor of more 'advanced'

Figure 6.2: In a Piegan Lodge — (before retouching).
Source: Smithsonian Institution, photo no. 75-11978.

Figure 6.3: In a Piegan Lodge — (after retouching) (E.S. Curtis, 1910).
Source: Smithsonian Institution, photo no. 90-14319.

Figure 6.4: Upshaw — Apsaroke (E.S. Curtis, 1905).
Source: Smithsonian Institution, photo no. 81-8708

cultures such as their own. But the ideological construction of Indian culture as mysteriously in tune with the natural world has been extraordinarily persistent, re-emerging in the 1970s when Indian culture was being championed as part of a general rise in environmental awareness. In the introduction to a catalogue of Curtis's photographs on exhibition at the Philadelphia Museum of Art in 1972, for example, Joseph Epes Brown argued:

> It is thus near to Nature that much of the life of the Indian still is; hence its story ... is a record of the Indian's relations with and his dependence on the phenomena of the universe — the trees and shrubs, the sun and stars, the lightning and rain — for these to him are animate creatures. (Brown 1972, 6)

Whether or not these observations are true, they enable the author to construct a picture of the Indian's 'special relationship with his natural environment' and to speak condescendingly about the 'childlike quality of the Indian's soul' (Brown 1972, 7–8).

Figure 6.5: A.B. Upshaw — Interpreter (F.A. Rinehart, 1898).
Source: Smithsonian Institution, photo no. 81-9647

Curtis's romanticised construction of Indian culture and landscape can be discerned in his aesthetic as well as in his choice of subject matter. He adopts the same visual aesthetic in many of his Indian studies as he employed in his early landscape photographs. The *Clam Diggers* is a particularly good example. Having won Curtis various honours in a national photographic exhibition, the same photograph later reappears in *The North American Indian*. Apart from cropping the original photograph, there is no difference in the aesthetic that Curtis employs in the two contexts despite the 'scientific' pretensions of Curtis's Indian research (for details, see Lyman 1982).

Given his claims to scientific objectivity, it is also relevant to judge Curtis's photographs by the standards of contemporary anthropology at a period when the discipline was only just beginning to emerge as a professional science. As a photographer with no formal training in anthropology, Curtis's relationship with the scientific establishment was basically deferential. Curtis was aware that he lacked the credentials of a trained anthropologist and wanted his work to be edited by 'men in the scientific field, recognised as authorities' in order to lend it 'unquestionable authenticity' (quoted in Lyman 1982, 60).

In the interests of 'authenticity', Curtis frequently deferred to professional anthropologists such as George Bird Grinnell, A.L. Kroeber, George A. Dorsey and Clark Wissler. In turn, several members of the anthropological establishment were lavish in their praise of Curtis's work. In his study of *The Crow Indians*, for example, the anthropologist Robert H. Lowie described *The North American Indian* as 'an excellent piece of work and while not written either by or for a professional anthropologist lives up to high standards of accuracy' (Lowie 1935, 355). Similarly, the *American Anthropologist* gave Curtis a favourable review, describing *The North American Indian* as a 'faithful representation of actualities', 'a noble monument to a passing race', and a 'trustworthy graphic memorial of our passing aborigines' (McGee 1910, 449).

Other contemporary observers were more critical, questioning the naturalness of Curtis's posed subjects. Writing in the photographic journal *Camera Craft* in 1903, for example, George Wharton James questioned Curtis's practice of posing his subjects, while the anthropologist James Mooney objected to Curtis's habit of referring to Indians as 'warriors' even when they were not at war. Similarly, in his attitudes to 'race', Curtis can be clearly situated in relation to the prevailing ideas of his time.

Representations of race

Photography and other forms of pictorial representation played an important role in scientific deliberations about 'race' during this period (Cowling 1989). Anthropological lectures were commonly illustrated by lantern slides, and expeditions regularly brought back photographic evidence of 'exotic' cultures and landscapes. Among Curtis's contemporaries, for example, Clark Wissler includes several carefully posed photographic portraits of different 'racial types' in his anthropological study of *The American Indian* (1917). Various conventions were established to improve the reliability of photographic images as empirical evidence. Guidelines, such as Louis Sullivan's *Essentials of Anthropometry: A Handbook for Explorers and Museum Collectors* (1923), were published giving detailed instructions about posing anthropological subjects against a regular grid in order to ensure accurate measurements of body shape and size.

By posing his subjects in 'naturalistic' settings, Curtis generally avoided the standard full-face and profile poses of contemporary anthropometric photography, described by Green (1984) as embodying a 'technology of power'. However, any notion of 'capturing' a person on film reflects an inherent inequality in the relationship between photographer and 'subject', whether or not permission has been given for the photograph to be taken and whether or not the photographer has paid for the privilege. Even today, representations of 'exotic' people, especially where these images are produced for sale, raise equally troubling political and ethical dilemmas. The description of Leni Riefenstahl's photographs of the Nuba and the Kau as 'fascinating fascism' (Sontag 1975) may be an extreme case, but readers of popular journals like *National Geographic* are regularly confronted with similarly commodified depictions of other cultures (Abramson 1987). It is the inequalities that different parties bring to the encounter (subject, photographer, publisher, viewer) that give photographic representation its political edge.

Despite his preference for outdoor settings and relatively informal poses, Curtis's work nonetheless reveals many of the contradictions of contemporary racist ideologies.

For example, Curtis's habitual reference to 'the Indian' (in the singular), implying that he believed in a discrete and homogeneous Indian 'race', was frequently contradicted by his acknowledgement of 'tribal' diversity. Many of his photographs claim to represent particular Indian 'types', such as *Typical Nez Perce* (1899) or *Typical Apache* (1906), and the text is full of passages such as the following which combine racist stereotyping with a crude form of environmental determinism:

> Physically the Mohave are probably superior to any other tribe in the United States. Men and women alike are big-boned, well-knitted, clear-skinned. Mentally they are dull and slow — brothers to the ox. The warm climate and comparative ease with which they obtain their livelihood seem to have developed a people physically superb; but the climate and conditions that developed such magnificent bodies did not demand or assist in building up an equivalent mentality. (Curtis 1908, vol. 2, 48)

Some of Curtis's more popular works, such as an article he wrote in *Scribner's Magazine* in June 1906, contain quite blatant forms of racism, such as his reference to the Indian's 'inbred desire for bloodshed' (quoted in Lyman 1982, 657). Elsewhere in Curtis's work, passages that contain a degree of circumspection, such as his argument that 'we cannot refer to the Indian as a unit ... but rather we must in a measure consider each group as a subject unto itself', sit uncomfortably beside more clearly racist stereotyping, such as his description of the Apache as 'warriors to a degree unparalleled' (quoted in Gidley 1987, 76–9). The general moderation of Curtis's 'scientific' tone occasionally gives way to more unbridled remarks, exposing more 'popular' forms of racism. Thus, 'scientific' assertions that the American Indian is 'one of the five races of man' with more than fifty 'linguistic stocks' are juxtaposed with more virulent forms of racism such as his description of the Apache: 'His birthright was craving for the warpath, and his cunning beyond reckoning. His character is a strange mixture of savagery, courage, and ferocity, with a remarkable gentleness and affection for his family' (quoted in Gidley 1987, 75–7).

Even his more serious work, like *The North American Indian*, is characterised by various forms of 'scientific' racism such as his description of the Apsaroke as embodying 'the highest development of the primitive American hunter and warrior. Physically these people were among the finest specimens of their race' (Curtis 1909, vol. 4, xi), or by more complex (but no less racist) arguments such as the following: 'To the workaday man of our own race the life of the Indian is just as incomprehensible as are the complexities of civilisation to the mind of the untutored savage' (Curtis 1907, vol. 1, xv).

For Curtis, Indian culture was primarily of interest as a reflection of 'the mind of the untutored savage', and, as Roosevelt's foreword makes clear, this was closely linked to an evolutionary theory of 'race'. Roosevelt explicitly compares contemporary Indian life with the 'conditions thru [sic] which our race past [sic] so many ages ago that not a vestige of their memory remains' (Curtis 1907, vol. 1, foreword). Despite these attempts to construct an image of a remote and idealised aboriginality, tempered by an evolutionary theory of human development, Curtis clearly recognised the disastrous effects of westward expansion on 'traditional' forms of Indian life. While he rarely referred to the massacres that had taken place during his lifetime, such as the slaughter of 300 Dakotas at Wounded Knee in 1890 (Brown 1970), Curtis's whole project can be seen as an implicit critique of current US policy towards the Indians. Though he generally avoided explicit criticism of government policy, he described the treatment accorded to the Indians as 'in many cases ... worse than criminal' (Curtis 1907, vol. 1, xv). He referred to the Indians' 'unequalled struggle against inevitable subjection' (Curtis 1911, vol. 6, xi), occasionally giving vent to more extended criticism, as in his condemnation of US policy towards the Californian Indians:

> All Indians suffered through the selfishness of our own race, but the natives of California were the greatest sufferers of all ... By what was supposed to have been a treaty they signed away their lands, in lieu of which they were to be granted definite areas much smaller in extent, together with certain goods and chattels, and educational advantages. This treaty was never ratified, yet we took advantage of one of its proposed provisions by assuming immediate possession of the Indian lands, by which cunning the majority of the natives were left homeless. Little by little, tardily and grudgingly, action towards providing homes for the surviving unfortunates has been taken; but what has been granted them in most cases only intensifies the outrage, for many of the reservations are barren, rocky hillsides of less than an acre for each individual — land the tillage of which is next to impossible. (Curtis 1924, vol. 13, xi–xii).

If Curtis constructed a particular view of Indian 'racial' difference, his attitude towards gender roles and relations is no less noteworthy. Although he was struck by the general lack of differentiation between the roles of Indian men and women, his representations of male and female subjects still conform closely to his contemporary viewers' expectations about patterns of masculine and feminine behaviour. Typically, men were photographed in active poses (on the warpath, fishing, dancing), while women were depicted in more decorative, passive poses (day-dreaming, waiting, watching). Curtis generally avoided visual references to the alleged sexual promiscuity of Indian women, unlike the gratuitous nudity in the portrayal of Indian women by several of Curtis's contemporaries. However, the titles of his photographs often give a sexual twist to their interpretation which is not immediately apparent from the visual image itself. *At the Trysting Place* (1921) is a case in point. Curtis's title refers unequivocally to a place of romantic assignation while the photograph itself carries no clear indication of such a motive. It simply shows two Hopi women in traditional costumes and hairstyles, waiting by the side of a path under a tree (fig. 6.6). The imputation of a sexual motive is entirely adventitious.

Whatever our judgement on these issues, it is evident that Curtis indulged in fewer fabrications as his work progressed. In the later phases of his project, particularly in volume nineteen of *The North American Indian*, published in 1928, there is less attempt to disguise the effects of acculturation than in the early volumes. Parasols and motor cars are clearly visible in several of these photographs where they would have been removed by retouching in earlier phases of the project. European commodities were, of course, more widespread by this point, but more cynical readings are also possible. It could be argued, for example, that Curtis's later work simply represents the final phase in the 'domestication' of the Indian: having removed the potential military threat to westward expansion, the American public could now afford the luxury of romanticising the Indian, a process in which Curtis's photographs were certainly implicated. Changing images of the American Indian, from savagery to nobility, and more or less idealised representations of the Indians' relationship to the land, must clearly be interpreted in terms of these changing material circumstances. So, too, must the revival of Curtis's popularity since the 1970s.

Figure 6.6: At the Trysting Place (E.S. Curtis, 1921).
Source: Smithsonian Institution, photo no. 90-14318.

Representing Curtis

Having discussed how Curtis represented Indian culture to the contemporary American public, it is also worth considering how Curtis has himself been represented since the publication of his work in the early decades of the twentieth century. If an examination of Curtis's work demonstrates that there can never be a 'correct' way of representing other cultures divorced from the material context in which those representations are made, then an analysis of Curtis's fluctuating fortunes demonstrates the equal impossibility of reaching a definitive judgement of the photographer's intellectual, moral and artistic worth. Soon after publication of the first volumes of *The North American Indian*, Curtis's reputation rose from that of local hero ('Seattle Man Triumphs', *Seattle Times*, 22 May 1904) to national celebrity ('the most talked of man in the United States in that line of work', *Seattle Times*, 11 June 1905). The support and patronage of President Roosevelt and J.P. Morgan ensured that Curtis's work was taken seriously, even if the project was never a great financial success.

The fate of Curtis's work was itself a reflection of the crisis of confidence through which the United States was passing during his lifetime. The Depression years were not an auspicious time for selling volumes of lavishly-produced photographs, costing several thousand dollars. However, even as the country's economic fortunes improved, national attitudes towards the treatment of American Indians were also beginning to change. Once the human cost of westward expansion began to be recognised, few people wanted to be reminded of Curtis's 'vanishing race'.

During the 1960s, however, Curtis's reputation began to improve with the rise of environmental awareness, civil rights campaigns and the growth of an increasingly politicised native rights movement. In the 1970s, major exhibitions of Curtis's work appeared at the Pierpont Morgan Library in New York and at the Philadelphia Museum of Art (Brown 1972), with complete sets of *The North American Indian* selling for over US $70 000. Curtis began to be lionised by anthologists and biographers, two of whom describe *The North American Indian* as 'the most remarkable undertaking by one man in the history of books' (Graybill & Boesen 1976, 109). With the publication of Lyman's (1982) critical study, accompanying the Smithsonian exhibition in 1982, Curtis's reputation once again hung in the balance. Lyman himself reflects generously on Curtis's benign intentions and on the constant financial pressure under which he worked, but still considers his work to have been guilty of deception. The repudiation of Curtis as the creator of a racist illusion was under way.

If anachronistic judgements are to be avoided, however, it is important to assess Curtis's work in relation to appropriate contemporary standards including the emerging scientific establishment of professional anthropologists and museum curators. Here, it is worth noting that Curtis's status was never fully assured. His work was spurned by several national institutions such as the Smithsonian Museum, which never bought a subscription to *The North American Indian*. Another point of comparison might be with the leading photographers of his day. Here, a more positive assessment is possible. Curtis's photographs bear favourable comparison with the work of many of his peers, avoiding the sexist stereotyping of Indian women and bloodthirsty shots of Indian men which were all too popular with other photographers. Neither was Curtis alone in posing his subjects or lending them props in order to achieve the desired ethnographic or artistic effect. Similar practices were common among Curtis's contemporaries, including such luminaries as John Wesley Powell and Edweard Muybridge. Clearly, there are dangers in judging Curtis by the moral and professional standards of another generation. Christopher Lyman's work and the Smithsonian exhibition run this risk, giving present-day viewers a sense of moral superiority in relation to Curtis's apparently more innocent contemporaries. A more balanced judgement might concede that portraits of other societies always contain elements of illusion, distortion and misrepresentation, especially where the encounter is characterised by such rampant inequalities as those separating the American Indian from Curtis's viewing public.

Curtis's work contains evidence of conscious manipulation and deliberate deception, but this merely highlights the extent to which all representations of other cultures are an ideological fiction — cultural constructions which reveal in their making the interests that they serve. Curtis's photographs may have their idiosyncrasies but they also reveal a characteristic 'way of seeing' that was common among Curtis's contemporaries. His romanticised portraits of Indian culture and his exaggeration of their harmony with nature helped soften the image of the primitive 'savage', but they also served to confirm the superior self-image of the white 'race'. For all their aesthetic qualities, Curtis's photographs cannot be divorced from their ideological role in the legitimation of white supremacy. In this sense, Curtis's photographic 'way of seeing' is inseparable from the imperialism that it both reflected and helped reproduce. This surely is their primary significance for cultural geographers.

Conclusion: constructions of culture

The interpretation of Curtis's photographs provides a good example of what anthropologists now refer to as a 'crisis of representation' (Marcus & Fischer 1986). The phrase implies that it is no longer possible to assume the mantle of scientific objectivity which Victorian anthropologists once confidently adopted in their descriptions of other cultures. The innocence that may once have informed such representations has long since been lost in the move towards a more critical sense of cultural politics.

Photography poses particular problems in this regard, with its illusion of objectivity and its beguiling sense of transparent meaning ('the camera never lies'). Uncovering photography's hidden codes is a complex and contradictory process, since the dominant code of photographic realism gives every appearance of being uncoded (Hutcheon 1989). However, art historians and cultural critics are becoming increasingly aware of what John Tagg has called the 'burden of representation' (Tagg 1988), challenging the notion of photography as a mere record of reality. Whether one considers the documentary tradition, the use of photography in official surveillance, or the 'science' of visual anthropology (Collier 1967), photography comprises a site of struggle in which the meaning of visual images and their political significance are often fiercely contested.

How then are we to view Curtis's photographs and what lessons does his work contain for contemporary cultural geography? The essential contradiction, it seems to me, is that native American culture is an integral part of US history and yet Curtis's photographs have always been valued for their evocation of a sense of cultural 'otherness'. At first, Curtis deliberately set out to record the 'primitive', to document what he saw as a 'vanishing race'. For a time, his photographs were praised for their anthropological interest as portraits of an exotic 'other' while, today, his work is being reassessed in the knowledge that America's westward expansion was achieved at enormous human cost. To judge the cultural significance of Curtis's work requires that we see his photographs not so much as the product of one man's unique vision as representative of a broader cultural 'way of seeing'.

If Curtis's work contains elements of demonstrable falsehood, misrepresentation and deception, it also raises general questions about the extent to which members of one group can ever fully and accurately represent the culture of another group, especially when the power differential between them is so great. Anthropologists have begun to reflect critically on the politics of representation in constructing ethnographic accounts of other cultures, but even they have tended to focus on verbal rather than on visual media (e.g. Clifford & Marcus 1986; Geertz 1988). As geographers enter the contested terrain of cultural politics, we will need to sharpen our sensitivity to the visual. However, most importantly, as this analysis of Curtis's photographs suggests, we must also insist on the inseparability of aesthetic, 'scientific' and political judgements. Though Curtis and his contemporaries would no doubt have denied it, his work provides ample evidence of the extent to which the cultural is political.

Note

I would like to thank the Librarian of the Museum of Mankind (British Museum, Department of Ethnography) for letting me consult a facsimile edition of Curtis's *The North American Indian* in the museum's collection. Also, many thanks to Jane Jacobs, Jan Penrose, Hugh Prince, Teal Triggs, Sarah Whatmore, Peter Wood and the editors for thoughtful criticism of previous drafts.

References

Abramson, H.S. 1987, *National Geographic: Behind America's Lens on the World*, Crown, New York.

Agee, J. & Evans, W. 1939, *Let Us Now Praise Famous Men*, Houghton Mifflin, Boston.

Anderson, K. 1987, 'Chinatown as an idea: the power of place and institutional practice in the making of a racial category', *Annals, Association of American Geographers,* 77, pp. 580–98.

Banton, M. 1987, *Racial Theories,* Cambridge University Press, Cambridge.

Barnes, T.J. & Duncan, J.S. (eds) 1992, *Writing Worlds*, Routledge, London and New York.

Barthes, R. (ed.) 1977, 'The photographic message', in S. Heath (trans.), *Image-music-text*, Hill & Wang, New York, pp. 15–31.

Berger, J. 1972, *Ways of Seeing*, Penguin, Harmondsworth.

Berkhofer, R.F. Jr 1978, *The White Man's Indian: Images of the American Indian from Columbus to the Present*, Alfred A. Knopf, New York.

Blackman, M. 1980, 'Posing the American Indian', *Natural History,* 89, pp. 68–75.

Brown, D. 1970, *Bury my Heart at Wounded Knee*, Barrie & Jenkins, London.

Brown, J.E. 1972, 'Introduction: mirrors for identity in the photographs of Edward Curtis', in *The North American Indians: A Selection of Photographs by Edward S. Curtis*, Aperture, New York, pp. 6–12.

Clifford, J. 1986a, 'Introduction: partial truths', in J. Clifford & G.E. Marcus (eds),*Writing Culture,* University of California Press, Berkeley, CA, pp. 1–26.

Clifford, J. 1986b, 'Identity in Mashpee', in J. Clifford, *The Predicament of Culture*, Harvard University Press, Cambridge, MA, pp. 277–346.

Clifford, J. & Marcus, G.E. (eds) 1986, *Writing Culture: the Politics and Poetics of Ethnography*, University of California Press, Berkeley, CA.

Collier, J. Jr 1967, *Visual Anthropology: Photography as Research Method*, Holt, Rinehart & Winston, New York.

Cosgrove, D.E. & Daniels, S.J. (eds) 1988, *The Iconography of Landscape,* Cambridge University Press, Cambridge.

Cowling, M. 1989, *The Artist as Anthropologist: the Representation of Type and Character in Victorian Art*, Cambridge University Press, Cambridge.

Cowlishaw, G. 1987, 'Colour, culture and the Aboriginalists', *Man NS*, 22, pp. 221–37.

Curtis, E.S. 1907-30, *The North American Indian* (20 vols and supplements, privately printed).

DeWall, B.B. 1982, 'Edward Sheriff Curtis: a new perspective on the North American Indian', *History of Photography*, 6, pp. 223–39.

Dippie, B.W. 1982, *The Vanishing American: White Attitudes and U.S. Indian Policy*, Wesleyan University Press, Middletown, CT.

Duncan, J. 1990, *The City as Text: The Politics of Landscape Interpretation in the Kandyan Kingdom*, Cambridge University Press, Cambridge.

Geertz, C. 1988, *Works and Lives: The Anthropologist as Author*, Stanford University Press, Stanford.

Gidley, M. 1976, *The Vanishing Race: Selections from Edward S. Curtis' 'The North American Indian'*, David & Charles, Newton Abbot.

Gidley, M. 1987, '"The vanishing race" in sight and sound: Edward S. Curtis's musicale of North American Indian life', *Prospects,* 12, pp. 59–87.

Graybill, F.C. & Boesen, V. 1976, *Edward Sheriff Curtis: Visions of a Vanishing Race*, Thomas Y. Crowell Co., New York.

Green, D. 1984, 'Classified subjects: photography and anthropology', *Ten.8*, 14, pp. 30–7.

Harding, S. 1986, *The Science Question in Feminism*, Cornell University Press, Ithaca, NY.

Hutcheon, L. 1989, *The Politics of Postmodernism*, Routledge, London.

Jackson, P. 1987, 'The idea of "race" and the geography of racism', in P. Jackson (ed.), *Race and Racism: Essays in Social Geography,* Allen & Unwin, London, pp. 3–21.

Jackson, P. 1989, *Maps of Meaning*, Unwin Hyman, London.

Jones, G. 1980, *Social Darwinism and English Thought: The Interaction Between Biological and Social Theory,* Harvester Press, Brighton.

Lowie R.H. 1935, *The Crow Indians*, Farrar & Rinehart, New York.

Lyman, C.M. 1982, *The Vanishing Race and Other Illusions: Photographs of Indians by Edward Curtis*, Smithsonian Institution Press, Washington DC.

McGee, W.J. 1910, 'Review', *American Anthropologist*, 12, pp. 448–50.

Marcus, G. & Fischer, M. 1986, *Anthropology as Cultural Critique*, Cambridge University Press, Cambridge.

Marshall, E. 1912, 'The vanishing red man', *The Hampton Magazine*, 28, pp. 245–53.

Rex, J. & Mason, D. (eds) 1986, *Theories of Race and Ethnic Relations*, Cambridge University Press, Cambridge.

Riis, J. 1890, *How the Other Half Lives*, Charles Scribner's Sons, New York.

Said, E.W. 1978, *Orientalism*, Random House, New York.

Samuel, R. (ed.) 1981, *People's History and Socialist Theory*, Routledge & Kegan Paul, London.

Samuels, M.S. 1979, 'The biography of landscape', in D.W. Meinig (ed.), *The Interpretation of Ordinary Landscapes*, Oxford University Press, New York, pp. 51–88.

Sayer, A. 1989, 'The "new" regional geography and problems of narrative', *Society and Space*, 7, pp. 253–76.

Sontag, S. 1975, 'Fascinating fascism', *New York Review of Books,* 6 February, pp. 23-30, reprinted in *A Susan Sontag Reader*, Penguin, Harmondsworth, pp. 305–25.

Sullivan, L.R. 1923, *Essentials of Anthropometry: A Handbook for Explorers and Museum Collectors,* American Museum of Natural History, New York.

Tagg, J. 1988, *The Burden of Representation: Essays on Photographies and Histories,* Macmillan Education, London.

Wissler, C. 1917, *The American Indian*, Douglas C. McMurtie, New York.

7 Outsiders in society and space

David Sibley

Introduction

Dirt, as Mary Douglas (1966) has noted, is matter out of place. Similarly, the boundaries of society are continually redrawn to distinguish between those who belong and those who, because of some perceived cultural difference, are deemed to be out of place. The analogy with dirt goes beyond this, however. In order to legitimate their exclusion, people who are defined as 'other' or residual, beyond the boundaries of the acceptable, are commonly represented as less than human. In the imagery of rejection, they merge with the non-human world. Thus, indigenous minorities like the Inuit (Eskimo) and other native North Americans have been portrayed 'at one with nature', as a part of the natural world rather than civilisation. Similarly, in racist propaganda, social groups have been dehumanised by associating them with, or representing them as, animals which are widely considered to be unclean or polluting, like rats or pigs. As Frederick Douglass, an American slave, observed in his biography, the slaves of an estate were valued together with 'horses, sheep, and swine. There were horses and men, cattle and women, pigs and children, all holding the same rank in the scale of being, and were all subjected to the same narrow examination' (Boime 1990, 211). Such associations effectively put the group outside society and, although mythical, the images become a part of common knowledge.

In this chapter, I will be concerned with the social construction of the outsider, examining both the stereotyped images which have entered popular consciousness and have confirmed marginal or residual status in advanced capitalist societies, and the nature of the spaces to which outsiders have been relegated. The perception of minority cultures as being beyond the boundary of 'society' is associated not only with characterisations of the group but also with images of particular places, the landscapes of exclusion which express the marginal status of the outsider group. I will illustrate my argument with reference to Gypsy communities in Britain, other European countries and North America, but the ideas could also be applied to groups other than racialised minorities. There are some similarities in the response to minority cultures, like Gypsies, and to groups who are inappropriately lumped together as 'deviant', particularly the mentally ill and mentally handicapped (Wolch & Dear 1987; Philo 1989). Here, we have a similar problem of misrepresentation and a desire to exclude in a social and spatial sense, expressed, for example, in the construction of isolated asylums in the nineteenth century. As Philo (1989, 284) observes: 'In the long term the practical consequence of having a network of 'closed spaces' devoted specifically to mad people was to produce and then continually to reproduce a population designated as different, deviant, and dangerous by 'mainstream' society'.

In order to understand how socio-spatial constructions of the minority have been shaped in the case of Gypsy communities, I will first look at the question of conflicting world views, the difference between the perceptions of Gypsy culture shared by members of the minority group, and the generalised and distorted representations which result inevitably from interpreting visible elements of the minority culture in the context of world views characteristic of the dominant society.

The romantic, the deviant and the other

In cultural geography, there is a growing concern with difference and otherness, with a recognition that relationships with other social groups and the environment are conditioned by shared perspectives which are quite diverse. This reflects a wider concern, evident particularly in feminist and post-modern literature, that general descriptive categories used in social science, like 'class' or 'woman', neglect significant social cleavages and forms of oppression. Michelle Barrett (1987, 30), for example, has argued to this effect, suggesting that to treat a category like class as essential or universal does violence to the range of collective experiences which are actually or potentially significant in a political sense. She suggests that 'the claims of nation, region and ethnicity, as well as age, sexual orientation, disability and religion are being pressed as important and politically salient forms of experiential diversity'. An increased sensitivity to difference is necessary if experience is to be represented authentically and this sensitivity is apparent in some academic writing, for example, where feminist theory has engaged with post-modern social anthropology (Mascia-Lees, Sharpe & Cohen 1989). However, it is more generally the case that difference is viewed as deviance because it is set against some notion of the 'normal'. This is evident, for example, in responses to travelling people in Britain (a term which includes both Gypsies and Irish and Scottish Travellers). A commonly held view of travelling people as not just different but deviant is expressed in a comment on Irish Travellers in a letter to an English local newspaper, the *Walsall Observer*: 'Why, in heaven's name, don't [these] members of a foreign republic stay in their own country and live in houses there, like normal people' (Sibley 1981, 23).

Acknowledging that there are a number of 'salient forms of experiential diversity', as Barrett puts it, or differences in world views, it is still difficult to register these differences because the world views of others are in varying degrees inaccessible or muted. Others may communicate in a different idiom and employ different categories to make sense of their world (Ardener 1975), and even without a language barrier it may be difficult to represent world views authentically. If the world views of others are partly hidden, there will be a danger of misrepresenting them and constructing stereotyped images. Clearly, this can work both ways. A minority's perspective on the larger society will also be partial and distorted, although in a practical sense this is not a problem in the way that it is for the majority. It is state agencies and antagonistic communities in the dominant society who have the power, the capacity to affect the lives of minority groups, and state policies for minorities may be oppressive because they are informed by partial and stereotyped views. This is the case for current policies for British Gypsies, for example, as I will attempt to demonstrate in this chapter.

The misrepresentation of Gypsies is evident in academic writing, novels and the media. They are portrayed both as romantic and deviant. The romantic image, which appears in cultural forms as different as opera (Carmen) and tourist brochures advertising the 'natural' attractions of the Camargue in the south of France (wild bulls, white horses, flamingoes and Gypsies) fits a world view in which Gypsies are seen as a part of nature or of an imagined pre-industrial rustic existence. The deviant consists of visible elements of Gypsy culture, associated with work, shelter and so on, which are seen out of context. That is to say, in deviant representations there is no understanding of the practical needs of a semi-nomadic people whose survival depends partly on recycling materials discarded by the dominant society. The people and their material culture are viewed as malignant and polluting. They comprise 'matter out of place', as Mary Douglas (1966) puts it. The romantic image is essentially mythical, associating nomadism with freedom, with escape from the constraints of settled society and 'the Gypsy personality' with passion, colour and mystery. This is expressed, for example, in Hermann Hesse's poem, 'Glorious World':

> Sultry wind in the tree at night, dark Gypsy woman
> World full of foolish yearning and the poet's breath

and rather more prosaically in advertising and the presentation of consumer goods. For example, a picture in a recent catalogue for Monsoon clothes, a firm with shops in trendy locations like Covent Garden, London, shows models dressed in 'ethnic' fashions draped around a bow-top Gypsy wagon (fig. 7.1) and the same romantic image has been used in a British advertisement for a bra and on the wrapping of Gypsy Cream biscuits.

Ironically, a mythical, romantic Gypsy culture is identified as real in popular responses, as distinct from the 'they are not real Gypsies' reaction to those actually encountered. Visible features of modern Gypsy culture, such as modern, chrome-trimmed trailers parked on waste ground in cities and surrounded by piles of scrap metal and wrecked cars, pram wheels and milk-churns for storing water (fig. 7.2), do not fit the romantic stereotype so, in this sense, the people observed are not 'real'. At the same time, they violate accepted notions of the appropriate use of land in cities. The 'real' Gypsy is seen as belonging in the past and usually in rural surroundings, part of a cosy image of rural life (fig. 7.3) whereas the people camped on waste ground are perceived as violating urban space, the world of the majority population. This is suggested in characteristic reports in English local newspapers, describing opposition to urban Gypsy sites. Consider for example 'City could be gipsy dump' (*Hull Daily Mail*, 7 November 1990), and similarly: 'A spokesman for [York] corporation said it was a long standing policy to clear the site and tipping refuse was part of that policy. "If you don't tip, you will get more gipsies", he said' (*The Guardian*, 4 September 1975). There is an association implicit in these media representations between residual matter, refuse and a residual population. In Britain, the urban Gypsy population, a large majority of the total Gypsy population, is often referred to in coded terms which signify their perceived deviance and illegitimacy, particularly 'tinker' and 'itinerant', and these ascriptions reinforce the view of the group as residual.

In popular perceptions of the Gypsy presence in modern English cities, the appropriate context for understanding Gypsy culture, that is, the world views which

Figure 7.1: Use of the romantic Gypsy image in advertising.
Advertisement produced by Phyllis Walters Ltd, London, for Monsoon Fashion Catalogues.

Gypsies articulate themselves, remain largely hidden. Gypsy beliefs about social organisation, about work and cleanliness, which make their use of land comprehensible, are viewed negatively because they do not correspond to notions of social and spatial order which prevail in the larger society. Their behaviour is viewed as 'anti-social', rather than reflecting an alternative conception of social order.

Figure 7.2: Illegal Gypsy encampment in Hull, 1979.

Figure 7.3: Gypsy encampment near Hull, 1972.

It is notable that in many respects the values of the dominant society are reversed in Gypsy culture, providing an instance of symbolic reversal associated with many minority cultures (Cohen 1985). Thus, the integration rather than separation of work, residence and recreation are valued; ritual taboos about cleanliness require defecation in an outside toilet or in the open air, not in a trailer; some domestic animals valued as pets by gaujes (non-Gypsies), cats for example, are considered mochadi (unclean). Thus, the boundary between Gypsy society and the larger society is confirmed through a series of reversals. While Gypsies are seen as polluting spaces controlled by the dominant society, gauje practices pollute Gypsy space. While the boundary is strong, the social distance between Gypsies and others is maintained and it remains difficult to uncover the hidden areas of Gypsy culture.

This is not to say that relations between Gypsies and the dominant society are entirely static or polarised. Some British Gypsies interact freely with gaujes and there is a long history of intermarriage. In the recent past, that is, since the early 1970s in England and Wales, there has been some recognition of the demands of Gypsies for education and secure settlements (with the gradual implementation of Part 2 of the *Caravan Sites Act* since 1970) and programmes designed to increase the social welfare of Gypsy families have prompted research which may have increased the awareness of Gypsy culture among officers of local authorities (Worrall 1979; Hyman 1989). In conflict situations, however, where the presence of Gypsies is perceived as some kind of threat to property or amenity, a different kind of knowledge — the partial, distorted view of Gypsy culture — is commonly articulated. The media, particularly the local press, continue to represent Gypsies as a deviant group.

This example demonstrates an important general point in regard to the mutedness of some social groups. Because they are muted, they remain partly invisible. This partial perspective on the 'other' renders them deviant in the sense that they do not fit into the categorical schemes of the dominant groups in society. This applies to some aspects of the relationships between adult and child, women and men, the able-bodied and the physically-disabled, for example, where children, women and the physically disabled may be represented as 'other', as well as to instances of cultural difference defined by race or ethnicity. Lack of awareness of other world views is not only a question of knowledge, however. It is also a source of oppression.

Landscapes of exclusion

Space is implicated in the cultural construction of outsiders in two respects. First, marginal, residual spaces, places with which groups like Gypsies are often associated (fig. 7.4), confirm the outsider status of the minority. They may be places which are avoided by members of the dominant society because they appear threatening — a fear of the 'other' becomes a fear of place. Associations are made between place and the minority community and both the image of the place and the image of the group are founded on mythologies. This is evident in press reporting of events in British inner cities, for example, with the effect that 'inner city' itself becomes a coded term for the imagined deviance of black minorities (Keith 1987; Smith 1989). The labelling of places as threatening confirms the otherness of the minorities with whom the places are associated, and relegation to marginal spaces serves to amplify deviance. Press reporting of supposedly deviant behaviour similarly has an amplifying effect (Cohen 1973). If

Figure 7.4: Gypsies camped under a motorway in Arles, south of France, 1990.

social and spatial distance are maintained by the exclusion of the minority, it is likely that stereotyped views will persist.

A second role for space in the constitution of the outsider group concerns the arrangement of spaces in the built environment. Spatial structures can strengthen or weaken social boundaries, thus accentuating social division or, conversely, rendering the excluded group less visible. In order to understand the role of space in this process, it is necessary to think about space in relation to the exercise of power. Space represents power in that control of space confers the power to exclude, but some spatial configurations are easier to control than others. I will first examine this general problem, and then consider the outsider issue as one instance of the exercise of power over space.

Historically, we can recognise an association between priestly, military and civil power, and built form. The design of cities has in various periods had an instrumental role in the exercise of power. Thus, in early urban societies, such as the meso-American civilisations, in cities like Teotihuacan in Mexico, the bounded, enclosed, central space was the centre of priestly power and one which could not be profaned. Similarly, Neusner (1973) suggests that in ancient Israel, the rabbis could proscribe a wide range of things as polluting and this effectively gave them the power to exclude from the temple and from the land of Israel. The list of pollutants included some animals, women after childbirth, skin ailments, and other bodily conditions deemed unclean. More recently, military power was expressed in the extensive central spaces of the Baroque city. Challenges to authority in the form of popular uprisings were conspicuous if they violated the purified spaces of authority and were more effectively put down than they would be in the winding alleys of pre-Baroque cities (Mumford 1961, 369–70). These symbolic forms are echoed in the modern city in the highly ordered spaces in centres of government power, whether in Bucharest under Ceaucescu, Canberra, Brasilia, Washington DC, or the centre of Baghdad. Power is expressed in grand designs and a simple geometry.

More generally, spaces which are homogeneous or uniform, from which non-conforming groups or activities have been expelled or have been kept out through the maintenance of strong boundaries, can be termed pure in the sense that they are free from polluting elements and the purification of space is a process by which power is exercised over space and social groups (Sibley 1988). The significance of such purified spaces in the construction of the 'other' is basically that difference is more visible than it would be in an area of mixed land use and social diversity. Residents in a socially and economically homogeneous suburb, for example, may erect barriers to those who are different because they pose a threat to the homogeneity which the residents have been conditioned to value. Dear (1980) examines this problem with specific reference to the rejection of the mentally ill and mentally handicapped by North American suburban communities, and the issue is discussed in socio-psychological terms by Richard Sennett in *The Uses of Disorder* (1970), where he argues that the North American suburb, as an ideal type of social area, is both exclusive and repressive. I think that the problem is more general than Sennett recognised, however. We can begin to understand it by looking at an analogous problem in education.

Spaces, boundaries and control

In an attempt to understand the relationship between the content of school curricula and control systems in education, Basil Bernstein (1967) has developed a number of schemata which focus on subject boundaries and content. As a control problem, the structuring and organisation of the transmission of knowledge is analogous to the question of regulating spatial boundaries and locating objects or social groups in spatial units. In 'Open schools, open society' (1967), Bernstein distinguishes between an open curriculum, which emphasises the interconnections between different branches of knowledge and thus the blurring of boundaries, and a closed curriculum in which knowledge is compartmentalised and boundaries between subjects are clearly defined. The former he associates with a democratic approach to learning, where students participate in making decisions about what is taught, and the latter with a hierarchical, centralised system where decisions are made at the top and transmitted downwards, with little opportunity for reconstituting knowledge through interdisciplinary work. In fact, it is in the interest of those in control of the closed curriculum to encourage the maintenance of boundaries between subjects. Their position is secured by the retention of strong boundaries around 'pure' subjects because this discourages new thinking across traditional subject boundaries which would present a challenge to authority.

Bernstein later formalised these ideas, describing the organisation of knowledge in terms of its classification and framing (Bernstein 1971). Classification, according to Bernstein, can be either strong or weak. With strong classification, boundaries are clearly defined and the knowledge contained within the boundaries is identified in unambiguous terms. Homogeneity is valued and a blurring of boundaries would be seen as a threat to the integrity of the subject. Thus, strong classification is characteristic of the closed curriculum. Weak classification, by contrast, signifies weakly defined subject boundaries and a concern for the integration of knowledge. Similarly, within subject areas, strong framing means that there are clear rules about what may and may not be taught, whereas weak framing means that many possible relationships and interconnections are explored.

Open/closed or strongly classified/weakly classified curricula could also be seen as alternative models for society, one where power is diffuse and the other where power is concentrated in the hands of a few at the top of a political hierarchy. In applying Bernstein's ideas to the organisation of space, it is the connection with the distribution of political power which should be recognised.

Strongly classified spaces have clear boundaries, their internal homogeneity and order are valued and there is, in consequence, a concern with boundary maintenance in order to keep out objects or people who do not fit the classification. Weakly classified spaces will have weakly defined boundaries because they are characterised by social mixing and/or mixed land uses. Difference in this instance will not be obvious and if mixture and diversity are accepted, policing of the boundaries will be unnecessary. Generally, strongly classified spaces will also be strongly framed, in that there will be a concern with separation and order, as there is, for example, in many middle-class suburbs. Weak framing would suggest more numerous and more fluid relationships between people and the built environment than occur with strong framing. Buildings may have multiple uses, either simultaneously or at different times of day, for example. Using this schema, it is possible to see how space contributes to the social construction of the outsider.

The spatial context of the outsider problem refers to the presence of a non-conforming group in strongly classified space or the fear that such a group will intrude into a space which is strongly classified. To give an example of the latter, Sennett (1971, 228–89) describes a middle-class suburban community in Chicago in the late nineteenth century, 'Union Park', where there was a panic following a spate of armed robberies in the city. Whatever the real circumstances of these crimes, in Union Park 'everyone knew immediately what was wrong, and what was wrong was overwhelming: it was nothing less than the power of the "foreigner", the outsider who had suddenly become dominant in the city'. The 'folk-devils' in this case were Italian anarchists. In response to this imagined threat, 'only a state of rigid barriers, enforced by a semi-military state of curfew and surveillance would permit [the suburban community] to continue to function'. External threat, however, may also lead to internal cleansing, an urge to expel anyone who appears not to represent collective values. This need to purify space and society is evident both in Sennett's example of the threatened suburban community and in earlier cases of witch crazes, such as the infamous Salem witch trials in seventeenth-century Massachusetts, when any woman behaving in a way which appeared to depart from an ever more narrowly defined set of community values was in danger of being accused of witchcraft.

I would argue, therefore, that there is a connection between the strong classification of space and the rejection of social groups who are non-conforming. Further, there is evidence that minorities who are obliged to live in strongly classified and strongly framed environments characteristic of planned settlements, which includes approximately half the Gypsy population in England and Wales and many groups of indigenous peoples in the Arctic and sub-Arctic, in Canada, Greenland and the former Soviet Union (Osherenko & Young 1989), may find the organisation of space in settlements, or on official sites in the case of English Gypsies, constraining and alienating. This is implied in a comment by a Dene (Canadian Indian) at Fort Macpherson, a planned settlement in sub-Arctic Canada (Berger 1977, cited in Sibley 1981, 172):

> Look at the housing where the transient government staff live. And look at housing where the Indian people live ... Look at how the school and hostel, the Royal Canadian Mounted Police and government staff houses are right in the centre of the town dividing the Indian people into two sides ... Do you think this is the way the Indian people chose to have this community?

To summarise, space is an integral part of the outsider problem. The way in which space is organised affects the perception of the 'other', either as foreign and threatening or as simply different. The strong classification of space, as in the archetypal homogeneous suburb, implies a rejection of difference so the presence of minority groups in such spaces accentuates their difference and outsiderness and the likelihood of exclusion is increased. Similarly, when a minority which does not make separations between activities like home and work is relegated to a strongly classified space and subjected to socio-spatial controls, its cultural practices are likely to appear deviant to the control agencies in the dominant society. In weakly classified space, minorities will be less visible, they may not be identified as non-conforming and, consequently, the potential for conflict over the use of space is reduced. Because behaviour is less likely to be recognised as deviant, control will not be so much of an issue. Thus, we can generally anticipate an association between the strong classification of space and the identification of outsiders as a social category.

Exclusion and adaptation: relationships between Gypsies and the dominant society

The aspects of Gypsy culture cited in this chapter so far have referred primarily to communities in the British Isles and I will make more detailed reference to a British example later in this essay. It would be inappropriate to generalise from these cases to the whole Gypsy population, however, because Gypsies exhibit considerable cultural diversity. Gypsies comprise a minority population in all European countries, parts of the Middle East, including Egypt and Iran, and in India and Pakistan. In addition, they have dispersed to the Americas, particularly Brazil and Argentina, the United States and Canada, and to Australia and New Zealand as a part of the large-scale intercontinental migrations in the nineteenth and early twentieth centuries. Thus, they have had to adapt to a variety of dominant cultures. These adaptations have been one source of difference within the Gypsy population.

Although Gypsies have an ethnic identity secured by language, economy and other cultural attributes, they have intermarried with other nomadic groups and with the settled population. Indeed, it is meaningless to talk about a racial identity although Gypsies have been racialised in the sense that aspects of their way of life viewed negatively have been described as racially inherent. This has provided legitimation for discrimination and exclusion.

In Britain and Holland, in particular, there are also culturally distinctive semi-nomadic groups with whom Gypsies compete for resources but who are similarly seen as outsiders by the dominant society. These are Irish and Scottish Travellers, living in

England and Wales as well as in their native countries, and Woonwagenbevoners (caravan dwellers) in Holland. Within the European Gypsy population, communities distinguish themselves by kin-ties, place associations and occupational traditions which have contributed to the emergence of distinctive cultural identities, although migrations have complicated any regional patterns which might have existed. Some of the larger groups include the Kalderas, traditionally metal-workers from Russia but subsequently settled in Paris, Gothenburg and other west European cities, and in the United States, notably in the San Francisco Bay area and Los Angeles; the Boyash, from Hungary and Romania, but also settled in western Europe and North America and with strong traditions in entertainment; the Sinti and Manus, in southern Europe; and the Vlach in Hungary. However, self-ascriptions are complex and refer to different groupings within Gypsy society and different national identities. Also, Gypsies may not refer to themselves as Gypsy because of the pejorative use of the word by gaujes. It is for this reason that most British Gypsies usually refer to themselves as Travellers while Rom or Roma, meaning 'the people' in Romany, are self-ascriptions more commonly used by continental European Gypsies. As Liegeois (1986, 46) observes: 'Gypsies ... are defined as such by the views and attitudes of others'.

The Gypsy economy is one of the most significant features distinguishing the minority as a distinctive culture. It is not occupations which are particularly distinctive but attitudes to work. Thus, it is possible to talk about the Gypsy economy as an aspect of culture, while recognising that the particular niches in dominant economies occupied by Gypsies in different places and at different times vary considerably. In general, Gypsies avoid wage labour where possible and try to maintain a dominant position in any transaction as a matter of ethnic pride. They value flexibility and opportunism, with several money-making activities often being pursued simultaneously within one family, such as scrap metal dealing, horse trading and hawking. To some extent, the economy confirms the boundary between Gypsies and gaujes. Okely (1979, 20) suggests that self-employment is crucial in defining this boundary but there are circumstances in which this may not be possible. In Hungary under the Communist government, for example, men were obliged to work in factories, but the Vlach Gypsies combined factory employment with horse trading, scavenging and cultivating their own plots of land. Even social security payments can be viewed as one acceptable source of income, for example, in the United States and England (Sutherland 1975; Okely 1979), because taking money from the gaujes does not signify dependency. It is essentially no different from begging, which is still practised by Gypsies in Spain and by Travellers in the Republic of Ireland, for example. Whatever their transactions with the dominant economy, however, Gypsies see gauje society as exploitable.

Living on the margin allows Gypsies to exploit the residual products of the dominant economy, such as domestic scrap, and to provide services where mobility and minimal capital outlay are advantageous. Examples include the repair of supermarket trolleys or car bumpers (fenders) by Kalderas in the United States (Sutherland 1975). These occupations put Gypsies on the outside but, at the same time, they are highly dependent on urban society. Theirs is an urban culture which popular imagery locates elsewhere, in rural settings. This false image has important consequences for Gypsy communities, creating opportunities but also constraining their activities. If Gypsies are not thought of as an urban culture, it may be possible for them to pass as non-Gypsy traders in the city.

In some occupations, a Gypsy stereotype of unreliability would be bad for business so the failure of gaujes to recognise the ethnic identity of urban Gypsies — who 'belong' in the countryside — can be economically advantageous.

The Kalderas in the eastern suburbs of Paris, for example, find that presenting themselves as gaujes, which is made easier by living in small houses or bungalows (pavillons) in working-class districts, helps in getting contracts for building repairs and other work which is not usually associated with Gypsies (Williams 1982). By contrast, when Gypsies are a highly visible urban minority living in trailers, the rural stereotype accentuates their 'deviance' in the eyes of antagonistic house-dwellers. In this sense, they are polluting because they do not belong in an urban setting and hostile communities attempt to exclude them. Gypsies are not accepted in rural areas either, however, because the visible features of their culture, the chrome-trimmed trailers, piles of scrap and so on, still render them deviant. There is no 'proper place' for Gypsies because, according to the romantic stereotype, they are always distant in space and time.

Prejudice in practice: separation, containment and control

In Europe, there is a long history of attempts by the state, or by local groups with government sanction, to remove Gypsies from national territory. The Nazi government in Germany was the last to attempt this, through genocide. In modern industrialised societies, the more general objective is to settle and contain Gypsies, to remove them from locations where they are perceived as a non-conforming outsider group, violating space valued by the settled society, particularly residential space. Separation rather than integration is the unstated goal of most settlement policies (Sibley 1987). An alternative response, evident in several East European countries, has been to deny that Gypsies have a cultural identity and to house them with other workers. In Romania, for example, Gypsies are not recognised as a 'nationality' or minority group, although the country has the largest Gypsy population in Eastern Europe.

Liegeois (1986) documents attempts by European states to eliminate or remove Gypsies. In the seventeenth and eighteenth centuries, sanctions included the hanging of Gypsy men, in Slovakia in 1710 and Prussia in 1721, for example; the mutilation of women and children; flogging, branding, forced labour and banishment, including deportation from Britain to North America and Australia. In France, a common sentence for being a Gypsy in the seventeenth century was to be sent to the galleys for life. The harshest penalties were eventually seen to be ineffective, however, and other measures were substituted, with the same objective of removing Gypsies from sight, through physical expulsion to remote locations, cultural annihilation or assimilation.

Local responses: the case of Gypsies in Hull

There is a connection between this history of exclusion and response to Gypsies in modern societies. Attitudes to Gypsies in the developed world still suggest that the minority constitutes a threat to social order and, in some countries, a threat to spatial order. Thus, in a country like Britain, where the land use planning system reflects widely accepted notions of spatial order and amenity, unregulated Gypsy settlements constitute deviant landscapes. The response of the state to this deviance is to impose order on Gypsy communities through the medium of official sites, to isolate and transform in a controlled environment. The way in which these controls are exercised locally can be demonstrated with reference to the recent history of the Gypsy population in Hull, in north-east England.

Gypsies have lived in Hull for at least one hundred years. In the 1970s, old people recalled spending the winter months during their childhood in rented houses in the inner city, and migrating for agricultural work in the summer. While some families maintained this pattern of movement and settlement until about 1975, most had by this time settled in the city. They camped, illegally, on roadsides or in fields close to a large peripheral housing estate, or on land cleared of housing in the inner city.

This was a period of persistent conflict. Evictions by the local authority were frequent and antagonistic comments by local politicians were publicised in the local press in a series of alarmist articles. One demonstration in the summer of 1973 by local authority tenants demanding the removal of a Gypsy camp close to their estate, illustrated the enduring negative image of Gypsies projected by hostile communities. Some placards referred to the deviant form of settlement: 'How much longer do we have to put up with this shanty town on our estate?' Others alluded to unregulated industrial activity: 'Smokeless zone — Gypsies burn car tyres, we would be fined'. Residents interviewed by the local press at this time made adverse comments about the Gypsies' lifestyle: 'They smell, they have rats, they make a noise'. This particular protest had all the elements of a moral panic but there were also more routine acts of violence and harassment, like bricks and iron bars thrown through caravan windows.

The conflict was defused by the construction of two sites in the city, both locations reflecting the local authority's desire to distance the Gypsies from the rest of the population in order to minimise conflict. The first was built in a heavily polluted industrial area which had been cleared of residential development. The second site was built in an old quarry, used for dumping rubbish, on the edge of the city. It could be argued that, through site development, Gypsies were consigned to residual space — a morally polluting minority was associated with physically polluted places. In a change of policy, a third site is now planned for a residential location in the inner city. The attitude of the settled population has not changed, however: 'Anger over Gypsy camp decision: estate residents plan protest to MP' (*Hull Daily Mail*, 13 March 1991).

Existing sites have reinforced the boundary between the Gypsy community and the rest of the city's population. The isolation of existing sites is coupled with site designs which represent a geometry of control, or strong classification, in Bernstein's terms. Both site layouts are based on models developed by a central government department (the Department of the Environment). Spaces for trailers are arranged in regular rows and this residential space is clearly separated from the warden's space. There are no work areas or play areas, although these are included in the model designs. Single-use zoning, characteristic of the Hull sites and most others built in England by local authorities, is important as a means of controlling residents. Families have been evicted from one site for 'misusing' space, for example, by erecting sheds in the residential zone. This kind of boundary enforcement causes discontent because the boundaries are imposed by authority and they are not those recognised as important in the Gypsy community, where work, play and residence are spatially integrated. A frequent comment by site residents is: 'You might as well be in a house as living on this site'. Boundary enforcement depends on effective policing. On the other site, the boundaries have been blurred through the construction of chicken runs, dog kennels and storage sheds around some of the trailers. Wardens have not attempted to maintain the separation of uses and, probably because of this, there appears to be a higher level of satisfaction with the site. Thus, while it seems legitimate to characterise official Gypsy sites as landscapes of control, at least in intention, it must be acknowledged that the dominated minority can act subversively and frustrate the efforts of the social control agencies.

These sites have been the only home for about forty Hull Gypsy families for a decade. Although there is some evidence of social change which may be attributed to site environments, they do not appear to have fundamentally affected the Gypsies' way of life. Extended families still interact intensively, usually occupying adjacent pitches, but less time is spent outside, talking around a fire, for example. Fires are banned but, in practice, they are simply lit less frequently. More time is spent watching television and videos. Satellite dishes and decoders have widened the range of viewing for a few families but with no noticeable effect on family values. There has been no transformation of Gypsy culture but it is clear that sites are constraining. They limit work opportunities and discourage social interaction beyond the family. They contribute to a resentment of authority, but it is the warden and other council officials rather than the police who serve as the agents of control. The Gypsies are occupying gauje space and have only limited success in making it their own.

Conclusion

The socio-spatial construction of certain groups as outsiders is a complex process but I have suggested that the problem can best be understood by focusing on boundary processes, the ways in which distinctions are made between the pure and the defiled, the normal and the deviant, the same and the other. Drawing on social anthropological concepts developed by Mary Douglas (1966), outsiders can be defined as those groups who do not fit dominant models of society and are therefore seen as polluting. In social space, such groups disturb the homogeneity of a locality and a common reaction of the hostile community will be to expel the polluting group, to purify space. For Gypsies, both their unregulated occupation of land and the controlled environments to which they are increasingly relegated, as in Britain and Holland, constitute 'deviant' landscapes which confirm their outsider status and reinforce the boundary between the minority and the dominant society.

Mythology plays an important part in the representation of the minority as deviant and not belonging to 'society'. In order to establish the threatening nature of the outsider group, it is necessary to attribute to it mythical characteristics which dehumanise and legitimate exclusion or expulsion. If the group is distinguished by culture and physical characteristics, racist myths become an important part of the negative representation of the minority. The case of European Gypsies demonstrates the importance of racism, but the sense of non-conformity is magnified by a fear of the nomad, notwithstanding the fact that many Gypsies are sedentary.

Perceptions of an outsider group, however, are also conditioned by its visibility. While an inability to gain a complete understanding of the world view of the minority is part of the problem of stereotyping which academic research may hope to rectify, to remain hidden, out of sight of the dominant society, may also be to the advantage of the minority. In the case of Gypsies, attempting to survive in a modern urban society, to maintain an economic system without state regulation, depends on retaining a degree of invisibility so myths associating Gypsies with a romantic, rural past may work to their advantage. In the city, the myths may help them to disappear. Visibility is also affected by structural factors, however, because to assume outward conformity depends on opportunities related to the management of the housing market and the built environment and these opportunities vary over space and time. Because their relationship to place varies and because of their cultural diversity, there can be no single representation of Gypsies as an outsider group. Gypsy territory might be 'invisible', a house or an apartment in the city, or it might be highly visible, a patch of waste land or an official site — a landscape of exclusion. While a consciousness of the boundary with the gauje world is a defining characteristic of Gypsy cultures, this boundary takes many shapes.

References

Ardener, E. 1975, 'The problem revisited', in S. Ardener (ed.), *Perceiving Women*, Routledge & Kegan Paul, Andover, Hants, pp. 19–27.

Barrett, M. 1987, 'The concept of difference', *Feminist Review*, 26, pp. 29–41.

Berger, T.R. 1977, *Northern Frontier, Northern Homeland,* Ministry of Supply and Services, Ottawa.

Bernstein, B. 1967, 'Open schools, open society', *New Society*, 14 September, pp. 351–3.

Bernstein, B. 1971, *Class, Codes and Control, Volume 1,* Routledge & Kegan Paul, Andover, Hants.

Boime, A. 1990, *The Art of Exclusion: Representing Blacks in the Nineteenth Century*, Thames & Hudson, London.

Cohen, A. 1985, *The Symbolic Construction of Community*, Tavistock Publications, London.

Cohen, S. 1973, *Folk Devils and Moral Panics,* Paladin, St Albans.

Dear, M. 1980, 'The public city', in W. Clark & E. Moore (eds), *Residential Mobility and Public Policy*, Sage, Beverley Hills, pp. 219–41.

Douglas, M. 1966, *Purity and Danger*, Routledge & Kegan Paul, Andover, Hants.

The Guardian, 4.10.75.

Hesse, Herman 1975, *Wandering*, Picador, London.

Hull Daily Mail, 7.11.90; 13.3.91.

Hyman, M. 1989, *Sites for Travellers*, London Race and Housing Research Unit, London.

Keith, M. 1987, 'Something happened: the problems of explaining the 1980 and 1981 riots in British cities', in P. Jackson (ed.), *Race and Racism*, Allen & Unwin, London, pp. 275–301.

Liegeois, J.-P. 1986, *Gypsies: an Illustrated History*, Al Saqi Books, London.

Mascia-Lees, F., Sharpe, P. & Cohen, C.B. 1989, 'The post-modern turn in anthropology: cautions from a feminist perspective,' *Signs*, 15, 1, pp. 7–33.

Mumford, L. 1961, *The City in History*, Secker & Warburg, London.

Neusner, J. 1973, *The Idea of Purity in Ancient Judaism*, E.J. Brill, Leiden.

Okely, J. 1979, 'Trading stereotypes: the case of English Gypsies', in S. Wallman (ed.), *Ethnicity at Work*, Macmillan, Basingstoke, pp. 17–36.

Osherenko, G. & Young, O. 1989, *The Age of the Arctic*, Cambridge University Press, Cambridge.

Philo, C. 1989, 'Enough to drive one mad: the organization of space in 19th century lunatic asylums', in J. Wolch & M. Dear (eds), *The Power of Geography*, Unwin Hyman, London, pp. 258–90.

Sennett, R. 1970, *The Uses of Disorder*, Penguin, Harmondsworth.

Sennett, R. 1971, 'Middle class families and urban violence: the experience of a Chicago community in the 19th century', in T.K. Haravan (ed.), *Anonymous Americans,* Prentice Hall, Englewood Cliffs, NJ, pp. 280–305.

Sibley, D. 1981, *Outsiders in Urban Societies,* Basil Blackwell, London.

Sibley, D. 1987, 'Racism and settlement policy: the state's response to a semi-nomadic minority', in P. Jackson (ed.), *Race and Racism,* Allen & Unwin, London, pp. 74–89.

Sibley, D. 1988, 'Survey 13: purification of space', *Environment and Planning D: Society and Space*, 6, pp. 409–21.

Smith, S.J. 1989, *The Politics of 'Race' and Residence,* Polity Press, Cambridge.

Sutherland, A. 1975, *Gypsies: the Hidden Americans,* Tavistock, London.

Williams, P. 1982, 'The invisibility of the Kalderas in Paris', *Urban Anthropology,* 11, 3-4, pp. 315–46.

Wolch, J. & Dear, M. 1987, *Landscapes of Despair,* Polity Press, Cambridge.

Worrall, D. 1979, *Gypsy Education: a Study of Provision in England and Wales,* Council for Community Relations, Walsall.

8 Gender in the landscape: expressions of power and meaning

Janice Monk

Introduction

It is not difficult to recognise the more obvious expressions of class, race or ethnicity in the material landscape. The quality of residences and their decoration, the signs on shop windows, the graffiti on walls, the manicured lawns or the jumble of weeds and rubble convey to us impressions of affluence or poverty, diversity or homogeneity, and feelings of familiarity or strangeness, comfort or anxiety. But gender? Superficially, since for the most part men and women occupy the same spaces, it seems that an analysis of the landscape focusing on gender would not be fruitful. Yet gender is a central element of human experience. It would therefore be surprising if the landscape did not reflect the ideologies that support distinct gender roles and the inequalities of power that they embody. Further, we might expect that gender socialisation would lead women and men to experience the landscape in different ways, and to attach different meanings to it. Because gender roles and relationships are largely taken-for-granted aspects of life, however, and because the experience of the masculine gender has been assumed to represent the universal rather than the particular in much geographic writing, the gendered nature of the landscape was rarely acknowledged until the development of feminist research in the 1970s (Monk & Hanson 1982).

The purpose of this chapter is to explore some of the ways in which power and meaning in the landscape are associated with gender. In dealing with gender I will be drawing on feminist thinking which distinguishes between sex, the biological differentiation of male from female which is universal, and gender, the cross-cultural and historically varying expressions of masculinity and femininity. To illustrate the variability and malleability of gender roles and relationships, I will present examples from a number of cultural settings and historical periods. I will argue that the often unspoken social and cultural beliefs, that is the ideologies which people hold about gender, are important in shaping landscapes. In turn, landscapes set the contexts within which men and women act and reproduce gender roles and relationships. Much of the discussion will demonstrate how landscapes, both materially and symbolically, reflect power inequalities between men and women by embodying patriarchal cultural values. These values support the dominance of men and the subordination and oppression of women; they are often interpreted as being universal and historically pervasive, though they vary in expression and in the intensity of their impact at different times and places.

As a counter to this examination of patriarchal domination in the landscape, I will also consider how women have resisted it by creating their own visions of landscapes and working to bring these visions into being. I will discuss the efforts of women to reform male-created architectural and urban spaces and to combat the environmental destruction they see stemming from masculine manipulation of nature and technology. Dealing with oppression and resistance, however, does not tell enough of the story. Studies of women's religious beliefs and rituals, their oral and written literature and their arts suggest that they draw on the landscape in expressing a sense of female autonomy and their identity as women. In other words, the meanings women draw from the landscape may empower them not only to resist patriarchal domination but also to validate themselves. In this chapter, I will describe how some women in the south-western United States have drawn on the landscape for such purposes. In summary, my approach is designed to show that gender and landscape are indeed connected and to argue that landscape expresses power and meaning in ways that have both negative and positive connotations for women.

Of heroes and horses, myths and maidens: the landscape of public monuments

At the south-eastern corner of Central Park in New York, in glistening gold, General William Tecumseh Sherman, astride his majestic horse, dominates a small plaza (fig. 8.1). However, the hero of the Union Army is not alone. His horse is preceded (not led) by a winged female figure holding aloft a palm frond. She symbolises Victory. Describing this noted monument, art historian H.W. Janson comments: '(W)hat is original about Saint-Gaudens's Victory is her delicate, virginal type, even the consciously awkward way she carries the palm frond, and the way she keeps pace with the forward movement of horse and rider' (Rosenblum & Janson 1984).

Though such monuments might seem to function largely as backdrops in daily life, they are intended to commemorate what we value and to instruct us in our heritage through visible expressions on the landscape. In western societies, their message of male power, reinforced by the commanding mounted position, is repeated frequently in tributes to military heroes. As Susan Gross and Mary Rojas (1986) have documented, the people who are commemorated by the outdoor monuments of Washington DC are mostly male military and political figures. Among the monuments listed on the Rand McNally tourist map of the city only one represents a woman, Joan of Arc (also mounted on a horse). Three other women are portrayed in the city's outdoor monuments — Queen Isabella I of Spain, another political figure, Mary McLeod Bethune, and Olive Risley Seward. Bethune is commemorated in her own right as a black educator, though she too served as a political appointee (Gross & Rojas 1986). Even the placement of female historical figures on the landscape may signify something other than the woman herself. Seward's statue, for example, honours her family for their political work, though she is recognised for her interests in the abolition of slavery and her influence on her father (Gross & Rojas 1986). Similarly, the stern figure of Queen Victoria in the square which bears her name in Sydney presents her complete with orb and sceptre, the symbol of

Figure 8.1: Saint-Gaudens monument to General Sherman, New York.
Source: Photo by Amy W. Newhall.

empire and colonial power. It bears little relation to the woman herself — one who chose to wear the black dress and bonnet of widowhood to the celebration of the jubilee of her reign though others attending were garbed in ceremonial dress (Benson 1985).

Though the few monuments commemorating individual historical women on the landscape favour the political realm, women from other spheres of life, for example those who have nursed soldiers in war, are sometimes represented in a generic way. Such commemorations are relatively rare, however. In Australia, among 2000 or more Anzac memorials to the First World War, only one local monument portrays a nurse (in Maryborough, Victoria), though figures of nurses are included in the major memorials in Melbourne and Sydney. However, as Ken Inglis notes 'you have to look hard' to see them on relief panels in Melbourne, and the official description of the memorial in Sydney turns the nurses into mothers of the race lovingly tending the weary and wounded (Inglis 1989, 37). Reports of efforts to build war memorials to women show how their roles in enterprises that cast men as the actors are deemed insignificant or rejected. Plans to build a sculpture commemorating women veterans of the Vietnam War in Washington DC have long been frustrated by bureaucratic regulations and conflicts over design, though a sculpture of male veterans was erected adjacent to the Vietnam Wall monument some years ago (Huyck, personal communication). Only recently does contention over the design appear to have been resolved but governmental authorisation of construction has not yet been given ('Women in war' 1990). Resisting the male monopoly of the commemorative landscape, the Women in Military Service For America Foundation obtained congressional authorisation to construct a memorial at Arlington National Cemetery to honour all United States women veterans of the past;

they are struggling to raise donations to begin construction before the authorisation deadline expires. Their proposed design is remote from the concept of the heroic figure on the horse. It incorporates a computer registry of the 1.6 million women who have served in the armed forces, and women may choose to have their photographs included (Vaught n.d.).

By contrast with the realism of this proposed monument, the representation of female figures in the urban landscape is usually of an abstract symbol, a mythical maiden, like the Victory with General Sherman. As Marina Warner writes: '(E)ven if executed with a high degree of naturalism, female figures representing an ideal or abstraction hardly ever interact with real, individual women. Devices distinguish them: improbable nudity, heroic scale, wings, unlikely attributes' (Warner 1985, 28).

She reports a staggering number of abstract female forms decorating official buildings in Paris, bringing together the French sense of the romantic and erotic. In Britain, she notes the female guardian of virtue symbolised in many monuments — an armed woman expressing the conquest of desire in the guise of Peace, Victory, Fortitude, Justice or Truth. The association of female figures with Liberty, whether the French Marianne or the American 'Miss Liberty', can only seem ironic given the history of restriction and political exclusion of real women in male-dominated democracies.

Thus, conveyed to us in the urban landscapes of Western societies is a heritage of masculine power, accomplishment, and heroism; women are largely invisible, present occasionally if they enter the male sphere of politics or militarism. Even representation of these women may only be achieved when other women work together to support construction. In their place are abstract female symbols, which may be interpreted as noble ideals for men but which reflect little of the worlds that women have made and inhabited. As indicators of patriarchal hegemony in Western cultures, these monuments set and reflect the context of gender relations in everyday life.

Home space: protective or constraining?

If gender distinctions are clearly evident in the landscape of public monuments, they are, on first reflection, not as obvious in the spaces of the home. Yet here too, if we examine a variety of cultures and historical periods, we can see how ideologies that shape gender roles and relations are expressed in architectural design and the ways that people behave in space. Examples across cultures reveal how patriarchal values, often ostensibly protecting women, in fact constrain them. Nevertheless, these same examples show that women may attach different meanings to spaces than men, that they may find ways to manoeuvre in them to meet their own needs, and that they make efforts to design spaces to reflect their own values. Which of these approaches women take will depend on the cultural and historical context.

For centuries, specific men's and women's spaces codified the social order of Confucian society in Imperial China. In the world of the middle and upper classes especially, dwellings consisted of a series of courtyards bounded by a wall. The women's quarters were isolated from the outside world, located at the rear along a windowless back wall, accessible only by passing through the other courtyards. Valued in the patriarchal culture for her reproductive capacities and central to assuring the identity of the male line, a woman was thus protected and secluded from outside contact, expected to devote her life to the household of her husband, his parents and her sons (Pollock 1981). What meanings and consequences derive from this prescribed segregation? Nancy Pollock, interpreting Chinese painting and poetry, argues that for the male artist the beautifully rendered interior rooms and gardens symbolised the ideal woman, subservient, humble and obedient. For the women poets, architectural barriers implied containment, exclusion and isolation 'loss of mobility and individuality ... being bound to the home and a limited sphere of activity' (Pollock 1981, 37).

Similar segregation has characterised the dwellings of Iranian households in support of patriarchal Islamic principles which prohibit contact between women and men unless they are mahram (that is, ineligible marriage partners) and are supported by the custom of secluding women in the home. For the devout Moslem, sharing space with people who are na-mahram (that is, not mahram) is to be avoided because it might lead to illegal sexual relationships outside of marriage. In order to entertain visitors at home, families set aside a space near the front of the house, separated from family quarters to the rear. Women withdraw from this space and are thus protected from view when male na-mahram visitors are present (Khatib-Chahidi 1981).

However, the rigidities of idealised seclusion may be used by women to serve their own purposes, or may be modified in daily life and by changing circumstances. Thus women use the private women's spaces for uninhibited female socialising; they also enter the publicly-visible spaces of Iranian villages and use them for their own purposes in daytime hours when men are absent (Khatib-Chahidi 1981). Urban living may also bring modifications to rigid gender separation in home space even when elements of seclusion persist. For example, the large central courtyard of the rural Irarian home from which the family could see a visitor without being seen may shrink to a modest family living area in an urban apartment, so that seeing becomes reciprocal. If a separate entertaining area is maintained in the apartment, this permits the more religious family members to avoid na-mahram visitors by withdrawing to some other room (Khatib-Chahidi 1981).

This example should not be construed to mean that modernisation necessarily reduces the negative consequences of spatial isolation for women. In other contexts, recent economic changes have reinforced the advantages of female seclusion for sustaining male power. The situation in Narsapur, India, provides a good illustration. Penetration of global capitalism into this community has generated increasing demands for the inexpensive lace produced there. To meet these demands, secluded women work long hours for little pay in their own homes. Their exploitation is supported by an ideology which defines them as 'housewives' rather than as workers, and the principal profits of their work redound to men in the community. Underlying this situation is a social history which links social prestige and female seclusion and which illustrates how class and gender ideologies may be intertwined. The lace-makers are Kapu, a class in which men's status is dependent on secluding women; they contrast with the lower class, untouchable Harijans in which women work openly in the fields. Today, the Harijan women are able to earn more than the Kapu. According to Maria Mies, with higher incomes and the enhanced sense of confidence and esteem derived from working collectively, Harijan women have come to look down on the Kapu women. Yet she argues, the Kapu women, constrained by the limiting patriarchal values that identify high status with female seclusion, shun manual work outside the home. We do not know if they fail to see how these values disadvantage them or if they are powerless to resist. The result of the pressures of economic change is that these women remain isolated and have been impoverished (Mies 1982).

It is often easier to recognise the implications of spatial forms in other cultures than in our own because we take so much of the everyday world for granted. A brief study of housing policies and plans and of the writing of social critics since the late nineteenth century in the United States and Britain shows how ideas about gender roles permeate the design of domestic space. These materials also reveal how conceptions of gender roles change over time and provide examples of some ways women have sought to define their own visions.

In the latter half of the nineteenth century, the notion that men were most properly associated with the public sphere of life and women with the domestic held strong sway in the United States, especially among the middle class. Articles in popular magazines such as the *Ladies Home Journal* and books like *The American Woman's Home* written by Catherine Beecher and Harriet Beecher Stowe in 1869 idealised a woman's duty as the spiritual centre and efficient manager of the home, which was portrayed as a retreat from the world for the working husband and the centre of domestic harmony. These ideas were still being promoted in the first decade of the twentieth century when the *Ladies Home Journal* published designs by Frank Lloyd Wright for homes in which high walls and leaded windows enclosed a truly protected environment while, within, continuous open space centred on the family hearth, a symbolic focus of harmony and togetherness (Rock, Torre & Wright 1980).

Such designs contrast with dwellings in Utopian communities built in the United States between the 1820s and the 1840s by followers of the British reformer Robert Owen and his French contemporary Charles Fourier. Exhibiting a concern for equality within the home and a priority for reducing the burden of individual women's housework, they constructed communal housing that incorporated private space for sleeping (and sometimes family living) but shared areas for cooking, dining, and childcare. Similarly, material feminists like Charlotte Perkins Gilman and Melusina Fay Pierce writing in the late nineteenth and early twentieth centuries in the United States and reacting against the ideal of female domesticity, advocated kitchenless houses or apartment hotels with co-operative kitchens, communal cafes and shared children's nurseries and play areas. Their goal was to free women from full-time isolated housework in the domestic sphere to make it possible for them to engage in wider social participation in the public sphere (Hayden 1981). Though their designs offered broader opportunities for middle-class women, they did not solve the needs of working-class women and their families, especially those who might be employed as providers of the collective childcare or food services. Nor did they fundamentally challenge the prevailing ideologies of the period that associated family and domestic care with women.

British feminists concerned about the needs of low-income women took a different approach in their reports for the Women's Housing Sub-Committee which was established by the British government in 1918 to plan state-built housing. Unlike earlier feminists who had been challenging women's inequality in the public sphere, the women on this committee wanted to ease women's lot within homes where the gender division of labour was accepted. Informed by detailed conversations with working-class women and seeing the inadequacies of homes in which families lived in a couple of rooms, shared sculleries, had no hot water, and often were required to carry water and slops up and down stairs, they aimed to save the women expenditure of money and energy. They suggested a separate room for cooking removed from the family living area, and a parlour where the woman could relax away from her unfinished work; and they paid special attention to economical means of providing hot water and cooking fuel. Their final report referred briefly to communal housing, but concluded that 'English women ... do not regard communal housing with favour. It is not, however, a reason for neglecting to consider schemes by which unnecessary drudgery would be saved' (quoted in Matrix 1984, 36). Their work contrasts markedly with that of a committee of men 'experts' set up by the Local Government Board in 1917. Its brief recommendations were confined to ideas about building housing quickly and cheaply. One of its most influential members, Raymond Unwin, attacked the notion of a separate parlour as inappropriate aping of the middle classes (Matrix 1984).

Whether Utopian and experimental or accepting prevailing gender roles, these designs and those which have prevailed in the second half of the twentieth century have generally assumed the patriarchal nuclear family as the norm and placed the burden of domestic responsibility on women. In the USA, by 1980 these assumptions resulted in a housing stock in which nearly two-thirds of the units were single-family detached homes, with those built after the Second World War of increasingly larger size. Yet in recent years, American households have been getting smaller and smaller, and housing prices higher and higher. Income tax structures favour home owners but, for the most part, only two-income couples have any hope of qualifying for mortgages and meeting payments (Hayden 1984). Scarce indeed is affordable and suitable housing for low-income households, especially for the rising proportions of single-parent, largely mother-supported, households.

Contemporary feminist writers and activists are again advocating design reform, but their proposals incorporate visions which seek to free women from oppressive domestic situations and to recognise their need to work outside the home. Among the projects publicised in feminist publications on the built environment are The Mothers' House in Amsterdam, the Constance Hamilton Cooperative in Toronto and the Nina West Homes in London which provide private and communal areas, spaces for childcare, counselling offices and the like (fig. 8.2) (Hayden 1984; Klodawsky & Mackenzie 1987). Feminists are also working to support refuges for battered women and their children, stressing locational and design features, not only the establishment of homes. They seek sites near public transportation, schools and other services, and larger old houses that include several bedrooms on upper floors with common spaces on the ground floor so that the women will have privacy as well as community support and security (Klodawsky & Mackenzie 1987). These projects reflect a new feminist recognition of the desirability of separate spaces to protect women from male violence and demonstrate a reconcept-ualisation of women's social needs compared with the domestic visions of the nineteenth century and the 1950s. They illustrate one form of resistance to male domination, yet they remind us of the gender inequalities still pervasive in western societies where such refuges remain necessary. Their construction, however, is hampered by inadequate finance and obstacles like zoning laws which in many communities in the United States prohibit the building of group homes in neighbourhoods zoned for individual family residences. In general then, power over the built environment remains in male hands and women have little control over its form.

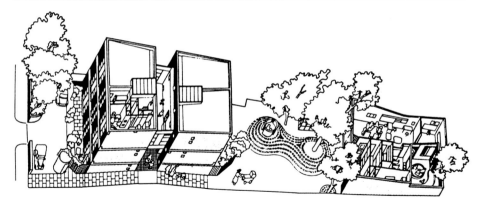

Figure 8.2: The Nina West homes in London are designed for the needs of single parents. Childcare facilities are built behind flats to meet the needs of parents who have to go out to work. Some can be employed at the centre. Corridors between flats also provide play areas that can be easily watched, and intercoms link units for easier baby-sitting.
Source: after Hayden (1984, 166).

The city and the suburb: patriarchal divisions of urban space

Expressions of gender in the contemporary urban landscape of Western cities transcend the individual dwelling. Indeed, the distinction between city and suburb reflects gender ideologies writ large. Feminist geographers have located the origins of this division in urban space historically in the rise of industrialisation, when the site of paid productive work moved out of the home into the factory, and the home became the locus of unpaid reproductive work. For the middle class especially, the division was supported by values which identified women with work in the home and cast men in the role of outside breadwinner (Hayden 1984; Mackenzie & Rose 1983; McDowell 1983). As the development of public transportation and acquisition of family cars made possible the greater spatial separation of home and work, and the promotion of appliances for the home reinforced this sphere as the place of the woman consumer, the distinction between the suburban home as the female domain and the urban workplace as male territory was strengthened (Miller 1983). Mortgage and zoning policies exacerbated the division, supporting the construction of single family homes and the separation of residential and commercial areas.

The gender politics underlying the form which has dominated twentieth-century urban development is clearly expressed in the documents promoting the construction of greenbelt towns in the USA in the 1930s. The chief promotional pamphlet for these planned new towns advocated putting 'houses and land and people together in such a way that the props under our economic and social structure will be strengthened' (quoted in Wagner 1984, 36). Husbands were identified as the commuter working outside the residential area and the women were expected to remain at home during the day, served by shops, schools and movie theatres which were intended to be within walking distance of their residences. Illustrations in the pamphlets featured aproned women in kitchens with modern appliances, working in the garden and taking care of children. The management agency which screened applicants for new homes rated them on a scale of one to ten on such criteria as 'family integration', with the highest points for families that were judged 'normal, home-loving, and self-respecting' (Wagner 1984, 38).

That the suburban form disadvantages women has become increasingly obvious, whether women are isolated in the home or struggle to maintain dual roles as paid workers outside the home and bearing the major responsibilities for household and family care. The diversity of women's needs has been invisible to planners of public transportation which is organised to serve 'regular' (that is full-time, male, city) workers and which remains inadequate for women who work part-time or have to combine shopping, delivering children to childcare, and carrying out other errands with their journey to work. Likewise, land use zoning that separates residential and commercial uses makes it more difficult to combine work and shopping or to conduct businesses in the home. Despite such known inadequacies, the creation of suburban estates continues apace, extending to new contexts. Jacqueline Coutras (1987) has identified the dilemmas of women who have recently moved to expanding suburbs in the Paris region, valuing residence there for their families, but personally caught between isolation and extended commuting. Other scholars are identifying situations in which employers in the United States, for example, in the San Francisco Bay area, are moving their routine clerical operations to new offices in middle-class suburbs to attract low-cost, well-qualified female workers who want to work close to home — a practice that exploits white suburban women and diminishes the availability of such work for minority and single women living in central city areas (Nelson 1986).

The examples above identify many of the daily inconveniences and economic costs to women of suburban residence, but other authors highlight its psychological costs to women. Quite widely written about since Betty Friedan identified the stultifying limitations of suburban domesticity for women in her book *The Feminine Mystique* (1963), these costs continue to be identified in social surveys and by women writers who are advocating change. William Michelson (1977), for example, encountered ambivalent feelings about suburbia among Toronto women. Sophie Watson highlights the contrast between her life in Canberra (as part of a male–female suburban couple) and her independent residence in inner Sydney:

> In my mind I see Canberra bringing the end of the relationship. I lost my sense of self in Canberra ... The lack of my own space, the suburban box, the long empty streets, the difficulty of meeting people, the social life based on couples, the lunchtime affairs, the absence of community ... that was Canberra. It was hard to build a life of one's own. I felt I had become the suburban wife. My centre slipped away.
>
> Sydney is another story. I've moved several times. Different arrangements. Inner city life. Community. Diversity. Possibility. Turmoil. Dirt. Waves. Beach. Breakfast on the roof at Bondi. Nino's. Enzo's. Real houses. Houses with thick walls. Bedrooms to play music in. Different coloured faces. People dropping by. Noise. Difference valued and created. (Watson 1989, 10–11)

Watson apparently is a single woman without children. Low-income single mothers living in inexpensive urban rental housing created by the Women's Development Corporation in Providence, Rhode Island, see their ideal residential environment in somewhat different terms. For many of these women, the vision is like the stereotypical suburb — it embodies privacy, peace and quiet, qualities that have been rare in their lives. Still, they value access to city services and indicate that having the affordable apartments provided by the project has given them a heightened sense of independence, confidence and control (Breitbart 1990). These examples remind us that as we interpret women's ideals and their reactions to the landscapes designed for the 'traditional' family, we have to be careful to recognise the diversity of needs and aspirations among women, a diversity which the conventional patriarchal model excludes.

Michelson, Watson and Breitbart have been discussing women's psychological reactions; other authors have suggested ways in which masculine identity and suburban living are also interrelated. Though he does not explicitly mention gender, Peter Muller's (1981) characterisation of movers to the burgeoning suburbs of post-Second World War suburbs in the United States implies that men are his subjects. He writes of them as 'earnest young war veterans, possessing strong familistic values, who desired to educate themselves, work hard, and achieve the "good life"' (p. 54) ... 'any major salary increase or promotion was immediately signified by a move to a "better" neighbourhood' (p. 35). Muller links this mobility to 'the drive for achievement' (1981). Similarly, Geraldine Pratt (1990) argued that home ownership is central to the identity of middle-class Canadian men, marking them as good providers.

The form of urban space thus simultaneously reinforces particular gender identities, roles and relationships, and creates obstacles to their change. Despite the fact that economic and socio-demographic conditions indicate we would be better served by more varied and flexible spatial forms which integrate home, work and services, outmoded gender assumptions continue to inform urban land use planning. The challenge is to adapt what we have to support not only the conventional nuclear unit but also diverse types of households, ranging from adolescent single mothers to dual-employed couples to elderly widows trying to cope without adequate community support in houses that are overly large for their circumstances. Individuals are creating alternatives, for example, by redesigning and redesignating home spaces to operate childcare services in neighbourhoods or conduct businesses from their residences (Mackenzie 1987). Private groups such as those who develop co-operative housing or women's shelters offer another model (Wekerle 1981), but it is critical to initiate institutional changes at local and national levels as well. We have models from the past of women translating their concerns into urban reform and public policy. Los Angeles women in 1920, for example, successfully overthrew a downtown parking ban that implied their convenient access to stores was unnecessary because women's time was inconsequential (Scharff 1988). Women reformers in the United States in the early twentieth century brought changes on a larger scale, supporting the development of settlement houses, urban parks, and improved sanitation (Cranz 1981; Gittell & Shtob 1981; Merchant 1984). However, as Cynthia Enloe (1990) points out, gender ideologies that have inhibited women's participation in the larger political sphere embody the same concepts of patriarchal power that favour public expenditure on militarism and policies that support international business while reducing expenditures for social welfare. Thus future transformation of the urban landscape in a significant way will require substantial changes in the prevailing cultural ideologies that underlie political and economic life.

Woman and nature: power, meaning and metaphor

Thus far, I have addressed ways in which ideas about gender roles and relationships are constituted in the built environment, emphasising the implications of these expressions for the material conditions of everyday life. I would now like to widen the scope of the discussion to address visions of natural as well as built landscapes and of the human transformation of nature, focusing on metaphors which link 'woman' and 'nature'. My intent is to show how the different meanings attached to such metaphors affect the ways in which cultural groups approach the management of their relationship with the natural environment.

An array of contemporary women scholars, writers and activists, especially those who identify themselves as 'ecofeminists', are challenging the ways western scientific and philosophical thought over the last several hundred years have constructed and associated the concepts of 'nature' and 'woman'. They argue that the values embodied in these conceptualisations have been deleterious to nature and supportive of the domination of women. They call for modifications if humanity is to achieve sustainable life in the future. Carolyn Merchant has made two significant contributions to this literature in *The Death of Nature: Women, Ecology, and Scientific Revolutions* (1980) and *Ecological Revolutions: Nature, Gender and Science in New England* (1989). She argues that 'forms of consciousness are power structures. When one world view is challenged and replaced by another during a scientific or ecological revolution, power over society, nature, and space is at stake' (1989, 22). *The Death of Nature* examines the transition in European thinking between the fifteenth and seventeenth centuries from an organic world view, in which the human, natural and spiritual are blended, to a mechanistic world view in which nature is conceptualised as an object to be manipulated and controlled by the human mind and technology. In the organic view, nature is valued and identified as a mother or goddess. In the mechanistic view, it is seen as a machine to be controlled by men. She claims '(T)he removal of animistic, organic assumptions about the cosmos constitute the death of nature' (1980, 193).

Merchant (1980, 1987), and a variety of other writers (for example, Ortner 1974) have pointed out a second way in which 'woman' and 'nature' are linked. Because of their capacity to bear children, women are portrayed as closer to 'nature', while men are linked to 'culture'. By extension, if it is legitimate for men to dominate 'nature', then it is also legitimate for men to dominate women. Commonly-used metaphors for nature reveal the connections between these conceptualisations. Thus nature is portrayed as a 'virgin' to be raped, tamed or possessed. The 'mother' metaphor also continues, with nature portrayed as a fruitful mother who exists to nurture men. Annette Kolodny, analysing literature by male writers about the American West, provides a psychosexual interpretation of the inspiration they have derived from such metaphors. In *The Lay of the Land* (1975), she argues that, like the growing (male) child choosing between independence and maternal dependence, the American (male) literary imagination found itself forced to choose between a landscape that promised total gratification in return for passive and even filial responses but also, apparently, tempted and even invited the more active responses of impregnation, alteration and possession (Kolodny 1975, 71).

Many ecofeminists respond to the devaluation of nature and woman in western thought by advocating conceptualisations that esteem nature as goddess and mother.

They draw a sense of female power from their association with nature, and demonstrate this empowerment in activism against the destruction of the natural environment by male-dominated technologies. Identification as mothers is an important element of a variety of ecofeminist protests. Targets like nuclear power plants, toxic waste dumps and polluted waters are portrayed as threats to the health of their children as well as to the survival of 'Mother Earth' (Merchant 1987). Not all ecofeminists emphasise maternal roles or identification with the earth goddess, however. Some, such as Merchant, base their analyses in the material realm of daily work with its gender divisions of labour. Nevertheless, they too seek new organic metaphors and a consciousness that will reintegrate nature, production and social reproduction, and reconstruct gender relations and human–nature relations in order to attain sustainable life. This is a consciousness that will recognise mutual obligations and interdependence rather than asymmetry and dominance (Merchant 1989).

Third world development is also being reinterpreted by feminist writers seeking alternative metaphors to support new approaches to living with the environment. In *Staying Alive: Women, Ecology, and Development* (1989), Vandana Shiva challenges the tenets of western masculine conceptions of science and development as they are applied to environmental manipulation in the third world. She posits that models that have been represented as embodying universal truths are, in fact, based on assumptions of power, violence, exclusion and reductionism which cast nature as woman, the passive 'other'. Shiva proposes the alternative of the feminine principle embodied in the Hindu deity, Prakriti, which in conjunction with the male principle, Purusha, incorporates a vision of the pursuit of harmony, diversity and sustainability as the key to saving nature and human life. By contrast with the passive woman, Prakriti is an active creative force.

Shiva presents the consequences of the western philosophy and behaviour as disastrous for the daily survival of women, peasants and indigenous peoples. She reviews problems in forestry, agriculture, and the control of water, exploring the ways rural women, such as those in the Chipko movement, have mobilised against the commercial exploitation of forests for lumber and the planting of fast-growing alien species. Instead they support the planting of ecologically appropriate trees that will protect soils and watersheds and sustain life. Shiva characterises these women's ecological struggles as 'new attempts to establish that steadiness and stability are not stagnation, and balance with nature's essential ecological processes is not technological backwardness but technological sophistication' (1989, 36). She sees such efforts to reaffirm the life of nature as essential because '(T)he killing of people by the murder of nature is an invisible form of violence which is today the biggest threat to justice and peace' (1989, 36). For her, liberation of the person and liberation of nature will only be accomplished through integrating such dualisms as male/female and human/natural.

The metaphors women use to relate to the land are not bounded by ecological concerns, however, nor are they concerned solely with countering male visions and domination. Across cultures, women find empowering meanings in the land which validate their own gender identity. They express these meanings in their religious beliefs and rituals, oral and written literatures, and arts. I will provide only a few examples from the writing and art of women of the diverse cultures of the south-western United States, but these examples suggest the richness of such expressions by women and reveal again that gender identity is both culturally varying and that its expressions may be linked to the landscape.

American Indian, Mexican American and Euro-American women writers in the Southwest refer to the land in female terms, but the woman is not a virgin to be raped or tamed nor is she restricted to the identity of mother. In this landscape, the vast spaces and extensive areas that seem free of human domination appear to liberate women from the traditional strictures of femininity that silence their voices. They identify the land as a woman who embodies traits that give them a sense of their own complexity, power and worth. Thus, Euro-American Mary Austin portrays the desert as a strong woman who has not been, and cannot be, mastered. Alice Corbin Henderson sees the land as an old woman, ancient and peaceful, 'Blinking and blind in the sun ... who mumbles her beads/ And crumbles to stone' (quoted in Rudnick 1987, 13). For contemporary Mexican-American Pat Mora, the landscape can also be an old woman, a teacher or *curandera*, the healing, wise woman of her culture, who mediates between human beings and nature and brings power and magic to the woman writer.

The women's visions also reveal a sense of vital female sexuality in an erotically charged energy that emanates from the land. This is most forcefully and consistently exhibited in the writing of American Indian women, who describe women having sexual relationships with the spirit beings that inhabit, and indeed are, the land; they draw personal and cultural sustenance from their encounters. Thus in her collection, *Storyteller*, Leslie Silko tells of Yellow Woman who goes out to rendezvous with the Sun around the time of the Fall equinox:

> She left precise stone rooms
> that hold the heart silently
> She walked past white corn
> hung in low rows from roof beams
> the dry husks rattled in a thin autumn wind.
>
> She left her home
> her clan
> and the people
>   (three small children
>   the youngest just weaned
>   her husband away cutting firewood)
>   (Silko 1981, 64)

Consummation of her relationship with the sun ensures that he will not leave the earth forever locked in winter (Smith with Gunn Allen 1987). This active sense of female sexuality is also clearly revealed in Mexican-American poetry. Pat Mora, for example, writes 'The desert is no lady ... Her unveiled lust fascinates the sun' (quoted in Norwood & Monk 1987, v).

Perhaps most common across the Indian, Mexican-American and Euro-American women are expressions of a sense of integration between self and land, rather than separation. It is pervasive in the Indians' communication with an animate nature, and illustrated by the creations of Euro-American artists Michelle Stuart and Nancy Holt who fuse their physical bodies with the land in the process of creating their works, finding spiritual communion with the land. Stuart, for example, rubs ground rocks and earth onto paper laid on the earth, then polishes the paper with her hand, through this integration allowing the earth to reveal its own patterns (Duvert 1987). Holt, in her work *Sun Tunnels,* a series of concrete pipes placed in the Utah desert in alignment with solar geometry, cuts holes in the pipes to allow the sun to play over the body of the occupant and to permit vision out to the heavens. On seeing the site she chose for the work, Holt felt 'my insides and outsides (come) together for the first time' (quoted in Duvert 1987, 212).

Ultimately, the meanings these women derive from the landscape empower them to survive ('Desert Women', by Pat Mora):

> Desert women know
> about survival.
> Fierce heat and cold
> have burned and thickened
> our skin. Like cactus
> we've learned to hoard,
> to sprout deep roots,
> to seem asleep, yet wake
> at the scent of softness
> in the air, to hide
> pain and loss by silence,
> no branches wail
> or whisper our sad songs
> safe behind our thorns.
>
> Don't be deceived.
> When we bloom, we stun.
> (Mora 1986, 80)

Conclusion

In writing this chapter I have tried to convey that ideologies about gender have shaped the form of landscapes and that representations of gender in the landscape contribute to defining our choices in life and the constraints we confront. Nevertheless, it should be clear from the examples I have incorporated that gender does not function in a simple way as a dichotomy between an essentialist masculine and feminine. Gender roles and relationships are historically and cross-culturally constructed and are mutable. So is their embodiment in the landscape. Culture, class and ethnicity all modify the ways that gender functions in specific times and places. Meaning and power relationships change as contexts and consciousness change.

Insofar as landscapes reflect power relationships, it is clear that patriarchal hegemonies have created spaces and places which deny or devalue women. For many women and increasingly, it appears, for the environment, such dominance has been damaging. But expressions of power do not go unchallenged. Women have found ways to manipulate restrictive landscapes for their own purposes and we have examples of how they have acted to create conditions more amenable to their interests and values. Because women and men draw meaning from landscapes, and use them in expressing their senses of personal and collective identity, landscapes can also empower people to creativity and action, to develop cultural alternatives that might contribute to the making of a sustainable and more socially equitable environment.

Note

I appreciate the assistance of Amy W. Newhall and Barbara Morehouse with the research for this chapter, and the clerical help of Mary Contreras and Roxane Martell Jones.

References

Benson, E.F. 1985 (1930), *As We Were: A Victorian Peep-Show*, Hogarth Press, London.

Breitbart, M. 1990, 'Quality housing for women and children', *Canadian Woman Studies*, 11, 2, pp. 19–24.

Coutras, J. 1987, *Des Villes Traditionelles aux Nouvelles Banlieues,* SEDES, Paris.

Cranz, G. 1981, 'Women in urban parks', in C.R. Stimpson, E. Dixler, M. Nelson, & K.B. Yatrakis (eds), *Women in the American City*, University of Chicago Press, Chicago, pp. 76–92.

Duvert, E. 1987, 'With stone, star, and earth: the presence of the archaic in the landscape visions of Georgia O'Keeffe, Nancy Holt, and Michelle Stuart', in V. Norwood & J. Monk (eds), *The Desert Is No Lady: Southwestern Landscapes in Women's Writing and Art*, Yale University Press, New Haven, pp. 197–222.

Enloe, C. 1990, *Bananas, Beaches and Bases: Making Feminist Sense of International Politics*, University of California Press, Berkeley.

Friedan, B. 1963, *The Feminine Mystique*, Norton, New York.

Gittell, M. & Shtob, T. 1981, 'Changing women's roles in political volunteerism and reform of the city', in C.R. Stimpson, E. Dixler, M. Nelson, & K.B. Yatrakis (eds), *Women in the American City*, University of Chicago Press, Chicago, pp. 64–75.

Gross, S.H. & Rojas, M.H. 1986, *But Women Have No History!: Images of Women in the Public History of Washington DC,* Glenhurst Publications, Inc., St Louis Park, Minnesota.

Hayden, D. 1981, *The Grand Domestic Revolution: A History of Feminist Designs for American Homes, Neighborhoods, and Cities,* MIT Press, Cambridge.

Hayden, D. 1984, *Redesigning the American Dream: The Future of Housing, Work, and Family Life*, W.W. Norton & Company, New York.

Huyck, H. 1990, personal communication (National Park Service, US Department of Interior, Washington DC).

Inglis, K. 1989, 'Men, women and war memorials: Anzac Australia', in J.K. Conway, S.C. Bourque & J.W. Scott (eds), *Learning About Women: Gender, Politics, and Power*, University of Michigan Press, Ann Arbor, pp. 35–59.

Khatib-Chahidi, J. 1981, 'Sexual prohibitions, shared space and fictive marriages in Shi'ite Iran', in S. Ardener (ed.), *Women and Space: Ground Rules and Social Maps*, St Martin's Press, New York, pp. 112–35.

Klodawsky, F. & Mackenzie, S. 1987, 'Gender sensitive theory and the housing needs of mother-led families: Some concepts and some buildings', *Feminist Perspectives Feministes*, no. 9, Canadian Research Institute for the Advancement of Women, Ottawa.

Kolodny, A. 1975, *The Lay of the Land: Metaphor as Experience and History in American Life and Letters*, University of North Carolina Press, Chapel Hill.

Mackenzie, S. 1987, 'Neglected spaces in peripheral places: homeworkers and the creation of a new economic centre', *Cahiers de Geographie du Quebec*, 31, pp. 247–60.

Mackenzie, S. & Rose, D. 1983, 'Industrial change, the domestic economy, and home life', in J. Anderson, S. Duncan, & R. Hudson (eds), *Redundant Spaces in Cities and Regions,* Academic Press, New York, pp. 155–200.

Matrix 1984, *Making Space: Women and the Man Made Environment*, Pluto Press, London.

McDowell, L. 1983, 'Towards an understanding of the gender division of urban space', *Environment and Planning D: Society and Space*, 1, pp. 59–72.

Merchant, C. 1980, *The Death of Nature: Women, Ecology, and the Scientific Revolution*, Harper & Row, San Francisco.

Merchant, C. 1984, 'Women of the progressive conservation movement, 1900-1916', *Environmental Review*, 8, 1, pp. 57–85.

Merchant, C. 1987, 'Ecofeminism', *New Internationalist,* 18-19 May.

Merchant, C. 1989, *Ecological Revolutions: Nature, Gender, and Science in New England*, University of North Carolina Press, Chapel Hill.

Michelson, W. 1977, *Environmental Choice, Human Behavior, and Residential Satisfaction*, Oxford University Press, New York.

Mies, M. 1982, 'The dynamics of the sexual division of labor and the integration of women into the world market', in L. Beneria (ed.), *Women and Development: The Sexual Division of Labor in Rural Societies,* Praeger, New York, pp. 1–28.

Miller, R. 1983, 'The Hoover® in the garden: middle-class women and suburbanization, 1850-1920', *Environment and Planning D: Society and Space*, 1, pp. 73–88.

Monk, J. & Hanson, S. 1982, 'On not excluding half of the human in human geography', *The Professional Geographer*, 34, 1, pp. 11–23.

Mora, P. 1986, *Borders*, Arte Publico Press, University of Houston, Houston.

Muller, P. 1981, *Contemporary Suburban America*, Prentice Hall, Englewood Cliffs, NJ.

Nelson, K. 1986, 'Labor demand, labor supply, and the suburbanization of low-wage office work', in A.J. Scott & M. Storper (eds), *Production, Work, Territory*, Allen & Unwin, Boston, pp. 149–71.

Norwood, V. & Monk, J. 1987, *The Desert Is No Lady: Southwestern Landscapes in Women's Writing and Art,* Yale University Press, New Haven.

Ortner, S.B. 1974, 'Is female to male as nature is to culture?', in M.Z. Rosaldo & L. Lamphere (eds), *Woman, Culture, and Society*, Stanford University Press, Stanford, CA, pp. 67–88.

Pollock, N.L. 1981, 'Women on the inside: divisions of space in Imperial China', *Heresies*, 11, 3, 3, pp. 34–37.

Pratt, G. 1990, 'On the reproduction of academic discourse: class and the spatial structure of the city', paper presented at the annual meeting of the Association of American Geographers, Toronto.

Rock, C., Torre, S. & Wright, G. 1980, 'The appropriation of the house: changes in housing design and concepts of domesticity', in G. Wekerle, R. Peterson & D. Morley (eds), *New Space for Women*, Westview Press, Boulder, pp. 83–100.

Rosenblum, R. & Janson, H.W. 1984, *Nineteenth Century Art,* Prentice Hall and Harry N. Abrams, Inc., Englewood Cliffs, NJ and New York.

Rudnick, L. 1987, 'Re-naming the land: Anglo expatriate women in the Southwest', in V. Norwood & J. Monk (eds), *The Desert Is No Lady: Southwestern Landscapes in Women's Writing and Art*, Yale University Press, New Haven, pp. 10–26.

Scharff, V. 1988, 'Of parking spaces and women's places: the Los Angeles parking ban of 1920', *National Women's Studies Association Journal*, 1, pp. 37–51.

Shiva, V. 1989, *Staying Alive: Women, Ecology, and Development*, Zed Books, London.

Silko, L. 1981, *Storyteller*, Seaver Books, New York.

Smith, P. with Gunn Allen, P. 1987, 'Earthy relations, carnal knowledge: southwestern American Indian women writers and landscape', in V. Norwood & J. Monk (eds), *The Desert Is No Lady: Southwestern Landscapes in Women's Writing and Art*, Yale University Press, New Haven, pp. 174–96.

Vaught, W.L. n.d., letter soliciting donations to the Women in Military Service For America Memorial Foundation, Inc.

Wagner, P.K. 1984, 'Suburban landscapes for nuclear families: the case of Greenbelt towns in the United States', *Built Environment*, 10, 1, pp. 35–41.

Warner, M. 1985, *Monuments and Maidens: The Allegory of the Female Form*, Weidenfeld & Nicolson, London.

Watson, S. 1989, 'Social spatial connections', in D. Modjeska (ed.), *Inner Cities: Australian Women's Memory of Place*, Penguin Books, Melbourne, pp. 7–13.

Wekerle, G.R. 1981, 'Women house themselves', *Heresies*, 11, 3, 3, pp. 14–16.

'Women in war' 1990, *Arizona Daily Star*, 12 November, A9.

9 The construction and deconstruction of women's roles in the urban landscape

Hilary Winchester

Introduction

This chapter examines the evidence in the urban landscape for the social construction of women's roles. The methodology combines radical feminist theory with the post-modernist technique of deconstruction. Radical feminist theory locates the oppression of women in the power structures of capitalism and patriarchy. These power structures constitute the dominant hegemony in contemporary Australian society, which constructs spaces to reflect and reinforce its own ideologies. These underlying ideologies are often masked by different layers of meaning in the landscape.

The study area is the city of Wollongong in New South Wales. The urban landscape of two contrasted areas of the city is critically examined. The mall in the central city is a landscape created in the 1980s by and for powerful societal structures. In contrast, the northern suburb of Bellambi, a landscape of public housing, is marginal to the dominant hegemony of capitalism and patriarchy. In both landscapes, the roles of women are deliberately constructed. This chapter attempts to deconstruct those landscapes by examining the layers of meaning contained within them.

'Reading' the landscape

Reading the landscape is a facet of cultural geography which has a long-standing tradition but which is undergoing resurgence through the influence of post-modernism. The tradition of studying landscape stems from work early this century when the Berkeley school of American cultural geographers recognised that waves of human occupation left distinct traces on the natural environment. In this traditional view, the human or cultural landscape was seen to consist of layers of interpretable artefacts, each related to a historical phase of occupation. These layers would not necessarily be easy to decipher, as, like layers of sediment, some would be covered completely, while others would be eroded. Nonetheless the landscape was viewed as a palimpsest, a scroll of parchment which had been etched time and again, with the traces of what went before still visible to those who cared to look. Culture was seen as a primary agent in the shaping of the landscape and regional differentiation as a reflection of cultural differences.

The resurgence of interest in the landscape stems from the ideas of post-modernism which have been absorbed into mainstream geography from about the mid 1980s. A key element in the methodology of post-modernism is that of deconstruction (Dear 1986). A landscape may be read in the same way as a text may be read; the layers of meaning within it may be dissected and analysed (Duncan & Duncan 1988). This technique, when combined with the study of semiotics, the language of signs, helps to unravel the cultural significance of a landscape. Geographers now increasingly recognise the importance of powerful individuals and organisations as agents shaping the landscape. So, for example, the appearance of a city's central business district (CBD) reveals not only the importance of commerce in contemporary post-industrial culture, but is a visible expression of the power of large multinational corporations, the size and shape of the buildings themselves constituting obvious symbols of dominance.

Many approaches within post-war human geography stress the role of human agency, where people are not passive, but actively shape their environment. Some post-modernists would also consider that differing interpretations of the same landscape may be of equal validity. A landscape may be viewed in different ways by different people, with the central business district being a place of power and prestige for some high-status business people, but a meeting place or place of work for others, and a place of fear and avoidance for women at night. Each person or group views, uses and constructs the same landscape in different ways; these are neither 'right' nor 'wrong', but rather are part of the many layers of meaning within one landscape. The landscape has layers of artefacts which may derive from historical usage; it also has layers of meaning which stem from the multiple uses of the same environment.

The urban cultural landscapes of Australia can be understood with reference to their historical development; their architecture reflects the influence of a number of immigrant groups. Hence the architecture of older Australian cities forms an intricate combination of British terraced houses, Italianate decoration, American sprawl and Australian verandahs and iron lacework, a combination which provides clues in the landscape to our present and former culture (see NSW Department of Housing and Construction 1980). However, it is also possible to move beyond this architectural specificity to examine the cultural significance of some of the ordinary features of the urban landscape. Ordinary features such as motels and garages are cultural indicators as much as the more prominent landmarks such as the Sydney Harbour Bridge and the Opera House (Lewis 1979). A logical development of the post-modernist tenet that every person's view is equally valid is that every landscape artefact is equally significant.

Many urban landscapes are deliberately constructed to reflect societal structures. This is clearly seen in the location of churches on hilltops, where the elevation of the church reflects the superiority of the sacred over the secular. Other examples occur with the control of building heights and sizes for people in different levels of the social hierarchy (White 1984, 3-15). Landscape serves not only to reflect societal structures but also to reify them, in other words it sets them in concrete and makes them real (see Anderson 1987; Duncan & Duncan 1988). If social hierarchies are embodied in bricks and mortar, not only do they become real, they become accepted as part of everyday life and as part of the natural order. Often, urban landscapes are created by powerful agents whose interests are served by establishing such a reality.

Powerful agents creating the landscape may make use of particular techniques to promulgate a natural order; the techniques include the processes of domination and legitimation. Domination may involve the taking of prime space, the control of space or the creation of space in such a way as to effect control. Legitimation may involve the use of other power or authority to validate this control. Both processes may involve symbols, myths and subconscious associations to establish that domination and legitimation. Two Sydney examples may clarify these ideas of legitimation and domination. The redevelopment of Darling Harbour from a derelict dockland area to a multipurpose place of consumerism, complete with shops, restaurants, museums and an exhibition and conference centre occurred during the 1980s. This space was dominated by the New South Wales state government, which created a special body, the Darling Harbour Authority, in order to circumvent existing planning controls. Its creation of prime space was legitimised by marketing the project to New South Wales as 'a Bicentennial gift to the nation' (Huxley & Kerkin 1988). The second example is the construction of the Sydney Tower, which dominates the skyline of the Sydney CBD. The Tower was deliberately constructed to symbolise Sydney's 'coming of age' as a world city, and to become in itself a symbol of Sydney, as the Eiffel Tower has become a symbol of Paris (Morris 1982). The structure of the Tower on top of 'Centrepoint' is an obvious symbol of domination because of its height, its visual distinctiveness and its name. The AMP Society, a major finance company which built the Tower, legitimised the consumerism of the Centrepoint shopping centre by the construction of a myth which became a tourist attraction. The Tower thereby becomes imbued with layers of meaning, as the 'heart of the city', as the 'city come of age', as Sydney itself and as a technological and educational experience. These layers of meaning both disguise and legitimate the Tower's purpose in extracting consumer dollars from visitors and tourists.

Feminist geography

This chapter brings together two important new threads in human geography; ideas from post-modernist deconstruction of the landscape and from feminist geography. Post-modernism and the new cultural geography focus attention on the many layers of meaning in and the multiple uses of cultural landscapes. Feminism in geography has focused attention on women both as geographers and as the subject of study. Recent feminist geography has developed from a study of 'women and geography' to a consideration of gender roles and gender relations. Feminist geography has moved through a number of overlapping phases — liberal feminism, Marxist feminism and radical feminism. Initial liberal feminist studies in the early 1980s were concerned with drawing attention to the invisibility of women; Monk and Hanson (1982) argued that women were excluded from human geography because their roles and experiences were either assumed to be the same as men's, in other words that studies were gender-blind, or were assumed to conform to a stereotype, usually of women as mothers and unpaid housekeepers. Such considerations helped to raise the consciousness of gender issues within geography, and to bring women's concerns, such as the provision of childcare, into the content of human geography.

A second phase of feminist geography, which draws on Marxism, has examined gender roles, that is the socially constructed roles taken by women and men. Marxism considers that status roles are determined by an individual's relationship to the mode of economic production, either as capital or labour. Marxist feminists consider that there are important differences between women's and men's views and experiences of labour. There are three fundamental differences, one being that women are often segregated into low-paid, insecure and low-status occupations in the paid labour force; they are greatly overrepresented in caring and clerical jobs. A second difference is that women are not only engaged in production but also in reproduction, and much of their work consists of unpaid labour in the home (see Bowlby 1990). A third difference is that part of women's reproductive role in caring for families involves them as primary consumers (Bondi & Peake 1988). Women therefore have more complex relationships to capital as producers, reproducers, and consumers, whereas men's relationship to capital is primarily as producers. There is also a clear male dominance in the ownership of capital.

Recent developments in radical feminist geography emphasise not only gender roles but gender relations which, like class relations, are based on power structures within society. Patriarchy is a system characterised by power, dominance and competition which historically has ascribed power to men and dependence to women. The oppression of women can best be understood when their relations to both capitalism and patriarchy are explicitly considered (see Gibson 1990).

Powerful agents within society construct space in a way which reflects the structure of power. This is true for gender as well as for the differences between sacred and secular, rich and poor. Feminist geographers have examined the ways in which space is constructed by patriarchal interests and used by women and men. Patriarchal spaces reflect the power of men and range from the CBD to the boardroom. Women's spaces are more often confined, especially to the suburbs and to domestic space (see Allport 1986; Johnson 1989, 1990). The suburbs are occupied by women in their reproductive role of caring for families; women are often disadvantaged in these areas and isolated from transport and services (Allport 1986). Spaces and places which are apparently for everyone and nominally gender-neutral are more likely in practice to be male spaces. This is true, for example, of spaces ranging from surfing beaches to the central city at night (Valentine 1989). Johnson (1990) argues that even in houses, which are seen as women's spaces, men may have their own inviolate places such as studies or garden sheds, whereas women have family rooms and 'dream kitchens' from which other people can be less easily excluded. In many ways, therefore, space may be considered to be 'not only gendered, but also patriarchal' (Johnson 1990, 21).

This chapter examines the levels of meaning evident in some of the ordinary landscapes of the city of Wollongong, New South Wales. Wollongong is a city of approximately 250 000 people, the centre of the urban Illawarra, located about 80 km (50 miles) south of Sydney. It is a city based on coal and steel, but undergoing forced restructuring as the industrial base is eroded. Two areas are examined, a landscape of patriarchal and economic power, which is the newly constructed mall in the central business district, and a landscape of relative powerlessness, the suburb of Bellambi, which is widely recognised as a 'problem' residential area (fig. 9.1). The construction, use and cultural significance of each area is examined, with a particular focus on the ideology of gender, its connection to power (the mall) and powerlessness (Bellambi), and its intersection with capitalism and patriarchy.

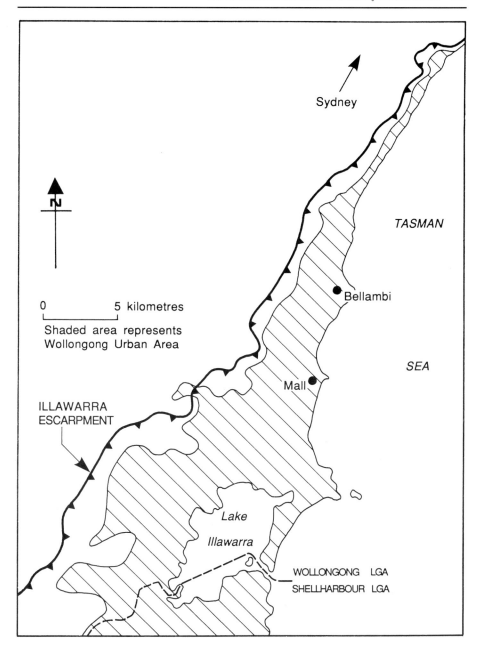

Figure 9.1: Wollongong urban area, showing the location of Wollongong City Mall and Bellambi.

'Reading' Wollongong Mall

The Wollongong Mall was opened on 20 October 1986 at a cost of $34 million as a joint venture between Wollongong City Council and a Sydney firm of developers, Kern Corporation. The mall was designed to improve the retailing facilities of the city centre

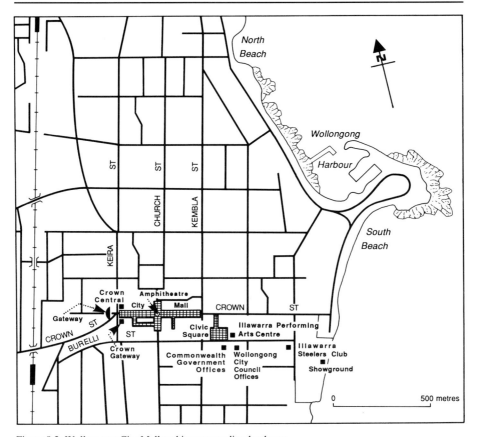

Figure 9.2: Wollongong City Mall and its surrounding land uses.

(Wollongong City Council 1982). The investment was to boost the city's economy after a period of severe local depression in the early 1980s (Schultz 1985). Wollongong has traditionally suffered from an underprovision of services of all kinds because of its reputation as an industrial city and as a Labor stronghold, and because of its proximity to Sydney (Robinson 1977). The mall was therefore also designed to remedy these historical legacies, and particularly to stop escape spending to Sydney, then estimated at around $17 million per year.

The mall was formed within the existing central business district by the pedestrianisation of Crown Street between Keira and Kembla Streets, and of a number of small lanes in the vicinity (fig. 9.2). The mall contains two major anchor stores, David Jones and Grace Bros, at the western (Keira Street) end, and a large number of smaller shops, banks and services. The two anchor stores each control a major arcade of shops, Crown Central and Crown Gateway respectively, and there are a number of other smaller and less successful arcades at the eastern end of the mall. Crown Gateway is the most luxurious of the arcades, with small luxury shops on the top floor and specialty food outlets on the lower ground floor. Crown Central, adjacent to David Jones, is a more mundane shopping centre with discount stores, a market day on Wednesdays, and more fast food and low-order stores, such as newsagents and confectioners' shops.

The heart of the mall consists of only the western block. This block is made distinctive by its architecture and by obvious landmarks constructed at either end. The Keira Street end is symbolically sealed from the noisy traffic of the Princes Highway by a very large pink illuminated gateway which acts as a shield to separate the workaday world outside from the 'consumer paradise' inside. The other end of the heart of the mall is at the former intersection of Crown and Church Streets, where a small raised covered stage has been constructed and rather grandiosely termed the 'amphitheatre' (fig. 9.2). Hilly Church Street to the north is paved with many steps, forming an area for people to gather and watch the entertainment provided. This is an area for display, entertainment and fashion parades, and is a real and symbolic meeting place, with a small children's playground to the east and an oversized chessboard to the south. Between the gateway and the amphitheatre the paved area of the heart of the mall is set beneath huge arches of steel supporting a domed steel mesh canopy, beneath which are draped great sails of canvas. This domed structure, painted a greenish blue, unifies the two sides of the former Crown Street and forms an area which is visually and architecturally distinctive.

The heart of the mall may be interpreted on several levels. At first glance, there is little difference between Wollongong Mall and similar structures elsewhere, whether in Cronulla or Coffs Harbour. However, at a symbolic level, the mall structures are evocative of Wollongong's past, present and future. The steel supports are indicative of the steel backbone of Wollongong's industrial heritage. The arches and dome have become part of Wollongong, replicated in the City Council's own notices and in the design of the Steelers' Club completed in 1990. The mall also indicates the future of the city. The celestial arches and the canvas sails invoke images of sky and flight, of sea and sailing. The eye is channelled by the arches and the amphitheatre towards the ocean beyond the eastern end. From the amphitheatre to Kembla Street is a vista created by arcades of palm trees, paving and fountains of running water. The industrial past looks to the future of the city at the heart of the Leisure Coast; the present is poised between the two. Wollongong City Council in 1989-90 renovated the area around Wollongong Harbour and North Beach; when combined with new developments at the Showground, the home of the Illawarra Steelers' Rugby League Football Club at the ocean end of Crown Street, these will physically link the mall to the recreation and leisure facilities planned for the city in the early 1980s (Wollongong City Council 1982) (fig. 9.2).

The mall as a setting of consumerism

A further level of interpretation is that Wollongong Mall is a symbol of western consumer society. The mall serves as an improved retailing facility for the city, and is located close to new and impressive City Council offices, the Illawarra Performing Arts Centre and Commonwealth government offices (fig. 9.2). The design of the governmental area continues the architectural theme of the mall with brick paving, foliage and archways. It may be argued that the close association of the mall with the offices of the local state provides a powerful legitimation function for consumerism. The mall is one of Wollongong City Council's proudest achievements in the restructuring of the city.

Consumer activity within areas such as the mall is disguised by including other layers of meaning within the landscape. Consumerism is overlaid with different associations by the use of signs and symbols. Two illusions are clearly embodied in the construction

Figure 9.3: The gateway to the mall looking east from Crown Street. The gateway is a real and symbolic entrance to the 'shopping paradise' of the mall. To the left, some of the formidable blank walls of the exterior of the mall can be seen.

of the landscape. The first is the idea of the mall as a paradise for shopping. The use of street furniture, lighting, advertising and the display of goods for sale is designed not only to make shopping easier and more comfortable but also to encourage spending. The gateway to the mall is not only a real but a symbolic entrance (fig. 9.3). The massive blank walls of the outside of the mall in Keira and Burelli Streets are reminiscent of the walls of the fortress that the shopper (heroine) must scale in order to obtain the 'promised land' of Grace Bros and David Jones. Once inside the gates, the music, foliage, arches and seating suggest that the struggle to attain the mall has indeed been worthwhile (fig. 9.4). The lavish piles of goods in the shops offer a veritable cornucopia, a vision of bounty. Yet the mall has a tension induced by the crowding of the street furniture and the enclosure of the steel birdcage. Paradise, to be worth achieving, has to be worth

Figure 9.4: Shoppers and housewives: women shopping in Wollongong Mall. The reality of women as consumers does not always match the image of women depicted in the shops. Note the arches and foliage of the mall interior.

competing for. If the mall is paradise, then the shopper is the pilgrim (Miner 1989). The repellent outside walls and the creation of tension within are apparently paradoxical. They are a representation of the idea that good results are only achieved by struggle. The symbolism draws on the idea of a soul (pilgrim) overcoming difficulties to reach heaven (paradise). The pink gateway to the mall is symbolic of the entrance to paradise. The shopper is cast in the role of pilgrim struggling towards the good things and just rewards to be found in the mall, which appears as paradise.

The second illusion which obscures the consumerist function of the mall is that the mall is an entertainment and social centre. The amphitheatre symbolises these functions. Many large sites of consumerism are able to overlay elements of fantasy and elsewhereness into their landscape (Hopkins 1990) although this exotica is much less developed in Wollongong than in larger and more prestigious consumption sites. Darling Harbour, for example, has a 'Disneyfied' landscape, with toy trains used as 'people movers', a fun fair and street artists. Wollongong Mall has few elements of fantasy and elsewhere, but is nonetheless promoted as a social centre and meeting place, indicated by the amphitheatre, children's playground and chessboard. Not only does the social function encourage people to linger and to spend, but it imbues shopping with a whole new set of associations. Shopping is presented as a pleasurable activity linked to entertainment and social interaction. The mall is presented as a contribution to lifestyle and to the image of the city. Consumerism (shopping) is legitimated by these layers of meaning.

The social function of the mall is to a great extent illusory. The meeting place is effectively not public space, but is heavily controlled by City Council Ordinance officers, police and private security firms. People using the mall for non-conforming, non-consuming purposes may be moved on for loitering, especially if they are unlicensed vendors or buskers or are perceived to be trouble-makers. In these ways the mall is an expression of the dominance not only of the consumer ideal, but of the type of consumerism which is authorised and legitimated. This expression of domination and legitimation is in many ways more subtle than the crude phallic symbols (Short 1989) of the modernist central business district.

Shoppers, housewives and fashion-plates: women's roles and the consumer ideal

The discussion of the mall as a landscape of power has considered so far the elements within it which have been built to reinforce the ideology of consumerism. This chapter now turns to an examination of the gender roles and expectations built into the landscape. The main participants in and targets of consumer activity are women. Shops in prime sites and major stores focus on women's fashion and clothing. The emphasis on women's consumption goods varies a little according to the time of the year, and can reach ridiculous heights around the consumer birthday of Mother's Day. Miner (1989) reports that one mall in New South Wales had to be closed temporarily because of the crush and hysteria brought about by shop assistants in period costume giving away flowers and perfume one Mother's Day. Prime sites focus much less attention on male fashion and clothing. Chapman (1988, 229) considers that 'the young male market had always been considered difficult to crack, because shopping and consuming had traditionally been regarded as female activities and thus incompatible with masculinity'.

The focus on women as consumers is a part of a complex patriarchal/capitalist structure. Bondi and Peake (1988, 25) argue that 'issues of consumption do have a particular salience for women'. The focus on women as consumers is important in two major respects. First, despite their relatively low individual incomes, they are often the major purchasers of goods not only for themselves but also for other members of their households (Game & Pringle 1983, 124). Women in their roles as wives and mothers are often the people who spend most time and money shopping and are therefore the main target for marketing. Women's role in consumption is underpinned by the ideology of women's caring role and a particular ideology of motherhood; Bowlby (1988, 62) considers that 'an important element in our present-day conception of womanhood and of female sexuality is the idea that women should love, nurture and tend their men and children' (see also Reiger 1991, 50). Secondly, women are consumers not only as nurturers but also as objects of sexuality and beautification. The focus of prime-site stores on female fashion indicates and perpetuates the notion of the woman as adornment, a decorative adjunct to the real business of the city which is conducted by men.

Although women may consume for their households as well as for themselves, the image of women projected in the shop displays rarely suggests any note of domesticity. Indeed the image of women presented in the shop fronts seems to conform to one of two stereotypes. The shops which sell jeans, cheaper clothing and shoes project a young sporty image. It is no surprise to find that all the models are tall, slim, young and white, but the image goes beyond these physical attributes to project a lifestyle of sport and fitness, fun, excitement, youth, vitality and independence. The more expensive shops and department stores present a more upmarket stereotype. The models are still tall, slim, young and white, but the ideal portrayed is the independent business or professional woman with taste, style and money. Women with dependent children, or who are over size fourteen or age forty, have no place in these projections. Even a specialty store catering for the 'large and elegant' seems to stress the elegance in the window and the largeness on the racks. In both stereotypes the image is one of independence and control rather than dependence and domesticity.

The image of independence is belied by many of the shop window displays. At the time of research in 1990, three fashion stores displayed women in either of the above modes, but in one case clad also in chain mail, in another hemmed in with wire, and in a third draped around fake animal skins. The message is clear if the observer cares to read it. Women's independence is illusory; women's fashion is not just an adornment but a construction to restrict women to a given role and a given image. Capitalism and patriarchy are here closely interlinked. A key element in this link is advertising. However, women's views do not necessarily conform to those of the advertisers. Game and Pringle (1983, 124) have pointed out that women often view shopping as work and pride themselves on their good economic sense in doing it successfully. Other women elect to wear self-styled clothing, and some weave their own.

At the time of research, there were only two obvious references to families in and around the mall. Woolworths' supermarket in adjacent Burelli Street dubs itself a 'Family Centre'. This is a realistic assessment of its role as a prosaic supplier of weekly provisions. However, it has no other obvious family connotations or services, except a coffee shop and home delivery of goods. There is not even a toilet, and certainly no mothers' room or short-term childcare. The other reference to families was an advertisement by a major bank for mortgages for a dream home, illustrated as a detached house with a white picket fence occupied by a family of Dad, Mum, child and dog. This imagery reflects other powerful ideologies of the owner-occupied house on the quarter-acre block (Kemeny 1986; Watson 1988). However, despite the importance of this form of housing for consumption, for example cars, consumer durables and white goods, the family forms little part of the consumer image. The advertisements for home and family-based consumption stress independence rather than dependence, the exciting rather than the mundane, just as the built environment offers fantasy and elsewhere rather than ordinariness and domesticity.

The majority of mall users are women (fig. 9.4). Student estimates made in 1990 revealed a 60:40 majority of women throughout most weekdays. The proportion of men was higher than anticipated. This may relate to the changing distribution of domestic duties within the household, but may be inflated in Wollongong by an unemployment rate (10 per cent in 1990) significantly above the average for New South Wales (7 per cent in 1990), and by the relatively high proportions of men engaged in shift work. The only area of the mall where men were in the majority was in the vicinity of the chessboard, used exclusively by older men of southern and eastern European origin.

The women using the mall conformed only in part to the image portrayed in the shops. Relatively few seemed to be tall, slim and white, unsurprising given the mixed age and ethnic composition of Wollongong's population (27 per cent overseas-born in the 1986 census). During the day, many were older women past retirement age, but there were also women of middle age who were least likely to be employed in the paid labour force. Younger women, some of whom were tall and slim, hardly conformed to the set image as they grappled with bags, strollers and preschool children. Other women, fitting shopping into the working day, conformed more to the stereotypical image. On Saturdays, women were more often seen with their families.

The mall is a cultural landscape that with the sanction of the state was built by capital interests to encourage consumerism. The landscape also incorporates significant patriarchal elements. It is a landscape which relies on women's domestic role but does not overtly recognise it. Women are targeted as consumers because of their ascribed gender role, but the mundane realities of household provisioning are hidden by layers of meaning in the landscape. In this landscape the woman is treated as an object and adornment while being offered an illusion of control and independence. The landscape reifies women's culturally constructed roles, and in subtle and unsubtle ways reinforces behaviour which conforms to the capitalist and patriarchal norm.

Women also act as agents in the landscape. Of course, women in many ways benefit from the improved retail and entertainment facilities in the mall, as shopping becomes more pleasant (if no less of a chore). Moreover, women can attempt to ignore the illusions of the mall, and instead use it for comparative shopping. It is also possible to resist the image by buying goods different from the mass-produced norm, although some may argue that these goods are merely part of the product differentiation and niche marketing rampant in the economic system of flexible accumulation. Thus it may be possible to resist the pressures of a patriarchal culture but almost impossible to avoid consumerism.

'Reading' Bellambi estate

Bellambi is one of the older residential suburbs of Wollongong, approximately 7 km (4.3 miles) north of the mall. The suburb grew up as a small town around Taylor and Walker's mine which was opened in 1861, and its fortunes in the nineteenth century closely followed those of the coal mining industry. Further development in the Bellambi-Corrimal area occurred with rapid post-war immigration from southern Europe. In the early 1970s, Bellambi was chosen as the site of a large new Housing Commission estate. During the period 1945-71, the NSW Housing Commission built 8858 houses and 722 flats in the Illawarra, but of these, only 117 were in Bellambi (Robinson 1977).

The development of the Bellambi Housing Commission estate began in 1972, on 67.5 ha (167 acres) of land between Cawley Road and the ocean, at a cost of about $8 million. The original estate comprised a total of 695 dwelling units and aimed to provide housing for between 2500 and 3000 people (*Illawarra Mercury,* 10 May 1972). The next development, in 1973, was the construction of six single-storey blocks of units for aged people, providing twenty-six bed-sitting units. Since this time, the estate has spread further, with a variety of housing types, including two and three-bedroom houses, townhouses and units. The suburb at the 1986 census contained 691 dwellings rented from the Housing Commission, comprising 53 per cent of the housing stock, by far the highest concentration in a city in which only 10 per cent of housing overall is rented from government agencies.

Bellambi is a place of powerlessness largely as a result of the concentration of public housing in the area. King (1986) has argued that public housing has increasingly become welfare housing and is a residual and declining sector of the housing stock. It has become a terminal housing sector for a large group of people who will never be able to afford the culturally-defined ideal of owner-occupation. The occupation of housing constructed by the state is in itself an indication of marginalisation from the capitalist system.

The stigma of a Bellambi address is somewhat surprising considering the nature and physical environment of the estate. The estate consists mainly of townhouses, which are of pleasant outward appearance if somewhat cramped by Australian standards (fig. 9.5). The original pensioner units have deteriorated and are cold and uncarpeted, although their inadequacies are not very obvious from outside or in summer. Nonetheless, Bellambi has been described as 'Hell Town' and 'Lego Land', and has received much unfavourable publicity which the residents are attempting to overturn (*Advertiser*, 19 April 1989). The whole estate is close to the ocean, with some of the Housing Commission (now Department of Housing) houses fronting the sweep of Bellambi Beach with views to the dramatic coastline of the northern Illawarra. The stigma derives not from the natural environment but from the culturally constructed landscape. The stigma of the area arises from its industrial past, which stimulated the construction of public housing, which in turn reified the existing stigma.

The current land use of Bellambi renders the suburb a marginal area occupied by people who are relatively powerless (Winchester & White 1988). The area is of potential value for private housing redevelopment, a value which is being realised at new subdivisions to the north. The suburb also has potential value in its reservoir of labour, as many residents are unemployed or unable to enter the paid labour force. However, at present, the area is of little concern to those in power who represent the cultural hegemony of capitalism and patriarchy. Unlike that of the mall, the landscape bears no imposing public landmarks. Bellambi has no equivalent to the pink gateway or the amphitheatre. The rows of small and shabby terraced houses are a physical reality which themselves symbolise alienation from the property-owning classes. Attempts to renovate the physical environment have recently been organised by the Healthy Cities Illawarra organisation; these improvements include trees, parks, playgrounds and a beach clean-up (*Advertiser*, 19 April 1989). Nonetheless, the built environment constructed by the NSW government expresses a form of dominance and oppression which cannot be fundamentally altered by cosmetic improvements, and which requires no other legitimation.

The community of Bellambi has succeeded in acquiring some services in the area, although these were provided several years after the construction of the estate. In 1980, a government grant of $17 500 was awarded to meet half the costs of construction of an amenities block at Bellambi Point. This formed part of an employment scheme for

Figure 9.5: Medium density public housing in Bellambi. These houses front Bellambi beach.

young people and was designed to help alleviate youth unemployment in the area. The block, adjacent to the rock pool and surf beach, still stands but the amenities have been totally torn out and vandalised, the walls are covered with graffiti and the floor with excrement. Youth unemployment at the 1986 census stood at over 40 per cent for the suburb. The other major facility provided has been the Bellambi Neighbourhood Centre, opened in 1987 and funded jointly by Wollongong City Council, the NSW Department of Housing and the Department of Family and Community Services. This centre provides a variety of services and activities, functions as a drop-in centre, and provides adult education, childcare, coffee mornings, crafts, video nights and as many other services as it can on a limited budget. A number of residents expressed reservations about using the centre, however, considering that it catered for mainly the 'rougher element' in the suburb.

Gender roles and marginal space

The gender roles and expectations built into the landscape differ markedly between the relatively powerless area of Bellambi and the mall. In Bellambi, the overall power structures of state and economy are superimposed over the assumptions and images of gender. The suburb, as with the majority of Australian suburbs, consists mainly of single-family housing. There are a few units for single people, originally designed for the elderly but now used as open housing and occupied by a variety of tenants including former psychiatric patients and young homeless people. Apart from these few units, the single-family housing provides little flexibility for changing household size and composition (Watson 1988). The construction of such housing, with very few alternative facilities such as laundries or cafes, inevitably necessitates the multiplication of domestic work usually undertaken by women (Hayden 1980). This domestic role of women is the very aspect which is ignored by the consumerist power brokers as being too mundane to form part of the social construction of consumer sites.

It has been argued for many years that the construction of low-density urban residential areas with sprawling housing far removed from facilities reflects a particular social construction of the family (see Allport 1986). The assumption involves a breadwinner (normally male) who goes out to work, and a carer (normally female) who works unpaid within the domestic environment, raising children and keeping house. The zoning of separate land uses, the separation of home and work, and the paucity of public transport and childcare effectively lead many women into that role. In this way, the built environment not only reflects the prevailing ideology of the family and gender roles, but reproduces those beliefs.

The cultural enclosure of women into domestic life is very marked in a low-income, working-class suburb. The housing in Bellambi is a long distance from employment and shops, while public transport and childcare is limited and expensive (Winchester 1992). Moreover, the welfare nature of the housing and the increasing feminisation of poverty have resulted in a preponderance of female tenants, many of whom are lone parents (Winchester 1990). These women, with sole day-to-day responsibility for bringing up a family, lack job opportunities, transport and childcare, and consequently may opt out of the paid labour force and work full-time at child rearing. They do not conform even to the image of domestic bliss suggested by the comforting Woolworths or by the mortgage advertisements. They are not the stuff of which images are made or for whom products are marketed. The majority of women in Bellambi do not conform to either of the consumer stereotypes. Very few women are visible in the public space in this suburb. Of the stereotypes portrayed in the mall, the upmarket independent business and professional woman is most notably lacking. For the women of Bellambi, shopping locally is a problem because of children and transport, and most do their shopping in the closer suburban centre at Corrimal for convenience rather than travelling into the city centre. Women in domestic and suburban space are too mundane to form part of the image of the mall, and to a great extent they are not part of the reality.

While Bellambi's women find it difficult to overturn the burden of patriarchal planning (although see Winchester 1992), certain male residents have responded to their economic marginalisation while deepening the overall powerlessness of local women. Groups which are effectively powerless, such as the unemployed youth in marginal Bellambi, are able to express their control over space in limited ways. They have no power to construct space, nor access to legitimising authorities, such as the City Council or the police. A key strategy for the control of space in these circumstances is its continuous appropriation and use (Harvey 1987). Continuous use is a form of legitimising authority, and is the basis of 'no-go' areas in more conflict-torn situations. The appropriation of space is most clearly seen around the so-called amenities block on Bellambi Beach. Its monopoly by lounging male teenagers and its lack of amenity are enough to deter other users of the beachfront. The graffiti and vandalism are not just the results of boredom or lack of discipline, but symbolise a deeper societal malaise and a rejection of the authority by which they themselves are rejected.

The cultural appropriation of public space on the Bellambi foreshore reveals a gender differentiation in the use of space. This public space, nominally for everyone, is in practice appropriated by young men, with very few or no women participating. Patriarchal assumptions ensure that men rather than women control space even when they are themselves part of an alienated class. Societal expectations allow men to be noisier, more violent and more aggressive than women. The young men can resist exploitation and alienation by appropriating space, which then becomes unavailable for use by other classes and by women. The appropriation of public space by male members of the working class can cause conflict with the police; in circumstances such as the Bathurst riots where motorbikers clashed with police, the spatial but not the sexist nature of the conflict has been recognised by researchers (see Cunneen & Lynch 1988).

Conclusion

This study has examined the built environment of two contrasting areas of Wollongong, one an area of power and the other an area of powerlessness. Wollongong Mall is a landscape of consumption which can be comprehended at a number of levels. It is now a symbol of Wollongong itself, its past and future, as well as being layered with other meanings that obscure its prime purpose of consumption. This area is shaped by the powerful pressures of profit-making which are legitimised by apparently unrelated functions such as entertainment, by the construction of layers of meaning and illusion in the landscape, and by the power of the local state. Bellambi, on the other hand, is marginal to the agents of power; it is a stigmatised suburb which has a negative image associated with the relatively powerless occupants of public housing. Still, resistance to this marginalisation process is possible, and at Bellambi it is shown by a competing process of continuous appropriation, by a subgroup of the residents. On the other hand, little overt resistance to the power of consumerism is tolerated in the mall, an area of prime space, although women may modify their shopping behaviour and attitudes.

The area of power may be contrasted with the area of powerlessness at a number of levels. The prime function of the area of status is consumerism (shopping), whereas the prime function of the area of stigma is residential. The built environment of the mall displays power, derived from ownership of capital and access to the local state, whereas Bellambi is in a sense outside capitalism, in that the state is providing welfare housing for those who cannot compete in the marketplace. In each area, myths, symbols or illusions are built into the landscape. The mall is symbolic of Wollongong itself, it contains a myth of attaining paradise and an illusion that it is a social and entertainment centre. In the case of Bellambi, the myth of the happy nuclear family is built into the housing. In both areas, however, resistance to the powerful forces is both possible and evident, although its form too is tempered by patriarchy.

These contrasting urban landscapes embody particular social constructions of women's roles. The mall, as a site of consumption, emphasises a particular image of women as consumers. The image of domesticity is considered too mundane for such a site, yet women's domestic role as major household providers is exploited by marketing goods directly to them. The significance attached to women's fashion incorporates the notion of female as object and as adornment, while projecting an illusionary image of independence and control. Supplementary constructions of women incorporate stereotypes which are ageist and ethnocentric. On the other hand, the construction of the public housing at Bellambi incorporates the powerful social construction of the stereotypical nuclear family and of women as users of domestic space. The image of women's roles projected in the landscape of power belongs to the ideologies of consumerism and patriarchy and provides at least the illusion of independence; in the landscape of powerlessness where consumerism is absent, the construction is domestic and dependent.

This chapter has argued that the two most powerful pressures shaping contemporary Australian society are capitalism and patriarchy. Both these powerful formations comprise groups who construct space which in turn reify particular ideologies. To deconstruct the landscape, both forces need to be examined. A radical feminist analysis acknowledging the impact of both patriarchy and capitalism as power structures in society, when combined with a reading of cultural landscape, provides some new insights into the construction and deconstruction of our urban cultural geographies.

Note

I am grateful to the Australian Research Council and the University of Wollongong for the provision of research funding which helped support this project. I am also grateful for the comments of Ms Lauren Costello, Mr Kevin Dunn and Dr Iain Hay on an earlier draft of this paper.

References

Advertiser, 19 April 1989, 'Residents declare "enough is enough".'

Allport, C. 1986, 'Women and suburban housing: post-war planning in Sydney, 1943-61', in J.B. McLoughlin & M. Huxley (eds), *Urban Planning in Australia: Critical Readings,* Longman Cheshire, Melbourne, pp. 233–48.

Anderson, K.J. 1987, 'The idea of Chinatown: the power of place and institutional practice in the making of a racial category', *Annals of the Association of American Geographers,* 77, pp. 580–98.

Bondi, L. & Peake, L. 1988, 'Gender and the city: urban politics revisited,' in J. Little, L. Peake & P. Richardson (eds), *Women in Cities: Gender and the Urban Environment,* Macmillan Education, Basingstoke, pp. 21–40.

Bowlby, S. 1988, 'From corner shop to hypermarket: women and food retailing,' in J. Little, L. Peake & P. Richardson (eds), *Women in Cities: Gender and the Urban Environment,* Macmillan Education, Basingstoke, pp. 61–83.

Bowlby, S. 1990, 'Women, work and the family: control and constraints', *Geography,* 76, pp. 17–26.

Chapman, R. 1988, 'The great pretender: variations on the new man theme', in R. Chapman & J. Rutherford (eds), *Male Order: Unwrapping Masculinity,* Lawrence & Wishart, London, pp. 225–48.

Cunneen, C. & Lynch, R. 1988, 'The social meanings of conflict at the Australian Grand Prix motorcycle races', *Leisure Studies,* 7, pp. 1–19.

Dear, M. 1986, 'Postmodernism and planning', *Environment and Planning D: Society and Space,* 4, pp. 367–84.

Duncan, J. & Duncan, N. 1988, '(Re)reading the landscape', *Environment and Planning D: Society and Space,* 6, pp. 117–26.

Game, A. & Pringle, R. 1983, *Gender at Work,* Allen & Unwin, Sydney.

Gibson, K. 1990, *"Hewers of cake and drawers of tea": women and restructuring on the coalfields of the Bowen Basin,* ERRRU Working Paper 2, University of Sydney, Sydney.

Harvey, D. 1987, 'Flexible accumulation through urbanization: reflections on "post-modernism" in the American city', *Antipode,* 19, pp. 260–86.

Hayden, D. 1980, 'What would a non-sexist city be like? Speculations on housing, urban design, and human work', *Signs: Journal of Women in Culture and Society,* 5, 3, Supplement, pp. 170–87.

Hopkins, J.S.P. 1990, 'West Edmonton mall: landscape of myths and elsewhereness', *Canadian Geographer,* 34, pp. 2–17.

Huxley, M.E. & Kerkin, K. 1988, 'What price the Bicentennial? A political economy of Darling Harbour', *Transition: Discourse on Architecture,* 26, pp. 57–64.

Illawarra Mercury, 10 May 1972, 'Bellambi homes for '72.'

Johnson, L.C. 1989, 'Making space for women: feminist critiques and reformulations of the spatial disciplines', *Australian Feminist Studies,* 9, pp. 31–50.

Johnson, L.C. 1990, 'Gendering domestic space: a feminist perspective on housing', *New Zealand Journal of Geography,* 90, pp. 20–4.

Kemeny, J. 1986, 'The ideology of home ownership', in J.B. McLoughlin & M. Huxley (eds), *Urban Planning in Australia: Critical Readings,* Longman Cheshire, Melbourne, pp. 251–8.

King, R. 1986, 'Housing policy: planning practice', in J.B. McLoughlin & M. Huxley (eds), *Urban Planning in Australia: Critical Readings,* Longman Cheshire, Melbourne, pp. 274–87.

Lewis, P.F. 1979, 'Axioms for reading the landscape: some guides to the American scene', in D. Meinig (ed.), *The Interpretation of Ordinary Landscapes,* Oxford University Press, Oxford and New York, pp. 11–31.

Miner, C. 1989, 'Maid/made to mall order,' paper presented at Claiming Space conference, Australian National University, Canberra.

Monk, J. & Hanson, S. 1982, 'On not excluding half of the human in human geography', *The Professional Geographer,* 34, pp. 11–23.

Morris, M. 1982, 'Sydney Tower', *Island Magazine,* 9/10, pp. 53–61.

New South Wales Department of Housing 1980, *Glebe Project,* Australian Government Publishing Service, Canberra.

Reiger, K. 1991, 'Motherhood ideology', in R. Batten, W. Weeks & J. Wilson (eds), *Issues Facing Australian Families: Human Services Respond,* Longman Cheshire, Melbourne, pp. 46–53.

Robinson, R. (ed.) 1977, *Urban Illawarra,* Sorrett Publishing, Melbourne.

Schultz, J. 1985, *Steel City Blues,* Penguin, Melbourne.

Short, J. 1989, *The Humane City: Cities as if People Matter,* Blackwell, Oxford.

Valentine, G. 1989, 'The geography of women's fear', *Area,* 21, pp. 385–90.

Watson, S. 1988, *Accommodating Inequality,* Allen & Unwin, Sydney.

White, P. E. 1984, *The West European City,* Longman, London.

Winchester, H.P.M. 1990, 'Women and children last: the poverty and marginalization of one-parent families', *Transactions of the Institute of British Geographers,* 15, pp. 70–86.

Winchester, H.P.M. 1992, Production and reproduction: needs and policy uptake of one-parent families. Paper presented at the Institute of British Geographers Conference, Sheffield, January.

Winchester, H.P.M. & White, P.E. 1988, 'The location of marginalized groups in the inner city', *Environment and Planning D: Society and Space,* 6, pp. 37–54.

Wollongong City Council 1982, *Crown Street Mall, Wollongong,* mimeo, Wollongong City Council, Wollongong.

Constructing geographies:
culture and capital

10 Modernity and post-modernity in the retail landscape

Jon Goss

At the heart of the New Times is the shift from the old mass-production Fordist economy to a new, more flexible, post-Fordist order based on computers, information technology and robotics. But New Times are about much more than economic change. Our world is being remade. Mass production, the mass consumer, the big city, big-brother state, the sprawling housing estate, and the nation-state are in decline: flexibility, diversity, differentiation, mobility, communication, decentralisation and internationalisation are in the ascendant. In the process our own identities, our sense of self, our own subjectivities are being transformed. We are in transition to a new era. *Marxism Today* (1988)

Introduction

There is widespread recognition of a profound shift of cultural sensibility in western societies over the last two decades or so. The various terms used to describe the 'New Times' — 'post-industrial society', 'information society', 'post-Fordism', and 'post-modernism' — suggest that it is complex and encompasses various dimensions of everyday life. This chapter will briefly examine the relationship between the material and symbolic — or more loosely, the economic and cultural — components of the ongoing transformation and its manifestation in the built environment, particularly in purpose-built places of consumption, or shopping centres or malls.[1] This is appropriate given the importance of consumption to our contemporary lives, and given the fact that it is in architecture that the new sensibility attains its most visible expression (Jameson 1984, 54; Sharrett 1989, 162).

First, without mass-produced consumer goods everyday life would be inconceivable for most of us, not only because they sustain our material living standards, but also because they help define individual and collective identities. In the consumer society you are 'what you buy' as much as 'what you do' and, as media constantly inform us, self-actualisation is only the next purchase away. Shopping now may be the second most important cultural activity in North America, and although watching television is the first, much television programming promotes shopping directly (through advertising) and indirectly (through depiction of consumer lifestyles). The existential significance of shopping is clearly recognised in popular culture by bumper stickers shouting slogans such as: 'Born to Shop', 'Shop 'Til You Drop', and 'I Shop Therefore I Am'.

Second, the built environment reflects material and symbolic changes in society: 'Architecture is the will of the epoch translated into space' (Mies van der Rohe 1926, cited in Frampton 1983, 40). For example, the development of the skyscraper in the nineteenth century was based on advances in technology (the elevator and structural steel), the organisation of production (mergers and the rapid growth of the corporation), and prevalent ideology (verticality symbolises corporate power and classical styles symbolise the civic function of business). The built environment, however, does not merely mirror historical change, for social relations and ideologies are partly reproduced through it. The argument of this chapter, then, is that material and symbolic transformations characterising the 'New Times' are manifest and at least partially realised in the retail built environment.

The history of the shopping mall

The planned shopping centre had humble beginnings before the Second World War: the first in the United States was built in Lake Forest, Chicago in 1916; in 1922 Country Club Plaza, a prototype shopping district with stylised architecture, landscaping, unified management and sign control was opened in Kansas City (fig. 10.1); and in 1931 Highland Park Shopping Village, the first centre based on a pedestrian mall, was built near Dallas. Other small centres were built at busy intersections, but the department stores generally remained downtown until the massive highway construction and residential suburbanisation of the 1950s. In 1950 there were less than 100 shopping centres in the United States (Urban Land Institute 1985, 16); today there are more shopping centres than post offices or secondary schools (Stoffel 1988). Nearly 35 000 shopping centres offer a total of almost 235 km^2 (2.5 billion ft^2) of gross leasable retail space (National Research Bureau 1990), and huge super-regional malls sprawl around suburban highway interchanges and squeeze into the decaying fabric of downtown. The largest shopping centre in the world is the massive West Edmonton Mall in Canada which is 1.5 km (1 mile) long, covers about 145 ha (110 acres), has a total floorspace of 483 000 m^2 (5.2 million ft^2) and parking for 14 000 cars.

The shopping centre is a place in which retailers sell and consumers shop, but it is more than that — it also provides for entertainment, edification, education and sustenance. It typically houses funfairs and fashion shows; hosts community dances and concerts; conducts fitness classes and courses in adult literacy; and provides food and drink. It is also a predictable, safe and sanitised alternative to the old city street, a place where families go on outings, old people idle and exercise, and teenagers hang out and grow up 'mall-wise'. The geographical spread of this cultural institution and its way of life has truly resulted in 'The Malling of America' (Kowinski 1985) and with the global export of the model we are perhaps witnessing 'The malling of the world'!

Before examining the development of these p(a)laces of consumption, and their changing characteristics and functions in these 'New Times', it is appropriate to consider the nature and role of consumption and of the built environment in advanced capitalist societies.

The culture of consumption

Consumer goods serve the double purpose of satisfying socially defined needs and 'materialising' cultural distinctions, providing a code that symbolically expresses personal and social difference (Sahlins 1976; McCracken 1988). This is not entirely

Figure 10.1: Country Club Plaza, Kansas City, Missouri, c. 1930.
Source: Chris Wilborn & Associates, Photographers, Kansas City, Missouri.

new, as 'consumer culture' has been in the making for several hundreds of years (Braudel 1967), and the first consumer revolution, which took place in the nineteenth century, had already established consumer goods as repositories of social meaning (Williams 1982; Miller 1981). It is only in this century, however, and particularly since the Second World War, that everyday life has been so thoroughly commodified that we can be persuaded to buy sexual attraction, happiness and personality, as well as status, in the form of consumer goods. Persuasion is the responsibility of specialists in the cultural institutions of advertising, marketing and the media. Identified as the 'captains of consciousness' (Ewen 1976, 19) these agents might better be called the 'high priests of capitalism' since their means of persuasion is summed up by the notion of 'fetishism of the commodity'.

A fetish is an object of religion in 'primitive' cultures that is invested with spiritual powers and regarded with dread or reverence. Commodities work similar magic in contemporary western cultures such that advertising is 'a highly organised and professional system of magical inducements and satisfactions, functionally very similar to magical systems in simpler societies, but rather strangely coexistent with a highly developed scientific technology' (Williams 1980, 185). Highly sophisticated advertising techniques maintain the superstition that possession of the physical object confers power over nature and others even if the 'real' power lies in the economic or political capacity of the owner.

A second sense in which the commodity is fetishised is in the 'masking' of the social relations necessary to produce it and the human labour it embodies. Although some commodities are marketed as the products of 'craft' labour (signifying quality), sensitive contemporary consumers would generally rather not be reminded of (or haunted by) the third world sweatshop labour that makes their designer clothes or the assembly lines that produce their household goods. Commodities appear in advertisements and the marketplace with the ghost of human labour thoroughly exorcised, so that very few consumers know, or can give thought to, what they are composed of, where they were made and who made them (Jhally 1987, 49).

However, one must not accord too much power to either the magician or to the advertiser, for their operations only work for an audience predisposed to believe in the illusion, wherein lies the real source of the 'magic' (Bourdieu 1986, 137). Designers, advertisers and retailers do not have to conspire consciously to deceive their audiences (although they often do), but may merely highlight 'latent correspondences' between the commodity and cultural symbols (Sahlins 1976, 217). It is not necessary to tell us that fast cars confer extra libido upon drivers, or that a particular cigarette brand will add 'cool' to the smoker. We take the attractive (female) passenger, or the elegant decor seen with the commodity and 'independently' make the connection. Consumers are asked to employ their accumulated cultural knowledge to actively weave together the natural, symbolic and social elements provided by the image-maker and so create the commodity's context — that is, the mode and manner of its consumption (Sack 1988). Moreover, consumers are never only the dupes that the 'captains of consciousness' might wish them to be. They may actively and imaginatively subvert the images presented and latent associations highlighted, perhaps by 'unmasking' the social relations embodied in the commodity, by consciously consuming out of context, or campaigning in general against the manipulative content of imagery.[2]

Finally, a critical component of the commodity's context is the real or imagined landscape in which it is advertised or marketed. The advertiser employs the power of place to suggest the appropriate mode of consumption. The consumer then imaginatively employs the commodity to locate him/herself in this place and to weave the appropriate context. The tropical beach, for example, symbolises relaxed, sensual luxury, and the consumer is able to experience this through the consumption of particular clothes, cigarettes or alcohol, while lounging on the back porch in a suburban subdivision.

The meaning of the built environment

The built environment is a rather unique cultural artifact in that it both symbolically expresses the social relations that structure ways of life, and functions physically as a spatial system that reproduces them. First, elements of the built environment are signifiers, that is, they refer to abstract concepts or relations. For example, the towering office block with its reflective skin signifies a powerful, anonymous authority, while a suburban residence signifies private property, territoriality and nuclear family life. Part of the signification resides in the function of these structures — as a corporate headquarters or as a home — but it also lies in the form and style that differentiates one office block or suburban house from another. Both functional and stylistic elements of the built environment constitute a complex system of signs which can be read critically as a cultural text (the practice of semiotics). Second, the built environment compartmentalises social spaces, for example, into public/private, day/night and backstage/frontstage, and thus separates various uses and users, and presents opportunities and constraints for their interaction. The configuration of physical spaces has socio-psychological effects that reproduce social relations. The floorplan of the suburban 'family', for example, is believed to play an important role in 'domesticating' women and children and defining privacy, sexuality and eating habits (Wright 1981). Shopping centres, as we shall see, employ various architectural elements and structural plans that through signification and control of segregated spaces facilitate the sale of commodities.

The built environment also plays a critical economic and political role. It facilitates the circulation of commodities, and is itself a source of profit to those engaged in its production. Real estate profit originates from human labour employed in its production, but as with other inherently limited commodities (such as works of art), also derives from speculation upon value, which rises with investment by other owners of capital. A building's value depends partly upon levels of investment in adjacent properties, which the individual owner is unlikely to be able to control directly. The state, however, whose tax revenues depend upon land values and whose power depends upon popular support, has the authority to control and co-ordinate this process and is increasingly drawn into 'growth coalitions' with fractions of capital and labour to promote and regulate development. Downtown shopping centres, which help reclaim the inner city both for profit and popular use, are often a feature of these joint projects.

The periodicity of capitalism

Capitalism has moved through distinct phases characterised by a given technology, labour process, medium of communication, spatial/organisational structures (Lash & Urry 1987, 16), role of the state and dominant culture. It is argued, for example, that organised or monopoly capitalism, which is associated with the culture of modernism, consolidated at the beginning of this century in the United States. Over the last two decades or so, however, it has been giving way to disorganised or global capitalism, associated with the culture of post-modernism (Lash & Urry 1987).

Organised capitalism is based on the concentration of industrial and financial capital in large corporations and cartels; mass production of standardised commodities under scientific management or Fordist regulation;[3] politics of national trade unions and workers' parties; the growth of an administrative middle class; and the corporate state which regulates the national economy and mediates class conflict through welfare legislation. Manufacturing dominates the economy; the main production technologies are the electric motor and the internal combustion engine; and the primary medium of communication is the printed word. The spatial structure consists of coherent regional economies focused on urban industrial complexes (Lash & Urry 1987, 3-4). Modernism, the cultural correlation of this stage of capitalism, entails mass consumption, technical rationality, glorification of science and a futuristic orientation.

The Fordist regime of accumulation began to falter in the late 1960s as labour costs increased in western economies, while more efficient competition developed elsewhere (particularly in Japan and Asia's newly industrialising economies). The result is a 'disorganisation' of capitalism, including the decentralisation of production; the incorporation of new (female and immigrant) labour markets through subcontracting and a relative shift in manufacturing towards the third world; a relative numerical and political decline of the 'core' (unionised male) working class; a massive expansion of services and the emergence of a service class; a growth of new (environmental, gender, race and urban) social movements; a decentralisation of financial capital; and a crisis of the state. The dominant technologies are nuclear power and the computer; and the mode of communication is the electronically-produced image and sound byte. The spatial manifestation is the decentralisation of industry, decline of industrial cities and disintegration of regional economies. Cultural life is fragmented and pluralistic, and cultural differences are broken down by tourism and the international media. Everyday life is aestheticised and consumption is individualised (see below).

The new 'cultural dominant' (Jameson 1984, 55) is not *caused* by changes in technology and economic organisation, but is a constitutive part of the complex social transformation. Moreover, culture is not a homogeneous field whose content can be 'read off' from the economy, but a locus of struggle. There are contradictory currents in intellectual, artistic and popular norms and practices, and conflict over the means and relations of cultural production. In the field of popular music, for example, consider the rebellion of punk against the institutions of rock during the 1970s, a struggle that erupted over who makes music and how it is made; it echoed the struggle that rock and roll waged in the 1950s against folk, country and easy-listening, and perhaps older struggles between popular and high cultural practices, and between youth and established authority.

Modernity and mass consumption

Enhanced productivity under the modern regime of scientific management makes possible increased wages and reduced working hours, concessions which in fact became socially necessary: first, at the level of the individual, to provide incentive to work even where tasks were repetitive and alienating; second, at the level of the firm, in response to demands of organised labour; and third, at the level of society, to sustain demand for mass-produced commodities. Workers were compensated for the loss of control over production by reduced working hours and increased wages (which they had long demanded). At the same time, the advertising industry, institutionalised credit, branches of the welfare state, and other forms of demand management developed to ensure that increased time and money would be properly spent on the acquisition of commodities. Mass consumption was born together with mass production in the struggle over relations in the workplace and distribution of the social surplus. Since the state was increasingly required to mediate in this struggle and manage production and consumption, there developed what has been called the 'bureaucratic society of controlled consumption' (Lefebvre 1971, 60).

This consumption regime was based on the commodities of suburban housing and the automobile. Both were mass-produced and were mutually dependent — suburban residence demanded a car, as the car demanded the construction of highways and the building of the suburbs. They combined to create the space for expanded commodity consumption, a space filled with other essential commodities — the refrigerator, washing machine, vacuum cleaner, lawn mower and the television. The 'captains of consciousness' mobilised America's romantic preoccupation with the rural frontier and the normative model of the nuclear family to promote a new 'design for living'. In the suburban home the male wage-earner and female domestic manager were surrounded by consumer durables that tamed any vestiges of nature intruding into their idyll and at the same time defined their relative success as breadwinner and homemaker. The modern consumer-couple pursued an acquisitive lifestyle where 'he' was constrained into a lifetime of waged labour to pay for it and 'she' into a lifetime of unpaid domestic labour necessary to maintain it. The spread of this 'American dream' resulted in a partial breakdown of qualitative cultural differences based on geography, ethnicity and social class, and established quantitative social distinctions based on status-assigning possessions.

The built environment of modernism

The modern built environment takes two forms: the high modern, which is meticulously planned and monumental, and ostensibly universal; and the modern vernacular, which is unplanned and practical, and was at first distinctly American. High modernism, or the 'International Style', provides an appropriate industrial architecture for Fordism. First, it celebrates modern technology by incorporating elements resembling railway lines, grain elevators, stacked TV sets and missiles. Second, like other commodities, high modern architecture is standardised for mass production. The same shoe-boxes built of steel beams and concrete function in the suburbs as factories, warehouses and shopping malls or are stood on end in the city as corporate offices and lower-income housing. Third, its monotonously regular geometrical forms and the hostility of its concrete and mirrored-glass surfaces show as much indifference to the occupier as the assembly line to the worker. Fourth, it turns its back on the city and the past. It violates sensuous urban space with abstract forms and harsh angles; it consciously separates itself from urban society with an impermeable facade and a moat of windswept concrete or asphalt, and it eliminates historical reference, reducing building form to a rationalist, minimalist aesthetic which shows contemptuous disregard for function and place (Jencks 1987, 15). Ironically, the original intent of high modern architecture was to unify work and art, and celebrate the potential of modern industry to sweep away the rigidities and inequalities of past societies symbolised in national architectures. However, the aesthetic that was a metaphor for liberation and progress was appropriated by the vertically integrated and anonymous institutions of corporate and state capitalism.

The popular architecture of suburban residential and retail landscapes is quite different, even if also practically subordinate to the machine (in this case the automobile), in that it operates on a human scale and acknowledges, albeit to a limited extent, the individuality of the consumer. Mass-produced, standardised houses exhibit variations based upon the Cape Cod, ranch, split-level or colonial styles, in what are otherwise monotonous subdivisions, while commercial strips that developed to serve the new automobile public in the 1930s and 1940s were composed of highly diverse and competitive elements clamouring for attention from passing vehicles.

The modern retail built environment

The shopping mall expresses both the high and vernacular forms of modernism. It grew out of the commercial strip and the small plazas common along highways, and was conceived as an alternative to the retail centre of the city, promising a sense of suburban community and market life without the congestion, crime, pollution and even weather of the real main street. Victor Gruen, the acknowledged pioneer of the shopping mall and designer of the first climate-controlled mall (Southdale, Edina, MN, 1956), intended that for the suburban residents the mall would be 'more than just a place where one may shop — it shall be related in their minds with all activities of cultural enrichment and relaxation' (cited in Gillette 1985, 451).

We need not doubt the sincerity of the developers of the first shopping malls, but the fact remains that they are artificial environments which, unlike the main street, have no prior reason for existence and no historic rootedness in place. The first generation of planned shopping centres were simply planted in greenfield sites where new highways converged and one suburban shopping centre was much like another. The 'mall rat', 'mallie' (Kowinski 1985, 33-4), or 'mall-walker' (Jacobs 1984), felt at home in Northland (Chicago) or Prestonwood, Dallas, and perhaps even in Brent Cross (London) or Parly 2 (Paris).

Figure 10.2: A 'greenfield' site. Les Pumerades-Saint Bruno near Montreal, Canada.
Source: Urban Land Institute, Washington DC.

The shopping mall expresses an 'instrumental rationality' (Gottdiener 1986, 289); its structural and architectural elements combine to construct an efficient 'machine for shopping'. It is an introverted space which sits in a barren desert of asphalt, presenting a bleak exterior except for the minimal landscaping suggestive of the oasis inside. Customers are drawn from their cars to the prominent entrances of classic columns, arches, towers or canopies, and are swallowed up, often swept by escalators to galleries or grottos where they lose their immediate bearings. Exits (even fire exits) are inconspicuous and unattractive. The 'machine' then circulates shoppers in a manner designed to optimise exposure to the merchandise on display. The concern to keep them moving is perfectly expressed in a shopping centre design manual:

Pause points for shoppers to rest, review their programmes and re-arrange their purchases etc. also need planning with care. Seating, while offering a convenient stopping point, must not be too luxurious or comfortable. Shoppers must move on and allow re-occupation of seating and the danger of attracting the 'down and outs' of various categories must be avoided. (Beddington 1982, 36)

The design of shopping centres varies with the number of department store 'anchors', but mall lengths are usually about 200 m (650ft) as it is assumed that this is the maximum distance pedestrians are willing to walk. Focal places are otherwise used to break the flow and distract the shopper from considerations of distance and time, and to give the mall a sense of exterior public place. Mall widths are restricted to about 6 m (20 ft) with perhaps an extra 3 m (10ft) of obstacles — seating, fountains, plants and temporary vendors — in the central zone to direct shoppers towards the storefronts (Gottdiener 1986).

The department stores, which draw the mall's customers and are able to dictate conditions to the developer, traditionally insist on straight corridors and sign control to protect sightlines to their logos across the ends of the mall. Smaller retailers depend more upon impulsive purchases by customers on their way to the 'big name' department store so their storefronts are designed to maximise the area of display and to entice the shopper inside. Everywhere, huge sheets of plate glass and mirrors unflatteringly reflect the shopper, imperfect compared with the mannequins and magical commodities in the looking-glass world of the dressed window.

In this retail wonderland reality is suspended through a number of subtle devices. There are no clocks to register the march of time; no windows to remind the consumer of an outside reality. Temperature control and constant lighting mask the passage of daily or seasonal time, and create artificial micro-climates, refreshingly cool in summer and comfortably warm in winter. Maintenance and security staff ensure that the environment is kept spotless and safe. Deliveries and services are kept 'backstage' in tunnels and hidden passageways so that commodities appear in a flawless retail context as if by magic.

Although the modern mall presents itself as public space, private ownership allows a degree of management that main street retailers cannot attain. Not only is the atmosphere not welcoming of the poor 'underconsumer', but those who disrupt consumption, such as political leafleteers, rowdy teenagers and street-people, can be escorted from the premises. Although this right has been challenged in the United States Supreme Court, conflict over public access versus private exclusion has been ruled a matter for individual states to decide, and in most cases private security has considerable control over everyday activity in the mall. The mall presents itself as a public place but does not accept the associated responsibilities and inconveniences. As Kowiniski (1985, 68) points out, the shopping mall is not so much a new downtown as a version of the romanticised model of the 'Main Street' pioneered in Disneyland: it is without the dangers of the automobile or the inconvenience of the natural elements. It is also uncorrupted by bars, liquor stores and betting shops; intolerant of those who might rudely challenge the illusion of the universality and normality of the culture of consumption; and without laundromats, repair shops and second-hand stores to remind us of the materiality of the commodity. Unlike downtown where the retailer and developer compete as best they can with their existing neighbours, here positive externalities, or 'spillover effects', are internalised with the appropriate tenant mix.

It would be uncharitable, however, to dismiss the shopping centre as merely an engineered instrument of mass consumption, since a variety of users have appropriated it for their own social purpose and forced developers and managers to recognise their needs. The mall is a place where youth, elderly and homeworkers of the suburbs can go and commune or pass time agreeably on a daily basis. The bottom line remains retail profit and rental income, but strollers and creches for shoppers with young children, amusement arcades and fairground attractions for teenagers, and rest areas and special activities for the elderly, are loss leaders necessary to service these populations. Of course, we could see these innovations as part of a strategic design (the amusement arcades, for example, 'contain' youth on the mall's peripheries), but the creative use of the mall environment has undoubtedly forced a partial compromise of the retail logic. The struggle of community and political groups over the legal status of the mall's territory must also be viewed in this light.

During the 1960s and early 1970s there appeared to be no limit to the construction of suburban shopping centres, and they were built with speculative abandon. While it is probably premature to predict that such centres 'will go the way of the dinosaur' (Gruen 1978, 9), there has been a marked slow-down in construction. Structural constraints include increased costs of land assembly and construction, saturation of local retail markets, reluctance of suburban government to provide infrastructure, and tightened environmental controls (Frieden & Sagalyn 1989, 82), trends which coincide with increased market segmentation and a changed retailing concept. Developers have adapted by renovating old shopping centres, adding food courts, galleries, soft landscaping, architectural flourishes (such as Art Deco and Victoriana) and sideshows, creating the 'hot mall' which sells shopping as entertainment (Stallings 1990, 14). They have also pioneered a new generation of malls which unite the scale and technology of modernist construction with the post-modernist affection for grand, chaotic spectacle. The 'megacentres', exemplified by West Edmonton Mall, Canada, the Mall of the Americas, under construction in Bloomington, Minnesota, and Metrocentre, in Gateshead, England, are monsters of planned spontaneity and prefabricated pleasure, total environments that satisfy every consumption need, even as self-contained tourist destinations for the whole family.

The truly post-modern retail environments, however, purvey a more or less particular consumption experience and are developed downtown, where post-modernism has rediscovered the city and history. Before discussing the form of post-modern retail landscapes, however, these must also be placed in their material and symbolic context.

Post-modernity and individualised consumption

Under the 'post-Fordist' regime of accumulation, mass production and consumption have given way to flexible production and personalised (as opposed to mass) consumption. Sophisticated production technologies and computerised distribution systems allow rapid turnover of product styles designed for the specific market segments identified and exhaustingly researched by the new 'disciplines' of geo-demographics and psychographics. The demand for high-quality information and sophisticated co-ordination has increased the number of specialists in the culture, knowledge and communication industries who provide services essential to commodity production and circulation. These specialists form the core of what has been called a 'new middle class' and their lifestyles and cultural orientations are critical to the consumption practices of post-modernism.

The new class is defined as a waged class because it does not own the means of production nor the product of its labour, yet has a degree of control over the production process and may claim intellectual ownership of the product. It is thus in a somewhat ambiguous class position, but because it is relatively well-educated, it is able to employ cultivated distinctions in taste, lifestyle, personal expression, sexuality and quality of living environment to define its cultural territory. These distinctions are expressed in consumption and are most readily employed by the subgroup of this class popularly known as 'yuppies'. They are stereotypically associated with commodities that, for example, exhibit cosmopolitanism (from Japanese paper lanterns to espresso coffee machines), eschew ostentation (minimalist furniture and natural finishes), boast quality (brand names and designer labels), and display privileged knowledge (gourmet coffees and the 'right' wines).

Class distinction is thus no longer quantitative (based on the value of commodities consumed) but qualitative (based on style of consumption). In fact, one might say that it is not primarily the material object that is consumed, but the image of ourselves consuming the object (Debord 1983; Baudrillard 1981). One no longer buys merely to 'keep up with the Joneses', but to appropriate a style for one's persona. Thus even with a practical household gizmo one gets literally 'The Sharper Image'; and with fashionable clothes one gets 'The Look', becomes a member of 'The Limited', or is seen to be on the right side of 'The Gap'. Ironically, however, as entrepreneurs expand the market behind the cultural avant garde and the 'masses' emulate the middle class by consuming its commodities, so the new class must develop new tastes to mark its distinction. The last fad is rapidly replaced with the latest, making for an extraordinarily rapid turnover of symbolic content in commodified experiences of tourism, leisure, sport, entertainment or body maintenance. Identity is dynamic and emphasis is on self-discovery and personal growth through self-improvement literature, personal improvement seminars and image consultants.

Disillusionment with the political failures of the 1960s and the rise of this 'culture of narcissism' (Lasch 1979) have translated societal problems into personal inadequacies, social concern into self-help, and public life (of the festival, voting and community) into appearance. Immediate personal gratification is pursued instead of life-long co-operative projects such as marriage and child-rearing, and pursuit of quick financial success replaces the career goal. Ironically, however, having been liberated from the constraints of these institutional projects post-modern individuals yearn for a sense of their history and place. Nostalgia manifests the post-modern desire for authenticity, for the continuity of tradition and for community lost. In an existential search for roots (Jager 1986) the post-modern voraciously consumes styles of past times manufactured by the 'heritage industry' (Hewison 1987) and of distant places produced by the tourist industry.

The past is commodified in 'pop images and stereotypes' (Jameson 1983, 118), such as old 'B' movies, retro clothing, and restored pinball and soft-drink machines. Historical artifacts are 'museumised', while the contemporary other is ransacked for signs of tradition and community. Consequently, the post-modern consumer has accumulated a 'well-stocked musée imaginaire' (Jencks 1987, 95), or fragments of experience from other times and places: (s)he has typically learned to eat muesli for breakfast and Ethiopian for lunch, drink Mexican beer and Chilean wine, wear Red Army surplus and sarongs, watch subtitled movies, listen to reggae, rai, opera and gamelan, and dance the hula or lambada. These souvenirs and disembodied gestures mark the cosmopolitan lifestyle and sophisticated taste of an individual, and show an obsessive desire for authenticity in an increasingly rootless culture.

Post-modernity and the built environment

Flexible accumulation has a profound impact upon the cities of the advanced capitalist world. As they lose population and employment, and suffer a relative divestment of capital, tax revenues decrease, while the costs of urban service provision and maintenance of the deteriorating built environment escalate. At the same time central governments have reduced support in an attempt to curb both their own expenditures and the political power of cities. 'Entrepreneurial' cities and their 'growth coalitions' must compete to attract increasingly footloose and speculative private capital, and one strategy has been to subsidise the development of urban space into office complexes, festival markets, convention centres and sports stadia to provide the work and play spaces of the new middle class who are attracted to the central city by prospects of employment in information and financial services, residence in gentrified or redeveloped districts and recreation in the restored bohemia.

Post-modern architecture employs pastiche and freely mixes metaphors, playfully combining paradoxical elements — old and new, local and global, high culture and vernacular. It is sensitive to its surroundings, and embraces the history and diversity of the commercial and vernacular built environment. While modernism repressed the free expression of symbolic capital in the built environment (Harvey 1989, 80) post-modernism celebrates connotative imagery and decorative play, combining, as the city does, baroque, classic, rococo, art deco, high modern, commercial and folk architecture. It appeals to popular tastes with landmarks of allusion and sentiment, consciously cultivating a 'sense of place' (Ley 1987, 44). However, it also communicates with a particular public, employing specific elements that allow 'those in the know' pleasure in the exercise of their cultural capital. Post-modern architecture bows condescendingly to popular culture but winks knowingly at the cultural elites. An example is Philip Johnson's AT&T Building in New York City(fig. 10.3).[4]

As with modernism, it is possible to identify both a high and a popular form of post-modern architecture. First are the 'hyperspaces' (Jameson 1984), complex structures that combine 'a mixture of last-gasp late modernism and interior-decorator postmodernism' (Cooke 1988, 75).[5] These structures (for example, the Peachtree Development in Atlanta, the Beauborg in Paris, the Bonaventure Centre in Los Angeles and the Eaton Center in Toronto) represent an aestheticisation of the finance capital that built them. They are hermetically sealed fantasy worlds. Their scale and complexity are spatial metaphors for the cultural experience of global capitalism. Transparent surfaces invite us into brightly lit worlds of motion, spectacle and theatre where the individual is said to experience a hallucinatory exhilaration, an excitement and terror felt at the instant of total alienation from historical and spatial reality (Jameson 1984). Moving through this space, a constant barrage of sight and sound bombards the user, allowing a glimpse

Figure 10.3: Philip Johnson's AT & T Building, a model.
Source: Bob Harr, Hedrich-Blessing, Photographers, Chicago, Illinois.

of a post-modern world in which signifiers refer only to each other, a 'hyper-reality' in which there is no distinction between the real and imaginary (Baudrillard 1983).

Popular post-modernism is more modest. It engages in restoration or reproduction of traditional and regional architectures, employing a mock vernacular of exposed brick cladding and timbers, painted woodwork, wrought ironwork, brass fittings, stained glass, antique signs and gaslights. It displays the contrived spontaneity, superficial charm and manufactured chic of 'quaintspace' (Relph 1987, 253) and it is presented free from the historical technological and social realities that would be intolerable to the contemporary consumer. Gaslights are really electric, the windows are double-glazed, and the well draws piped water. It is typified in the renovated working-class neighbourhoods and waterfronts of the Victorian city oblivious to the depredations of the factory and the excesses of colonialism; in reproduction small towns of New England or the Mediterranean village divorced of socio-sexual repression and inequality; and in plantation-style houses of the south ignoring the inhumanity of slavery. The context asks the selective consumer to form associations only with the 'positive' traditional values of family, community and honest labour.

The post-modern retail environment

The essential forms of the post-modern retail environment — the specialty centre and the downtown 'megastructure' — reflect the vernacular and high forms of post-modernism respectively, while a hybrid form — the festival marketplace — combines elements of both. The specialty centre is an 'anchorless' collection of upmarket shops and restaurants pursuing a specific retail and architectural theme. It is prone to quaintification. Typical designs in North America include New England villages (Pickering Wharf, Salem, Massachusetts); French provincial towns (The Continent, Columbus, Ohio); Spanish-American haciendas (The Pruneyard, San Jose); Mediterranean villages (Atrium Court, Newport Beach, California); and timber mining camps (Jack London Village, Oakland, California). Pride of place must, however, go to The Borgota in Scottsdale, Arizona, a mock thirteenth-century walled Italian village, with bricks imported from Rome and shop signs in Italian (Kowinski 1985, 233), and to The Mercado in nearby Phoenix, Arizona, modelled on traditional hillside villages of Mexico, with original components imported from Guadalajara, and buildings given Hispanic names (fig. 10.4).

The details may be so accurate that authenticity is displaced and the stylised copy appears more real than the original. The restaurants with their architectural elements, textual fragments, objects of material culture attached to walls and ceilings, and of course the modified cuisine may be more convincingly Italian or Mexican than those in Italy or Mexico. The consumer ignores or forgets that the tortillas are factory-made, the entrée warmed in a microwave oven, and the decorative handicrafts probably produced for export under elaborate subcontracting systems. While the consumer is presented an opportunity to display acquired exotic tastes, the commodity on sale is perfectly fetishised.

The downtown megastructure, on the other hand, is a self-contained complex including retail functions, hotels, offices, restaurants, entertainment, health centres and luxury apartments. Typical examples include Water Tower Place in Chicago, the Tower

Figure 10.4: The Mercado, Phoenix, Arizona.
Source: Reddie Henderson, Horizon Photography, Phoenix, Arizona.

City Centre in Cleveland and Town Square in St Paul. These structures are part of the challenge to the separations (between moments of production, reproduction and consumption, and between workplace, living place and leisure space) on which modernist culture is founded. At the same time, these small worlds ensure that the needs of affluent residents, office workers, conference attenders and tourists can be met entirely within a single hermetically sealed space.

Several features distinguish the downtown megastructure from the suburban shopping mall, although by now many of these have been extensively 'retrofitted' in the post-modern style. After studies found that 70 per cent of all energy consumed in malls was spent on lighting, the calculus of economics and fashion have combined to return daylight in glazed malls reminiscent of nineteenth-century European arcades. These afford a sense of grand public space, and natural light allows the planting of ficus, bamboos and 'interiorised' palms to simulate the tropical environments of tourism, to indicate a respectable age for the establishment and to suggest care for the environment. Water has always been an important element in the mall as a means of soothing tensions and refreshing shoppers, but now elaborate watercourses and waterfalls simulate nature, rather than urban fountains. These three effects combine to turn things inside-out, so that pure and perfected nature, the ideal place of leisure, is ironically found indoors within the city, and no longer in the deteriorating environments of the suburbs beyond.

The downtown malls are also no longer primarily 'machines for shopping', although the aesthetics of movement are retained in the sweep of huge escalators and the trajectory of 'bubble' elevators. Now passage through the mall is an interactive experience, an adventure in winding alleys resembling the Arabian souk or medieval town, with the unpredictability of 'pop-out' shop fronts — glass display cases which jut out into the mall — and mobile vendors. Shopping at the downtown mall is not merely the necessary purchase of goods, but is a form of retail tourism where the individual makes her/his own itinerary.[6]

Clocks have returned and are even displayed as central ornaments. They are invariably antique analogue clocks, visual puns for past time, and evocative of historic public spaces. The presence of the clock is no longer a threat to consumption perhaps because post-modern time is flexible, neither linear nor compartmentalised into specific everyday activities. The present moment expands, the time is always now, and the pleasure of consumption in these purpose-built places transcends temporality measured by the clock. It does not compete with the mundane activities of everyday life, but becomes an integral, regular part of it.

No mall experience is complete without food, which has become a critical marker of social taste. Food courts and full-service restaurants now offer not merely sustenance to the hungry shopper, but a full range of culinary experiences, from fast food to five star, and from international to local ethnic cuisine. The food court is also a place to rest and a vantage point from which to view the spectacle of the new middle class at play.

Entertainment is more than ever the key to success, and attractions such as ice rinks, carousels, roller-coasters, local and historical exhibits, and staged events are an essential part of the show. The contemporary retail environment is an exercise in Disney's 'imagineering', the employment of fantasy and engineering technology (Relph 1987, 129) which effectively enlivens, or conceals, the practical activity of shopping. Also significant in this regard is the fact that shopping centres are increasingly graced by 'high' cultural activities. Developers have commissioned artists to create special works integrated into the design of the centre, established valuable collections of artists' works in permanent displays, sponsored temporary exhibits and hosted shows of classical music. For example, the Bel Canto opera competition is held in shopping centres across the country; a Shakespearean Festival is held in Lakeforest Mall, Gaithersburg, Maryland; sculptures by Henry Moore and Jonathan Borofsky are exhibited in 'sculpture courts' at North Park Center, Dallas; South Coast Plaza in Costa Mesa, California boasts 'one of the most important outdoor sculpture environments in the world' (*Shopping Center Age* 1989, 108); and South Coast Plaza, Faneuil Hall Marketplace in Boston, The Mercado in Phoenix and Horton Plaza in San Diego all have art centres or museums on the premises. This aestheticisation of the shopping experience enables the new middle class to develop and display its cultural capital while obviating charges of vulgarity associated with conspicuous consumption.

The festival market combines these elements with an idealised version of historical urban community and the street market, typically in a restored waterfront district after the model of Faneuil Hall Marketplace in Boston. These environments reflect a nostalgia for manual labour, public gatherings and the age of commerce. Buildings and vessels are restored, and there is usually a historic museum on site. The marketplace is typically decorated with antique signage and props which casually suggest an authentic stage upon which the modern consumer can act out a little bit of history. The street entertainers, barrow vendors and costumed staff often support this stylised image.

The aestheticisation and historicisation of shopping is appropriate because an increasing amount of cultural education is required to appreciate commodities. As both the audiences and the techniques of the 'captains of consciousness' (Ewen 1988) have become more sophisticated, the cultural symbols employed in advertising are more complex. The young professional selectively shopping for quality goods in specialist boutiques is employing perhaps as much accumulated cultural knowledge in creating the context of the commodity as (s)he would in interpreting an oil painting, theatre performance or historical novel. Through design strategies employed in the post-modern shopping centre the act of consumption itself is fetishised: the material activity of shopping resonates with the symbolic activity of leisure, entertainment, education and artistic appreciation.

Conclusion

The history of the planned built environment of retailing is more complex than this brief sketch can show, but in general the unitary 'shopping machine' of the suburbs is being replaced by the mixed-use 'consumer spectacle' originating in the city. This shift in form and function illustrates and reproduces some of the economic and cultural determinations of the 'New Times', a more or less fundamental transformation in the nature of western capitalism. Consumption has replaced production as the driving force of social life. The dynamic connection between the cultural and economic dimensions of existence, however, ensures that the increased significance of consumption and the symbolic ordering of social life is linked to profound changes in the nature of production and the material basis of existence. The argument that has been made here is that the built environment is a particularly useful social object through which to explore the linkages between them.

Notes

1 A mall is technically an enclosed or partially enclosed pedestrian thoroughfare, but in North American usage it also refers in general to the collection of connected buildings of any large shopping centre.

2 Consumer boycotts have been very successful in undermining the magic of commodities such as Coors beer, Burger King fast foods and Ratners gold jewellery (Smith 1990) and consumer advocates have perhaps less successfully campaigned for 'truth in advertising'.

3 Scientific management, or Taylorism (after F.W. Taylor whose *Principles of Scientific Management* was published in 1911), refers to a system where managers rigidly control and co-ordinate mechanised production employing deskilled workers, while Fordism (after Henry Ford) refers to large-scale assembly line production such as in the Model T factory where such practices were first systematically applied in 1913.

4 This building fulfils the functional requirements of standard office space, but was greeted as a rejection of modernism by critics who celebrated the broken 'Chippendale' pediment and the triumphal arch at the base modelled on the Pazzi Chapel. The combination of the classical language of architecture and this humorous touch appeals precisely to 'those in the know'. The historic reference and the joke is probably lost on everyone else.

5 Late modernism itself is best typified by the Pompidou in Paris, the Hong Kong Shanghai Bank in Hong Kong, the Lloyds Building in London and the Sainsbury Centre for the Visual Arts, University of East Anglia. It is a self-conscious modernism, an attempt to relieve the boredom of modernist aesthetic by taking it to an extreme and exaggerating the functionalism and technical elements to amuse or please (Jencks 1987), but without the pastiche and playfulness of post-modernism proper. Typically this involves a display of heating and ventilation ducts and cleaning gantries, and an aesthetic of motion.

6 Some shopping centres have organised self-guided tours or employ tour guides (Kowinski 1985, 21) and others, such as the Riverchase Galleria in Birmingham, Alabama, even offer weekend shoppers' specials combining hotel rooms with retail discounts.

References

Barthes, R. 1972, *Mythologies*, Hill & Wang, New York.

Baudrillard, J. 1981, *For a Critique of the Political Economy of the Sign*, Telos, St Louis.

Baudrillard, J. 1983, *Simulations*, Semiotext(e), New York.

Beddington, N. 1982, *Design for Shopping Centres*, Butterworth Scientific, London.

Bourdieu, P. 1986, 'The production of belief: contribution to an economy of symbolic goods' in R. Collins, J. Curran, N. Garnham, P. Scannell, P. Schlesinger & C. Sparks (eds), *Media, Culture and Society*, Sage Publications, Beverly Hills, pp. 131–63.

Braudel, F. 1967, *Capitalism and Material Life 1400-1800*, Harper & Row, New York.

Cooke, P. 1988, *Back to the Future*, Unwin Hyman, London.

Debord, G. 1970, *Society of the Spectacle*, Black & Red Books, Detroit.

Ewen, S. 1976, *Captains of Consciousness: Advertising and the Social Roots of Consumer Culture*, McGraw-Hill, New York.

Ewen, S. 1988, *All Consuming Images: The Politics of Style in Contemporary Culture*, Basic Books, New York.

Frampton, K. 1983, 'Towards a critical regionalism: six points for an architecture of resistance' in H. Foster (ed.), *Postmodern Culture*, Pluto Press, London and Sydney, pp. 16–56.

Frieden, B.J. & Sagalyn, L.B. 1989, *Downtown, Inc.: How America Rebuilds Cities*, MIT Press, Cambridge, Mass.

Gillette, H. 1985, 'The evolution of the planned shopping center in suburb and city', *Journal of the American Planning Association*, 51, 4, pp. 449–60.

Gottdiener, M. 1986, 'Recapturing the center: a semiotic analysis of shopping malls', in M. Gottdiener & A.Ph. Lagopoulos (eds), *The City and the Sign*, Columbia University Press, New York, pp. 288–302.

Gruen, N. 1978, 'Gestalt magnetism or what is special about speciality shopping centers?', *Urban Land*, January, 3–9.

Harvey, D. 1989, *The Condition of Postmodernity: An Enquiry into the Origins of Cultural Change*, Blackwell, Oxford.

Hewison, R. 1987, *The Heritage Industry*, Methuen, London.

Jacobs, J. 1984, *The Mall: An Attempted Escape from Everyday Life*, Waveland, Prospect Heights.

Jager, M. 1986, 'Class definition and the aesthetics of gentrification: Victoriana in Melbourne', in N. Smith & P. Williams (eds), *Gentrification of the City*, Allen & Unwin, Boston, pp. 78–91.

Jameson, F. 1983 'Postmodernism and consumer society', in H. Foster (ed.), *The Anti-Aesthetic*, Bay Press, Port Townsend, WA, pp. 111–25.

Jameson, F. 1984, 'Postmodernism, or the cultural logic of late capitalism,' *New Left Review*, 146, pp. 52–92.

Jencks, C. 1987, *The Language of Post-Modern Architecture* (5th edn), Academy Editions, London.

Jhally, S. 1987, *The Codes of Advertising*, Frances Pinter, London.

Kowinski, W.S. 1985, *The Malling of America: An Inside Look at the Great Consumer Paradise*, William Morrow, New York.

Lasch, C. 1979, *The Culture of Narcissism: American Life in an Age of Diminishing Expectations*, Warner Books, New York.

Lash, S. & Urry, J. 1987, *The End of Organised Capitalism*, University of Wisconsin Press, Madison.

Lefebvre, H. 1971, *Everyday Life in the Modern World*, Harper & Row, New York.

Ley, D. 1987, 'Style of the times: liberal and neo-conservative landscapes in inner Vancouver, 1968-1986', *Journal of Historical Geography*, 13, 1, pp. 40–56.

McCracken, G. 1988, *Culture and Consumption: New Approaches to the Symbolic Character of Consumer Goods and Activities*, Indiana University Press, Bloomington.

Marxism Today, 1988, 'Introduction' (Special Issue on the New Times), October.

Miller, M.B. 1981, *The Bon Marche: Bourgeois Culture and the Department Store, 1869-1920*, Princeton University Press, Princeton.

National Research Bureau 1990, *Shopping Center Directory 1990,* Chicago, NRB.

Relph, E. 1987, *The Modern Urban Landscape*, Johns Hopkins University Press, Baltimore.

Sack, D. 1988, 'The consumer's world: place as context', *Annals of the Association of American Geographers,* 78, 4, pp. 624–64.

Sahlins, M. 1976, *Culture and Practical Reason*, Chicago University Press, Chicago.

Sharrett, C. 1989, 'Defining the postmodern: the case of SoHo Kitchen and El Internacional', in D. Kellner (ed.), *Postmodernism/Jameson/Critique,* Maisonneuve Press, Washington, DC, pp. 162–71.

Shopping Center Age 1989, '...But is it art? Museum, living or "plop" — artwork is good business for malls,' November 1989, pp. 104–12.

Smith, N.C. 1990, *Morality and the Market: Consumer Pressure for Corporate Accountability*, Routledge, London.

Stallings, P. 1990, 'Essay — the call of the mall', *MacNeil/Lehrer Newshour*, 27 November, transcript, WNET, New York.

Stoffel, J. 1988, 'What's new in shopping malls', *New York Times,* 7 August.

Urban Land Institute 1985, *Shopping Center Development Handbook,* Urban Land Institute, Washington DC.

Williams, R. 1980, *Problems in Materialism and Culture: Selected Essays*, New Left Books, London.

Williams, R.H. 1982, *Dream Worlds: Mass Consumption in the Late Nineteenth Century France*, University of California Press, Berkeley.

Wright, G. 1981, *Building the Dream: A Social History of Housing in America*, Pantheon, New York.

11 World's Fairs and the culture of consumption in the contemporary city

David Ley and Kris Olds

Introduction

The City of Toronto licked its wounds after failing, by one vote, to secure the World's Fair for the year 2000 for, despite a promotional campaign costing almost $5 million, the city's boosters were unable to dissuade an international panel from awarding the Fair to Hamburg, representative of a united Germany. Toronto was also one of the six finalists bidding for the 1996 Olympics, a bid which cost considerably more. Within Canada, Toronto is not alone in its pursuit of 'hallmark events' (Hall 1989). The trend was begun by Montreal with its celebrated Centennial Exposition of 1967, followed by the notorious billion-dollar Olympic Games in 1976. Since then the Commonwealth Games have come to Edmonton, the Winter Olympics to Calgary, a World's Fair to Vancouver, and in 1994 the Commonwealth Games return to Canada, to Victoria. Other smaller cities including London and Halifax have been unsuccessful finalists in bids for major events. The pursuit of the spectacle is not confined to Canada. Besides Toronto, another of the six finalists for the 1996 Olympics was Melbourne, which triumphed in a spirited contest with Brisbane and Sydney to serve as the Australian flag-bearer. In 1988 Brisbane had its own World's Fair, and other cities are in on the act. Perth was put on the map by hosting the America's Cup yacht race, while Adelaide closes its streets each year to host a Grand Prix (for these and other Australian examples, see Syme et al. 1989). In 1988 it seemed as if parts of Australia had embarked on a year-long carnival in recognition of the bicentennial of white settlement.

The cost of these ventures is immense, and raises fundamental political and moral questions about resource allocation. In 1989 the City of Toronto opened its $560 million covered sports stadium and in 1990 fundraising was well along for a new ballet and opera house ($230 million), while estimated costs for the Olympics reached $2.52 billion, and for the World's Fair, $1.3 billion. The opportunity cost of this scale of investment is breathtaking, not least in a city with serious environmental problems and in urgent need of affordable housing. An anti-poverty coalition, Bread Not Circuses, assailed the Toronto media and City Council about the justice and wisdom of such conspicuous consumption in a metropolis with seventy-five food banks and perhaps 20 000 homeless.

The apparent multiplication of hallmark events is part of a broader trend toward the playful and the aesthetic in contemporary society (Ley 1980, 1983). The places of leisure and recreation are expanding to whole regions: in developed nations a number of growth regions, including Australia's Gold Coast, California, Florida, and parts of the western Mediterranean evoke a leisure lifestyle as a major component of their human geographies. There is every indication that these trends will accelerate in the future. The futuristic Japanese proposal to build a new city, the 'multi-function polis', in Australia with an integral leisure function indicates the resilience of the concept of recreation in private as well as public planning. Japanese investment is centrally implicated in leisure and resort projects elsewhere around the Pacific Basin. In the Canadian Rockies, Japanese and other Asian interests have bought into the major winter sports centres of Banff and Whistler, and are involved (or targeted) in some of the proposals to construct upwards of forty golf courses within a ninety-minute drive of Vancouver. The same is happening within the city, as new palaces to the arts and culture — Mozart in the metropolis (Whitt 1987) — new stadia for sports and recreation, and whole districts, like Sydney's Darling Harbour or Baltimore's Inner Harbor, are being recreated as emporia of the pleasure principle. The proliferation of conference centres and their attendant brood of hotels point to the growing synthesis of business and leisure. Recreational pursuits have also become major elements of a new generation of mega-malls like Gateshead's Metrocentre in England or the West Edmonton Mall, a billion-dollar facility which has 600 stores and services, and under the same roof a range of attractions including a beach and wave pool, skating rink, fun fair, miniature golf course, sea aquarium with dolphins, operational submarines and a replica of Christopher Columbus' vessel, *Santa Maria* (Hopkins 1990). The same conjunction of business and fantasy has been achieved by the London marketing company Imagination, which creates for its corporate clients a concept of marketing as theatre (Whatmore 1990), a dramatic and total environment for the extolling of a corporate product.

In its manipulation of a total environment, a company like Imagination is a magic-maker, committed to moulding a new way of seeing, or rather a new way of sensing, for its temporary fabrications offer a fuller sensual environment of sight and sound. In its marketing strategy the aestheticisation of space is a key concern: 'there is no such thing as neutral space' (Whatmore 1990, 18). A similar revaluing of *urban* space has been a feature of the past twenty years, including a heightened sensitivity to landscaping, heritage preservation and urban design. Does the urban visitor sense this newly aestheticised urban landscape as a participant or as a spectator? Is the manipulative intent of Imagination a model for new post-modern city landscapes? There are those who see only spectacle and social control in the aesthetic halo of new consumption-based landscapes (Harvey 1987; Huxley & Kerkin 1988). Others see a more active engagement between city residents and the 'liveable city', with its new range of leisure opportunities. There are many questions which remain unanswered. What is the meaning of these landscapes of consumption, some temporary, some more enduring, which provide such a stark counterpoint to the industrial areas and port waterfronts of Sydney or Brisbane which they replace? How are these landscapes of a public mass culture received by their visitors? What are the intentions of the elites who shape them, and how are these dominant meanings internalised or reconstructed by the majority of urban dwellers? These are questions we shall address in this chapter, as we examine the 1986 World's Fair in Vancouver and place this event in a broader theoretical literature which debates the meaning of contemporary public culture.

Mass or popular culture?

The problem of the masses has been a central, perhaps the central, preoccupation of social theory for well over a century. For Kierkegaard, authentic individuality, real human nature, was being submerged in the nineteenth century before the relentless flood of the urban crowd, the masses. Gustave Le Bon's *Psychologie des Foules* (1895) was an important reflection of a widespread sentiment, and an inspiration to other theorists, including Freud. 'The substitution of the unconscious action of crowds for the conscious action of individuals', observed Le Bon, 'is one of the principal characteristics of the present age' (cited in Brantlinger 1983, 166–7). From the generally disapproving view of the masses emerged the generally disparaging view of mass culture. Le Bon summarised this viewpoint:

> Crowds being only capable of thinking in images are only to be impressed by images ... Bread and spectacular shows constituted for the plebeians of ancient Rome the ideal of happiness, and they asked for nothing more. Throughout the successive ages this ideal has scarcely varied ... The crowd state and the domination of crowds is equivalent to the barbarian state, or a return to it. (cited in Brantlinger 1983, 168)

This is an argument with a contemporary ring, for the values of mass culture, and by extension its consumers, have been a consistent butt of criticism, as television, film and popular music, in particular, have been challenged as sources of latter-day decadence.

While these sentiments are often an expression of conservative morality, they reappear in a more radical reading, where mass culture, often represented as the culture or consciousness industry, is indicted as an instrument of false consciousness, as a form of social control by an economic elite in the advancement of its own interests. This depiction of mass culture as thought control was advanced by members of the influential Frankfurt School during the interwar period. The enlightenment promises of democracy and freedom were beset by a new bondage as 'the culture industry has molded men as a type unfailingly reproduced in every product' (Horkheimer & Adorno 1972, 127). Resistance is inconceivable, for hegemonic power from above is complete: 'The misplaced love of the common people for the wrong which is done them is a greater force than the cunning of the authorities' (Horkheimer & Adorno 1972, 134). The consumer is trapped, and in an alienated life 'becomes the ideology of the pleasure industry, whose institutions he cannot escape' (Horkheimer & Adorno 1972, 158). In *Society of the Spectacle*, Debord (1973) extends this uncompromising picture of social and mental control. His argument elaborates the initial thesis that 'The entire life of societies in which modern conditions of production reign announces itself as an immense accumulation of *spectacles*' (Debord 1970, par. 1). The scope of the spectacle is total; it has invaded 'The entire life ... Everything that was directly lived'. For Debord, the spectacle defends unequal class power, extending to the masses only 'the impoverishment, the servitude and the negation of real life' (par. 215). It neutralises resistance as 'the sun which never sets over the empire of modern passivity' (par. 13). It casts a deceptive but seductive unreality of images and signs. This is a thesis which to varying degree has a number of advocates (Harvey 1987).

Other perspectives in popular culture challenge this watertight system of hegemonic control, of powerful elites and passive, deluded consumers (Lears 1985; Williams 1977). Such a system oversimplifies. It presents the consciousness of the masses as monolithic and unproblematic, passive and without the potential for resistance. It locates mass culture ultimately in economic relations, overlooking very real status dimensions such as race, religion, gender and lifestyle. Government is either absent from analysis or treated unsubtly as an extension of dominant elites. Societal flux, the pervasive change which constantly dislocates and provides opportunity for opposition, is missing and society is portrayed as frozen and hermetic. The question of *why* the masses so readily internalise the allegedly manipulative values of mass culture is not addressed. One set of answers suggests that commodities supply a set of both material and symbolic needs deemed important by people (see Diggins 1977). Investigation of the relations between definitions of the good life by the public and the critic is, then, a significant issue, but one notable by its absence in the literature we have reviewed. Moreover, the view of mass culture expressed by its critics is distant and elitist. The interpretation of mass culture is invariably inferred rather than direct. There is a surprisingly consistent gap between the theory of social control and any empirical examination of the meaning of mass culture to its market. A web of interpretation is thrown over the experience of mass culture, but it is a web which is not informed by utterances from the consumers themselves.

A number of works in popular culture studies have reacted strongly against a posited mass culture. 'With the notion of "mass"', writes Laba (1986), 'the social reality of the forms of popular culture is either generalised and trivialised or ignored completely'. The influential view of mass culture as manipulation homogenises both the cultural product and its consumers, reduces them to passivity, and does not consider culture as an actively-negotiated process. It overlooks, for example, the common regularity that entrepreneurs follow styles as often as they create them, that commodities frequently emerge from expressive forms of popular culture (Laba 1986; Martin 1981), that the garment industry, for example, is organised on the premise that manufacturers cannot tell which of their current fashions will be successful (Scott 1988). A second perspective argues that popular culture is more complex, diverse and shifting, containing its own purposes which may be oppositional to elite intents.

Many of the social movements of the past twenty years have been associated with the liberal culture and politics of the new middle class, including environmentalism, civil rights, feminism, cultural nationalism and the anti-nuclear and democracy movements. In conservation, heritage and particularly neighbourhood protest, opposition has focused on the nexus of place (Eyles & Evans 1987; Hasson & Ley 1993). Oppositional subcultures which do not present a face of passivity are also found on the margins of mainstream society. In Britain the empirical research of the Centre for Contemporary Cultural Studies in Birmingham has documented numerous examples of resistance, particularly in youth subcultures (Hall et al. 1980; Willis 1977). Similarly in the American inner city, the stylised social worlds of the street gang member and the graffiti artist include rituals which invert the value system of 'straight' society. Like mainstream models, these adolescent subcultures seek to excel but, unlike the mainstream, the contours of their own existence encourage them to excel at being outrageous, at being bad (Ley & Cybriwsky 1974). Ethnic displays also present an opportunity to nurture alternative realities, through the performance of an ethnic carnival (Jackson 1988) or the creation of street murals reviving folk histories. The Chicano murals of the East Los Angeles *barrio* present a particularly resilient expression of folk culture, and it is within the *barrio* that a distinctive popular music has developed, a music which like the murals includes a cultural politics of historic folk memory and contemporary community struggle against poverty and cultural prejudice (Lipsitz 1986-87).

The debates around mass and popular culture have been focused with renewed intensity on post-modern cultural forms. Employing much of the vocabulary of the critique of the culture industry, post-modern design is attacked as superficial, tasteless, deceitful and manipulative (see Foster 1985). However, this criticism characteristically overlooks the active negotiation of symbolic forms that *may* occur in post-modern design. The use of recognisable popular elements is a key element of post-modern design, but their rearrangement may permit an ironic or parodic interpretation which challenges their taken-for-granted status. Post-modernism offers, in short, 'a model that is profoundly implicated in, yet still capable of criticising, that which it seeks to describe' (Hutcheon 1986-87). The critical potential of post-modernism is apparent when we remember its adversarial stand against the elitist designs of modern architecture and planning and their patrons in corporate capitalism and the corporate state. Not the least significant of Jane Jacobs' arguments against centralised modern planning thirty years ago was her challenge of its elitist way of seeing, against which she posed a radical populism based in part upon the everyday experience of the sights, sounds and rhythms of her own street in New York (Jacobs 1961). Her new appreciation of the strength of folk and personal knowledge was extended politically to advocacy of a participatory method which established direct communication between everyday life and planning practices. In this manner the ways of seeing and doing from below were reformulating the perception from above. The success with which Jacobs' argument infiltrated public planning challenges any view of hegemony which denies the place of active negotiation in popular culture, the capacity for opposition and penetration from below.

World's Fairs: instruments of social control?

Like mass culture, the modern world's fair has a nineteenth-century origin, and has invariably been the project of social elites. Their intent, it is held, was to consolidate '"ideologically coherent" "symbolic universes" confirming and extending the authority of the country's corporate, political, and scientific leadership ... (they were) triumphs of hegemony as well as symbolic edifices' (Rydell 1984, 2–3). Walter Benjamin was more specific in his denunciation of the nineteenth century Parisian expositions, which:

> opened up a phantasmagorical world, where man entered to be entertained. The amusement industry made this easier for him by elevating him to the level of a commodity. He had only to surrender himself to its manipulations, while enjoying his alienation from himself and from others. (Benjamin 1970)

Let us examine more closely this interpretation of the world's fair as an instrument of social control. In the United States, the initial sponsors of a major exposition invariably hailed from the municipal boosters of the chamber of commerce, but the role of the state should not be oversimplified. The public sector in the United States underwrote in grants and bonds 76 per cent of the cost of San Antonio's 1968 Fair, over 80 per cent of Spokane's 1974 Fair and 74 per cent of Knoxville's 1982 Fair. Indeed, senior government funds have commonly been procured through expositions to finance lasting public legacies, such as a new transportation system (e.g. Montreal 1967,

Knoxville 1982), urban redevelopment on the margins of downtown (San Antonio 1968, Spokane 1974, Knoxville 1982, New Orleans 1984), and cultural, sporting, recreational and convention facilities (Seattle 1962 and many others). However, besides the dominant economic and municipal objectives of increasing trade, tourism and public infrastructure, international objectives have added a separate dimension to a number of world's fairs. The Anglo-French Exhibition of 1908 celebrated the *entente cordiale* between the two nations, and the 1855 Fair in Paris had the major objectives of fostering a *rapprochement* between Britain and France and consolidating the legitimacy of Louis Napoleon (Chandler 1986).

Trade, local support and political ambitions are insufficient to draw a mass public to an exposition site. Here we encounter the second theme in the social control argument — the place of spectacle, fantasy and entertainment in enchanting and diverting the masses from more serious matters. From the beginning the fairs were certainly a dramatic expression of mass society, and grandeur was a ubiquitous theme. The main building of the 1867 Paris Exposition was 1.5 km (a mile) in circumference, while the 1889 Fair built heavenwards with the Eiffel Tower. A beaux arts White City of considerable splendour at Chicago in 1893 propelled American planners toward city beautiful principles for a generation. A jewelled tower was the glory of the 1915 San Francisco Fair, while by 1939 pervasive modern design tendencies prescribed the primitive geometries of a 185 m (610 ft) high triangular tower, the Trylon, and a globular Perisphere as the New York Fair's central symbols. The aesthetics of architecture, colour, decoration and lighting added to the sense of spectacle, particularly at night (Harrison 1980). However, a tone of moral and educational improvement has challenged too simple a view of spectacle. In 1893, the Chicago midway included extensive ethnological exhibits and public education 'ran riot' at the Exposition (Rydell 1984, 46; Harris 1978). It was at the same Columbian Exposition that Frederick Jackson Turner presented his frontier thesis to the American Historical Association meeting which was only one of many congresses and conventions coincident with the Exposition and conveying an erudite tone to the proceedings. By 1915, over 900 congresses convened at the San Francisco Fair, representing medicine, science, religion, social policy and the arts. Indeed, display of the arts was a major feature of international expositions. In the Parisian fairs, arts and education commonly ranked first. Both Gauguin and Picasso were inspired in their own artistic experimentation by the presence of 'primitive' art at the Paris expositions (Greenhalgh 1988).

It would seem that while the trading function is central it is incorrect to see the fairs as only merchandise marts. Education and entertainment have also been high-ranking goals, as have municipal, national and international political objectives. Nor should we oversimplify the response of visitors. We need then to broaden our understanding of fairs and their visitors beyond a simple bread and circuses metaphor: 'the fairs were not only selling goods, they were selling ideas: ideas about the relations between nations, the spread of education, the advancement of science, the form of cities, the nature of domestic life, the place of art in society' (Benedict 1983).

Does this simply broaden the potential scope of hegemony to a wider range of social experience? The ethnological exhibits pre-1914, for example, were strongly influenced by social Darwinism and as such reinforced racist attitudes. Moreover, the values displayed in the fairs were contained within the limits of middle-class society. Part of the fantasy of the expositions was their optimistic portrayal of a middle-class present and future, aesthetic, hygienic, pleasurable, self-improving and consensual where conflict and scarcity were no more evident than in any other middle-class setting. Indeed, the fairs were primarily stories a middle-class society told itself about itself. Admission charges barred large elements of the poorer population from entry. At Philadelphia's Centennial Fair a 'poor man's day' with reduced admission was held. In 1939 a Gallup poll indicated that 63 per cent of respondents who had not visited the New York Fair had stayed away because they could not afford the costs of attendance (Susman 1980). The obstacle of high admission charges to the entry of large sections of the population has been cited as recently as the ill-fated 1984 Fair in New Orleans (O'Brian 1985).

Imputations of hegemony and social control remain, moreover, inferences from above, and even detailed studies include minimal evidence of the actual ways of seeing of the public (Greenhalgh 1988). The New York exposition set out self-consciously to be 'the People's Fair' for 'the average American', but even here few documents have survived to assess how the people themselves perceived the Fair and the degree to which they internalised its values (Susman 1980). In this context the existence of a large (if imperfect) data set of visitors' perceptions of the 1986 Exposition in Vancouver is of particular interest for the light it throws upon the meaning of this landscape of heroic consumption to its audience.

Expo 86: learning within a context of fun

As much as any recent fair, the 1986 World Exposition in Vancouver opened an instructive window on its time and place (fig. 11.1). It represented both an integration of themes common to most world's fairs with the personalities, interests and opportunities of a unique setting (see the varying accounts in Anderson & Wachtel 1986; Government of Canada 1986). Expo 86 was planned and operated by the provincial government of British Columbia and managed by the Expo 86 Corporation, a crown corporation responsible to cabinet. The theme of the Fair was transportation and communications (originally its title was Transpo 86), to commemorate the centennial of the City of Vancouver and the arrival of the first transcontinental passenger train. In an initial press release in June 1979 the provincial government declared that 'The primary purpose of the Exposition is not, however, to make money. It is to mark this important double anniversary' (Province of British Columbia 1979). The objectives of Expo 86 were varied and changing. At an early stage, an important objective was to secure federal funds for urban redevelopment, including a convention centre, a sports stadium and a rapid transit line. The best chance of gaining these funds was through their amalgamation in a package including a world's fair. Promotion of the Fair was also intended to raise the sagging fortunes of the provincial government (Ley 1987). As the economic recession deepened, job creation and economic development were given pride of place in government press releases.

The organisation of Expo 86 captured a number of pervasive regional themes. Bitter disputes raged between all three levels of government about the financing and even the holding of the Fair, with the Mayor of Vancouver in opposition, and by early 1982 these conflicts seemed likely to lead to its cancellation. A second crisis followed, concerning labour disputes. Upon the insistence of the right-wing provincial government, the Expo Corporation awarded construction contracts to non-union firms, despite the high level of unionisation in the building trades (Mickelburgh 1986). With building contracts

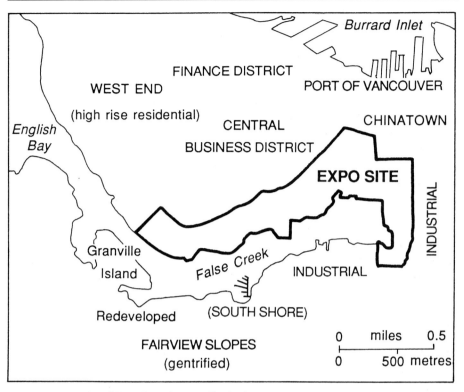

Figure 11:1 Location of Expo site and surrounding land use.

valued at between $600 and $900 million, the stakes were high for the unions, and disputes including work stoppages and demonstrations led to renewed crisis. On this second occasion, the Chairman of the Expo Board recommended cancellation of the Fair but was overruled by a deeply-divided cabinet. At this stage, the Fair, far from establishing social order, was deepening social conflict. A third theme, symptomatic of the neo-conservatism of British Columbia during the 1980s, was the dominant private enterprise orientation. The Chairman of the Expo Board (also President for the final fifteen months) was the province's most eminent entrepreneur, a rags-to-riches multimillionaire. The Board itself was dominated by businesspeople, though on a number of occasions it was overruled by direct intervention of cabinet. The true architect of the Fair was the Premier of British Columbia, who publicly announced the concept in January 1980 and who became ever more closely identified with it. By 1984, facing a growing deficit and labour unrest on the site, he described himself 'as the father of Expo suffering through its birth' (*Toronto Globe and Mail*, 12 April 1984).

The political mandate of the Fair gave it remarkable powers. The legal status of a crown corporation conferred empowerments upon Expo 86 greater than those of a private corporation. It enjoyed the freedom to raise and disperse its own funds (under the advantageous credit rating of the provincial government), the power of expropriation, and authority to override all city bylaws, zoning regulations and planning policy. With easy access to the public purse, a megaproject mentality toward spending readily arose.

Any comparison between Expo 86 and the calamitous 1984 Fair in New Orleans was, according to an Expo director, 'like comparing the Queen Mary to a canoe'. The distinction he saw was significant: while the New Orleans Fair 'had a total budget of $400 million to work with, Expo 86 and its participants are spending more than three and a half times that — $1.5 billion' (*BC Business Bulletin* 1985). Of this figure, $800 million was to be spent by the Expo Corporation, $300 million by the federal government, and the remainder by other Fair exhibitors. Government control gave a new meaning to the bottom line, as it had earlier to Expo 67 in Montreal. The project deficit grew from $12 million in 1980, to $75 million in 1982 and $311 million at the beginning of 1985. In the Fair's closing ceremonies, the Chairman of the Expo Corporation triumphantly announced that Expo 86 had been achieved on budget — what he had in mind was the projected deficit of over $300 million.

Advertising material highlighted entertainment rather than science and education, though the latter were certainly included. However, the matrix of the Fair, into which other activities were cast, was having fun, putting on and enjoying a good show (Kahrl 1986). Its Creative Director described the concept as 'learning within a context of fun' (Murray 1986, 6): 'I try to bring people to a teachable moment. To charm and delight and make them laugh while introducing some new information' (Orr, Deaton & Sturmanis 1986). The planning theme which emerged was intended to integrate pleasure and knowledge in a celebration of individual and social creativity. Against the spectre of social disillusionment, the message of the Fair was to be the achievement of human ingenuity in all fields. As such the Fair would counterpose its historic context: 'the look, feel and content of Expo 86 above all responded to the event's moment in time. It was imperative that this expression transcend the reality of a troubled decade' (Government of Canada 1986, 75).

Expo 86 had the air of a carnival, a colourful animation of space and time, whirling in the density of its stimuli. For its site design 'Images rather than words were stressed, with colour as the backbone of the vocabulary' (Government of Canada 1986, 9). Here, perhaps, is the disembodied realm of fantasy, the persuasive architecture of the sign, achieved to perfection. The design theme was 'festive technology', its vocabulary 'Exuberance. Festivity. Exhilaration. Charisma. Fantasy. Vibrancy. Surprise. Optimism. Spirit. Joy. The objective was to satiate the site with a level of colour and kinetics so intensely stimulating that the resulting memory would last a lifetime' (Government of Canada 1986, 76).

The pavilions themselves carried on the mix of 'learning within a context of fun'. The sixty-five pavilions included international, regional, and corporate sponsors (fig. 11.2). They varied widely in their exhibits: some offered little more than national gift shops and travel promotion. Others were resolutely serious and scientific. A few showed considerable artistic flair. A number displayed themes which revealed more diversity than a tightly-woven view of hegemony might accommodate. Of the forty national pavilions, seven came from socialist states, including China, the Soviet Union and Cuba — a catholic selection for a free-enterprise host government. The United Nations pavilion was devoted to the achievement of peace, the perils of war and the capacity of individuals to effect positive change. Two pavilions offered strong religious themes, Christian and Muslim (Saudi Arabia). Two regional pavilions presented significant themes from local popular culture: a sensitive examination of native culture (Northwest Territories) and the human face of outmigration (Saskatchewan). The folklife area

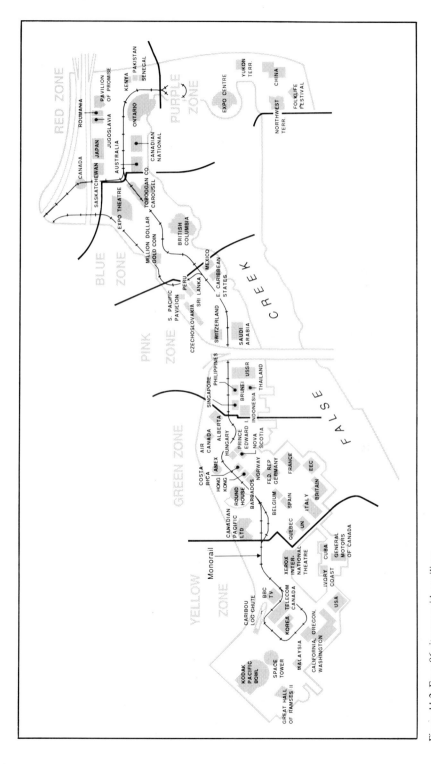

Figure 11.2: Expo 86 site map with pavilions.
Source: *The Expo Celebration*, 1986, Whitecap Books, Murray/Love Productions.

focused on different aspects of ethnic, native and popular culture. Most interesting of all was the ambivalent view of technology included in two of the corporate pavilions. The Canadian Pacific exhibit had two imaginative shows presenting social impacts of new technology and user conflicts. Equally unpredictable was General Motors' 'Spirit Lodge', a reflection on the meaning of new technology. In a pavilion which included an automobile display, the narrator of 'Spirit Lodge', an old Indian, challenged the claims of new technology and offered his own standard: 'Are our machines making us more like humans? Or are they making us more like machines?' (Fulford 1986). The final report of the Expo Corporation suggested in retrospect that the Fair's 'mood was post-technological' (Government of Canada 1986, 75). Oppositional themes may appear in the most improbable of sources, hegemony does not appear without paradox and inconsistency. So how stupefied were the visitors?

The meanings of Expo 86: public perceptions of a hallmark event

In the final weeks of Expo, a city newspaper included a questionnaire asking readers to send in their perceptions of the Fair. Five questions appeared.

1   What will you remember most about Expo?
2   Has it made us a world-class city?
3   What was its single best aspect?
4   Its worst?
5   Expo's deficit is now estimated at $300 million. Was it worth it?

To the editor's surprise over 2200 replies were submitted. About a quarter were received from the City of Vancouver, and about half from its suburbs; 99.5 per cent had attended the Fair. While the representativeness of this sample cannot be gauged, the results indicate a group well disposed to the Fair, with 85 per cent claiming that its large deficit was well justified. The perceptions of so large a group are significant in their own right for any insights that might be offered on the nature and extent of hegemony and social control over the public.

For the respondents the single best aspect of the Fair had little to do with the economic goals the government had been declaring repeatedly for several years. Fewer than 10 per cent mentioned economic objectives, and neither did educational objectives loom large, only 3.5 per cent of replies seeing education as the Fair's major achievement (though educational themes did appear as a secondary theme elsewhere). Instead of these lofty goals, the majority of respondents measured Expo in more personal terms, reflecting their own experience of the Fair, its activities and people.

The most memorable features of Expo have been classified and appear in table 11.1. Positive reaction to a 'successful' fair monopolises the categories; to a sympathetic eye even the line-ups could present an opportunity to speak to strangers and watch street entertainment ('the wonderful line-ups which enabled me to meet the world'). Perhaps the most predictable group of responses refer to the aesthetic quality of the site (categories 5, 6, 8, 11, 12). References to the waterfront setting, the rainbow colours, landscaping and sculptures indicated that the design process had been effective: 'The whimsy and colour of its beautiful land, sea and air plazas ... the smell of the sea from the quiet promenades.' 'The combining of colour and architecture with local landscape

Table 11.1:　'What will you remember most about Expo?'

		Numbers	**Per cent (n = 2216)**
1	Friendliness of people/happiness	758	34
2	Atmosphere/excitement	392	18
3	Entertainment/party	382	17
4	International/national meeting place	322	15
5	Pavilions/exhibits	295	13
6	Colour/colour coding	241	11
7	Pride/sense of community	241	11
8	Cleanliness	234	11
9	Courteous staff	234	11
10	Well organised	105	5
11	Setting/site itself	103	5
12	Beauty/aesthetics/architecture	100	5
13	Fireworks and lasers	98	4
14	Line-ups	70	3
15	Education received	60	3
16	Miscellaneous (30 other features)	482	22

in beauty, fantasy and wit.' Expo 86 had also learned the lessons of successful theme parks in the cleanliness of the site and the courtesy of staff: 'The cleanliness of the entire Expo site. The clean cut appearance of the staff gave the province a definite classy look.'

A second major theme explored a suspension of reality, Expo as a time and a place that was enchanting, set aside from a humdrum world. Consider the following: 'It has shrunk this year. This year didn't start till May 2 and will end in mid October.' 'Going through the entrance turnstile and being touched by the magic ... Going through the exit turnstile and it's back to reality, the real world.' 'I had so much fun. It was a fantasy place where you sensed people had left their problems outside the gate. There was a carefree atmosphere.' There are a number of questions to ask about this spell. How permanent was it? To what extent could people make the separation between the fantasies and the real? To what extent did the world of Expo invade life outside the fairgrounds? For some, a large number, the spell was that of a carnival spirit, it was entertainment, fun, a party. As such, it was the deficit not the show which had an air of unreality: 'Yes Expo was worth it ... worth it above all, *because we had fun!'* 'Emphatically, yes! The fair gave literally millions of hours of pleasure. The deficit is an unbeatable entertainment bargain.' 'A party always costs us some and this was an incredible party.'

For some respondents, the party became their party, and their identification with the exposition became almost obsessive. Here, most clearly, a confusion of realities was occurring: 'What a fantastic five months we have had — Expo has indeed been one big party and we shall miss it very much. I wish we could keep more of it intact ... I hate the thought of more high-rises going up on our beloved Expo site.' Note the personalisation of the Fair which occurs in the final sentence. As such, no cost it seems could be too high: 'What deficit? It is like putting a price on every hug we get from a child.' 'With the closing of Expo 86 I personally feel sad to have to say good-bye to such a dear friend, but this friend has left me with such wonderful memories that I will cherish forever.'

Such personification of the Fair is possessive, and indeed obsessive. One writer sent in a poem extolling 'My beautiful, colourful enchanting lady'. Another wrote:

> The feeling remembered is the excitement, the expectation, the pride that I got as opening day approached. A great love affair was happening, to me, to Vancouver, to the World. A sound and sight so wonderful that only the music and fireworks could come close to expressing it. EXPO 86, I remember you with passion, colour, lights, music and most of all giving the World exactly what you said you would: the biggest party of the century.

A number of respondents held season tickets and some attended frequently: 'It was a fantastic once-in-most lifetimes' experience and I'd do it all again. To date I've been 85 times.'

Such obsession is symptomatic of the spectacle. Augustine relates the seduction of a friend by the Roman games (in Brantlinger 1983, 79–80). Initially resistant, its sights, sounds and excitement became an opiate blinding his moral judgement. While allusions to bread and circuses were made only by correspondents critical of Expo, it is in such obsessive perceptions that the responses came nearest to the theoretical portrait of willing victims of the culture industry. The distraction of the public from broader issues is accompanied by a preoccupation with amusement and spectacle and its elevation to 'a dear friend', an 'enchanting lady'. There is a further question to ask. How abiding is this seduction, how lasting the spell? For a number of respondents the boundaries of fantasy and reality were clearly defined: 'Let's not worry about the deficit. Let's just accept it. The party's over. Let's pay for it now.'

A third group of categories (1, 4, 7, 9, 15) in table 11.1 reflect a more active and positive engagement with the Fair. They refer to intersubjective relations of happiness, friendship, a sense of community and mutual learning. Very few visitors attended Expo 86 alone. They came in clusters of friends and relatives, and the Fair was an occasion, a forum for *advancing* these social bonds. Many households in the region organised family reunions during 1986: 'We invited 60 members of the family and friends; 42 said they were coming, so far we had 52 ... We enjoyed every one of them and had the greatest summer of our life. We are in our 70s.'

The Fair was an opportunity for binding nuclear and extended family relations in learning and pleasure: 'I'll remember the leisurely hours we spent there — walking around the grounds, enjoying the entertainment, absorbing the information in the displays, watching the happiness of our children's faces.' The Fair's events and memories were *social* occasions: 'Remembering the time I sang with my friends in front of the world live in a studio was something extraordinary for me.' The Fair provided an opportunity for visitors to promote *their own* social purposes, to engage in the spectacle from their own way of seeing. Social bonds extended also to strangers, to other societies and cultures in a celebration of multiculturalism. Mutual learning offered many benefits: 'How educational it was. You could get a real feel for life in other countries and for their people. Prejudices were replaced with friendships.' 'The cultural events presented by international communities ... These have not only been a banquet for eye and ear, but have also helped to promote greater appreciation of one another's culture. Nations clearly have more in common than differences, and the audiences have felt this.' 'My 9 year old daughter will have a view of the world as a whole. Whatever else she learns, the world will remain a community.' Within responses such as this are conveyed not only the active engagement of people with the opportunities presented by a mass event. Perhaps also there is indication of learning which may engender independent world views, Jameson's (1979) 'utopian potential' within all mass culture which can challenge hegemonic values.

Conclusion

Expo 86 offers a further example of the increasingly ludic nature of urban life, the growing intrusion of leisure and the aesthetic into the urban landscape. The culture of consumption has an important playful dimension. What do we make of this tendency? How is it to be theorised? How intoxicating are these landscapes to their audience, to what extent a diversion and a delusion, an instrument of social control imposed upon an uncritical public? We should note that the planning of Expo was fraught with conflict. Indeed, it exposed and aggravated the deepest regional tensions: conflict between different levels of government and, above all, labour unrest with the decision to make Expo an open work site. While the extravaganza of Expo was being planned, the deep cuts of a provincial restraint programme led to the formation of a popular opposition movement, the Solidarity Coalition, and carried the province within a few hours of a general strike. The deflection of funds into Expo aggravated these tensions. During the pre-opening period the Fair was a source of social unrest rather than social control.

We have seen that among our respondents, memories were vivid and positive, indeed for some the Fair became virtually an obsession. In this displacement of reality, the data come closest to describing the manipulation of consciousness posited by mass culture theorists. How permanent though, was this psychosis? Moreover, another large group of respondents were far less spellbound. They engaged the Fair more actively, used it as a resource for advancing family and friendship ties, were less riveted by its fantasy, and were more intent on learning, including the more expansive issues of global citizenship posed by some of the pavilions. Among this group we have no basis to assume a displacement of reality. The cultural dupes posed by mass culture theorists are much less visible on the ground.

The hallmark event has become a major tool of economic development, and in some circumstances plays a role similar to that anticipated for heavy industry in earlier decades. The successful event may act as a regional multiplier, propelling waves of investment and economic activity. Overseas tourism to British Columbia, which had remained sluggish from 1980 to 1985, increased by 25 per cent in 1986, the year of Expo, and has sustained this higher level since. The growth of tourists has occurred particularly in Pacific Rim source countries, notably Japan, Hong Kong and Australia. Since 1986 there has also been a significant growth of 'business category' immigration to British Columbia, over half of it from Hong Kong. While other factors are no doubt at work, Expo's role in advertising Vancouver to the Pacific Rim market seems to have achieved its objectives.

The significance of a major hallmark event is indicated by preparations for the 1992 World's Fair in Seville. With a budget of $7-8 billion to improve regional infrastructure, the Fair was regarded as, in the words of a senior bureaucrat 'the motor that will enable the economy of Andalusia to take off' (Riding 1989). The provision of public infrastructure and a plan for regional economic development did not, however, exhaust the objectives of Expo 92. Both the Prime Minister and his Deputy were from Seville and well aware of the advantages of consolidating their own power base. Beyond party politics there was also a national objective, incorporating politics, economics and culture, to project the image of a new Spain into a newly united Europe. According to the chief engineer at Expo 92, 'Spain wants Expo 92 to show it as a modern country that is more than just bulls and flamenco' (Riding 1989). The hallmark event is anything but trivial; with its political, economic and cultural dimensions it has the capacity to remake human geographies.

Note

An earlier and longer version of this paper 'Landscape as spectacle: World's Fairs and the culture of heroic consumption' appeared in *Society and Space* 6, 1988, 191-212. It is reprinted with the kind permission of the publisher, Pion Limited.

References

Anderson, R. & Wachtel, E. (eds) 1986, *The Expo Story*, Harbour Publishing, Madeira Park, BC.

Benedict, B. 1983, 'The anthropology of world's fairs', in B. Benedict (ed.), *The Anthropology of World's Fairs*, Scolar Press, London, pp. 1–65.

Benjamin, W. 1970, 'Paris, capital of the 19th century', *Dissent,* 17, pp. 439–47.

Brantlinger, P. 1983, *Bread and Circuses: Theories of Mass Culture as Social Decay*, Cornell University Press, Ithaca, New York.

BC Business Bulletin 1985, 'Expo 86: a business with a future', *British Columbia Business Bulletin,* 1, 5, pp. 1–2.

Chandler, A. 1986, 'Fanfare for the new empire: the Paris Exposition Universelle of 1855', *World's Fair,* 6, 2, pp. 11–16.

Debord, G. 1970, *Society of the Spectacle*, Black & Red, Detroit.

Diggins, J. 1977, 'Reification and the cultural hegemony of capitalism', *Social Research,* 44, pp. 354–83.

Dobkin, M. 1983, 'A twenty-five million dollar mirage', in B. Benedict (ed.), *The Anthropology of World's Fairs*, Scolar Press, London, pp. 66–93.

Eyles, J. & Evans, M. 1987, 'Popular consciousness, moral ideology, and locality', *Society and Space,* 5, pp. 39–71.

Foster, H. 1985, *Recodings: Art, Spectacle, Cultural Politics*, Bay Press, Port Townsend, Washington.

Fulford, R. 1986, 'Only fair', *Saturday Night*, October, pp. 9–12.

Government of Canada 1986, *The Expo 86 General Report,* Department of External Affairs, Ottawa.

Greenhalgh, P. 1988, *Ephemeral Vistas: The Expositions Universelles, Great Exhibitions and World's Fairs, 1851-1939*, Manchester University Press, Manchester.

Hall, C. 1989, 'The definition and analysis of hallmark tourist events', *GeoJournal,* 19, pp. 263–8.

Hall, S., Hobson, D., Lowe, A. & Willis, P. 1980, *Culture, Media, Language*, Hutchinson, London.

Harris, N. 1978, 'Museums, merchandising and popular taste: the struggle for influence', in I. McQuimby (ed.), *Material Culture and the Study of American Life,* W.W. Norton, New York, pp. 140–74.

Harrison, H. 1980, 'The fair perceived: color and light as elements in design and planning', in H. Harrison (ed.), *Dawn of a New Day: The New York World's Fair, 1939-40*, The Queens Museum and New York University Press, New York, pp. 43–55.

Harvey, D. 1987, 'Flexible accumulation through urbanization', *Antipode,* 19, pp. 260–86.

Hasson, S. & Ley, D. (eds) 1993, *Neighbourhood Organisations and the Welfare State*, University of Toronto Press, Toronto.

Hopkins, J. 1990, 'West Edmonton Mall: landscapes of myths and elsewhereness', *Canadian Geographer*, 34, pp. 2–17.

Horkheimer, M. & Adorno, T. 1972, 'The culture industry: enlightenment as mass deception', in *Dialectic of Enlightenment*, Herder & Herder, New York, pp. 120–67.

Hutcheon, L. 1986-87, 'The politics of postmodernism: parody and history', *Cultural Critique,* 5, pp. 179–297.

Huxley, M. & Kerkin, K. 1988, 'What price the Bicentennial? A political economy of Darling Harbour', *Transition,* Spring, pp. 57–64.

Jackson, P. 1988, 'Street life: the politics of Carnival', *Society and Space*, 6, pp. 213–27.

Jacobs, J. 1961, *The Death and Life of Great American Cities*, Random House, New York.

Jameson, F. 1979, 'Reification and utopia in mass culture', *Social Text*, 1, pp. 130–48.

Kahrl, W. 1986, 'Vancouver and the hall of dynamos', *World's Fair*, 6, 4, pp. 1–5.

Laba, M. 1986, 'Making sense: expressiveness, stylization and the popular culture process', *Journal of Popular Culture*, 19, 4, pp. 107–17.

Lears, J. 1985, 'The concept of cultural hegemony', *American Historical Review,* 90, pp. 567–93.

Ley, D. 1980, 'Liberal ideology and the post-industrial city', *Annals of the Association of American Geographers,* 70, pp. 238–58.

Ley, D. 1983, *A Social Geography of the City*, Harper & Row, New York.

Ley, D. 1987, 'Styles of the times: liberal and neoconservative landscapes in inner Vancouver, 1968–1986', *Journal of Historical Geography,* 13, pp. 40–56.

Ley, D. & Cybriwsky, R. 1974, 'Urban graffiti as territorial markers', *Annals of the Association of American Geographers*, 64, pp. 491–505.

Lipsitz, G. 1986-87, 'Cruising around the historical bloc — postmodernism and popular music in East Los Angeles', *Cultural Critique,* 5, pp. 157–77.

Martin, B. 1981, *A Sociology of Contemporary Cultural Change*, Basil Blackwell, Oxford.

Mickelburgh, R. 1986, 'A fair wage', in R. Anderson & E. Wachtel (eds), *The Expo Story*, Harbour Publishing, Madeira Park, BC, pp. 125–48.

Murray, D. (ed.) 1986, *The Expo Celebration*, Whitecap Books, North Vancouver, BC.

O'Brian, B. 1985, 'Going bust: a case history', *World's Fair*, 5, 2, pp. 7–10.

Orr, S., Deaton, S. & Sturmanis, D. 1986, 'The Expo 86 gamble', *Western Report*, 21 April, pp. 49–51.

Province of British Columbia, 1979, 'Transpo 86: BC seeks 1986 international exposition to mark Vancouver centennial', news release, Ministry of the Provincial Secretary, Victoria, BC.

Riding, A. 1989, 'World's Fair a new world in Andalusia', *New York Times*, 20 August, p. 5.

Rydell, R. 1984, *All the World's a Fair*, University of Chicago Press, Chicago.

Schreiner, J. 1985, 'Selling Expo 86 to Canada and the rest of the world', *The Financial Post*, 25 May, p. 35.

Scott, A. 1988, *Metropolis,* University of California Press, Berkeley.

Susman, W. 1980, 'The people's fair: cultural contradictions of a consumer society', in H. Harrison (ed.), *Dawn of a New Day: The New York's World's Fair, 1939-40*, The Queens Museum and New York University Press, New York, pp. 17–27.

Syme, G., Shaw, B., Fenton, M. & Mueller, S. (eds) 1989, *The Planning and Evaluation of Hallmark Events*, Avebury, Aldershot, UK.

Tafler, S. 1984, 'Abandon $1.2 billion fair, Expo head tells BC Cabinet', *Toronto Globe and Mail*, 12 April, p. 1.

Whatmore, C. 1990, 'Marketing as theatre', *TD & T*, Summer, pp. 14–18.

Whitt, A. 1987, 'Mozart in the metropolis: the arts coalition and the urban growth machine', *Urban Affairs Quarterly*, 23, pp. 15–36.

Williams, R. 1977, *Marxism and Literature*, Oxford University Press, Oxford.

Willis, P. 1977, *Learning to Labour*, Saxon House, Farnborough, Hants.

Wyman, M. 1986, 'That's culture', in R. Anderson & E. Wachtel (eds), *The Expo Story*, Harbour Publishing, Madeira Park, BC, pp. 215–30.

12 Cultures of the past and urban transformation: the Spitalfields Market redevelopment in East London

Jane M. Jacobs

Introduction

Preserving and celebrating the past is a persistent and variably manifest feature of western and other societies (c.f. Lowenthal 1986). The past that is celebrated or reified is not 'given'; it is refracted through the present. Histories claimed as being of importance or value are a testament to a range of differently empowered interests and ideologies. Some histories dominate and may even become part of national imaginings, while others may be suppressed, ignored or marginalised (Anderson 1983). At times, dominant interests may use the past in order to consolidate or legitimate power. Officially or popularly sanctioned pasts are rarely static; they are embellished, transformed and even challenged (Hobsbawm & Ranger 1983). In Britain, for example, the national heritage once centred around events and artefacts associated with dominant interests. The icons of British (actually English) heritage were the grand events of Empire and the monuments of the powerful, like the country house (Wright 1985). However, the national identity of today's Britain is equally constituted around an industrial (albeit sanitised) heritage or more diminutive village heritage. What is officially or popularly sanctioned as a valued past has implications for those groups who are, or are not, represented; for those settings which are, or are not, preserved. Thus understood, the past is politically-weighted and has an impact on the geography and form of our cities.

In recent years the interest in the past has taken a peculiar new form in western capitalist societies. Museums burgeon, the tourist industry actively promotes and enhances history, shopping malls are designed to look like village high streets and products of all kinds are marketed wrapped in the imagery and rhetoric of past times (Hewison 1987; Horne 1984; Lumley 1988; Wright 1985). The past has become part of the processes of production and consumption associated with capital accumulation. The past has become commodified. Hewison (1987) has dubbed this the 'heritage industry'. It is within the expanding service sector that the link between heritage and capital is most clearly manifest: tourism, museums and retailing (Thrift 1989).

This chapter takes as its focus this politically-weighted and increasingly commodified heritage and explores the role it is playing in processes of urban transformation in contemporary London. The specific case of urban redevelopment dealt with is the recent proposal to relocate the inner-city Spitalfields Wholesale Fruit and Vegetable Market and redevelop the site essentially to meet the office and service requirements of the adjoining City of London. The chapter seeks to disclose the mutually constitutive relationship between capital (as represented by urban redevelopment) and culture (as represented by heritage values). In doing so the analysis works away from traditional explanations of urban transformation which have tended to privilege economic and political processes. Instead, it builds on the work of some recent analysts who have consciously sought to highlight the constitutive role played by culture in urban transformation. Culture, once seen as the superstructural icing on the Marxist economic cake, is now accepted as central to the process of urban transformation (Agnew, Mercer & Sopher 1984; Harvey 1985, 1989; Ley 1987; Zukin 1986, 1988).

Heritage has received considerable attention from those seeking to instate cultural factors in explanations of urban form. Heritage, particularly conservation of the historic built environment, has been seen as a counter-force to cycles of capital accumulation expressed in new redevelopment; an example of cultural values (as opposed to economic values) shaping the urban scene. For example, a number of studies have documented the rise of a conservation mentality in both popular opinion and in planning ideology and practice (e.g. Ford 1979; Fusch & Ford 1983; Relph 1987). These studies provide much insight into the way in which the historic built environment holds meaning and has become an important part of the planning agenda through conservation policy. However, at times the impulse to conserve the historic built environment is depicted as an unquestionably positive and exclusively 'cultural' process which operates separately from or as a check on the cycles of capital accumulation manifest through urban redevelopment. This chapter demonstrates that the depiction of the heritage impulse as the beleaguered and often marginal counter to capital is increasingly inadequate.

In Britain conservation of the historic built environment gained increasing legitimacy as a planning concern throughout the last century. Early legislation, such as the *Ancient Monuments Act 1882*, was concerned with only the oldest and grandest of building types. Preservation of the historic built environment reified the interests of the nation state and the expert interests of the lobby groups. During the twentieth century this limited emphasis expanded. New pressure groups emerged: the Georgian Group (1937), the Victorian Society (1958) and, most recently, the Thirties Society. Legislation responded and was reformed to embrace an increasing variety of building types and ages. Under the 'thirty year rule', introduced into policy in 1988, it is now possible to list some of the more typical glass and steel structures of the 1950s and 1960s. An important development in the broadening of conservation practice was the emergence of the idea of townscape and its legitimation through Conservation Area legislation (the *Civic Amenities Act 1967*). This provided the basis for identifying and designating whole areas of special historical and architectural character.

The emergence of conservation legislation provides an example of how one form of the heritage impulse can gain legitimacy through government policy. This legal legitimacy clearly meets an ever-growing concern to see the historic built environment conserved, yet it also veils some problematic dimensions of the conservation impulse in

Britain. Just as a new building can represent the interests of capital, so too can the historic building represent the interests of those groups influential enough to ensure its preservation. In Britain, for example, conservation of the historic built environment has been primarily the concern of an educated elite of art historians and architects, drawn from the middle and upper classes. The buildings preserved reflected their own expert ideas and class allegiances (Hewison 1987; Wright 1985). Since the 1970s this image and practice of conservation has changed dramatically with the emergence of pressure groups which consciously sought to popularise and democratise the conservation agenda.

The new democratic and populist tone of conservation in Britain, and its emergence as planning common sense, means that the relationship between empowered interests and conservation are not always as clear as they have been previously. While industrial and working class buildings are likely to be valued and listed, which will generally have popular support, this does not mean that the process of conserving the built environment is purged of its ideological and political implications. The Spitalfields case to follow will demonstrate that the conservation of the built environment and the heritage values associated with this process continue to empower certain interests above others and reify certain pasts above others. Further, the focus of planning legislation on preserving the artefactual past — the historic built environment — has worked to marginalise and disempower those who seek to protect and enhance pasts which are not grounded in the built environment. These pasts are no less real in their contribution to the character and functioning of the city, but their protection in the context of continual cycles of capital reinvestment and urban transformation is often far more problematic.

Only recently have studies of heritage values in the urban scene made explicit the hegemonic potential of a heritage impulse, its capacity to express and legitimate the status and power of certain interests. This has been done primarily through attention to the relationship between heritage and capital (Bommes & Wright 1982; Dear 1986; Knox 1987). An exemplary study is Sharon Zukin's account of the revalorisation of redundant loft space in New York's SoHo (Zukin 1986, 1988). Her study is remarkable in its detailed depiction of the way in which the economic revalorisation of urban space and built fabric works through and is dependent upon transformations associated with a range of cultural factors; artists, the art market, and an aesthetic which favours historic built forms. Others too (e.g. Dear 1986; Harvey 1989; King 1988, 1990; Knox 1987) have noted the increasing interdependence between heritage values and the more flexible cycles of capital accumulation which characterise late capitalism. Heritage values are now acknowledged as playing a constitutive part in the process of urban transformation, such as gentrification, in which older parts of the urban fabric are 'revalorised' both aesthetically and economically (see also Jager 1986; Mills 1988).

This chapter, too, highlights the nexus between capital accumulation and heritage values in city transformations, but it reiterates and locates this commodified past within the continually renewed and variably manifest power implications of the heritage impulse. The urban environment is not simply a site of capital accumulation, whether flexible or not. Other interests, such as conservationists, seek the preservation of the historic built environment. Others again may seek to protect the local community or a way of life. Each draws from the city a different history and past. Each seeks to preserve and enhance that past in the context of, and in differing relationships with, the continual cycles of capital reinvestment and urban transformation associated with the city.

Seeing the city as a product of contests and negotiations between differently empowered interests which ascribe to it different meanings, values and intents, raises important issues of method. To understand the circulation of meaning in this variably empowered context it is necessary to look beyond the cityscape itself to the discourses and representations associated with it and to their producers or authors (see Duncan & Duncan 1988). As Knox (1982, 294) suggests, it is important not simply to know that the environment is meaningful but to know who is communicating through the environment, to what audience and to what purposes. Townscapes and urban localities must be seen as part of a discursive communicative realm, replacing the idea of a 'language of the City' with an understanding of the 'language on the city' (Choay 1986, 173). In undertaking this methodological programme it is also necessary to contextualise the discourses thus explored, through an attention to history, to ethnography, to politics and economics. Acknowledgement of the fruitfulness of this emphasis has produced a number of studies which look specifically at contextualised urban discourses, such as the views of planners, architects and social visionaries (Bagguley et al. 1990; Knox 1987; Ley 1987; Schorske 1980). This chapter explores the contextualised discourses produced by a selection of interest groups associated with the proposed redevelopment of the Spitalfields Market site in the inner East End of London.

Spitalfields: pasts and presents

Spitalfields is one of the most deprived areas in London yet it abuts the eastern edge of the City of London, one of the three main finance centres in the world. It retains a popular reputation as a deprived and, at times, depraved place. It is part of the infamous East End, site of the Jack the Ripper murders and once a stronghold of petty criminals (Samuel 1981). It was to the East End and to areas like Spitalfields that many of the Victorian social reformers turned to provide documentation of the appalling conditions of urban life for the labouring poor (e.g. Booth 1892). Yet Spitalfields also has other connotations.

In the 1950s and 1960s, when British sociology was recovering the idea and the reality of 'community' in the urban scene, it was to the East End that they looked to confirm the persistence of the close-knit community in the city (Young & Wilmott 1957). In the contemporary popular imagination the idea of a persistent, if troubled, community spirit was portrayed in the television soap opera *East Enders*. Spitalfields' role as a home for successive waves of immigrants has added much to its community reputation. Beginning in the early eighteenth century, when the French Huguenots settled in the area after fleeing the Edict of Nantes, there has been a succession of immigrant settlers. The Huguenots were followed in the nineteenth century by the Irish and then Polish and Russian Jews. Most recently, Spitalfields has become home for Bengalis from the Sylhet district of Bangladesh. One eighteenth-century building in the area has, during its lifetime, served as a church, a Jewish synagogue and a mosque. Also associated with the community image of Spitalfields is the long-standing market culture. The Wholesale Fruit and Vegetable Market, which is the focus of redevelopment, is central to the area and has operated on its current site for three centuries. Equally long-standing are the large number of informal street markets. On weekends many of the streets of Spitalfields are given over to the jostle, noise and colour of such markets. This vibrant street life reiterates contemporary perceptions of the surviving urban community (Berman 1982; Jacobs 1964).

Spitalfields and the East End generally are equally renowned as a site of radical Left politics. The local borough of Tower Hamlets, of which Spitalfields is a part, has been a Labour stronghold for decades. It is the East End that provides the grand events of popular socialist resistance in London's history: the battle of Cable Street, the Poplar resistance, the anti-sweating protests (c.f. Fishman 1988; Rose 1988). Raphael Samuel, radical historian and founder of History Workshop, moved to the area in the 1960s in search not only of his own Jewish ancestry but also his radical intellectual ancestry.

The Spitalfields thus far described disguises a grander Spitalfields that once was. During the eighteenth century the Huguenot silk weavers brought to the area an economic prosperity and a way of life based not only on industry but also on intellectual societies, royal patronage and a rather elaborate and grand social life. Some of the more influential and prosperous of London families today trace a lineage to the Huguenot weavers of Spitalfields.

Spitalfields is a place and a community of many histories: immigrant, radical, informal trade and respectable Georgian. The Spitalfields of today shares much with the Spitalfields of old. The prime source of employment is still the garment trade which remains confined to overcrowded backstreet workshop spaces. The local population is primarily Bengali, continuing the area's role as a home for racialised minorities. The ward of Spitalfields remains a Labour stronghold. The street markets continue to operate, with Petticoat and Brick Lane markets now attracting large numbers of foreign tourists. The prosperous Georgian Spitalfields retains a presence through a substantial stock of the original eighteenth-century terrace houses.

The last two decades have brought a number of significant changes to the area. The first of these changes came in the mid 1970s with the emergence of an active conservation presence which sought to restore the remaining Georgian built fabric. A more recent change has been a shift in local political behaviour. While Spitalfields still remains a Labour stronghold, it now operates as a minority ward in a borough which since 1986 has been under Liberal control.

The most dramatic change has resulted from the eastward push of functions previously confined to the 'square mile' of the City of London (fig. 12.1). In 1986 the 'Big Bang' and deregulation expanded and transformed the financial practices of the City. New technology required new types of office space with open plan and large floor–ceiling heights to accommodate cabling. The new financial sector seeks out upmarket office space with an architectural style which enhances corporate image. At the end of the 1980s there were over 24 ha (60 acres) of large-scale redevelopment proposed for the Spitalfields area. The market site was at the vanguard of this massive speculative push eastwards. Since the early 1980s there has been a major effort to relocate the Spitalfields Wholesale Fruit and Vegetable Market and place on the 4 ha (10 acre) site a 140 000 m² (1.5 million ft²) development, predominantly for City service sector use (offices and retailing), but with some housing and local amenities.

The Spitalfields area sees the coming together of a number of deeply contradictory tendencies: a radical Left political tradition closely associated with the long-standing, racialised, working-class population of the area and the persistently poor living conditions; a more recent conservationist push led by professional middle and upper classes; and an even more recent transformation of the area into a prime office redevelopment site. The recent proposal to relocate the Spitalfields Wholesale Fruit and Vegetable Market and redevelop the site for offices and retailing has brought these

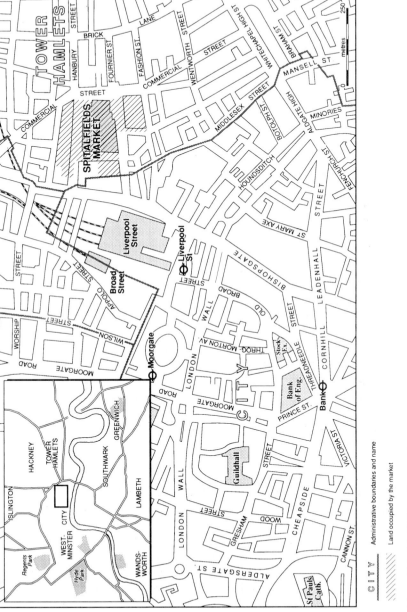

Figure 12.1: Spitalfields and surrounds.

varying strands of Spitalfields together in open conflict and collusion. In what follows, this case of urban redevelopment is explored through the discourses produced by three divergent interests: the conservationists, the developers and the local Left. The case reveals the pervasiveness of 'heritage' values in urban change, as the conflict in Spitalfields is not so much a conflict between the old and the new as between competing notions of valued pasts.

Spitalfields I : the conservationists' past

Spitalfields was one of the first areas of London to be developed outside the confines of the original City boundaries. During the early eighteenth century a substantial enclave of terraces was developed. Their original occupants, the French Huguenots, were weavers and added work-space lofts to many of the houses. These lofts are considered a distinctive architectural feature of the Georgian houses in the area (fig. 12.2). Since the Second World War there has been increasing official recognition of the area's historic built form. In the 1950s the Survey of London, the first systematic record of London's historic built fabric, produced a volume on Spitalfields (Survey of London 1957). When official listing procedures were introduced soon after, the majority of the Georgian terraces in Spitalfields were immediately placed on the register. In the late 1960s and early 1970s the local authority designated three conservation areas in Spitalfields. The controversial market site is surrounded by these designated conservation areas and the listed Georgian terraces.

Recently, the official recognition given to the architectural merit of Spitalfields' historic fabric has been transformed into passionate direct action. In the mid 1970s a small group of architects and architectural historians formed the Spitalfields Historic Buildings Trust. When the Survey of London recorded the built fabric of Spitalfields in

Figure 12.2. The gentrified Fournier Street showing the distinctive weaver lofts.

the 1950s, it recorded 230 eighteenth-century buildings in the area. By 1977, when the Spitalfields Historic Buildings Trust was formed, only 140 remained (*Spitalfields Trust Newsletter* 1978, 1).

From the outset the Trust followed a unique course of direct action, unprecedented in British conservation societies of the time. Its first highly publicised and successful effort in 1977 was to squat in two Georgian houses earmarked for demolition. Such direct action has become a favoured and much publicised Trust strategy but it belies a more systematic effort to ensure the historic housing stock of the area is restored to its former Georgian glory. The Trust became an active agent in the process of transferring the historic housing stock in the area into the hands of sympathetic and strictly vetted buyers who undertook a voluntary obligation to restore the houses in accordance with guidelines laid down by the Trust. The Trust did this either by directly purchasing houses and selling them on to selected buyers or by advertising houses on the market under private estate agents in the Trust newsletter. The Trust newsletters read like an estate agent brochure. As one of the founders noted, the Trust has operated less like a conventional conservation group and more like an 'unofficial inner city development organisation' (Blain 1989, 9).

The Trust's project of conserving the built environment of Spitalfields relied upon buyers who were both financially and aesthetically equipped to conform with the Trust's vision of a restored Georgian Spitalfields. The Trust consciously sought to attract the 'right sort of people' to the area. The newsletters are very explicit in informing the readership of who was moving in and their 'credentials' to undertake the task of sympathetic restoration. Thus the Trust was not only active in creating a revalorised urban fabric but also in the creation of a new social and cultural enclave. The Spitalfields case is one of self-conscious, engineered gentrification.

The impact on the area has been dramatic. The revalorisation and restoration of the Georgian housing has created a primarily residential enclave of writers, artists, architects and other professionals, some of whom are quite literally of the British gentry. All members of the new community lovingly restore their houses and some even make a living from the neo-Georgian enclave created. One resident offers private dinner parties with eighteenth-century cuisine. Another has transformed his home into an off-beat museum where the more adventurous tourist or Georgian enthusiast can experience the smells, the noises, the conversations and the surrounds of a Huguenot silk weaving family. High class heritage commodification.

The most significant impact has been on the Bengali garment industry. Prior to the conservation interest in the Georgian buildings of Spitalfields, most were in a poor state of repair. They were either so dilapidated they were uninhabitable, or they were rented out cheaply as workshop space to the Bengali garment industry. The conservation of the built environment has resulted in the displacement of Bengali users. The restoration efforts of the gentrifiers and the new life those interested in these houses gave to the property market have added to the marked rises in property values in the area. This market trend was consolidated through local authority conservation policy which introduced a specific use policy for the conservation areas. Since the late 1970s there has been a systematic rejection of all light industrial use applications and an encouragement of 'traditional' and 'more sympathetic' residential use. The Spitalfields Trust has been highly influential in ensuring such stringent local planning policy, actively campaigning and lobbying local planners to adhere to national conservation legislation and soliciting a number of local initiatives to enhance the conservation areas, such as the reinstatement of street cobbles and the addition of 'period' street fixtures.

The conscious restoration of a material and a social world around the Georgian aesthetic has also placed the Trust in conflict with the Spitalfields Wholesale Fruit and Vegetable Market. Initially the Trust saw the market as part of the 'local colour' of the Spitalfields area. However, as the Trust's Georgian Spitalfields became increasingly fixed in the built and social fabric, as more houses were restored, more streets cobbled, more (Victorian) lampposts installed, more property interests accumulated, its tolerance of the market as a source of 'local colour' diminished. Extensions made to the market site this century have been responsible for the loss of some of the original Georgian housing stock. The traffic, congestion, noise and litter problems associated with the increasingly modern trading practices of the market have become a concern for the Trust, as they damage and deface the increasingly restored residential enclave. The Trust has repeatedly tried to buffer the surrounding conservation areas from the activities of the market by building walls, planting trees and purchasing buildings on the borders of the market. When the current proposals to relocate the market and redevelop the site for offices and retail use were first mooted in 1986 the Trust responded thus: '[d]espite its long history and its colour and picturesqueness, the residents and the Trust will happily wave it goodbye provided it is replaced by something the design of which is worthy of this important and historic site' (*Spitalfields Trust Newsletter* 1986, 2).

The removal of the market and the redevelopment of the site was seen as providing not a threat but an opportunity for the further enhancement of the Georgian environment so treasured by the conservationists. The opportunity to see a particular historical vision of Spitalfields reinvented through the market redevelopment opened the way for a relationship of co-operation between the conservationists and the developers. The redevelopment came to be seen as an opportunity in the Trust's ongoing efforts to transform Spitalfields into a restored monument to early Georgian London and to rid the area of a local feature which was seen as increasingly incongruent with this vision.

In part, Trust negotiations with the developers centred on assisting with the restoration of the existing Georgian fabric. The Trust asked that the developers provide funds for the ongoing restoration of Hawksmoor's Christ Church, the only grand-scale Georgian building among the otherwise diminutive domestic architecture of the area. The Trust also asked that any new scheme for the market site reinstate Spital Square, which had had its northern edge demolished during market expansion. However, as will be shown in the following section, a considerable amount of Trust attention was given over to influencing the style of the proposed redevelopment. So fixed were the conservationists on re-creating Georgian Spitalfields, they were willing to see 'contradictory' elements of the area's past, such as the market, eradicated. They were willing to co-operate and trade with the developer in the pursuit of their Georgian vision. The full extent of this co-operation is only clear when the developers' views and their treatment of Spitalfields 'heritage' is fully explored.

Spitalfields II: the developers' past

The developers contending for the market redevelopment contract were more than willing to respond to the requests made by the Spitalfields Historic Buildings Trust. They readily incorporated the ambitions and aesthetics of the conservationists in pursuit of their own vision of transforming the market site into an extension of the City of London. There were two main contenders for the market redevelopment: Rosehaugh Stanhope and the Spitalfields Development Group. Each had as its base objective the transformation of the market site, on the edge of the financial core of the City, into a commercial and retail centre which would offer high returns. Yet the architectural and urban design language in which this process of capital accumulation was encased were highly sensitive to the conservation status of the local area. Faced with a local authority predisposed to protecting the Georgian architecture of the area and encouraging its transfer to residential use, and an influential and vocal conservation interest, the developers were only too aware of the importance of addressing this aspect of the heritage of Spitalfields in their quest for planning approval. Both developers tendering for the site consciously drew upon Spitalfields' history, but it was not just any aspect of the multivariate and at times contradictory Spitalfields of old. The developers addressed that part of the Spitalfields past which was already empowered by the conservationist lobby, already functioning in terms of the economic revalorisation of Spitalfields, and already legitimated by local and central state planning policy.

For example, Rosehaugh Stanhope actively sought a design team which addressed the conservation status of the area, and specifically the aspirations of the active and influential local conservation interests. One of the first actions undertaken by Rosehaugh Stanhope was to seek the advice of the Spitalfields Trust and the Spitalfields-based Georgian Group on the architects they should appoint. The conservationists provided a list of architects who worked exclusively in a neo-Georgian, neo-classical style. The developers followed the advice of the conservationists and retained architects who would produce designs 'in the genuine Georgian vernacular'. The architects were to 'ensure the creation of a new architecture, totally in sympathy with the surrounding Conservation Areas' (Rosehaugh Stanhope, press release, 7 August 1986). The final master plan was produced by Quinlan Terry in a bold and uncompromising classical style (fig. 12.3). The Quinlan Terry scheme imposed on the market site a rigidly formal and at times grand street pattern, including wide streets and large spacious squares. The scheme instated this Georgian recreation at the cost of a group of Grade II Victorian buildings on the eastern edge of the existing market. These were to be demolished in the proposed scheme to make way for the creation of a street which would open out a grand vista of the baroque centrepiece of the area, Hawksmoor's Christ Church.

In its selection of architects, Rosehaugh Stanhope had clearly attempted to address the Georgian aesthetic promoted by the Spitalfields Trust and consolidated and supported by the planning policies of the heritage-minded local authority. Ironically, while the local authority was prepared to grant provisional planning approval, the conservationists were less enthusiastic about the results. The Trust felt the scheme was too grand and it disapproved of the proposed demolition of the listed Victorian buildings, although demolition would allow a new vista of Hawksmoor's Christ Church. The Rosehaugh Stanhope scheme failed in the eyes of the conservationists not because of its disregard for the Georgian aesthetic but because of its too formal and too grand appropriation of it.

The successful contender in the market redevelopment was the Spitalfields Development Group (SDG). SDG also attempted to provide a development scheme that was sympathetic to the surrounding conservation areas, fully aware that this would help ensure planning permission. To this end it commissioned a design from an architect

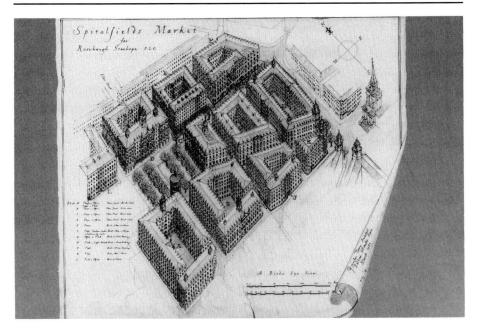

Figure 12.3: The grand neo-classical scheme of Quinlan Terry.
Source: 'Spitalfields Redevelopment Scheme 1987', reproduced from Charles Jencks, *The Prince, The Architects and New Wave Monarchy*, Academy Editions, London.

who was both a founding member of the Spitalfields Historic Buildings Trust and a resident of one of the Trust's 'rescued' buildings. Richard MacCormac's design style explicitly worked with local motifs and idioms derived from historical forms and patterns. The architect was familiar with conservation and conversion work as well as new building, and had long expressed his own vision for the area. The vision had no loyalty to the Spitalfields Market, and viewed relocation of the market and redevelopment of the site as an important step in the reconstitution and revitalisation of the area.

The MacCormac scheme (fig. 12.4) was more diverse in design and conception than the grand Rosehaugh Stanhope scheme. It provided a series of 'architectural conversations' between the different buildings on the site and the surrounding townscape. In plan, the scheme paid much attention to recreating a fine-grained block and street pattern which was compatible with that of the surrounding conservation areas. It reinstated the controversial north side of Spital Square and provided for additional small-scale squares and open spaces. The architectural style drew upon local architectural idioms but 'teased' with them, creating new architectural forms. The Grade II listed buildings on the market site were incorporated into the scheme.

It was not only in design that SDG consciously adopted the conservation aesthetic. As part of a community gain package SDG earmarked funds for the restoration of Christ Church. The promotion of the scheme was also strongly influenced by historical references. The logo of SDG was based on the friendly domestic form of the nineteenth-century listed buildings on the site. Its pitched roofs and chimney stacks provided a logo with an almost village quality which disguised the massive development planned behind the facade (fig. 12.5). A special promotional booklet entitled *Spitalfields: A Continuing*

Figure 12.4: The Richard MacCormac scheme.
Drawn by Richard MacCormac of MacCormac, Jamison & Prichard, for the Spitalfields
Development Group.

Story, adorned with the village logo and soft focus photographs presented the scheme as
the most recent chapter in the ongoing history. The text implied that the new
development would slip into the Spitalfields area almost unnoticed.

> The people of Spitalfields will still be doing much the same things as before. Spitalfields
> will be somewhere to live, relax, be entertained and shop; a place for people to work and
> prosper. All traditional pursuits, watched over by the weavers' houses, medieval precincts
> and Dickensian alleys and, above all, Hawksmoor's Christ Church. (SDG 1986, 12)

Thus, in rhetoric and action, development interests were quick to appropriate the
conservation agenda and the Georgian Spitalfields it celebrated in the design and
promotion of their schemes. Such a strategy was essential in legitimating the

Figure 12.5: The quaint facade of development did not go untouched by local protest.

development in the eyes of the influential conservationists and the conservation-minded local authority. Although the Trust had some reservations about the MacCormac scheme (in particular about its height and bulk) it did publicly endorse the scheme, which was granted planning permission.

Critical to the co-operation between the developers and the conservationists was the potential of the conservation agenda and aesthetic to serve the interests of capital. It worked to provide an acceptable facade (both architectural and rhetorical) to a large-scale redevelopment which was anything but compatible with the historical character of the area and which could only proceed at the cost of relocating the market operations. It was one aspect of Spitalfields history which could be appropriated without seriously jeopardising or compromising the development agenda. Furthermore, co-operation was possible because the developers were willing and able to speak a language familiar to the conservationists: the language of architecture, urban design and townscape.

Other interests in Spitalfields found the development, regardless of its architectural form, deeply contradictory to their vision of the area and the local pasts that they valued. These alternative interests did not express their views in the language of architecture, aesthetics and urban design but brought to the planning controversy a different Spitalfields' history, expressed in a different language. This was a past more deeply challenging to and less easily incorporated into the processes of capital reinvestment which generated the market redevelopment proposal.

Spitalfields III: the Left's past

The proposals to relocate the market and redevelop the site for office and retail use was opposed by the local Left, working under the campaign title of Save Spitalfields from the Developers (see fig. 12.5). Its active membership was essentially white local Left activists and a handful of Bengali people living in the area and active in local Left politics. The campaign was not concerned with the Georgian architecture of the area.

Indeed, its participating members had, in alternative forums, consistently opposed the gentrification occurring at the hands of conservationists. The campaign did not see the redevelopment as providing opportunities for the area. It saw it as an expansion of City interests into the East End and sought to protect the local community against this 'invasion'. In the rhetoric of the campaign, historic Spitalfields had an innately radical, working-class character which established it as a 'natural' counter to the forces of capitalism represented in the conservation activities and more explicitly in the proposed office redevelopment. The campaign was protecting 'indigenous' local qualities which it portrayed as holding the key to socialist reform in the city. The idea of the 'indigenous community' and local resistance is central to New Left political ideology in Britain which advocates a political programme of reform at the 'community' level. As such, the current socialist project of radical change is as deeply rooted in a romanticised and localised past as is the more overtly expressed historicism of the conservation movement.

It was through the evidence of Raphael Samuel, socialist historian and local resident, that the special character of the Spitalfields community was most clearly elaborated. Samuel and the campaign were united in seeing Spitalfields as 'that unique and historic area ... a community of working class and industrious people: a multi-ethnic community ... a historic place which for over 3 centuries has harboured both refugees and immigrants ... that has given the area a distinctive working character' (CSSD Briefing for Labour MPs, May 1988). In Samuel's often romantic evocations, Spitalfields was depicted as almost untouched by the forces of modern life. The Spitalfields he found in 1962 when he moved to the area was decidedly rustic in its social and cultural practices. There were one-room pubs which sold only beer, grocers still sold kindling and coal for fires, and there were two functioning dairies (Samuel 1989, 138–9).

The past evoked by the campaign centred around Spitalfields as a village-like working and trading community. The garment industry, which has been the prime economic base of Spitalfields since the Huguenots, in many ways defies the image of modern industry. Most businesses are still small-scale and run on a family basis. People still walk to work in Spitalfields. The campaign does not deny the poor conditions that are suffered by many of those employed in the garment industry, however, it lauds the anti-modern feel of the garment industry, its informality and recent revival through the participation of the Bengali community, both as workers and manufacturers. In this sense, the campaign's case for protecting the garment industry also became, somewhat paternalistically, a case for the protection of the most recent immigrant population of the area.

The campaign also tied the working character of Spitalfields to the tradition of marketing in the area, both the Wholesale Market and the street markets. In a protest statement the campaign described Spitalfields as having 'perhaps the best open air market in the world' (House of Commons 1987). As an arena of private enterprise, marketing does not fit so readily into the traditional concerns of the Left, but the market tradition of Spitalfields was depicted by the campaign as small-scale, informal, at times vaguely criminal, and as such deeply contradictory to the High Street retailing proposed in the redevelopment scheme. Spitalfields' marketing tradition as represented by the campaign was more redolent of the village market in its informality and colour. It was depicted as a site of anarchic and subversive opportunity and initiative, the 'natural home of the working class' shopper (Campaign protest exhibition, Bishopsgate Institute 1988).

The Spitalfields Wholesale Fruit and Vegetable Market was hardly of this informal, village nature, its 4 ha (10 acre) site being served by giant lorries bringing produce from around the world. Yet this larger-scale version of the market enterprise was given its own intrinsic charm by the campaign and depicted as reiterating (in function, if not in form or scale) the broader market character of the area. The campaign stressed that until the 1960s the practices of the Wholesale Market were decidedly 'pre-industrial': fetching was done by barrow or pony and cart and loads of produce were carried on the head (Samuel 1989, 135–6).

Thus the Left valued a past which was a complex intersection of industry, 'race' and trade; a way of life, as opposed to a built form; a living history as opposed to a conserved history. The traditional socialist Spitalfields was not captured in the built environment but in the people and practices of the area. The Wholesale Market was depicted as crucial to the retention of both the garment industry and the more informal street market tradition. These differing local functions were seen as in 'harmony' and having an 'elective affinity' in which one worked to protect and sustain the other. More importantly, the Wholesale Market kept more antagonistic or less tolerant land uses at bay. Its continued presence on the existing site was seen as essential to the maintenance of the industrial/trading base of Spitalfields, that is, the working-class Spitalfields.

The market battle reiterated for the campaign the traditional battle of socialism. The campaign enemy was not the wrong architectural aesthetic, but capitalism itself. The enemy was seen as 'big money', and expressed locally through the market redevelopment proposal. More potently, in this particular struggle, capitalism was manifest through the forces of a grand national symbol of capital, an expanding City of London, financial heartland of Britain. Spitalfields would be transformed under the 'enemy' into the home of 'millionaire corporations' and 'international banking'. The unique, organic community would become 'just one more line on the computer screen linking Wall Street and Tokyo' (*Spitalfields Defender* 1987).

The local Left which formed the basis of the campaign against the market redevelopment clearly imagined a Spitalfields past different from that of the Trust or the developers, and spoke of that past in an entirely different language. The Trust's ideology is one of reverence for the past, expressed primarily in architectural and urban design terms. The Left shares a reverence for the past but it is a different past which is expressed through the idea and language of community. In Spitalfields the traditional political voice of the oppressed working class and marginalised Bengali minority, the radical Left, has become disempowered in one of the most potent traditional sites of its power. The campaign's loyalty to a Spitalfields past which was deeply contradictory to the development agenda worked to disempower it in an urban scene where transformation is increasingly mediated through a far less challenging discourse of historicist architectural aesthetics and urban design.

Conclusion

The examination of the cases for and against the Spitalfields redevelopment reveals that while the conservationists and the developer ultimately have different agendas, they share a common desire to see the Spitalfields area rid of the market. The developers were in pursuit of a centrally located office development which could provide enormous returns. The conservationists were in pursuit of a vision to recreate a Georgian enclave.

The shared desire to relocate the Spitalfields Fruit and Vegetable Market provided the basis for co-operation and collusion between the traditional 'enemies' of developer and conservationist. The collusion was further consolidated by their use of a shared language of architecture and urban design.

Opposition to the Spitalfields Market redevelopment came from the local Left who lauded and guarded a radical, racialised, working-class Spitalfields. This group was marginalised in its opposition because its interests were deeply contradictory to those of the developers. It opposed the redevelopment outright and sought to keep the market on its present site. Its arguments in defence of the market were couched in the language of community rather than architecture and urban design. The opposition group in the Spitalfields case was concerned not with the preservation of historic buildings but with the preservation and protection of a particular social and cultural character in the area which was essentially radical and oppositional to the processes of capital.

The preceding examples of conflict and co-operation associated with the Spitalfields Market redevelopment reveal how heritage tendencies are variable. Different interests hold different pasts to be of value and at times these pasts are deeply contradictory. Further, these pasts have differing degrees of legitimacy depending on the power and interests of those who promote or revere them and on the extent to which they contradict processes of capital accumulation.

The Spitalfields case demonstrates that heritage is not always the sole possession of those opposing development and change in the city, but can equally act as the agent of change. The conservation efforts of the Spitalfields Trust brought changes to the area well before large-scale development arrived. It forced out garment workshops in the revalorised areas and changed the social, economic and cultural character of the gentrified enclaves. The developers were able to appropriate and exploit the heritage values asserted by the influential conservationists to legitimate and facilitate even more wide-reaching and dramatic change in the form of a large-scale commercial redevelopment. The Spitalfields example shows how interests which speak in an overt and conscious rhetoric of conservation and heritage can actually pose a threat to alternate, challenging and resistant pasts.

The Spitalfields Market controversy was in part a conflict of differently empowered pasts and discourses. In the current state of British planning, histories which are embodied in the built environment and which are less challenging to redevelopment objectives are clearly privileged. Pasts with more deeply oppositional potential and which are present in forms and practices less readily appropriated into redevelopment objectives, are marginalised. Such pasts can only be incorporated into urban processes of capital reinvestment if bleached of their radical and oppositional character. Increasingly, such histories are present in the urban scene, less as ongoing practices and more as sanitised, restored artefacts incorporated into capital projects of tourism or retailing. Much of the contemporary city may appear to have histories but increasingly they are histories of artefacts not ways of life.

References

Agnew, J.A., Mercer, J. & Sopher, D.E. 1984, *The City In A Cultural Context,* Allen & Unwin, Boston.

Anderson, B. 1983, *Imagined Communities: Reflections on the Origins and Spread of Nationalism,* Verso, London.

Bagguley, P. Mark-Lawson, J., Shapiro, D., Urry, J., Walby, S. & Warde, A. 1990, *Restructuring: Place, Class and Gender,* Sage Publications, London.

Berman, M. 1982, *All That Is Solid Melts Into Air: The Experience of Modernity,* Verso, London.

Blain, D. 1989, 'A brief and very personal history of the Spitalfields Trust', in M. Girouard , D. Cruickshank & R. Samuel (eds), *The Saving of Spitalfields,* Spitalfields Historic Buildings Trust, London, pp. 1–19.

Bommes, M. & Wright, P. 1982, 'Charms of residence: the public and the past', in R. Johnson, G. McLennan, B. Schwartz & D. Sutton (eds), *Making Histories: Studies in History Writing and Politics,* Hutchinson, London and CCCS, Birmingham, pp. 252–302.

Booth, C. 1892, *Life and Labour of the People of London: Volume. 1 East London,* London.

Campaign to Save Spitalfields from the Developer, 1988 *Briefing for Labour MPs,* CSSD, London.

Choay, F. 1986, 'Urbanism and semiology', in M. Gottdeiner & A.Ph. Lagopoulos (eds), *The City and the Sign: An Introduction to Urban Semiotics,* Columbia University Press, New York, pp. 160–75.

Civic Amenities Act 1967

Cosgrove, D. & Daniels, S.J. (eds) 1988, *The Iconography of Landscape,* Cambridge University Press, Cambridge.

Dear, M.J. 1986, 'Postmodernism and planning', *Environment and Planning D: Society and Space,* 4, pp. 367–84.

Dickens, P.G. 1980, 'Social science and design theory', *Environment and Planning B,* 7, pp. 353–60.

Duncan, J.S. & Duncan, N. 1988, '(Re)reading the landscape,' *Environment and Planning D: Society and Space,* 6, pp. 117–26.

Fishman, W. 1988, *East End 1888,* Duckworth, London.

Ford, L.R. 1979, 'Urban preservation and the geography of the city in the USA', *Progress in Human Geography,* 3, 2, pp. 211–38.

Fusch, R. & Ford, L.R. 1983, 'Architecture and the geography of the American city', *The Geographical Review,* 73, 3, pp. 324–39.

Harvey, D. 1985, *Consciousness and the Urban Experience,* Oxford University Press, Oxford.

Harvey, D. 1989, *The Condition of Postmodernity,* Basil Blackwell, London.

Hewison, R. 1987, *The Heritage Industry: Britain in a Climate of Decline,* Methuen, London.

Hobsbawm, E. & Ranger, T. 1983, *The Invention of Tradition,* Cambridge University Press, Cambridge.

Horne, D. 1984, *The Great Museum: The Re-Presentation of History,* Pluto Press, Sydney.

Jacobs, J. 1964, *Death and Life of Great American Cities,* Pelican, London.

Jager, M. 1986, 'Class definition and the aesthetics of gentrification: Victoriana in Melbourne', in N. Smith & P. Williams (eds), *Gentrification of the City,* Allen & Unwin, Herts, pp. 78–91.

King, A. (ed.) 1980, *Buildings and Society: Essays on the Social Development of the Built Environment,* Routlege & Kegan Paul, London.

King, A. 1990, *Global Cities: Post-Imperialism and the Internationalisation of London,* Routledge, London.

King, R.J. 1988, 'Urban design in capitalist society', *Environment & Planning D: Society & Space,* 6, pp. 445-74.

Knox, P.L. 1982, 'The social production of the built environment', *Ekistics,* 49, pp. 291–7.

Knox, P.L. 1987, 'The social production of the built environment: architects, architecture and the post-modern city', *Progress in Human Geography,* 11, 3, pp. 354–78.

Ley, D. 1987, 'Styles of the times: liberal and neo-conservative landscapes in inner Vancouver, 1968-1986', *Journal of Historical Geography,* 13, 1 , pp. 40–56.

Lowenthal, D. 1986, *The Past is a Foreign Country,* Cambridge University Press, Cambridge.

Lumley, T. 1988, *The Museum Time Machine: Putting Cultures on Display,* Comedia, London.

Mills, C.A. 1988, '"Life on the upslope": the postmodern landscape of gentrification', *Environment and Planning D: Society and Space,* 6, pp. 169–189.

Relph, E. 1987, *The Modern Urban Landscape,* Croom Helm, London.

Rose, G. 1988, 'Locality, politics and culture: Poplar in the 1920s', *Environment and Planning D: Society and Space,* 6, pp. 151–68.

Samuel, R. 1981, *East End Underworld: Chapters in the Life of Arthur Harding,* Routlege & Kegan Paul, London.

Samuel, R. 1989, 'The pathos of conservation', in M. Girouard, D. Cruickshank & R. Samuel (eds), *The Saving of Spitalfields,* Spitalfields Historic Buildings Trust, London, pp. 135–71.

Schorske, C.E. 1980, *Fin-de Siècle Vienna: Politics and Culture,* Alfred A. Knopf, New York.

Spitalfields Historic Building Trust, 1978 *Newsletter,* SHBT, London.

Survey of London 1957, *Spitalfields and Mile End New Town,* vol. XXVII, The Althone Press for LCC, London.

Thrift, N. 1989, 'Images of social change', in C. Hamnett, L. McDowell & P. Sarre (eds), *The Changing Social Structure,* London, pp. 272–9.

Wright, P. 1985, *On Living in an Old Country,* Verso, London.

Young, M. & Wilmott, P. 1957, *Kinship and Family in East London,* Routledge & Kegan Paul, London.

Zukin, S. 1986, 'Gentrification: culture and capital in the urban core', *Annual Review of Sociology,* 13, pp. 129–47.

Zukin, S. 1988, *Loft Living: Culture and Capital in Urban Change,* Radius, London.

Original sources

Spitalfields Trust Newsletters, 1975-89.

The Spitalfields Defender, campaign broadsheet.

Records The Campaign to Save Spitalfields From the Developer: *Bishopsgate Exhibition* Text, Letters and Public Statements, 1986-89.

House of Commons Select Committee Proceedings, Spitalfields Market Bill, 1987.

SDG/Rosehaugh Stanhope promotional material 1986-89.

Constructing geographies:
culture and nature

13 A 'green' vision: the evolution of Australian environmentalism

Kevin Frawley

Introduction

In mid 1989 the Australian Prime Minister Bob Hawke launched a substantial Commonwealth government commitment to environmental protection over the next ten years (Hawke 1989). This first ever comprehensive statement on the environment by an Australian Prime Minister is an indication of how, two hundred years after the European settlement of Australia, environmental matters have become prominent on the national political agenda despite federal constitutional limitations in this area.

The rise of the environmental movement and 'green politics' in Australia, while appearing to be almost entirely the product of the last few decades, has deeper roots that need to be explored from a historical/cultural perspective. The growth of Australian environmentalism can be related to a particular national historical experience and cultural context as well as continuing international influences. It has evolved out of a process of learning about and coming to terms with the environment since the relatively recent European settlement of the ancient Australian continent. Visions and expectations brought by successive waves of immigrants who were faced with establishing new cultural identities in a country of highly unfamiliar environments have also been influential. Very recently, long rejected or ignored Aboriginal conceptions of the land have begun also to permeate the European Australian consciousness. Still-evolving Australian images of environment and sense of place involve therefore, a blend of Eurocentric images of environment, a distinctive colonial or Australian view, uneasy adaptations to a harsh sprawling landscape, and an equally uneasy relationship with an ancient culture which modified but sustained the land through thousands of years prior to European settlement.

This chapter first considers some conceptual considerations relevant to environmentalism. It then outlines the history of Australian environmental ideas and the development of a public policy framework related to the environment, with a broad division of legislation into 'protective' and 'exploitative'. Finally, it considers the political struggle between opposing development and conservation paradigms in the recent period (fig. 13.1).

Culture and environment

The central question of this chapter is how a culture views itself in relation to the environment. It focuses on the dynamic relationship between cultural conceptions and landscape forms and meanings. This is not a new question for geographers, but is one that is now a central human concern as the consequences of past interactions are seen to threaten future human survival on earth. We have to assume that many of the questions now asked about the relationship between people and the environment are new forms of very old ones. As Simmons (1989, 2) has noted, it is scarcely surprising that humankind began early to formulate abstract ideas about its relationship to the environment. Mental constructs regarding the relationship of people to the environment were rooted in everyday practical concerns for individual and group survival.

These ideas progressively developed into a body of intellectual thought on the interactions of 'nature' and 'culture', traced for the west by Glacken (1967). Through this history, not only have the nature–culture interactions remained problematic, but so have the meanings surrounding the terms themselves. Discourse regarding the natural world is inseparable from cultural constructions of reality. For example, European Australians continue to debate what is meant by the 'natural environment' when the continent was occupied by Aboriginal people for at least 40 000 years prior to European settlement.

Glacken identified three main questions that humans have persistently asked about the earth and the relationship between nature and culture. One of these, the effects of human action in changing the earth from its hypothetical pristine state, has become central to modern environmental concerns. It has been most strongly articulated since the nineteenth century, when the potential for devastating human effects on the environment could be seen in the combination of a confident rational spirit of resource development and advances in the technological means to achieve this with the products of the industrial revolution. The second question concerning the influence of environment on people and culture has had a much longer currency, reaching its peak in the nineteenth-century view that the environment determined the course of human development. There is a strong element of determinism in the world view of the modern environmental movement which at the global scale sees the limits of human economic activity determined by biophysical parameters (Simmons 1989).

In western intellectual traditions a persistent feature of the human–environmental relationship has been the idea that the human species stands apart from the rest of the animal world and nature in general. Christianity, the dominant western religion, provided the foundation of beliefs in this regard but there is no single world view. Philosophers have identified three major positions and at the broadest level, the environmental relationships of European Australians can be framed within them (Attfield 1983). They are the belief that there are no constraints on the way in which humans may treat nature; the concept of stewardship (humans have obligations to care for nature); and the idea that humans can work with nature to perfect it. The latter is relevant to the Anglo-Celtic view in which perfectibility and the rural landscape (blending nature and human design) often appear to be synonymous. This notion is expressed by W.G. Hoskins in his *Making of the English Landscape* (1955) when he describes the 'perfect landscapes' of the English countryside, prior to the impacts of

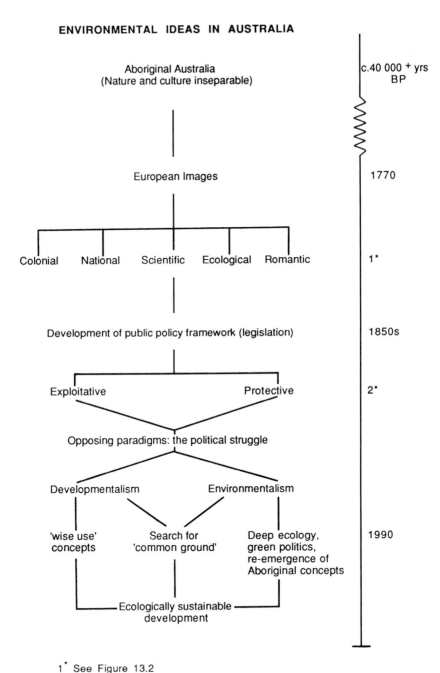

ENVIRONMENTAL IDEAS IN AUSTRALIA

Aboriginal Australia
(Nature and culture inseparable)

c.40 000 + yrs
BP

European Images

1770

Colonial   National   Scientific   Ecological   Romantic

1*

Development of public policy framework (legislation)

1850s

Exploitative   Protective

2*

Opposing paradigms: the political struggle

Developmentalism   Environmentalism

'wise use'   Search for   Deep ecology,
concepts   'common ground'   green politics,
                                                  re-emergence of
                                                  Aboriginal concepts

1990

Ecologically sustainable
development

1* See Figure 13.2

2* See Figure 13.3

Figure 13.1: Structure of environmental ideas, Aboriginal Australia to present.

large-scale mechanisation. There are also lesser traditions that have been influential in environmental thought, especially primitivism, romanticism and mysticism.

Perhaps the most important element in the cultural constructions that provide the filter between people and environment in the west has been science, seen as both a body of established knowledge and a method of enquiry into real world phenomena. The empirical method of science has been instrumental in constructing the modern view of the world. Science is equated with truth and provides apparently coherent and logical explanations of the way the universe operates that have replaced explanations constructed from religious beliefs. Established from the sixteenth century, modern science is based on the separation of humans from nature. Its approach to nature, refined in Newtonian physics, is reductionist. The latter has been subject to growing critique because many see as a major cause of environmental damage the failure to see nature in a holistic way. However, the Newtonian paradigm still constitutes the foundation of the modern popular conception of science and is the basis for the dominant, technically focused approach to environmental management.

The foregoing has aimed to show that ultimately the relationship between people and their environment is founded on certain beliefs which may not be explicitly articulated, but which are absorbed through a cultural framework which itself is being constantly remade by the outcomes of the relationship. If, for example, it is assumed that nature may be treated in any way without constraints, then ethical questions (such as, is it right to kill animals for sport?) simply do not arise. On the other hand, a belief in stewardship ideally leads to consideration of the survival and perpetuation of nature as well as future human generations. Care is needed, however, in making such links because duality of thought and action is common in the human relationship with the environment across all cultures.

It is these kinds of considerations that lie at the heart of environmentalist visions of reform of the human–environment interaction, leading to the search for a new environmental ethic. However, the means of achieving this are less clear. While a change in beliefs and values may be necessary for such social change to occur, it is also necessary to consider what material aspects of contemporary culture lend support to particular ideas and philosophies (Pepper 1984). For example, education is often seen as instrumental in changing attitudes towards those which are more ecologically supportive, but attempts to change the curriculum in this way normally confront other educational imperatives derived from the productive base of society.

Environmentalism

For the purposes of this discussion, environmentalism will be taken as embodying a range of thought and action concerned with the relationship between people and their environment. Environmentalism is considered here to include concern for both the natural and built (human modified) environment. It is directed in the widest possible sense to the protection and conservation of that environment. On a global scale it has also become increasingly concerned with equity, especially with regard to resource transfers, environmental quality and the ecological sustainability of regional economic systems. Environmentalism is the basis of a social and political movement which advocates a new philosophy of human conduct towards both nature and the cultural artefacts of human civilisation, as well as towards other human beings.

A generalised pattern of environmental ideologies has been presented by O'Riordan (1981, 376). One end of the spectrum is characterised by the 'technocentric' mode. Essentially this remains a developmentalist viewpoint, but one in which some consideration is given to the environment. Ideas of material progress, efficiency in managing resources, rational or objective approaches to that management (often relying upon scientific expertise), and faith in human ability to control physical, biological and social processes are hallmarks of the technocentric mode. In western countries, including Australia, governments have begun to move from this position to further accommodate environmental concerns, on the assumption that economic growth and resource exploitation can continue, provided regulatory and public participatory structures are established. The concept of ecologically sustainable development finds its place largely within this 'accommodating' mode. Authors such as Sandbach (1980) argue that this move to accommodation is the limit of pluralist style reform in democratic systems as the agenda for change has been co-opted by dominant political and economic interests which are able to repel or deflect more radical approaches to change.

The opposing end of the spectrum, the 'ecocentric' mode, is based on concern that the earth's life support systems are already overtaxed and threatened. It contains the view that no habitable future is possible without a fundamental change away from the belief in technological mastery of the planet to more humble lifestyles in harmony with ecological processes. The ecocentric view is a radical one, opposed to the dominant values and institutions of industrial society. Perhaps the most fundamental difference is the view of nature, which in the ecocentric mode is held in reverence, considered to have intrinsic value or worth rather than being valued only for serving human ends, and deemed to command certain moral obligations on the part of humans. The opposing modes of environmentalism presented here, in fact connect as a continuum. Organisations and individuals within them commonly embrace elements of both the technocentric and the ecocentric modes, invoking contradictions which are not easily resolved or conceptualised.

Modern environmentalism challenges both the ecological relationships and the social organisation that characterise the industrialised, energy intensive, high military spending economies which have developed over the last 150 years, partly as products of the industrial revolution. As a differing world view, it has been clearly articulated only from the 1960s and mainly in western countries. However, as Pepper (1984, 4) notes, the type of society which many see as ecologically sustainable and therefore socially desirable, would be based on ideas and values which may have existed already for a very long time, but now run counter to the prevailing economic ethos and conventional wisdom. Central to this is a questioning of the assumption about societal progress, which simply equates material prosperity with greater wellbeing.

'Reading' the environment: an approach

It is evident from the above that the unravelling of diffuse environmental ideas and their expression in the landscape is not a simple task. We can begin by trying to delineate significant visions of the environment, seeing these as cultural constructions of reality which draw on the long traditions outlined. These are given contemporary sanction by reigning economic and political forces or stand in opposition as a competing set of ideas. The way in which these visions gain ascendancy over one another and become the force behind private and public policy and action in the landscape must be related to power relations in society and its productive basis. Ultimately this contest of ideas and power finds expression in landscape form and meaning, but the landscape always remains contested space embedded with past ideas overlain by newly emerging ones. In attempting to read the landscape (or the environment in general) we find that despite the messages which emanate from it, it still remains obscure as if written in a form of code (Lewis 1979). Landscapes must also be seen as dynamic and transitional in form and meaning, requiring great care in interpretation of the motivations shaping them. This is because differing visions may produce similar landscape consequences; the ascendancy of particular visions may disguise the conflicts that were involved; and there is the great danger of transferring out of context, current ideas and concepts to an analysis of past landscape decisions.

The view taken here is that despite the persistence of dualism, a people's cultural identity is forged and evolves in part through the interactions with the environment part of which becomes existential or 'lived in space' (Relph 1976, 12). In a circular process, the cultural identity so established contributes to new visions which influence future environmental interactions. An important element of environmental concern is a sense of place developed at different scales. Encompassing a range of emotions, sense of place expresses oneness or connection with environment rather than the externality of the environment, and hence availability for capricious manipulation.

History of Australian environmental ideas

Australia, as one of the 'Settler Empires' of the New World, provides a rich source for the study of environmental images and the imprint of European ideas and concepts on the landscape. Modern concern for the environment is all the more significant because of the way it represents a dramatic overturning of previous images in which derogatory views of, or indifference to, the natural environment dominated. The central paradox in Australian environmental attitudes relates to the post-1788 peopling of the continent by those whose cultural traditions, aspirations and environmental knowledge derived from a fundamentally different physical environment (Seddon 1976). It was inevitable that it would take generations for a new view to emerge, an affinity with place, but all the time the European (especially Anglo-Celtic) perceptions were continually reinforced by immigration. This was particularly significant in the case of Australian elites in the churches, schools and universities whose ranks were continually replenished from Britain (Birrell 1987).

Aboriginal Australia

For Aboriginal Australians nature and culture are inextricably bound together in the Dreaming — the time when the world, including Aboriginal people and their law, were created (see chapter 15). Belief systems associated with the Dreaming link specific places with Dreaming events and give every person, living and dead, a place within a physically and spiritually united world (White & Lampert 1987). The landscape is not therefore a composite of external physical objects but is made up of culturally defined features of mythical significance (ancestors of the Dreaming).

The dispossession of Aboriginal Australians from their land after 40 000 or more years of occupation was remarkably swift. Despite the evidence to the contrary, English law persisted with the description of the continent as 'waste and uninhabited' (Reynolds 1987). Subsequently, much of the accumulated Aboriginal knowledge of the environment (e.g. plant chemistry) was lost. Though given little acknowledgement, Aboriginal skills and knowledge were instrumental in building the European rural economy, especially pastoralism.

Europeans found an Australian landscape which lacked apparent evidence of a human past. There were none of the familiar artefacts of established civilisation, such as buildings and ruins, cultivation or domestication. They did notice the common occurrence of bushfire — observations sharpened perhaps by prior experience of a landscape where such fires were uncommon. The role of fire in Australian biological systems and the practice of Aboriginal burning would eventually become a key question in Australian ecology, and feature prominently in current debates over how protected natural areas should be managed.

European images

Five significant visions or 'ways of seeing' the Australian environment since European settlement have been identified by Heathcote (1972) (fig. 13.2). These visions are culturally constructed lenses which have evolved through time, sometimes in combination with one another. Scientific visions, for example, complement both the colonial and the ecological.

Initially, within the *scientific* vision there was a spirit of enquiry into the natural phenomena of the continent motivated by intrinsic interest and curiosity. Exploration of the South Pacific inspired much thought on the relations between humans and nature in both science and art (Smith 1960). The period also saw the ascendancy of empiricism in science and rejection of neo-classical representations of nature. In the nineteenth century, scientific knowledge assisted in resource development but also began to appear in critiques of development, especially pioneering exploitation. By 1900, scientific knowledge and research methods were being applied to the natural resource industries such as forestry and agriculture. Later, scientific values were used in the argument for the preservation of natural ecosystems. New and positive images of the Australian environment are strongly based on a marriage of scientific discovery and aesthetic sensibilities. The powerful position of science in our culture has led some to view it as a final arbiter in environmental conflicts. However, these conflicts demonstrate how science cannot be divorced from values, as pro-development 'establishment' science and an 'oppositional' science have stood opposed on many issues (Mercer 1986).

The *romantic* vision encapsulates the aesthetic responses to the landscape. Initially the vision engendered a sympathetic response to both the Aborigines and to the 'uncivilised' landscape, apparently unmodified by human activity. This vision owed much to the picturesque movement which formed part of the flowering of Romanticism in the late eighteenth and early nineteenth centuries. The picturesque was closely related to empiricism in science. Nature was to be seen in all its roughness and irregularity, not reconstructed to conform to some classical ideal. The related concept of the 'sublime' brought enthusiasm for vast, chaotic and wild scenery. From about 1900 the romantic image motivated the bushwalking/conservation and later National Park and wilderness preservation movements. This vision with its mystical and spiritual extensions has become increasingly significant. Evidence for it in Australia can be found in the large number of individuals and groups defending the preservation of the natural environment,

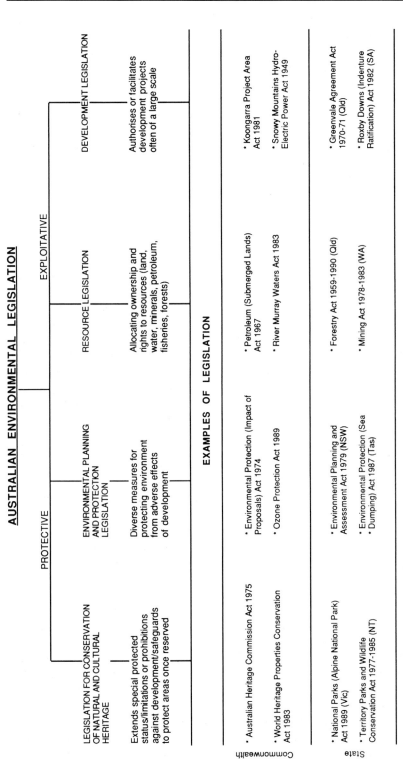

Figure 13.2: Images of the Australian environment 1770–1990

Source: Adapted from Frawley (1987), image categories from Heathcote (1972).

and the substantial areas now protected from development, in National Parks and World Heritage areas, for example.

The *colonial* vision has been the dominant one throughout Australian history. Its characteristics are an emphasis on economic development, progress and improvement of nature, as a corollary to which the vision is notable for its indifference to the natural landscape. It most strongly shows the lack of affinity for the native landscape of the immigrant European population who sought to transform it to be more like the landscapes with which they were familiar. Part of the rejection of the native flora and fauna derived from their perceived lack of economic value. This colonial vision was also supported from abroad. Much Australian development was ultimately controlled from Britain, serving the needs of Empire and British capital (Jeans 1987). Until recently, generations of young Australians learnt through the education system of the priority of Empire and the uselessness of the bush which — it was taught — needed to be developed and improved.

Three main stages may be identified within the colonial vision. The first was one of unregulated exploitative pioneering which through the nineteenth century increasingly applied the products of the Industrial Revolution to the exploitation of resources. Steam-powered machinery, for example in sawmills, revolutionised raw material processing. The second stage involved some tempering of this exploitation by the application of the concept of 'wise use' of resources. The 'wise use' conservation philosophy which derived from North America was founded on the idea of the 'greatest good for the greatest number over the longest time'. Its focus was on rational planning and scientific management of natural resources. Its rise partly reflected the growth of a class of technically qualified professionals who wished to assert their role in managing natural resources. In Australia, wise use concepts slowly came to underpin most state intervention in resource management and initially were particularly evident in water management. The third stage, since the 1960s, has seen the colonial image challenged by the ecological (see below). However, wise use concepts remain highly influential, and a century after their introduction are being written anew under the mantle of 'sustainable development'.

The *national* vision is related to a sense of pride in the achievement of development goals and confidence in Australian potential. It is both nationalistic and expressive of the establishment of a cultural identity. By the latter part of the nineteenth century, financial success in pastoralism, farming and mining brought confidence in and changed attitudes towards the land (Heathcote 1972, 91). Integral to the vision was a new optimism and patriotism which would be expressed in closer settlement schemes, water resource developments, and plans for northern Australia. The literary and artistic nationalist movement of the 1890s also affirmed an Australian view of the landscape in which the Australian bush featured prominently. It has also been argued that inland (mainly pastoral) Australia was the setting for the establishment of 'typical Australian' character traits (Ward 1958). The national vision was tied in with reconstruction plans after both World Wars and the mineral boom of the 1960s. However, the vision also began to take an alternative form at this time, with growing pride in Australian natural and cultural heritage.

The *ecological* vision has enjoyed popular support only since the Second World War and forms the context for the modern environmental movement. However, it is clearly linked to the scientific, romantic and national visions with their earlier origins. The ecological vision is characterised by its opposition to the development ethos and its rejection of the domination and careless exploitation of nature. It has also challenged the original national vision, with a more pessimistic view of Australian resource development potential. The ecological vision is now increasingly focused on ways of achieving an ecologically sustainable economy.

The evolution of Australian environmental thought and public policy: a brief review

The link between these visions of the environment, their incorporation in public policy and effects on the landscape can be examined in the progressive accumulation of a large body of state and federal legislation. Conceptually, environmental law is considered to embrace all legislation covering human interaction with the environment. This legislation can be broadly classified as 'protective' or 'exploitative' (fig. 13.3). The 'protective' component is legislation which has the aim of protecting the environment from undue degradation by human activity as well as that which provides for the conservation of natural and cultural resources. The 'exploitative' component is legislation for the disposal (sale, lease, granting) of natural resources and for facilitating development activity. In some instances, a specific piece of legislation incorporates both components (AEC 1986).

From earliest European settlement, the Australian landscape has been space contested by different and competing claims. Contemporary environmental conflicts are the most recent expression of a continuum of changing views on how the environment should be used and managed. These views are cultural constructions deriving from both long traditions and particular visions as previously outlined. European conflict with the Aborigines over the basic resource of land was the source of a first fundamental conflict. In the nineteenth century we can see the influence of British culture in the deliberate attempts to emulate both the physical form of the closely settled rural landscape, and its class structure dominated by a landed gentry. The contest, in the form of a class struggle between pastoral interests and small farmers (agrarians) is one of the enduring themes of nineteenth-century Australian social history. British cultural influences related to property rights can also be seen in the high value placed on the ability to obtain freehold land. However, there were also adaptations of ideas to Australian conditions. These solutions to Australian problems contributed to the national vision noted earlier. Given the dryness of the Australian continent, for example, the British derived common law rights to water were replaced at the turn of the century by state control (Bates 1983, 126).

It is in the second half of the nineteenth century that the first roots of what was to become Australian environmentalism are identifiable. There were two distinct influences. The first was a growing concern about reckless exploitation and waste of resources, in particular the effects of rural settlement and forest clearing. Some of this concern was reinforced by the highly influential book *Man and Nature* by G.P. Marsh (1864) which gained a wide Australian readership. The second aspect related to the affirmation of Australian cultural identity, nationalist sentiment and the attempt to see the landscape through Australian rather than European eyes evident in the Australian literary and artistic movement of the 1890s (Birrell 1987).

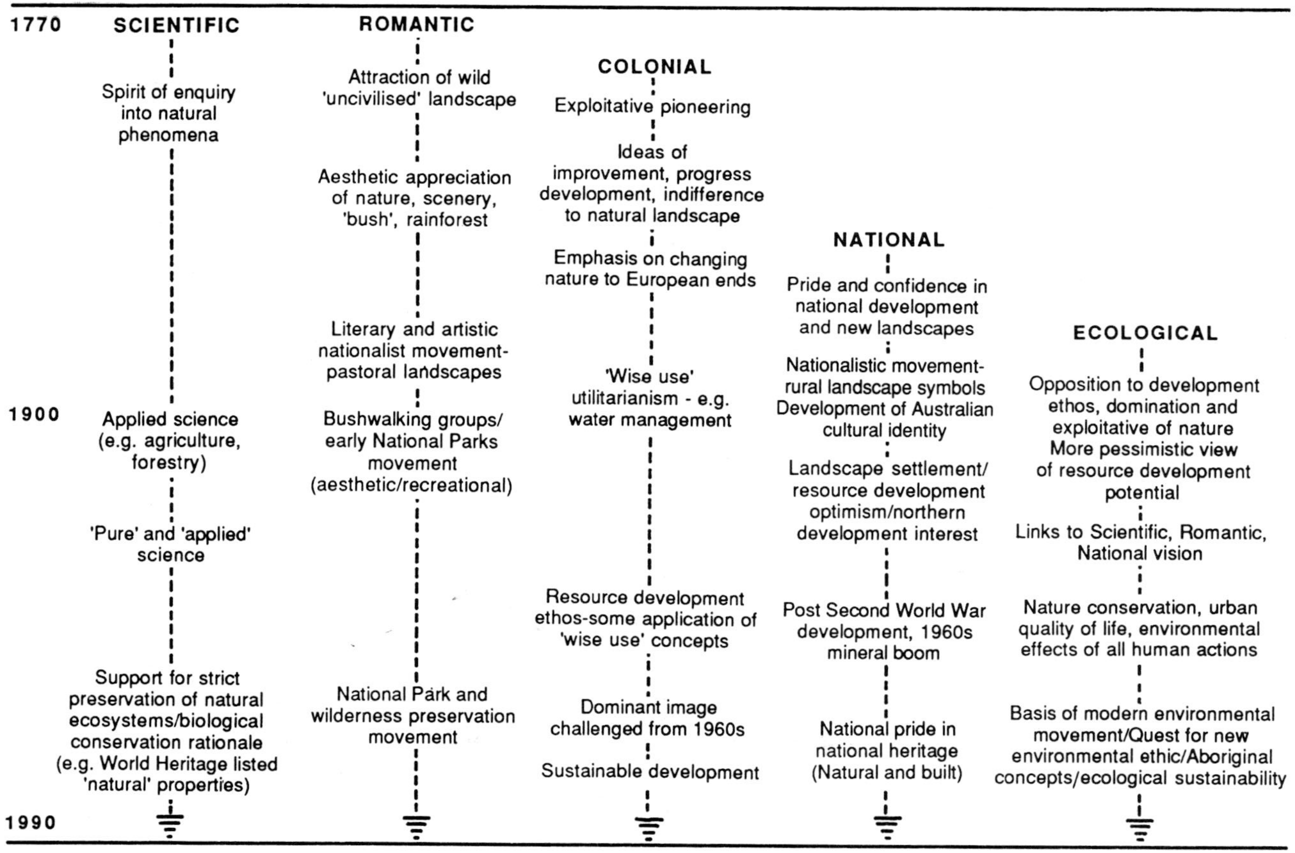

SCIENTIFIC

1770

Spirit of enquiry into natural phenomena

Applied science (e.g. agriculture, forestry)

1900

'Pure' and 'applied' science

Support for strict preservation of natural ecosystems/biological conservation rationale (e.g. World Heritage listed 'natural' properties)

1990

ROMANTIC

Attraction of wild 'uncivilised' landscape

Aesthetic appreciation of nature, scenery, 'bush', rainforest

Literary and artistic nationalist movement-pastoral landscapes

Bushwalking groups/ early National Parks movement (aesthetic/recreational)

National Park and wilderness preservation movement

COLONIAL

Exploitative pioneering

Ideas of improvement, progress development, indifference to natural landscape

Emphasis on changing nature to European ends

'Wise use' utilitarianism - e.g. water management

Resource development ethos-some application of 'wise use' concepts

Dominant image challenged from 1960s

Sustainable development

NATIONAL

Pride and confidence in national development and new landscapes

Nationalistic movement-rural landscape symbols Development of Australian cultural identity

Landscape settlement/ resource development optimism/northern development interest

Post Second World War development, 1960s mineral boom

National pride in national heritage (Natural and built)

ECOLOGICAL

Opposition to development ethos, domination and exploitative of nature More pessimistic view of resource development potential

Links to Scientific, Romantic, National vision

Nature conservation, urban quality of life, environmental effects of all human actions

Basis of modern environmental movement/Quest for new environmental ethic/Aboriginal concepts/ecological sustainability

Figure 13.3: 'Protective' and 'exploitative' categorisation of Australian environmental legislation.
Source: Detail partly from AEC (1986).

From the 1880s through to the First World War, there was the beginning of some systematic critique of the development ethos and pioneering exploitation. A number of new ideas and movements for change in environmental management practices took hold in Australia. For example, significant steps were taken in water management and all states had established forestry administrations by 1920. Also, following the first initiative in 1879, all states accepted the idea of reserving areas of land as National Parks. Inspired by the romantic vision, there was an expansion of 'protective legislation' for nature conservation and for the establishment of parks and reserves.

Government involvement in resource management between the 1880s and the First World War was subject to two important and distinct overseas influences. The first was experience in other British Empire colonies. The second was the North American 'wise use' conservation philosophy noted earlier. Wise use concepts were promoted for industrial imperatives. In the case of the timber industry, they provided a rationale for state intervention to safeguard the large capital investments being made in steam sawmilling. The state could allocate the resource among competing mills, regenerate the forest crop and reserve the forest against competing agricultural claims. The interests of millers were aligned with the public good, expressed as the supply of timber in perpetuity.

These initiatives were not followed, however, by sustained reform of environmental management practices or public agitation for such. Throughout the interwar and post-Second World War period of reconstruction, resource development linked to population growth — in turn related to defence of Australia's 'open spaces' — remained the central national vision. This period saw the beginning of specific 'development legislation' to facilitate large scale projects, such as the Snowy Mountains Hydro-Electric Power Scheme (fig. 13.4). Nevertheless, there were some questioning voices and even stalwart opponents to the direction of development. Such questioning remained largely within the colonial vision but was motivated by concepts of wise use. These were promoted by a slowly expanding professional elite of resource managers, such as foresters, water engineers and agricultural scientists.

Following the Second World War, Australia entered a period of substantial economic growth, boosted by the immigration programme and national development objectives. However, social and political changes were also afoot which would lay the basis for the modern environmental movement of the last two decades. Australia became a culturally more diverse society, more affluent, better educated, less tied directly to natural resource-based occupations, and more open to the international flow of ideas. At the international level, a particular unease was beginning to develop by the late 1950s regarding the application of the products of expanding science and technology to the environment. The major shadow was the threat of nuclear holocaust but another threat was widely publicised in 1962 in Rachel Carson's biting polemic *Silent Spring* which attacked the unwitting destruction of life and habitat by massive pesticide use. In effect, Carson's book was a critique of narrow reductionist science, and triggered the expansion of alternative holistic thinking with regard to the environment.

In considering the social origin of Australia's environmental movement, Birrell (1987) has explored the role of nationalistic sentiment and the development of an Australian cultural identity. Australian nature had to be valued by Australians before they would campaign for its preservation and for so much of the nation's European history, obeisance to all things British and inculcation of the view that Australian nature

Figure 13.4: Guthega Dam on the Upper Snowy River, New South Wales. The Snowy Mountains Hydro-Electric Power Scheme was one of Australia's largest post-war development projects and a powerful symbol of the 'wise use' of resources.
Source: *Australian Panorama*, Pictorial Collection, National Library of Australia.

was worthless, conditioned thought. The role of nationalist sentiment in promoting interest in the Australian heritage in the modern period is traced by Birrell to Left and reformist nationalist intellectuals of the 1930s and 1940s. After the war this interest expanded, but from the 1960s Australian nationalism was increasingly identified by social critics as aligned with the Right of politics, for example, in concern for defending the 'Australian way of life'. Nevertheless, an underlying current of nationalistic feeling that was to some extent separate from other nationalistic expression but linked to the romantic vision of the country, motivated ideas of a 'national heritage'. This feeling was closely associated with landscape symbols such as the distinctive flora and fauna and the harsh beauty of the inland. Nationalism is now a limited component of the conservation ideology expressed by the major organisations. At the grass roots level, however, identification with and caring for the landscape, flora and fauna as well as the country's cultural heritage was probably the way that many Australians found sympathy with conservation goals.

While from the resource development viewpoint, the immediate post-war period in Australia was largely 'business as usual', changes in community attitudes were being expressed through conservation groups which lobbied for improvements in the provisions for nature conservation. By the late 1960s Australia was experiencing a minerals boom. Logging in the overcut forests was continuing to expand into remote country. There were new land development and dam construction schemes. In a short space of time a number of conflicts arose, with mining being prominent, for example, the proposed mining and oil drilling on the Barrier Reef (see Wright 1977). In Victoria, the conflict over proposed farm development of the Little Desert and abandonment of the scheme in 1970 represented a watershed in the uncritical acceptance of development in that state (Powell 1988, 234–45).

This period witnessed the birth of modern environmentalism in Australia related to a wider tide of cultural change in the western world. Some of the movement was allied to critiques of capitalism, protest about Australian and American involvement in Vietnam, and a counter-culture which rejected the materialism produced by the post-war economic boom. The earlier utilitarian conservation concept of 'wise use' was increasingly seen as deficient, as it allowed the destruction of other values. There was also growing cynicism about whether the professed scientifically-based wise use management of resources was in fact being practised — evidenced by the rundown of productivity in the native forests. Environmental groups, along with other movements for social change, were no longer satisfied to leave resource decisions with the 'experts' or accept passively the outcome of the close relationship between governments and development interests. Instead, they demanded public involvement in resource decision-making and were prepared to use direct protest as well as more conventional means to achieve their goals. The real necessity, however, was to place environmentalism on the political agenda and legitimise environmental protection and planning in the Australian political process. This was central to developments from 1970 when there was substantial expansion of the other 'protective' category of legislation — that which established structures for environmental planning and protection.

In summary, Australian environmentalism has evolved through three main stages. The foundations were laid early this century in the adoption of 'wise use' concepts in resource management and the beginnings of advocacy for nature conservation inspired by the romantic and scientific visions of the environment. The second stage, dating from the mid 1960s, was one of placing environmental matters on the political agenda so that they would be a continuing concern of government. Part of this involved establishing the legitimacy of the cause. The third stage, reflecting the maturing of the movement, has been one of direct involvement in the political process: attempting to influence votes at election time, standing 'green' candidates for election, and forming 'green' political groupings or parties.

Environmentalism on the political agenda post-1970

Viewed in the historical context outlined above, the distinctive feature of the post-1970 period has been the formal involvement of Australian governments with environmental matters. Since the early 1970s, environmental protection and planning have been progressively incorporated into state and Commonwealth government policy-making in the form of both legislation and administrative measures. Environmentalism now forms an opposing social paradigm to the long-dominant developmentalist view and is also critical of many of its technocentric and wise use modifications.

Contemporary environmentalism is a complex movement incorporating a great diversity of goals and methods for their achievement. In the Australian context we can identify a number of key elements of modern environmental consciousness. The first is international in coverage involving a major contrast with the 'core values' of industrial societies which centre around materialism (economic growth), instrumental valuation of the environment (resources), and the domination of nature (Cotgrove & Duff 1980). The alternative environmental paradigm focuses on non-material benefits (self-actualisation and quality of life), intrinsic valuation of the environment and harmony with nature. The second element relates to the culturally-situated intellectual traditions outlined in the first part of the chapter. Environmentalism promotes as a key question for society the environmental impact of its actions, and stresses deterministically biospherical limits to human action. It also raises the need for a new environmental ethic in which moral judgements are extended to the human–environmental relationship. The third element is the continuation of visions of the Australian environment since European settlement and the re-emergence of Aboriginal conceptions of the land. While the ecological vision is the most significant, modern 'green' consciousness incorporates elements of all the visions earlier outlined, including some acceptance of the 'wise use' concepts of the colonial vision in particular contexts.

The most significant development in Australian environmental thought and practice since 1970 has been the emergence of 'green politics'. The green political movement has grown out of dissatisfaction with existing political philosophies. Liberalism and the traditional Left are both human-centred, with visions of social improvement that do not give much consideration to the environmental relationships of humanity (Hutton 1987). Also, though environmentalists have challenged the central values and ideology of industrial society and capitalism and might therefore seem to have something in common with Marxists, the environment is given scant consideration in both the Marxist critique and the capitalist perspective. Both positions tend to see the environment as something to be manipulated for human ends. Traditional class-based conflict is mainly about the share of the productive cake, which both sides have an interest in expanding. In the post-war period of economic growth, employees gained higher wages and living standards and were co-opted into the capitalist system of production. However, the problems which environmentalists identify are seen as deriving from that ever-expanding cake. They now argue that economic growth should be checked because of its increasing raw material inputs and environmentally degrading and life-threatening outputs.

The rise of Australian environmentalism and its mounting political force since 1970 can be traced through a number of key issues and events. Influential in the early 1970s was a flood of consciousness-raising literature which for the first time in human history took a global perspective on the state of the earth and its capacity to sustain an ever-growing population. Probably the most significant event in the birth of modern Australian environmental politics was the 'green ban' movement in Sydney and Melbourne in the early 1970s (fig. 13.5). This linked a range of concerns including quality of life issues, urban politics, class struggle and union attempts to take greater control over the labour process (Jakubowicz 1984). The social and political action involved was underlain by a radical critique of capitalism and the bureaucratic state. Though ultimately crushed, the movement was highly significant in demonstrating the usefulness of direct protest action in the democratic political process.

In the mid 1970s, the flooding of the aesthetically acclaimed Lake Pedder in Tasmania for hydro-electric power generation marked a turning point for the dominance of the colonial vision. Tasmanian developmentalist ideology and the technocratic arrogance and lack of public accountability of the Hydro-Electric Commission incurred

Figure 13.5: 'Green Ban' graffiti on railway pillar, Woolloomooloo, Sydney, portraying some of the prominent protagonists in the conflict.
Source: Anton Cermak/John Fairfax Group.

conservationist wrath. More importantly, perhaps, there was a deep sense of loss and grief which is still expressed. Lake Pedder was the issue which most clearly brought out the sense of national identification with the Australian landscape. It was a symbolic site for a changed Australian environmental consciousness.

In the following years, a wide range of issues were pursued by conservation and heritage organisations. Forest management, mining (including uranium mining and export), nature conservation and national parks, urban and regional planning, energy and population issues were prominent. By 1980 conservation organisations had a membership of 250 000. There was also considerable legislative activity. Between 1975 and 1982, 102 pieces of environmental legislation were passed (seventy-nine state, twenty-three federal) with about 80 per cent of this being 'protective' (fig. 13.3) (Grinlinton 1990).

While a wide range of issues engaged the efforts of environment groups in the 1980s, two particular issues caught widespread national attention. One was the future of the remaining rainforest in New South Wales and north Queensland. By this time, rainforests had begun to assume a prominent place in changing aesthetic appraisals of the Australian natural environment and this response was deepened with the popularisation of scientific discoveries. Rainforests became assimilated into emerging holistic and ecological views which stood in opposition to long-standing exploitative attitudes towards the forests. Following protracted political disputes, especially in Queensland where there were Commonwealth–state differences (Frawley 1991), both areas of rainforest were eventually inscribed on the World Heritage list.

The *cause celebre* of the early 1980s, however, was the conflict over the proposed Gordon-below-Franklin dam in south-west Tasmania. The anti-dam campaign raised environmental concerns to be a key element in the 1983 federal election campaign (fig. 13.6). Subsequently, the Commonwealth was able to intervene in what was formerly a state jurisdiction by means of Australia's nomination of south-west Tasmania to the World Heritage list. Once the area was inscribed on the list, Commonwealth constitutional power could be invoked to implement international treaty obligations. The validity of the exercise of Commonwealth power was later upheld by the High Court of Australia.

By 1990, environmentalism was established on the political agenda, raised from being a matter of limited or peripheral concern to government by a significant and growing constituency for environmental reform. For government, bringing environmental considerations into all aspects of policy making has been no easy task: the information base to do so is limited, environmentally sound economic restructuring is likely to be socially disruptive at least in the short term, and the majority of the electorate is still highly sensitive to government policies that might be seen in any way as reducing the community's standard of living. In this context, in the search for 'common ground', by 1990 the Australian government was embracing the concept of 'ecologically sustainable development'. The principles of this had already been outlined to some extent in the National Conservation Strategy for Australia formulated in 1983, but globally it gained wide publicity with the publication of the report of the World Commission on Environment and Development (Brundtland report) in 1987 (WCED 1987).

Figure 13.6: Evocative campaigning in the 1983 federal election for protection of the Franklin River in south-west Tasmania.
Source: *Habitat Australia* 15, 5, 1987, p. 8.

The concept of ecologically sustainable development has appeal to government trying to chart a course through the often contradictory messages coming from the community. It does provide some common ground for traditional development and newly ascending conservation views. While the developmentalists, however, appear to see the concept largely as a more sophisticated extension of the pragmatic, managerial 'wise use' principles established through this century, many of the conservationists are sceptical of the ability of government to recognise the fundamental ecological constraints within which, it is believed, economic development must be restructured.

Conclusion

This chapter has examined the development of Australian environmentalism from the historical perspective of still-evolving culturally framed understandings of the environment. Evident in this has been the formation of particular images or visions of the Australian environment over the last two hundred years, weighted heavily by Eurocentrism but showing also the progressive development of an 'Australian' view, and the influence of particular ideas and concepts from overseas. Significant was the early lack of recognition and rejection of the complex Aboriginal understandings of the environment except where these were valuable in establishing the rural economy. Aboriginal concepts are now re-emerging, however, as some non-Aboriginal Australians develop an affinity with the landscape and in turn are better able to appreciate Aboriginal environmental knowledge.

While modern environmentalism is often considered mainly in its contemporary political and social dimensions, it can only be fully understood by examining its challenge to long traditions in the way nature has been treated in the West. It brings new ways of seeing to the relationship between people and their environment which result in conflict as they clash with attitudes and values derivative of longer standing exploitative traditions. Australian environmentalism has been shown to be linked to international environmental concern and a wave of social change which dates from the 1960s. Viewed historically, there are parallels to other profound social changes in western society such as the rise of the labour movement, the emancipation of women, and universal suffrage.

To a greater or lesser degree (stressing again the great diversity of environmental thought) environmentalism presents an alternative, competing, though as yet minority paradigm to that which dominates in developed western countries such as Australia. Since the 1970s environmentalism has formed an oppositional culture to centralised, materialistic, industrial society; it has created fragile alliances with other minority and marginalised groups as well as the mainstream Left of politics. In Australia, as elsewhere, the movement tends to draw its most politically active members from that well-educated section of the middle class who do not draw their livelihood from the industrial or commercial sectors of the economy.

From the 1960s, the movement in Australia struggled to place environmental matters permanently on the political agenda. The evidence, politically in the form of legislation and administrative procedures, and culturally in changed community attitudes and modes of behaviour, suggests that much has been achieved in this regard. There is also considerable landscape imprint. In 1990 there were more than 40 million ha (100 million acres) of National Parks and other reserves. Eight areas were on the World Heritage List, some covering extensive land areas, for example the Queensland Wet Tropics, 896 500 ha (2.2 million acres). The Register of the National Estate contained 9633 places. In rural Australia, government-supported 'Land Care', Soil Conservation and 'Greening Australia' programmes were being implemented. While these structures and programmes are likely to have enduring effects, green politics in Australia will, by contrast, remain highly volatile being influenced by changing economic, social and political factors as well as continually evolving images of the Australian environment and its place in national cultural identity.

References

AEC (Australian Environment Council) 1986, *Guide to Environmental Legislation and Administrative Arrangements in Australia* (2nd edn), Australian Government Publishing Service, Canberra.

Attfield, R. 1983, *The Ethics of Environmental Concern*, Blackwell, Oxford.

Bates, G. 1983, *Environmental Law in Australia*, Butterworths, Sydney.

Birrell, R. 1987, 'The social origin of Australia's conservation movement', *Journal of Intercultural Studies*, 8, 2, pp. 22–38.

Carson, R. 1962, *Silent Spring*, Penguin, Harmondsworth.

Cotgrove, S. & Duff, A. 1980, 'Environmentalism, middle class radicalism and politics', *Sociological Review*, 28, 2, pp. 333–51.

Frawley, K.J. 1987, *Exploring Some Australian Images of Environment*, Working Paper 1987/1, Department of Geography and Oceanography, University College, Australian Defence Force Academy, Canberra.

Frawley, K.J. 1991, 'Queensland rainforest management: frontier attitudes and public policy', *Journal of Rural Studies*, 7, 3, pp. 219–39.

Glacken, C.J. 1967, *Traces on the Rhodian Shore*, University of California Press, Berkeley.

Grinlinton, D. 1990, 'The "environmental era" and the emergence of "environmental law" in Australia — a survey of environmental legislation and litigation 1967-1987', *Environment and Planning Law Journal*, 7, 2, pp. 74–105.

Hawke, R.J.L. 1989, *Our Country Our Future: Statement on the Environment*, Australian Government Publishing Service, Canberra.

Heathcote, R.L. 1972, 'The visions of Australia 1770-1970', in A. Rapoport (ed.), *Australia as Human Setting*, Angus & Robertson, Sydney, pp. 77–98.

Hoskins, W.G. 1955, *The Making of the English Landscape*, Penguin, Harmondsworth.

Hutton, D. 1987, 'What is green politics', in D. Hutton (ed.), *Green Politics in Australia*, Angus & Robertson, Sydney, pp. 1–33.

Jakubowicz, A. 1984, 'The green ban movement: urban struggle and class politics', in J. Halligan & C. Paris (eds), *Australian Urban Politics: Critical Perspectives*, Longman Cheshire, Melbourne, pp. 149–66.

Jeans, D.N. 1987, 'The incorporation of Australia', in D.N. Jeans (ed.), *Australia — A Geography, Vol. 2, Space and Society* (2nd edn), Sydney University Press, Sydney, pp. 1–23.

Lewis, P.F. 1979, 'Axioms for reading the landscape', in D.W. Meinig (ed.), *The Interpretation of Ordinary Landscapes*, Oxford University Press, New York, pp. 11–32.

Marsh, G.P. 1864, *Man and Nature: or Physical Geography as Modified by Human Action*, Scribner, Armstrong, New York.

Mercer, D. 1986, *Institutional and Counter-Institutional Forces in Australian Environmental Decision-Making*, Working Paper No. 21, Department of Geography, Monash University, Melbourne.

O'Riordan, T. 1981, *Environmentalism*, Pion, London.

Pepper, D. 1984, *The Roots of Modern Environmentalism*, Croom Helm, London.

Powell, J.M. 1988, *An Historical Geography of Modern Australia: The Restive Fringe*, Cambridge University Press, Cambridge.

Relph, E. 1976, *Place and Placelessness*, Pion, London.

Reynolds, H. 1987, *The Law of the Land*, Penguin, Melbourne.

Sandbach, F. 1980, *Environment, Ideology and Policy*, Blackwell, Oxford.

Seddon, G. 1976, 'The evolution of perceptual attitudes', in G. Seddon & M. Davis (eds), *Man and Landscape in Australia: Towards an Ecological Vision*, Australian Government Publishing Service, Canberra, pp. 9-17.

Simmons, I.G. 1989, *Changing the Face of the Earth: Culture, Environment History*, Blackwell, Oxford.

Smith, B. 1960, *European Vision and the South Pacific 1768-1850*, Oxford University Press, London.

Ward, R. 1958, *The Australian Legend*, Oxford University Press, Melbourne.

WCED (World Commission on Environment and Development) 1987, *Our Common Future*, Oxford University Press, Oxford.

White, J.P. & Lampert, R. 1987, 'Creation and discovery', in D.J. Mulvaney & J.P. White (eds), *Australians to 1788*, Fairfax, Syme & Weldon Associates, Sydney, pp. 3–24.

Wright, J. 1977, *The Coral Battleground*, Nelson, Melbourne.

14 The cultural politics of nature conservation and economic development

Jacquelin Burgess

Introduction

In this chapter, I want to explore the role being played by the media in representing the conflicts between economic development and nature conservation. My case study is the proposal by the Music Corporation of America (hereafter MCA) to build film studios, a theme park and associated commercial developments on a site which is located on the outer eastern fringes of London in the UK. Much of the land chosen by MCA is designated as a site of special scientific interest for nature conservation. The discourses of the different groups involved in the MCA proposal and the actions taken by these groups to progress or oppose the scheme highlight the profound importance of understanding cultural as well as environmental, economic and social issues involved in change.

Cultural geography, politics and the mass media

Geographers could usefully pay much closer attention to the print and broadcast media, as they are part of a complex cultural process in which meanings are produced and consumed (see Burgess 1990; Burgess & Gold 1985). Reality is constructed through shared, culturally specific, symbolic systems of visual and verbal communications and the media play a fundamental role in the construction of that reality, by selectively providing knowledge about the lives, landscapes and cultures of different social groups (Hall 1977).

It is useful to think of this cultural process of communication as a circuit of production, text, and consumption (Johnson 1986). At each stage of the circuit, transformations occur, transformations of meaning and form. For example, a journalist wishing to write a story about the impact of the loss of a particular habitat will contact expert ecologists who will tell the journalist about aspects of their work and its likely significance. These discussions will be phrased in scientific language and hedged by caveats about problems with data collection, the difficulties of assessing impacts in complex ecosystems and the need for more research. The journalist will endeavour to tell the story in a way that is intelligible to the readers of the paper. The science of nature conservation will be transformed, both in the selection and interpretation of the key issues felt to be significant and, more basically, through the production of the newspaper text itself. The science will be 'encoded' in a system of visual and verbal symbols — words, pictures, graphs etc. — creating a discourse which conforms to the basic constraints of newspaper production, the characteristics of the readers and the news values which help determine how the story is constructed. The circuit can only be completed when media texts are consumed, that is, when they are purchased and read. A second transformation occurs as consumers 'decode' or make sense of newspaper reports. There is no necessary equivalence between the meanings that are encoded in texts and the meanings that different readers decode from those same texts. Preferred meanings may well be accepted by readers but, just as often, they will be resisted, subverted and contested (Hall 1980; Morley 1986). The characteristics of audiences play a profoundly important role in determining how people interpret media discourses: making sense is 'a function of a complex environment, that of personality, of the family, of the neighbourhood, of work, of ideology' (Silverstone 1985, 182). The circuit is completed as diverse aspects of environmental, economic, social and political contexts within which people live and the activities in which they participate provide the basis for further transformations in the production of news. To return to our nature conservation example, inspired perhaps by newspaper reports of effective protests against developers in another part of the country, local people may well undertake a campaign of their own which will attract and generate new press coverage, and so the circuit continues.

Conservationists are indeed locked in battle with national and international capital interests seeking to exploit or destroy habitats in many different locations around the world. The discourses through which such developments are attacked or defended represent different social constructions of nature and its meanings/values: from the unbridled economic view that developers have the inalienable right to extract the maximum possible economic returns from all natural resources to the expressions of 'deep green' philosophy which seek to respect and protect the rights of all living things above all else. Such conflicts have a long history in terms of construing relations between nature and culture (Pepper 1984; see also ch. 13). In their current expressions, conflicts between nature conservation and economic development reflect a greater realisation than ever before of the rate and scale of the loss of habitats and species.

It is helpful to conceptualise the conflicts between these different ways of seeing and using nature as a form of cultural politics — different groups representing sectional interests are locked in struggles over the meanings and values of plants, animals and landscapes threatened by development. The crucial point is that these groups are differentially empowered, depending, for example on whether or not they have access to political elites, whether they are able to draw upon finance to support their proposals, whether they are able to mobilise the mass media to promote their particular ways of seeing, classifying and explaining actions and events. For example, we shall see in the case study that MCA used its economic power and political influence to persuade both decision-makers and a significant proportion of the local people who would be most directly affected by the development, that its proposals were exciting, innovative and of real economic, social and conservation benefit. Ranged against these powerful forces, the conservation/environmental groups found it difficult to fight effectively and their own distinctive ways of seeing nature did not ultimately carry the same weight. The major public arenas within which these kinds of battles will be fought are the print and broadcast media.

In this chapter I want to explore some of these issues by focusing on the ways in which MCA were able to exploit some of the tensions between different social constructions of nature and landscape which arose during the debate about the future of Rainham marshes. I shall do so by concentrating on the ways in which the local media represented these different ways of seeing the marshes, both present and future.

Hollywood-on-Thames?

For many years Universal Studios, owned by MCA, has invited tourists into its studios in Hollywood to see how films are made and to participate in what the company calls 'themed attractions'. These are technologically sophisticated rides which replicate the key scenes in some of Universal Studios' most famous films such as *Jaws, ET, Back to the Future* and *King Kong*. In late 1988, MCA began to search for two locations — one in Europe, the other in Japan — where the development concept might be applied. Having looked at sites in several European countries, the company narrowed the choice to two possible locations: one in Paris and the other in London.

The context: Rainham and the lower Thames grazing marshes

MCA chose a location some 24 km (15 miles) east of the centre of London in the outer London Borough of Havering (fig. 14.1). The site comprised some 650 ha (1600 acres) of low-lying pastureland on the north bank of the River Thames. This green space was sandwiched between the huge Ford motor car factory at Dagenham and the industrial/dockside activities of the Port of London going down to Tilbury. Rainham village, with a population of approximately 2500, was situated immediately to the north of the site. Rainham grew rapidly during the middle decades of this century as families moved out from the slums of East London. To many of these people, moving to Rainham provided an opportunity to escape to the countryside from the poverty and squalor of the inner city. The most significant feature affecting the quality of life in Rainham was the A13. This major road, which carries both commuter traffic and all the heavy transport between central London and the lower Thames docks, cut the village in two. During the rush hour, it could sometimes take half an hour to cross from the northern suburbs to the village main street south of the A13.

Land uses on the marshes were varied. Aveley marshes and part of Wennington marsh (225 ha; 560 acres) were used by the Ministry of Defence as an army firing range. Cattle and sheep grazed the pastures, but the public had very limited access to them. The remainder of Wennington marshes and part of Rainham marshes (140 ha; 350 acres) was covered by three silt lagoons, large, embanked areas in which silt dredged from the main channel of the River Thames was dumped. Along the river bank, factories were engaged in engineering, food processing and container transportation. These were protected by a 210 cm (7 ft) high, flood-protection wall which effectively prevented access to the river foreshore. There was also a large landfill site (100 ha; 250 acres) where domestic waste from central London was tipped and compacted prior to being re-

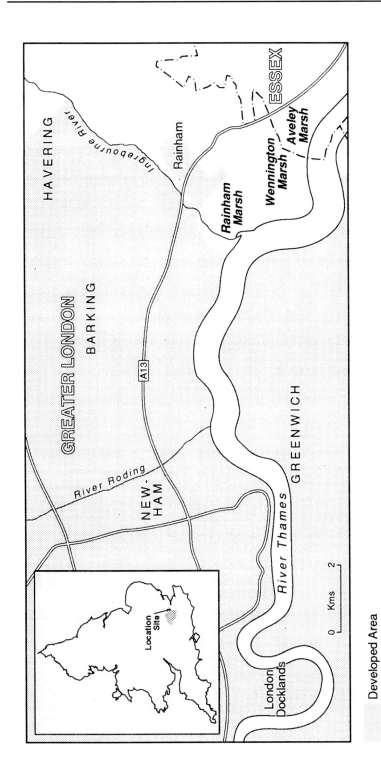

Figure 14.1: Location of Rainham and the site of the proposed MCA development.

landscaped. At the western side of the site, Rainham marsh (93 ha; 230 acres) was no longer managed for agricultural use and was used, illegally, as a motorcycle track.

The grazing marshes, the silt lagoons and the riverside were important for nature conservation, of such value that 505 ha (1250 acres) were designated as a site of special scientific interest (hereafter SSSI) in 1986. SSSI designation does not, however, guarantee protection. The Nature Conservancy Council (hereafter NCC) can only comment on changes and make suggestions about more sensitive management; it cannot legally enforce protection of SSSIs. Many SSSIs in different areas of the UK are under threat from both public and private sector development proposals.

There were several reasons why nature conservation organisations valued the Rainham site (NCC 1990), and the reasons put forward to justify the SSSI highlighted the way in which the scientific case for nature conservation was constructed. First, the NCC argued, the grazing marshes were ancient. The pattern of land use was established between the twelfth and seventeenth centuries meaning that the biotic communities had evolved over a long period of time. Second, it was the largest remaining area of grazing marshes in the inner Thames estuary — 65 per cent had been lost either to industrial and housing development or to more intensive agriculture, since the 1940s. Third, the NCC had identified many rare plants and invertebrates on the site: over thirty rare plants, including six which were nationally scarce. There were thirty species of invertebrates, such as butterflies, moths, dragonflies, water beetles and snails which were nationally scarce and seven which were in danger of extinction in the British Isles. The emerald green damsel-fly was thought to be extinct until it was rediscovered on Rainham marshes in 1983. Finally, the site was considered important for its breeding and wintering birds. One hundred and seventy different species had been recorded, including merlins, hen and marsh harriers and short-eared owls. For several years, the marshes had sufficient numbers of wintering teal to merit recognition as an internationally significant wetland. The importance of the site had been recognised by conservationists for many years, although it was not designated as an SSSI until 1986. As one conservationist said: 'In theory, because it was owned by public authorities including the Ministry of Defence and the London Borough of Havering, it was not thought to be under threat from development'. Thus, for the conservationists, Rainham marshes were of major importance and they fought hard to protect them from development (fig. 14.2).

Universal City: the proposal

If the Rainham location was chosen, the developers proposed spending £2.4 billion on the scheme.[1] The major elements of the plan included film and television studios, a theme park, cinemas, an arena, hotels with 4000 beds and a 173 ha (428 acre) nature reserve.[2] There would be 30 000 m^2 (320 000 ft^2) of festival retailing, 46 500 m^2 (500 000 ft^2) of office space, 112 000 m^2 (1.2 million ft^2) in a business park, 418 000 m^2 (4.5 million ft^2) of industrial and warehousing space, 2000 dwellings, 2800 m^2 (30 000 ft^2) of shopping and community facilities, and a new river pier. A 70 ha (175 acre) ecology park would be created on the landfill site. The company predicted that five million tourists a year would visit Universal City and estimated it would create some 20 000 jobs, of which 14 000 would be new to the local economy.

Figure 14.2: Protesters outside Romford Town Hall, 27 February 1990.
Source: *Romford Recorder*, 2 March 1990.

The political and economic contexts of the proposal were important. Both Labour and Conservative governments were committed to regenerating the economy of East London following the closure of the upper docks in the late 1960s and 1970s. Since the abolition in 1986 of the Greater London Council, which was responsible for strategic planning in London, each of the thirty-two boroughs have had primary responsibility for determining the future plans of its locality. Central government was involved through the function of the Secretary of State at the Department of the Environment, a cabinet minister who was responsibile for deciding whether development proposals which were not within the scope of local plans, should go to public inquiry.[3] The MCA proposals were important for both the national, and the local economy, so both central and local governments were involved in the complex negotiations about the site.

Researching the cultural politics of the Rainham marshes scheme

Cultural geography is distinguished by a variety of research styles which are often described as qualitative rather than quantitative, concerned with the interpretations of forms, images, texts, talk and actions. Within cultural geography, we will readily find studies of the production and the transformations of built environments, visual representations of landscapes and places, and the construction of meaning in literary texts (see Jackson 1989; Cosgrove & Daniels 1988). By comparison, empirical field research which focuses on the talk and actions of 'ordinary' people is rather less well developed although a growing number of geographers are turning to participant

Table 14.1:   Timetable of events and research strategies

Timetable of events

Nov. 1988 – June 1989	• MCA search for UK site; select Rainham (Feb. 1989) • initial private discussions with national/local politicians, planners etc.
5 June 1989	• press conference for local journalists announcing interest in the site
June – November 1989	• appointment of ecological consultants • preliminary negotiations • construction of master plan
29 November 1989	• press conference for national and local media to announce submission of planning application
Dec. 1989 – Feb. 1990	• public consultations • three public meetings held in early December • conservationists present petition against proposal to the Department of Environment (8/1/90) • continuing negotiations with NCC • liaison with national/local government
27 Feb. 1990	• planning permission granted by London Borough of Havering • £16 million mitigation package agreed with NCC
March 1990	• plan referred to Secretary of State (DOE) for decision on whether planning inquiry needed for proposal. • FOE release evidence suggesting low-level radioactive waste has been dumped on the site

Research strategies

May 1989 – Jan. 1991	• repeat, semi-structured interviews with developers' consultant, conservation personnel and local planners • monitoring of all national and local media items on Rainham
29 Nov. 1989	• attendance at press conference
Dec. 1989 – Feb. 1990	• attend public meetings • social survey conducted in Rainham (4 – 11 Jan.) • attend photo-call at DOE
27 Feb. 1990	• attend planning committee meeting to decide on application
March – June 1990	• recruit first in-depth discussion group in Rainham. Ten members to meet for six weeks • group runs 15/5/90 – 20/6/90
6 April 1990	• Secretary of State decides that planning inquiry is unnecessary • planning permission approved
April 1990 – Jan. 1991	• MCA still to decide between Rainham and Paris • television documentary on issue screened 8 June 1990 • MCA team disbanded in October 1990 • public inquiry on the rerouting of the A13 across the marshes (Nov. 1990 – Jan. 1991)
Aug. – Nov. 1990	• recruit second in-depth discussion group of local members of conservation/environmental organisations. Ten individuals participate for six weeks • group runs 10/10/90 – 14/11/90 • attend public inquiry on A13

observation, in-depth interviews with key informants and group interviews (see Eyles & Smith 1988; Burgess, Limb & Harrison 1988). Our study required a research strategy that would enable us to combine images, texts, talk and actions. This was because, in the critical pre-construction phase of any large commercial development, the idea or concept of the project is literally that — an idea, an imagining. Nothing tangible exists on the ground. At that stage, people are dealing exclusively with images, representations and with projections of economic, social and environmental impacts. Battles are won and lost; planning permissions granted or denied; millions of pounds committed or withdrawn on the basis of fantasies — images of the future which are to be weighed and tested against current realities. How can we research the production and consumption of such fantasies and tie them into the actions taken by different groups to promote or contest them?

Table 14.1 describes the main events over the history of the MCA proposal and shows elements of our research strategy. We tracked the project through repeated semi-structured interviews with the consultant for the developers, the local planning authority and the key actors from all the conservation and environmental groups. At the same time, we collected all the national and local coverage of the issue in press and broadcast media. We interviewed journalists and press officers. We attended all the press conferences and public meetings as observers and took full transcripts of the proceedings. In terms of understanding what the conflict meant to local people, we employed both quantitative and qualitative methods. In January 1990 we carried out a random survey of 254 households in Rainham village, using a questionnaire which incorporated attitude statements drawn from people's comments at the public meetings. We needed some indication of public opinion at a stage when the proposal was out to public consultation and a survey was the quickest way to obtain it. However, we followed the survey with a very different approach, much more in sympathy with the aims of ethnography. We conducted two in-depth discussion groups with local people over the early summer and autumn of 1990. This strategy enabled us to explore both the production and consumption of discourses about the development and to link these to the strategies and actions taken by the different groups involved in the conflict. I shall be concentrating here on the critical phases before planning permission was granted in spring 1990.

The production of news about the plans to develop on the SSSI

MCA selected the Rainham site in early 1989 (Dane 1991) and negotiations with government ministers, civil servants, land owners and the local authorities continued privately until the end of May. The company would have preferred its negotiations to remain private for longer, not least because it would have enabled the company to prepare its case without opposition from the public or environmental organisations. However, rumours were circulating: a few articles were published in the specialist press and then reported in the *Times* and *Guardian* newspapers. There was also local talk which caught the attention of a journalist on the weekly newspaper, the *Romford Recorder*. In his routine reading of local planning committee agendas, he came across an item which referred to MCA. Putting things together, the result was a front-page exclusive: 'Film giants roll in' (26 May 1989). MCA declined to comment but the story forced its hand. Two weeks later, on 5 June 1989, MCA held a press conference to which it invited representatives of the local press and radio (fig. 14.3). Significantly, the national news media were not invited because the company wanted, at this stage, to keep publicity to a minimum.

As table 14.1 shows, between June and December 1989 the company was involved in detailed research and negotiations with different levels of government. These included

Figure 14.3: Front page news, *Romford Recorder,* 9 June 1989.
Source: *Romford Recorder.*

discussions with NCC officers about the nature conservation value of the site and the beginnings of negotiations about a mitigation package — a deal which the developers claimed would compensate for the loss of most of the SSSI by providing sufficient money to purchase marshes elsewhere along the Thames estuary.[4] On 29 November

1989 MCA and Havering Council hosted a second press conference. MCA was ready to go public, and invited representatives of all the national papers plus the regional television news.

The environmental groups had been active during this time. NCC officers had been aware of the proposals early in the year and there was a history of involvement in the site dating back to 1985 when plans to reroute the A13 across the SSSI were opposed. The most active group in this campaign was the London Wildlife Trust (hereafter LWT) and it was an LWT officer who responded most quickly to the potential threat to the site by MCA. He issued a press release prior to the 5 June press conference which alerted the regional television news teams and a few of the national papers. While the developers wanted to minimise the amount of publicity and debate about their plans, the environmental groups needed to attract as much media coverage as possible. The media were the major vehicles through which to raise public awareness of the issues and the perceived value of the site for nature conservation. The hope was that people would be persuaded of the case and would lobby local and national politicians to reject the MCA proposal.

By January 1990, many different kinds of communications about the proposal were circulating in the community. There was continued local press coverage; the November press launch of the planning application had made the national press and been reported on regional television news broadcasts. Approximately 1000 brochures had been distributed by MCA. Leaflets advertising the public meetings were displayed around the village; a small exhibition was held in the local library. Leaflets from the Royal Society for the Protection of Birds (hereafter RSPB), LWT and Friends of the Earth (hereafter FOE) were put through people's doors. People were talking about the plans and many had attended the public meetings.

Media texts: coverage of the MCA plans in the local press

It is possible, superficially through the household survey and in more detail through the in-depth discussion groups, to explore the extent to which these different communications enabled people to acquire knowledge about the project. The survey of 254 households showed that the majority (61 per cent) first found out about the plans through coverage in the local newspapers, compared with television (13 per cent), national press (5 per cent) and local radio (2 per cent). The dominance of the local press as the major source of information reflected the extent to which the proposal had been given wide coverage since the initial announcement. The MCA plans had been discussed almost continuously since 26 May 1989. By contrast, the national media gave little coverage to the proposal and certainly not in the same depth. For example, only one of the nationals, in its reports of the November press conference, mentioned that there was opposition from conservation groups whereas this had received considerable coverage in the local press. Sixty per cent of the sample were aware that conservation groups were fighting the plans.

Newspaper texts have a number of distinctive characteristics with which readers are deeply familiar and take for granted (see van Dijk 1988a, 1988b). For example, each story is organised hierarchically, with the headline and lead sentence summarising the main topic of the item — what the story is 'about'. Progressively, as we read down the text, less important items and supporting details are introduced. This top-down structure

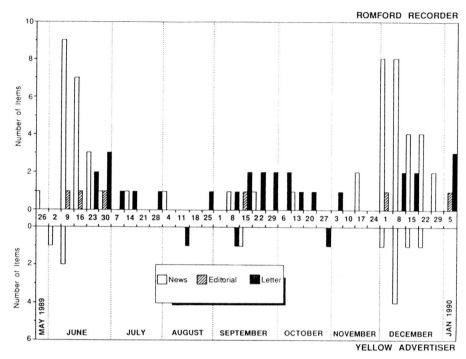

Figure 14.4: Local newspaper coverage of the MCA plans, 26 May 1989 – 5 January 1990.

enables readers to grasp the essential points without necessarily reading the whole item. It also enables news editors to cut articles to fit the page without losing the sense of the report. So readers come to a text with the expectation that what comes first is most important. Newspaper discourse is also characterised by distinctive styles of writing and presentation, and a distinctive rhetoric: compare the sensational language of the tabloids with their bold and exciting arrangements of words and pictures on a page with the more densely typed and sober language of the 'serious' press.

The *Romford Recorder* is a tabloid newspaper reporting events in a dramatic and eye-catching way. In terms of its apparent news values the paper favours the dramatic and the sensational. Typical headlines have included 'Hooligans go berserk', 'Flies plague horror', and 'Pub mob terror'. In reporting the MCA story, the American company was personified as 'Movie moguls' and 'Film giants', and the subeditor had a field day with film industry puns: 'Movie-makers take two' headlined an article about the choice between Rainham and Paris (30 June 1989), 'Movie men roll-in' on the November press conference (1 December 1989) and 'Cut — this isn't reel life' on a 'star letter' from the Havering Green Party candidate (8 December 1989). Beneath these stylistic devices, individual journalists believed they had a duty to get their facts right and were critical of some of the factual inaccuracies in the national press reports of the project.

Turning to the coverage in the local press in more detail, figure 14.4 shows the number of news items, editorials and letters published over the period 26 May 1989 to 5

January 1990. In total, there were fifty-two separate news stories, six editorials on the issue and thirty letters. The peaks on the graph coincide with the two press conferences in June and November with coverage tailing off in the intervening period. What is remarkable, given the speed with which national daily papers drop individual stories, is the persistency shown by the local paper, in reporting news and opinions about the plans for the marshes. Something appeared every week except five, and in three of those the free newspaper carried a story or letter.

From the beginning, the paper chose to frame the story in terms of conflict: first, the battle between Rainham and Paris to win the development and second, the battle between the conservationists and MCA about whether or not the plans would destroy the value of the area for wildlife. In total, thirty-eight news items dealt with some aspect of the conflict between economic development and nature conservation while thirteen explicitly focused on the issue. In most cases, the economic argument was given more prominence, forming the main topic, with ecological concerns relegated to the bottom of the article. The editor was always strongly supportive of the MCA plans but maintained fairness and balance by giving space to opposing views, primarily by publishing letters opposed to the scheme. One of the local journalists said he felt that the paper had not done as well as it might in reporting the conservation views, largely because it seemed difficult to get a 'positive angle' on conservation. The conservationists' case seemed very negative when set against the perceived excitement and economic benefits of the theme park.[5]

So the opposition was voiced primarily in letters to the editor, mostly written by members of local FOE groups, LWT and the local Green Party. It must be recognised that letters do not carry the same political weight as opinions and comments from the key actors cited in news reports. Further, the highly emotive style of one individual — who at one point likened the 'Mass Climatic Abuse' of MCA to child abuse — whose views received most coverage enabled the editor effectively to marginalise the environmental opposition:

> No doubt, doughty environmental campaigner Aubrey Pope and his Friends of the Earth will redouble their opposition but interviewing local people and business contacts, I am left with the impression that most favour the scheme ... As I write, I just know that Mr Pope and the rest of the environmental lobby will be queuing up to object. (1 December 1989)

From the conservationists' perspective, however, having letters published provided an opportunity to mobilise public support, especially when the national press were not picking up any of their press releases.[6]

Encoding different ways of seeing the marshes

What is particularly interesting for cultural geographers is the way in which the 'true' value of the site for nature conservation was constructed and contested in the discourses of the different groups involved. No one disputed the economic benefits that would accrue from the MCA proposal — only where it should be located. How to justify the loss of 70 per cent of the SSSI was the significant issue. A struggle over the real and symbolic meanings of the marshes was carried on over the period under review. The major rhetorical strategies of the developers were designed to undermine the current value of the site as an SSSI. They did so in a number of ways: by emphasising the use of part of the site as a landfill tip; by constantly referring to the silt lagoons (the most important habitat for birds) as 'man-made' structures and therefore not 'natural'; by making repeated reference to the destruction of the marsh habitat by motorcyclists; by emphasising how, in their plans, the nature reserve which they would 'create' by not developing on Aveley and part of Wennington Marshes, comprised 'the most important and most valuable area' in terms of plants and invertebrates.

At the same time, MCA projected itself as an environmentally concerned organisation: in an early article in the *Recorder* headlined 'Nature is safe, say company' (16 June 1989), the consultants outlined their plans to develop a nature reserve and ecology park, stressing the role of MCA in managing Yosemite National Park in the USA and offering to meet the conservation groups. In a different article published that week, a journalist wrote 'the film studios, theme park and nature reserve alongside the Thames will be kind to the environment' (16 June 1989). The crux of the argument about nature conservation on the marshes put forward by MCA was that the SSSI was badly managed and would face continued degradation without the capital investment that MCA could put into managing a nature reserve as part of its scheme. At the same time, it argued that without this development, the SSSI would be under continued threats from development which would not be as sensitive to nature conservation interests.

The developers' encoding of the meaning of the marshes and the value of the project dominated public communications. They organised and made presentations at the press conferences and the public meetings. They produced an expensive and highly sophisticated brochure outlining their plans; they responded quickly to requests for information from journalists; they supplied promotional photographs from Universal Studio tours in the USA. The conservationists' case was much less well orchestrated, reflecting the different levels of power and access to resources of both material and symbolic kinds. The voluntary groups were separate organisations, funded primarily by membership subscriptions; they lacked the financial resources available to the developers. The groups could not, for example, fund a central press office to deal with queries from journalists. Additionally, the NCC as a government body was unable to engage publicly in a campaign to oppose a project which had considerable support from several central government departments. The voluntary groups could do little but react to the developers' initiatives by endeavouring to counteract the claims being made by MCA.

The environmental and conservation groups had different ways of valuing the marshes and their importance for nature. The RSPB, for example, was primarily concerned with the birdlife to be found on the site and regarded the marshes as an important link in the chain of bird feeding sites which covers northern Europe; LWT were more concerned to slow or halt the loss of green spaces within London to any form of development. Despite these differences, all were agreed on the basic principle that SSSIs should be protected at all cost and should not be subject to development. As one of the officers of the Essex Naturalists' Trust argued: 'If we have a national strategy for nature conservation, then you can't jiggle around with sites. The principle is too important. You've got to protect them, otherwise we're on a slippery slope and will lose everything'.

His view reflected the argument put forward by the NCC for the ecological significance of the site, as the largest remaining example of grazing marshland habitat in London. The hope was to encourage people to see the marshes as a unique ecological exhibit — a kind of living heritage — to be protected and studied. This nature museum would also provide opportunities 'to educate people for a wider concern for wilder nature' as Ratcliffe, chief scientist for the NCC, argued in 1981. The rational, scientific way of seeing the marshland habitat was amplified in the communications of the local FOE groups who tried to locate the marshes in a global ecosystem. In press releases and letters to the local paper, members argued that the MCA plans should be rejected because they would have a severe impact on the greenhouse effect through increased levels of carbon dioxide pollution from cars bringing the five million tourists a year to the site. From this standpoint the loss of Rainham marshes was seen as equally significant as the loss of tropical rainforest.

The emotional appeal — the intrinsic value of the marshes to the environmentalists, which is often masked by a scientific rationale — was more direct. The area was full of wildlife and birdsong, a unique remnant of a world which had long since vanished from the rest of the Thames estuary. The marshes provided a haven of peace, tranquillity and endless opportunities for people to wonder at the beauties of the natural world. As an officer of RSPB wrote to the *Recorder* (23 June 1989): 'Let us save these atmospheric marshes with their flowers and birdsong, and manage them for the quiet enjoyment of generations to come'. It was unthinkable that this reality should be destroyed in order to create a Hollywood 'dream factory', 'a frivolous theme park'. Underlying this view was a powerful sense of real and potential loss. As one of the local conservationists said: 'The natural side of life is here for ever if we preserve it ... But once you've destroyed all the wildlife it's gone for good'.

The consumption of meanings: local knowledges and experiences

So far, the chapter has focused on different ways of seeing the marshes and how they were encoded in newspaper texts. It will now turn to the public consumption of these different meanings. A straw poll published in the local paper on 23 June 1989 suggested that there was considerable enthusiasm for the MCA plans, while a household survey in January 1990 showed that 69 per cent of local people supported the proposal. Some people had reservations about the increased traffic that would be generated, but no one interviewed made any reference to the impact of exhaust gases on the global climate. Others were worried about the impact of the proposal on wildlife. People's views about the plans were ascertained in different ways in the questionnaire, perhaps the most valuable of which was a series of ten statements taken directly from comments at the three public meetings. Responses to these statements revealed that the developers' case was largely, but not uncritically, accepted by the local population. These local views were amplified in the in-depth discussion group with local residents recruited after the survey.

Most people (72 per cent) agreed that the development would secure the economic future for the Rainham area, recognising that the scale of the project, the level of investment, the number of new jobs and the income generated by tourists would benefit the local economy. Only a minority (28 per cent) wanted to see the marshes remain as they were: few shared the conservationists' delight at the wonders of nature to be found there. A man said: 'If it was good countryside, I'd feel different. But it's a dump down there. There's nothing but rats and mosquitos and rubbish dumps'. The majority wanted to see something happen to the marshes, which were perceived as a wasteland, a badly polluted tip, an area which needed to be improved and managed so that people could enjoy it.

Not surprisingly, therefore, the widely-reported promise made by the developers to improve the environment was well-received. One possible reason why there was so much support for the MCA plans was that since the 1960s land use changes on parts of the marshes had significantly reduced public access. Many local people were bitter about how access had been denied by the waste-tips, the industrial estate, the dumping of silt, fly tipping and car-dumping, and the lack of management or control exercised over those who used the area for motorbike riding and falconry. Many people regretted these changes and believed the project would offer opportunities for more local recreation in a better-managed setting. Increased access would also allow more people to see animals and birds in a natural setting, a pleasurable experience desired by many (Harrison, Limb & Burgess 1987). MCA had argued this case in its publicity material and its views were emphasised in local press reports.

The desire to see the project built on the marshes also reflected considerable anxieties about the area's future if the scheme did not go ahead. Just over half said they thought it would stay as it was, a derelict wasteland which would probably be used for more tipping. Some thought it would be used for more factories. A few expressed the hope that it could be turned into a nature reserve or a wildlife park but did not know how that could happen. It was evident from these comments and from later discussions that very few local people knew that the area had SSSI status. Even some members of our environmental discussion group were surprised at the richness of wildlife on the site. As one woman said: 'I've lived in the area for a long time. And for a long time it's been associated in my mind with scrubland, bleak factories. And I hadn't thought it was that important for wildlife at all'.

Although the evidence presented so far might suggest that MCA had managed to gain unquestioning acceptance for its plans, this was not so. People were well aware of the motives behind the exercise and strongly resisted attempts to manipulate their views through the selective re-presentation of information in media reports. Local people were sceptical about the claims of the editor of the *Romford Recorder* that his press reports were impartial, and there was general cynicism about MCA's claim to be genuinely concerned about protecting wildlife on the marshes. Some said that the company were planning the development purely for commercial gain, while others thought the conservation elements in the proposal were there as 'tokenism', as a way of keeping the interest groups happy and improving the public relations image of the company. Within enviromental groups, considerable discussion was devoted to the 'greed' of large developers such as MCA and the threats that their projects posed more generally to open land and the countryside. Many people, in fact, agreed with the conservationists that wildlife would be driven away as a result of the development, although there was considerable confusion about the connections between habitat and species survival. Some people argued that there was not enough 'conservation space' in the area and that 'the birds will have nowhere to go' while others thought that the birds could go elsewhere as there was plenty of space and waste ground for them to use.

Turning finally to the balance of argument about nature conservation and economic development: the views of the local political elite in Havering, as reported in the local paper, were strongly in favour of seizing the opportunities offered by the development not least because the conservation element in the plans was deemed as 'adequate' to protect the wildlife on the marshes. These views were reflected in the household survey where the majority replied that they thought that the economic benefits from the project should be given more weight than the wildlife losses, arguing that people and jobs should come before wildlife. As we have seen, the conservation groups had been repeatedly marginalised by being described in the local press as an unrepresentative lobby. There was also a widespread feeling locally that the conservationists were an elite who were not really concerned with the quality of life of local people. As one woman said: 'the wildlife concern is felt by outsiders — it's not a local view. But the wildlife people don't live here. They live in nice leafy parts of London.' For these reasons, the conservationists failed in their attempt to encourage people to make connections between the immediate realities of their daily lives and the largely abstract arguments about the ecological significance of the SSSI. The case was lost and MCA was granted planning permission in the spring of 1990.

Conclusion

Underlying this case study of MCA's proposal to build a theme park on a small piece of largely unloved and unregarded wetland on the outskirts of London, are important issues to do with people's understanding of present realities, their hopes and aspirations for the future, and the exercise of power. Multinational corporations and environmentalists both see the world as a very small place. The former search hungrily for new development opportunities and are able to devote enormous financial and political resources to achieving their goals, the latter are deeply perturbed about the impacts of their activities on the global ecosystem. Both are served by media technologies which continue to 'shrink' the world and fundamentally change global and local relations.

The MCA plans had national and international economic implications and involved a considerable degree of private political activity, but were publicly described by government ministers as being a matter for local politicians to decide. The local newspaper played the most important role in informing people and helping to shape private and public actions, while the national media largely ignored the issue until it was too late to influence the planning decision. The developers were able to use the local press to help produce a sequence of images and discourses which meshed with local aspirations and desires. The fantasy world on offer in the MCA proposal, although people knew it was a fantasy, was attractive because it resonated with desires to see improvements in the locality which would contribute to a better quality of life. The value of the site for nature conservation, the need for the scientific study of this distinctive biotic community, the intrinsic worth of species and the 'right' of nature to exist undisturbed by human activities were not, in the main, ways of seeing re-presented in the local media; nor did such views accord with those of local people.

Notes

This research was funded by the ESRC and the NCC (grant no. W110251001). Dr Carolyn Harrison and Mr Paul Maiteny were the co-researchers on the project.

1   At the time of writing (December 1991) MCA has still not announced whether it will locate in London or Paris. It would seem that the plan is dead.

2   The original plan allocated 125 ha (310 acres) for a nature reserve. This was increased to 173 ha (428 acres) during negotiations in early 1990.

3   Havering Council granted outline planning permission on 27/2/90. The plans were referred to the Secretary of State for Environment because they contravened existing local plans. Conservation groups lobbied hard for a public inquiry which might have deterred MCA from continuing with Rainham because of the lengthy procedure. The Secretary of State decided on 6/4/90 not to call the application in for an inquiry.

4   The view of the NCC, expressed by one of the officers directly involved in negotiations over the site, was as follows:

> In all its dealings with MCA, NCC did not seek to negotiate a package which would provide benefits equating with losses, since natural variations between sites mean that there is no 'common currency' through which such balance could be attempted. In other words, since each site is unique, and since the resource is finite, compensation must remain an elusive concept. The term mitigation in its literal sense ('to make less harsh') is appropriate.
>
> NCC entered into negotiations with MCA for two reasons; first, the organisation felt that the initial offer from MCA was 'grossly ineffective'; second, the NCC was, by law, one of the consultees in the planning procedure and had been required to provide information to the ecological consultants who carried out the Environmental Assessment of the scheme. The eventual mitigation package was worth £16 million in financial terms — an unprecedented sum to be allocated for nature conservation.

5   Partly in recognition of this, conservation groups developed an alternative plan for the marshes in spring 1990. It would turn them into a wetland park, managed for conservation and recreation.

6   The national press only took up the story when the national FOE announced in late February 1990 that low-level radioactive waste had been dumped on the site. That was newsworthy!

References

Burgess, J. 1990, 'The production and consumption of environmental meanings in the mass media: a research agenda for the 1990s', *Trans. Inst. Brit. Geog. NS*, 15, pp. 139–61.

Burgess, J. & Gold, J.R. (eds) 1985, *Geography, the Media and Popular Culture,* Croom Helm, London.

Burgess, J., Limb, M. & Harrison, C.M. 1988, 'Exploring environmental values through the medium of small groups', *Environment and Planning A,* 20, pp. 309–26, 457–76.

Cosgrove, D. & Daniels, S. (eds) 1988, *The Iconography of Landscape,* Cambridge University Press, Cambridge.

Dane, R. 1991, 'Rainham Marshes: the process and the lessons', *Ecos,* 12, pp. 47–50.

Eyles, J. & Smith, D.M. (eds) 1988, *Qualitative Research in Human Geography,* Polity Press, Cambridge.

Hall, S. 1977, 'Culture, media and the "ideological effect"', in J. Curran, M. Guravitch & J. Woollacott (eds), *Mass Communication and Society,* Edward Arnold, London, pp. 315–48.

Hall, S. 1980, 'Encoding/decoding', in S. Hall, D. Hobson, A. Lowe & P. Willis (eds), *Culture, Media, Language,* Hutchinson, London, pp. 128–38.

Harrison, C.M., Limb, M. & Burgess, J. 1987, 'Nature in the city: popular values for a living world', *Journal of Environmental Management,* 25, pp. 347–62.

Jackson, P. 1989, *Maps of Meaning,* Unwin Hyman, London.

Johnson, R. 1986, 'The story so far and further transformations?', in D. Punter (ed.), *Introduction to Contemporary Cultural Studies,* Longman, London, pp. 277–313.

Morley, D. 1986, *Family Television: Cultural Power and Domestic Leisure,* Comedia Press, London.

Nature Conservancy Council 1990, 16th Report, HMSO, London.

Pepper, D. 1984, *The Roots of Modern Environmentalism,* Croom Helm, London.

Silverstone, R. 1985, *Framing Science: the Making of a Television Documentary,* British Film Institute, London.

Van Dijk, T. 1988a, *News as Discourse,* Lawrence Erlbaum Associates, Brighton.

Van Dijk, T. 1988b, *News Analysis: Case Studies of International and National News in the Press,* Lawrence Erlbaum Associates, Brighton.

The land in cultural context

15 Hunter-gatherer concepts of land and its ownership in remote Australia and North America

Elspeth Young

Introduction

The physical landscapes around us, their topography, aesthetic appeal and the evidence of human ingenuity which they present to us in a visual sense, mirror our societies. In observing and interpreting the landscape we are often immediately aware of the human use of the resources within that particular environment. We can see the results of the development of its soils and water supplies for agricultural purposes, or the exploitation of its minerals, and we can assess its locational value for human settlement and activity. However, such an observation of the landscape is only one component of the picture, a visible scene existing at a particular point in space and time. The landscape also consists of 'layers', reflecting historical processes which have resulted in its continuous transformation, and which stem from changing economic, political, cultural and demographic factors affecting a particular society. Visible evidence for the existence of these factors may be almost non-existent, and hence people tend to ignore their presence in the landscape. Cultural geographers concerned with landscape interpretation have been aware of this hidden 'authorship', however, and no longer approach the landscape primarily from a descriptive, visually-oriented point of view (Ley 1983, 271). Duncan and Duncan (1988), in discussing the idea of landscape as a 'text', stress that the reading of that text should encompass the idea of how it is linked both historically and in the present to social and cultural organisation.

However, it is not only recognition of the influence of hidden cultural processes on landscape construction which is important. It is also the realisation that social groups do not necessarily observe and interpret environments in the same way. Our own experiences, along with those which we have learned and accepted through contact with others, affect our interpretations and reveal something of the particular social and cultural environment within which we exist. Thus 'landscape is defined by our vision and interpreted by our minds ... [it] displays us as cultures' (Meinig 1979, 3). It 'is an ideological concept' (Cosgrove 1984, 15); 'a way of seeing' (Jackson 1989, 181); an unwitting autobiography, revealing the tastes, values, aspirations and fears and the very structure of society into which we fit (Lewis 1979, 12). For social scientists interested in understanding people's different reactions to and interpretation of their world, recognition of this subjectivity requires them to decipher how the actors themselves see and arrive at such understandings.

Cultural geographers have for decades attempted to demonstrate that our landscapes are reflections of the cultures that perceive and mould them. More recently, such geographers have introduced a more dynamic perspective to their approach to landscape interpretation, arguing that landscapes 'exist' in contingent, not static, relation to the images and actions of the beholder. One effective approach that demonstrates this point, that the landscapes we 'see' around us are formations undergoing cultural construction, is that of intergroup comparison. In cultural terms some of the clearest contrasts today occur in remote parts of Australia and North America, where hunter-gatherer societies, such as Australian Aborigines, North American Indians and Inuit (Eskimo) share the same geographical spaces with members of the advanced industrialised societies. This chapter first outlines the major elements in the landscape interpretation of hunter-gatherer and industrialised societies; second, identifies sources of conflict between these two visions; and finally, with the use of a central Australian case study, demonstrates how contemporary Anmatyerre constructs of the land are themselves fluid and changeable, adapted to the geographic, economic and political contexts within which different groups of these people are situated.

Hunter-gatherer concepts of land and ownership

The landscapes of hunter-gatherer societies and those of the industrialised world differ because of contrasts in their interpretation of the origin and structure of the universe, and in their economic and political structures. A major cosmological contrast concerns the perceived relationship of people and land. For most hunter-gatherer societies the land has been an inextricable part of their lives; it provided not only their sustenance in the form of game, fish and vegetable foods but also the foundation of their spiritual beliefs and hence of their social control mechanisms. Thus Watkins (1977, 95) comments that the reason for the Dene Indian land claim to Canada's Mackenzie Valley is not only a settlement of their desire for legal recognition of present and future hunting and trapping rights, but is also a political statement — a declaration of their long-standing cultural beliefs and their right to practise them. Usher and Bankes (1986, 13) confirm the intimacy of the people-land relationship for the neighbouring Inuit of the eastern Arctic in their description of the people being *of* the land rather than owning it, and stress that Inuit cosmology explained that relationship. Even the animals hunted by the Inuit were perceived not solely as food sources, but as entities with which the people were closely related, and the husbandry of them was a prime Inuit responsibility.

Similar concepts emerge in considering the people-land relationships of Aboriginal[1] Australians. For Aborigines the landscape, as Peterson (1975) and Strehlow (1970) have emphasised, provided nourishment and also expressed their spiritual beliefs, power relationships and relative group and individual status. Within the Aboriginal landscape ancestral beings, including human, flora and fauna, and natural phenomena such as water, lightning or thunder, acted to create physical features and to ensure the continuance and productivity of the land's resources. In that process they travelled across the country along clearly defined routes marked by experiences and actions occurring at different points and recorded through song, dance, painting and ceremony. These routes are today commonly referred to as the 'Dreamtime Tracks' and in popular literature as 'Songlines' (Chatwin 1987). Present-day Aborigines, particularly those who still have some links with traditional society, trace their descent from these beings and identify wholly with them so that in performing the rituals associated with their own particular tracts of country they effectively become the ancestors. Thus, when discussing the activities of ancestral 'bush plums' with an elderly Anmatyerre woman on Ti Tree station in Australia's Northern Territory in 1984 I was firmly told that the informant's grandfather, camping at the spring at Aliyawe, was himself a 'bush plum'. In those circumstances it is clear that the linkages between people and landscape are inseparable, and not surprising that, as Stanner (1979, 230) wrote: 'No English words are good enough to give a sense of the links between an Aboriginal group and its homeland ... When we took (from them) what we call "land" we took what to them meant hearth, home, the source and focus of life, and everlastingness of spirit'.

While all hunter-gatherer groups appear to hold these strong ties with the land, the actual expression of these linkages on the landscape, however, has varied with resource base and hence with population density. In what follows, some examples of this local adaptation and internal variation of hunter-gatherer visions are outlined.

In Australia, distant and environmentally distinct parts of the country, such as monsoonal Arnhem Land, the central desert and the Bight coasts of South Australia were spiritually linked by dreamtime tracks, along which the ancestors are believed to have moved freely. However, the traditional territories used by Aboriginal groups, particularly in economic terms, were much more restricted and were delineated somewhat differently according to the physical environment. In the northern monsoonal country of Arnhem Land, where the resource base was much richer and more reliable, traditional territories seem to have been more firmly circumscribed by boundaries than those of the desert people, where food supplies were often far less abundant. Thus, although Arnhem Land people ranged on a seasonal basis between the seashores, riverine wetlands and escarpment, the region within which they moved was recognised as the responsibility of a specific group (Altman 1987). In the central desert, where the seasonal round was less predictable, people ranged very widely, especially in drought periods. In such times those from resource-deficient areas ranged into the country of their better endowed neighbours, and such incursions were wholly acceptable as a survival mechanism with which all might ultimately be faced. Usher and Bankes (1986, 12) comment on the existence of a similar basis of mutual support and understanding in the harsh northern environments of Inuit hunters. In contrast, in the richer boreal forest country of their Athapaskan Indian neighbours, specific traplines clearly mark where, for generations, hunters have sustained their families through their use of the land's resources. Each family's country can therefore be clearly described in terms which all understand, and using another's trapline without permission would be culturally unacceptable. Evidence of land ownership presented in the Mackenzie Valley inquiry (Berger 1977) and the Dene land claim (Department of Indian and Northern Affairs [DIAND] 1988) relies heavily on information about the location and continuing use of such traplines.

Such differences, because they affect the definition of land responsibilities, also have spiritual significance. In arid central Australia different countries are identified with extended family groups rather than with leading individuals (bosses) within those groups, and permission to use territory is sought collectively rather than individually; in Arnhem Land the request must be made to the appropriate individual. Moreover, in the desert, where country is delineated by criss-crossing and intersecting 'dreaming' tracks rather than by continuous boundaries, people hold joint responsibility for many sites and regions. For non-Aborigines such overlaps complicate the process of understanding Aboriginal perception of the landscape, but among Aborigines they do not appear to cause conflict. Wonders (1983, 81–2) made similar comments in his study of overlapping native claims in the Mackenzie Valley in Canada. While he noted that overlapping claims existed, he stressed that the Dene/Metis, Inuvialuit and Nunavut people did not seem to see these as barriers to the resolution of land claims; it was the non-native Canadian bureaucrats who anticipated that there would be problems.

The principles by which hunter-gatherer land responsibilities are handed on add further complications. Inuit and Dene, mindful of the problems of survival in harsh northern environments, have not only totally accepted people of different native origin who have married into their groups, but have also been sympathetic towards the needs of non-native settlers who display an understanding of native customary behaviour. As Usher and Bankes (1986, 14) point out, they have often allowed them access to traditional resources, such as caribou, for skins and meat.

Australian Aboriginal land-related groups have also absorbed individuals and families with inherited spiritual responsibilities which belong elsewhere. This has involved a deliberate process of education, through which the incomers have been taught the stories and rituals appropriate to the country in which they were living. In the past such practices were probably extremely important, particularly in the desert where groups were small in number and might on occasion die out. By transferring spiritual responsibilities to others the continued health of the land was assured, and the health of future generations of its people. In more recent times (Young 1987), these mechanisms have helped people to deal with the social and economic disruptions arising from the dispersal of Aboriginal population groups whose country has been taken over by non-Aboriginal settlers. People who have been forced to live elsewhere have been deliberately taught to carry out the spiritual responsibilities relevant to their new abode.

Land inheritance and lineage add further complexities to Aboriginal concepts of land ownership. Despite earlier assumptions that land was inherited patrilineally, and hence that women had a subordinate role in caring for land, the evidence from land claims in the Northern Territory shows that people inherit land responsibilities through both maternal and paternal grandparents. This also appears to be the case elsewhere, for example in Queensland's Cape York peninsula and in the Kimberley region of Western Australia. Each individual therefore looks after more than one country, albeit in different ways. Those who trace their responsibilities through the paternal line are commonly called 'owners' (Warlpiri — *kirda*) and those with maternal links are referred to as 'guardians' (Warlpiri — *kurdungurlu*). In rituals *kirda* perform the ceremonies while the *kurdungurlu* organise and direct them, ensuring that the songs and dances are correctly presented and the paintings properly executed. Without people of both genders none of the components of the ceremony can be properly performed. Moreover, if land is to be properly cared for both in the economic and spiritual sense, it is expected that members of both paternal and maternal groups live on it.

Concepts of land and ownership in industrialised societies

The intrusion of non-aboriginal settlers — miners, traders, pastoralists, missionaries and public servants — into remote territories such as Canada's Arctic and the rangelands of Australia's deserts transformed land, often dramatically and visibly. The boreal forests of the Mackenzie River Valley and Australia's arid interior are carved up by criss-crossing seismic lines surging away into the distance; networks of roads traverse the landscape; boundary fences divide properties from one another; and a sparse spread of small towns, isolated station homesteads and mining camps provides evidence of a very different type of human occupation from that of the past, one of visible resource exploitation. Many non-aboriginal people perceive these spaces principally as sources of potential material wealth, to be used for both individual and collective monetary gain. Thus commercially valuable minerals are to be developed, forests and marine products to be harvested, and rangelands to be grazed by domesticated stock. Despite the fact that some sections of the non-aboriginal population now question such resource uses, the underlying concepts of the worth of the land and its resources still remain dominant. Non-aboriginal settlers who have, through time, developed a less materialistic attachment to the land which they have come to control, are in a minority. When such people leave the desert or the Arctic they may well feel a wrench at losing contact with familiar and loved places, but their departure does not signify a social and spiritual fission threatening the future survival of their group. When they describe these places most of them emphasise their barren nature rather than their beauty, their dearth of resources rather than their wealth of fish, game or other foods. To them such areas are the 'outback' rather than the 'homeland', places to be tolerated, hopefully for only a short period of their lives.

Two visions in conflict

The main contrasts between hunter-gatherer and industrialised society concepts of land and resources lie in the emphasis on spiritual as distinct from economic worth. Hunter-gatherers stress spiritual values. Many hold the culturally binding conviction that land is not a commodity which can be bought or sold, or used as a means of creating profits, and in their assessment of economic values they emphasise husbandry for the future and the use of resources for human survival rather than increasing material advantage. Industrialised societies, on the other hand, stress economic values, with exploitation of resources for continuing material gain as the perceived route to 'development'; spiritual values receive scant attention.

Such contrasts inevitably lead to conflict. Because of the superior technology, political and economic power of the industrialised societies the main losers in these conflicts have been the hunter-gatherers. Their understanding of the land, in both spiritual and material terms, has been submerged by that of the incomers. That does not mean that it has been entirely eliminated, but signs of its presence are hard for many non-aboriginal people to recognise. Many of the attributes of Aboriginal and native Canadian land responsibility and use are not actually visible on the landscape. Unless asked, Inuit and Indians do not disclose the patterns of their hunting and trapping territories to outsiders, and it is only pressures such as those imposed by intrusive development projects or by the need to justify their land claims which will force them to do so. Brody's fascinating study of Beaver land use and occupancy in north-eastern

British Columbia (1981), the monumental Inuit land use and occupancy study of the 1970s (Freeman 1976), and the Mackenzie Valley pipeline inquiries (Berger 1977) all stem from such pressures. In Australia, much of what the outside world has learned about the complexities of traditional Aboriginal land ownership has emerged in the course of land claims, lodged primarily in the Northern Territory since 1975. Thus more than ever we are now aware that, whether visibly or invisibly, many contemporary hunter-gatherers today retain their traditional concepts of land and its ownership, in the face of great pressures exerted by economic, social and political interests which are part of the industrialised world and which now, irrevocably, affect them.

Changes in the landscape, and resultant conflicts between hunter-gatherers and non-aboriginal settlers, are part of relatively recent history in many remote parts of Australia and North America. In semi-arid areas of central Australia, for example, where there was sufficient water for stock, much of the land was alienated for the pastoral industry in the early twentieth century. A new physical landscape of fence lines, cattle and vehicle tracks, dams, ponds, tanks and windmills for water and homesteads appeared. Straight lines marked by barbed wire separated neighbouring properties and created physical barriers to the journeys of the modern day representatives of the dreamtime ancestors. They were hindered from following the tracks marked by song and ceremony, and hence also failed in their spiritual duties, both to their predecessors and to their children. Ultimately, as evidence presented in recent land claims has illustrated, they believed that the whole viability of the land as their spiritual home and subsistence resource base would be threatened. Witnesses have expressed this in different ways, talking of their fears that the land would lose its fertility, and of how their continued presence on the land 'holds it up'. By this they mean that through the appropriate ceremonies the edible plants and animals on which they depended would be sustained. Their presence also ensured that important land management practices, such as mosaic burning of vegetation to ensure the continuation of suitable wild-life habitats, would be carried out. The depth of these feelings has become very obvious in recent times when Aborigines, having once more obtained secure tenure to their ancestral land, have moved back to establish small outstations in their traditional country. Often their first deliberate action has been to 'burn the country', because, after many years of abandonment, the spinifex grass has grown out of control and other more palatable species have virtually disappeared. To them, country in that state has become 'rubbish'.

In economic terms the major conflict in these rangeland areas concerned access to water. Permanent springs and soakages, such as the original spring at Alice Springs, were important meeting places for Aboriginal groups which, especially in drought times, might come from distant areas to camp at such spots. They were also major focal points for the pastoralists, wanting water for their stock. Many of the station homesteads were built close to these sites, and Aborigines were actively discouraged from camping nearby either to collect water or to carry out the relevant ceremonies associated with the location. Resultant disagreements led directly to violence on both sides, with the Aborigines — despite attempts at resistance — invariably the overall losers. In the Coniston massacre, which occurred in 1928 on a remote cattle station about 300 km (185 miles) north-west of Alice Springs, around 100 Aborigines are thought to have been shot by cattlemen and police in retaliation for the murder of Brooks, a dingo scalp collector who camped on the waterholes and was also said to be interfering with Aboriginal women (Cribben 1984).

Such violence today would be unlikely, but the conflicts remain, and the old people have not forgotten. Aboriginal 'refugees', forced to live in the town camps of Alice Springs because of the seizure of their land, have been thwarted in their efforts to obtain suitable excisions of small living areas back in their own country because they usually request those locations of both spiritual and economic importance to them — the water sources. Most have had to accept compromises.

Another source of conflict, common to hunter-gatherer groups in Australia, Canada and the United States, has arisen because some natural resources which form part of the native subsistence base are also perceived to be valuable by the incomers. This has particularly affected Indian and Inuit communities in Canada and Alaska, where, through the hunting and trapping and tourist industries, aboriginal and non-aboriginal interests may be in opposition. Fish such as salmon or big game such as moose, grizzly bear or wolf are targets of white hunters as well as food and clothing for hunter-gatherers, and control over the use of these resources affects both groups. Within native land, subsistence priorities can be stressed. There is, however, no guarantee that this will occur elsewhere. Different perceptions of the value of these natural resources have recently caused conflict in the case of the harvesting of seals and other furred animals. Total bans on such activities by animal rights and conservation groups in Canada have effectively destroyed the livelihood of northern aboriginal communities. These attitudes reveal a complete lack of understanding of Indian and Inuit modes of resource use, or a deliberate refusal to acknowledge the existence of such practices (Keith & Saunders 1989).

Perhaps the most visible evidence of conflict between hunter-gatherer and industrialised society concepts of land ownership and control lies in the settlement patterns themselves. Both in northern parts of America and in outback Australia, formerly fluid patterns of human occupation, reflecting semi-nomadic societies, have been largely replaced by fixed, centralised settlement patterns. These changes were primarily deliberate, aimed at fostering the assimilation of surviving hunter-gatherer groups into the wider society, both through enforced resettlement in permanent shelters and incorporation into the wage economy. Large mission and government settlements, both in Australia's Northern Territory and in Canada's Northwest Territories, became the main 'towns' for remote-dwelling Aborigines, Inuit and Indians. Smaller nucleated settlements developed around the homesteads of the new pastoral properties and mining camps, where people could exchange their labour for prized goods such as tobacco, flour, tea, sugar and blankets. Only in recent decades has there been a resurgence of more dispersed settlement patterns. This change stems from the resumption of aboriginal control over the land, directly attributable to land rights legislation. It clearly indicates the lifestyle preferences of many aboriginal people, and reveals the continuing underlying struggle to assert their rights and beliefs. Indeed it suggests that, despite the superior power and technology of the incomers, the original inhabitants of these remote areas have been able to retain much of their specialised knowledge and understanding of land and resource use.

What we see today, therefore, are landscapes which reflect not only differing concepts of land ownership and control, but also their everchanging interaction with political and economic factors. The visible signs — roads which follow straight boundary lines, connecting white settlements and ignoring other places which to the hunter-gatherers might be significant; water supplies which are harnessed through complicated introduced technology even although this might disrupt the natural attributes of the resource; and schools, health clinics and stores which are located at points of central importance to non-aboriginal rather than to the aboriginal people — suggest that the land ownership concepts of the industrialised society have been overwhelming. However, signs of hunter-gatherer valuations of land are also present and, with the granting of indigenous land rights in many remote areas, increasingly visible. The existing 'mix' of land 'paradigms' from hunter-gatherer and industrialised society is not uniform, but varies geographically, culturally and linguistically, and according to the operation of different political and economic factors at different times. Moreover, neither aboriginal nor non-aboriginal constructs of the environment are static embodiments of some timeless essence. Rather, they display internal variation, and capacity for change, adaptation and struggle. The following case study illustrates such cultural responses as they relate to the Anmatyerre people of Central Australia.

Land tenure and Anmatyerre responses: contemporary examples

To the north and north-west of Alice Springs lies the country of the Anmatyerre people, a relatively small Aboriginal linguistic group which today numbers over 1000 individuals. Although semi-arid, their territory is well-endowed with surface and ground water and its outcropping ridges and sheltered valleys provide an attractive environment for a wide range of native flora and fauna. Not surprisingly, this country was also attractive to incoming non-Aboriginal settlers. From 1916, when Coniston station was first established, Anmatyerre country was progressively alienated for pastoralism and by 1950, when the Mt Allan property had finally been declared, the people had lost direct control over most of their land (fig. 15.1). Instead of ranging freely over their family territories most people camped in semi-permanent fashion around the station homesteads where they formed the backbone of the labour force for each stock-camp. Quite quickly, their landscape became visibly transformed by land-use practices that reflected a different environmental perception and economic system. It was crossed by roads and tracks of various grades ranging from the main road to Darwin, the Stuart Highway, to smaller access roads to homesteads and bores and tanks providing water for the cattle, and it was bounded by paddock fences. Less immediately obvious, but ultimately of great importance, were the effects of heavy grazing by hard-hoofed animals — changes in drainage patterns, development of erosion channels, introduction of new vegetation species, and the disappearance of some types of native flora and fauna. Nevertheless Anmatyerre interpretations of land ownership, while largely dormant, did not disappear. Since the mid 1970s these have re-emerged, particularly in those communities which, through government purchase programmes and the implementation of land rights legislation, have regained full control over their ancestral territories. Other Anmatyerre, whose land lies within the boundaries of adjacent non-Aboriginal held stations, lack such decision-making power and have not been able to reassert their concepts of land ownership and occupation to the same extent.

Two pastoral properties, Ti Tree and Mt Allan, were purchased for their traditional owners by the federal government in 1976 and were subsequently the subject of land claim investigations for conversion to Aboriginal freehold title under the Northern

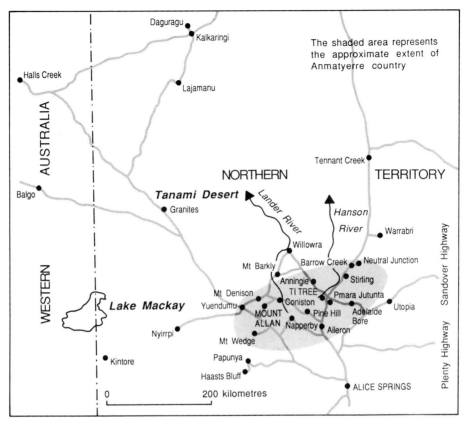

Figure 15.1: Anmatyerre country, Central Australia.
Source: *Aboriginal History*, vol. 11, 1987, p. 159. Courtesy Elspeth Young.

Territory *Land Rights Act 1976*. The Mt Allan claim has been granted and, while arguments over details have delayed final approval of the Ti Tree claim, its acceptance has been recommended in principle by the federal government. Thus to all intents and purposes the Aboriginal owners of both of these properties can now determine how to use their land. Aborigines living on neighbouring stations in Anmatyerre country, such as Napperby, Coniston or Anningie, may be heavily restricted in their choice of modes of land use. Thus, although they share language and culture, belong to the same kinship 'mob' and move freely between each other's camps, the cognitive and physical relationships of contemporary Anmatyerre to the land vary.

Anmatyerre social organisation still forms the basis of a land ownership system. In social terms all Anmatyerre are classified into one of eight major subsections, with membership being determined patrilineally by parentage. Thus the children of Mpetyane fathers belong to Ngale subsection, while those of Peltharre fathers belong to Kngwarraye subsection (table 15.1). These pairs of subsections are called patricouples. Subsections are also arranged into two groups of four, called moieties, between which preferred marriages occur. Thus Mpetyane people, men or women, should marry Pengarte, and Kemarre are expected to marry Peltharre.

Table 15.1:   Anmatyerre subsection terms and linkages

Mpetyane	=	Pengarte
Kemarre	=	Peltharre
Perrwerle	=	Penangke
Ngale	=	Kngwarraye

= This symbol links first choice marriage partners   [This symbol links fathers with children

Figure 15.2a: Photograph of a painting by Jeannie Nungarrayi Egan (1989) from Yuendumu, Northern Territory. It shows the tracks of ancestral faunal beings (possum, goanna, kangaroo and emu) and human ancestors (Jungarrayi and Nangala), to and from Yurnipirli waterhole. The artist's explanation of the painting, in Warlpiri and English, follows:

Nyampuju kuruwarri yirrarnurna janganpkurlu manu kuyu panu kari kuja kalu yanirni ngapa kurra. [This dreaming is about possum and other meat (edible animals) or animals coming to the waterhole.]

Yangka kardiyarlu manu yapa karirli yungulu milya pinyi junga nyarni kuruwarri yapa kurlangu ngurrararla, kuja karlipa purami manu kijirni. [(This painting is made by) all the 'bosses' so other people in their families can know the dreaming properly and learn.]

Yamuju jukurrpa Jungarrayi Nungarrayi kirlangu manu Japaljarri Napaljarri kirlangu. [This dreaming belongs to all these family skin groups (Jungarrayi/Nungarrayi and Japaljarri/Napaljarri).]

Source: Reproduced by permission of the artist.

Patricouples, such as Mpetyane/Ngale or Pengarte/Penangke, hold ritual responsibility for specific dreaming tracks which cross Anmatyerre land. Marriages between subsections create linkages between dreaming tracks and associated countries. The stories describing this system have been orally transmitted through many generations and are illustrated through dance, song and painting. Paintings are therefore essentially Aboriginal 'maps' of country, describing the association between the people and the land. They graphically illustrate Aboriginal cosmology. Figure 15.2 a and b presents one such map of an area immediately to the west of Mt Allan, on the former Yuendumu

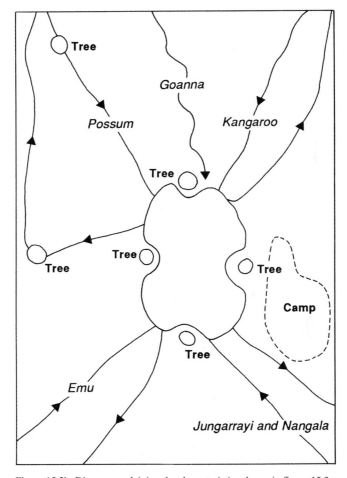

Figure 15.2b: Diagram explaining the characteristics shown in figure 15.2a.

Reserve. It shows the journeys of the ancestral faunal beings (goanna, kangaroo, possum, emu) and the human ancestors (Kngwarraye and Ngale) who cared for Yurnipirli, a waterhole still of great spiritual significance to the present representatives of these moieties.

Anmatyerre perceptions based on this land ownership system bear little relationship to the proofs of ownership imposed by non-Aboriginal pastoral use. The fences

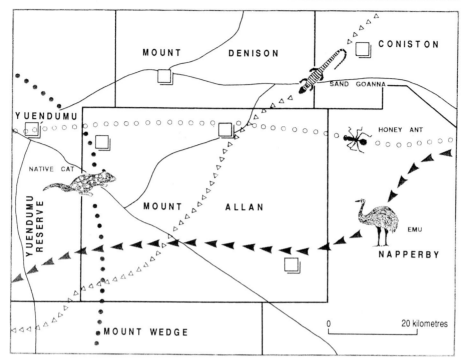

Figure 15.3: Anmatyerre and non-Aboriginal delineations of property on Mount Allan.

bounding Mt Allan, for example, cut straight across Anmatyerre delineations of the property (fig. 15.3). In the northern section the station is traversed by the honey ant ancestral track, associated with Penangke/Pengarte subsections; on the west lie the tracks made by the possums and native cat ancestors of Kngwarraye and Peltharre; and to the south is the emu track of Ngale and Mpetyane. Diagonally from the south-west to the north-east travelled the sand goannas, also ancestors of Kngwarraye and Peltharre groups. All these tracks intersect at certain points and all also continue beyond Mt Allan's boundary fences. As was clearly demonstrated during hearing of evidence for the Mt Allan land claim in 1982, the co-existence of these Aboriginal and non-Aboriginal systems of delineating land can cause some confusion. Because the actual land claim was legally restricted to the area included within the boundary fence of the pastoral lease, witnesses were asked to describe their ancestral countries in a somewhat artificial fashion, as if these territories ceased to exist at the fence line. Knowledge of country beyond the boundary fence was in many cases essential to understanding the details of their stories. Thus many witnesses did find it necessary to talk about land outside the actual claim, particularly if that land included places of great spiritual significance. As one key witness stated, that country needed to be described to the judge, both because it was linked to the actual area under consideration and also because, being on a non-Aboriginal held property (Napperby), it was more vulnerable. He and other witnesses found it very hard to accept that, while evidence proving ownership of the land under claim was presented according to Anmatyerre concepts, the land itself was spatially delineated according to non-Aboriginal concepts.

Because Mt Allan and Ti Tree are now Aboriginal-owned, their residents can use the land as they wish. They can accord with traditional Aboriginal modes of land use, they can accept non-Aboriginal conventions, or they can combine the two. In both cases they have chosen this last course. These are working cattle stations, with significant Aboriginal populations (about 150 on Mt Allan and 350 on Ti Tree). They carry Aboriginal labour forces of around fifteen during the mustering season and have the potential to provide significant community incomes when prices are favourable. Inevitably this means that some of the non-Aboriginal landscape icons are reinforced. These include the fences, bores, tanks and roads. There is also evidence for a re-emergence of more traditional Aboriginal values in land use. Mt Allan's Aboriginal residents no longer all congregate in the camp beside the station homestead. Some families have dispersed and established small outstations (or 'homeland centres') near sites of spiritual importance to them. For example, groups associated with honey ant dreaming are now living near the western boundary of Mt Allan, within easy access of Yuelamu. This site is of great significance not only to them but also to all their other classificatory kin, including Anmatyerre, Warlpiri and Alyawarre who trace their descent from honey ant ancestors. Similarly, people who are spiritually descended from emu and dingo ancestors have moved to the east, to the country for which they are responsible.

This type of population dispersal, apparent on both Mt Allan and Ti Tree, not only changed the human occupation patterns, but has both social and economic implications. Residents of these smaller settlements belong to closely linked extended families. Hence social conflicts, commonly observed when people from different groups were forced to live close to each other in large centralised settlements such as neighbouring Yuendumu, have declined. The move to smaller settlements has improved people's access to bush tucker and game. These natural resources had been heavily depleted near the central homesteads because, with the large concentrated populations, too many people were trying to make use of them. Thus the reassertion of Aboriginal concepts of land use and protection has helped to improve people's quality of life.

Population dispersal following the legal reacquisition of traditional land may, however, have other apparently less favourable implications. This is particularly noticeable when the use of the land still follows the non-Aboriginal mode, in this case commercial pastoralism. The former non-Aboriginal owners of both Mt Allan and Ti Tree stressed large-scale, centralised management. This included forcing Aborigines to live beside the station homesteads, both because they provided the labour for the stock camps and because the owners felt that if they camped elsewhere on the property cattle operations might be disrupted. The present Aboriginal owners, however, seem to be less concerned about such disadvantages. Ti Tree station, both during its previous European history and in its more recent period of Aboriginal ownership, provides an interesting example of the kind of dilemmas which arise from overlapping concepts and uses of land.

The area covered by the present Ti Tree station includes two smaller properties, Ti Tree on the west and Woola Downs on the east. Each of these had distinct Aboriginal populations who were drawn from the traditional land-owning group and provided the local workforces. After the stations were amalgamated in 1950 the eastern Woola Downs Aboriginal camp disappeared, and families dispersed to Utopia station, to the east, and to the western homestead camp at Ti Tree itself. The new Ti Tree station then had only one Aboriginal camp, and was run as a large-scale, centralised enterprise. However, following the purchase of Ti Tree by the Aboriginal Land Fund Commission in 1976 the former Woola Downs mob expressed a desire to move back on to their country and established their Adelaide Bore camp in 1979. This move arose partly from the need to reassert Aboriginal concepts of land-ownership. However, the new settlement also became linked to the cattle operations. Once the camp was set up the Woola people intimated that they wanted to split the control of the pastoral enterprise, with the erection of a new boundary fence between themselves and the remainder of the group at Ti Tree station. This fence, interestingly enough, followed the Aboriginal concept of the boundary, marking the hand-over point on the *ahakeye* (bush plum) dreaming track where western families in the Ngale/Mpetyane group transfer spiritual responsibility to their eastern kin. In this case the Aboriginal concept of land boundary coincided in space with one which was essentially associated with non-Aboriginal ideas on land ownership. Arrangements for the two separate enterprises were also to include an allocation of funds from Puraiya, the Ti Tree station cattle company, and the granting of their own cattle brand. Although the two Aboriginal groups agreed and the boundary fence was completed in 1982, the split was not then finalised. Because of threats from government agencies, primarily the Aboriginal Development Commission, that funding would be cut off unless commercial viability was the main priority, the plans for the split were not implemented.

This was not the end of the Ti Tree story. Between 1983 and 1985 the Ti Tree people went through the process of collecting evidence for the presentation of their claim to have the land title converted to Aboriginal freehold, resulting in lengthy and detailed discussions about traditional land ownership, and reinforcing the desire on the part of a number of Ti Tree groups to move into smaller communities on their own country. The whole issue of splitting the cattle operation was also reopened. As yet no major changes have occurred, but they may occur in the future, particularly after the claim is finally ratified. The people will then be free to decide on their own future — large-scale centralised pastoralism, smaller-scale fragmented pastoralism or subsistence, with little or no commercial pastoralism. These complexities affecting both Ti Tree settlement patterns and land use demonstrate the practical problems that can arise when Aboriginal and non-Aboriginal concepts of ownership are combined.

Most other Anmatyerre people form smaller population groups than those on Mt Allan and Ti Tree. In Yuendumu they account for only about fifty individuals out of a total population of 600. The former reserve, recognised as lying at the interface between the Anmatyerre and their Warlpiri neighbours, is Aboriginal freehold land and people can exercise their land use rights freely. The Yuendumu Anmatyerre, all closely related to Mt Allan families, are involved with Ngarliyikirlangu, the Yuendumu cattle company; they also use the area for subsistence purposes and maintain their ceremonial responsibilities. The western Mt Allan boundary fence is seen only as a barrier separating the two herds of cattle. The amalgamation of Aboriginal and non-Aboriginal concepts of land ownership by the Anmatyerre owners has been harmonious, and the compromise has posed no real problems.

Anmatyerre with interests elsewhere, on non-Aboriginal owned stations such as Mt Denison, Coniston, Napperby or Anningie (fig. 15.1), are much more restricted in how they can use land. Only two of these stations, Napperby and Anningie, still have resident Anmatyerre populations (respectively numbering about 200 and seventy). Both groups live on small leases of land excised from the properties. These areas, no more than 3 sq km, provide only for living space. There is little or no potential for the development of a community economic base and the allocated land may also lack social and spiritual significance. In the case of Napperby the original Anmatyerre application for a living area near a place of great spiritual value was refused because the non-Aboriginal pastoralist felt it was too close to the homestead and would have to tap into the same permanent water supplies. The excision which was finally agreed upon is some 5 km distant, on a piece of undisputed and neutral country.

Aboriginal communities on excisions on properties like Anningie and Napperby are today forced to depend heavily on the government for their economic base. Although they formerly worked in the station stock camps, few are now employed — the introduction of award wages for Aborigines, and more capital intensive management techniques such as helicopter mustering have reduced demand for their skills. Most families therefore derive their cash incomes primarily from social security. Despite retaining their commitment to more traditional responsibilities for the land, the means for discharging such responsibilities are blocked. They, along with Anmatyerre visiting traditional country on properties where they no longer have permanent camps, such as Coniston or Mt Denison, can find their movements heavily restricted. They are discouraged from semi-permanent or even brief overnight camps elsewhere. Thus carrying out ceremonies, such as initiation rites which involve lengthy preparation by the main adult participants and, for the initiates, days or weeks living in the bush close to the ceremonial area, is extremely difficult. As the actual locations for such meetings are specifically chosen to reflect individual and family relationships with land, this could mean that people are unable to fulfil their spiritual responsibilities properly. Hunting and foraging can also be restricted. Although non-Aboriginal pastoralists, under the terms of their leases, are supposed to allow such activities, they can and often do indirectly discourage Aborigines from hunting. Methods used include locking gates, such as those on the roads linking Mt Allan with Napperby and Mt Allan with Coniston; blocking up entrances between Aboriginal camps and adjacent country to all but walkers; and generally intimidating people by stopping vehicles and requesting information about where people intend to go and how long they intend to stay. It is not uncommon for Anmatyerre foraging on these properties to hide whenever they see a station vehicle approaching, and they will go to considerable lengths to avoid contact if at all possible. In general they do not feel free to use the land as they wish. Under these circumstances it would not be surprising if they had abandoned their efforts to maintain traditional activities. That they have not done so is a clear demonstration both of the strength of their cultural foundations and their capacity to adapt their behaviour so that this social stability can be maintained.

Differences in Anmatyerre access to their country because of variations in land tenure also affect the transfer of vital knowledge to future generations. If children and young people cannot undergo initiation or even visit their ancestral country they lack the knowledge to carry out the appropriate ceremonies or make proper use of resources. Resettlement of Anmatyerre following the alienation of the land for pastoralism has had a marked effect on the continuity of spiritual responsibility (Young 1987). Some individuals have been 'adopted' into other country because they have been permanently resident there, and have lost contact with their ancestral lands; others, primarily of part-European ancestry, have spent most of their lives in Alice Springs, and only learned about their heritage through their direct involvement in the land claims; and still others, although resident elsewhere, continually return to maintain their spiritual linkages.

Conclusion

Different cultural groups do indeed see and interpret landscape in different ways — physically, in the case of boundaries or in the use of contrasting environments, and culturally, in their constructs of the values of land and resources. From childhood we are encouraged to accept those interpretations emanating from our own culture, and those belonging to others may be largely invisible to us. This obviously detracts from the richness of our understanding of the world around us. More seriously, it potentially leads to lack of recognition of other modes of land and life. This can have quite negative results, both for people and their environment in general and for specific population groups. In the context discussed here, with the recent occupation of highly fragile environments by people who lack a detailed and long-term understanding of the consequences of their modes of land and resource use, failure to pay attention to land-use concepts practised by their hunter-gatherer predecessors has been detrimental to resource sustainability. Moreover, the hunter-gatherers, whose lives have been economically and politically dominated by the superimposed industrialised society, have been forced into accepting an unhappy compromise. Such problems would have been less severe if the land ownership concepts of hunter-gatherer and industrialised societies had been mutually recognised. Moreover, acceptance of hunter-gatherer land ownership concepts by industrialised societies can be of practical relevance.

Possible contributions of hunter-gatherer concepts of land use to resource sustainability have been mentioned both generally (World Commission on Environment and Development [WCED] 1987) and specifically (Zarsky 1990). Examples referred to in this chapter include Inuit attitudes to seal and caribou harvesting in Canada, and Aboriginal perceptions of the importance of natural resource subsistence as an alternative to extensive cattle grazing in arid rangelands. Countries like Canada, the United States and Australia would do well, as has been argued elsewhere (Coombs et al. 1990), to incorporate such ideas into their future policies for sustainable development.

Deeper understanding of hunter-gatherer concepts has implications not only for remote hunter-gatherer communities but also for all tax-payers. Service provision for the sparse populations in remote areas is very costly, and hence services must be located in places most convenient for the clients. As the Anmatyerre case study shows, population consolidation, a major outcome of the clash between the two cultural groups, has recently been disrupted by renewed dispersal of the hunter-gatherers into small scattered settlements. This, as has been described in detail elsewhere (Australia 1987; Young & Doohan 1989), poses a challenge to government agencies responsible for service delivery. Schools and health clinics, located at places which bureaucratic policy-makers judged to be central, are no longer conveniently situated for their Aboriginal clients. As a consequence their facilities are underused and some are in danger of becoming expensive government-financed 'white elephants'. Plans for service delivery could be made much more relevant if the cultural and economic reasons for the new Aboriginal settlement patterns were taken into account. These to a large extent reflect Aboriginal concepts of land use and ownership; people move to places which are central to them, often because of the coincidence of a number of spiritual threads which enable them to explain their world. They need services in these new settlements, but because the populations are so small, the costs of service provision could be prohibitive. Possible responses from government agencies could include an increased number of smaller, locally staffed schools, health clinics which combine central location with regular mobile services, and retail stores which link smaller units to larger central outlets. This could be expensive in the short term. However, in the long term it is surely more efficient to provide people with appropriate services in the right locations, and hence prevent unnecessary waste of resources. Ultimately, recognising that the cultural realities of people's contemporary worlds inform their practical day-to-day lives might help to provide better forms of support for their future development.

Note

1   The term 'Aboriginal' refers only to members of the indigenous population of Australia; the term 'aboriginal' refers to members of Australian and North American indigenous populations.

References

Altman, J. 1987, *Hunter Gatherers Today*, Institute of Aboriginal Studies, Canberra.

Australia 1987, *Return to Country: The Aboriginal Homelands Movement in Australia,* House of Representatives Standing Committee on Aboriginal Affairs, Final Report, AGPS, Canberra.

Berger, T. 1977, *Northern Frontier, Northern Homeland: The Report of the Mackenzie Valley Pipeline Inquiry*, Minister of Supply and Services, Ottawa.

Brody, H. 1981, *Maps and Dreams*, Jill Norman & Hobhouse, London.

Chatwin, B. 1987, *The Songlines*, Cape, London.

Coombs, H.C., Dargavel, J., Kesteven, J., Ross, H., Smith, D.I. & Young, E.A. 1990, *The Promise of the Land: Sustainable Use by Aboriginal Communities*, Working Paper 1990/1 CRES, ANU, Canberra.

Cosgrove, D.E. 1984, *Social Formation and Symbolic Landscape*, Croom Helm, London and Sydney.

Cribben, J. 1984, *The Killing Times*, Fontana/Collins, Sydney.

DIAND 1988, *Dene/Metis Comprehensive Land Claim: Agreement in Principle,* DIAND, Ottawa.

Duncan, J. & Duncan, N. 1988, '(Re)reading the landscape', *Environment and Planning D: Society and Space,* 6, pp. 117–26.

Freeman, M.M. (ed.) 1976, *Inuit Land Use and Occupancy Project,* DIAND, Ottawa.

Jackson, P. 1989, *Maps of Meaning,* Unwin Hyman, London.

Keith, R.F. & Saunders, A. 1989, *A Question of Rights: Northern Wild-life Management and the Anti-Harvest Movement Canadian*, Arctic Resources Committee, Ottawa.

Lewis, P.F. 1979, 'Axioms for reading the landscape: Some guides to the American scene', in D.W. Meinig (ed.), *The Interpretation of Ordinary Landscapes,* Oxford University Press, Oxford.

Ley, D. 1983, 'Cultural/humanistic geography', *Progress in Human Geography,* vol. 7, no. 2, pp. 267–75.

Meinig, D.W. (ed.) 1979, *The Interpretation of Ordinary Landscapes*, Oxford University Press, Oxford.

Peterson, N. 1975, 'Hunter-gatherer territoriality: the perspective from Australia', *American Anthropologist*, 77, pp. 53–68.

Stanner, W.E.H. 1979, *White Man got No Dreaming: Essays 1938-72*, Australian National University Press, Canberra.

Strehlow, T.G.H. 1970, 'Geography and Totemic Landscape in Central Australia: a functional study', in R.M. Berndt (ed.), *Australian Aboriginal Anthropology*, University of Western Australia Press, Perth, pp. 92–140.

Usher, P. & Bankes, N. 1986, *Property, the Basis of Inuit Hunting Rights — A New Approach,* Inuit Committee on National Issues, Ottawa.

Watkins, M. 1977, 'From underdevelopment to development', in M. Watkins (ed.), *Dene Nation: The Colony Within*, University of Toronto Press, Toronto.

Wonders, W.C. 1983, *Overlapping Land Use and Occupancy of Dene, Metis, Inuvialuit and Inuit in the Northwest Territories*, DIAND, Ottawa.

World Commission on Environment and Development (WCED) 1987, *Our Common Future*, Oxford University Press, Oxford.

Young, E.A. 1987, 'Resettlement and caring for country: the Anmatyerre experience', *Aboriginal History*, 11, 1-2, pp. 156–70.

Young, E.A. & Doohan, K. 1989, *Mobility for Survival: A Process Analysis of Aboriginal Population Movement in Central Australia,* NARU, Darwin.

Zarsky, L. 1990, *Sustainable Development, Challenge for Australia*, Commission for the Future Occasional Paper No. 9, AGPS, Canberra.

Index

Subject index

Aboriginal Development Commission 268
Aborigines *see* Australian Aborigines
Adorno, T. 180
advertising 149, 159, 161–162, 164, 175
African Americans 38
Alexander, J. 79
America's Cup 178
American Museum of Natural History 92
'American West' 74, 133
Ancient Monuments Act (1882) 195
Anglophile identity 41, 45 *see also* identity,
    Anglophile
Anglophile landscape 42, 43, 44, 46, 48, 50
Anglophilia 39–41, 46
anthropology 2, 38, 91–92, 98–99, 104,
    105, 108
anthropometry 99
architecture 5, 72, 81, 140, 145, 159, 160,
    165, 166, 170, 172, 182, 183, 186, 189,
    206, 209
    corporate 72, 73, 82, 83, 84
    Georgian 198, 200–202, 203, 206
    modern 73, 83, 84, 182, 183
    postmodern 84, 170, 172, 182
    Renaissance revival style 76, 79
    Victorian 195, 202, 203
AT & T building, New York City 170, 171
Austin, M. 135
Australia, environment 221, 224, 229, 231,
    233 *see also* environmental visions
Australia, national identity 7, 226
Australian Aborigines 1, 4, 7, 8, 17, 220,
    221, 224, 256, 256–7, 258, 260, 261,
    263, 267, 269
    Alawarre people 267
    Anmatyerre people 256, 262–270
    conceptions of land 215, 220, 232, 258,
        268
    spiritual beliefs 256, 257, 258, 265

    Warlpiri people 267, 268
authenticity 92–95, 99, 169, 170, 172

Barrett, M. 108
Beecher, C. 128
behavioural geography 9
Belich, J. 22, 24
Bellambi Housing Commission Estate 139,
    150–152, 153–155 *passim*
Bellambi Neighbourhood Centre 152
Bengalis 197, 206, 207, 208
Benjamin, W. 182
Berger, J. 89
Berkeley School of Geography 3, 4, 10, 139
Berkhofer, R. 90, 91
Bernstein, B. 114–115, 119
Berry, B. 132
Bethune, M. 124
Birrell, R. 226, 227
boundaries
    cultural 5, 107, 112, 113, 114, 117, 119,
        120, 121
    physical 22, 27, 114, 115, 119, 120, 257,
        258, 259, 261, 262, 266, 267, 268,
        270
boundary maintenance 107–121 *passim*
Breitbart, M. 132
Brody, H. 259
Brown, J. 97
built environment 82, 84, 113, 115, 121,
    129, 133, 149, 151, 153, 154, 159–160,
    162–163, 165–168, 170–172, 175, 195,
    196, 198, 200, 201, 202, 208, 209, 218,
    240
Bureau of Indian Affairs 91
business connections 5, 72, 73, 83, 84, 246
    see also class, business
business people 42, 44, 74, 84, 140, 149,
    153, 185, 191

Place index